M0002401...

MANAGING
THE DATA-BASE
ENVIRONMENT

TELEPROCESSING
NETWORK
ORGANIZATION

DISTRIBUTED FILE
AND DATA-
BASE DESIGN
↔
STRATEGIC
DATA-PLANNING
METHODOLOGIES

YSTEMS ANALYSIS
FOR DATA
TRANSMISSION
↔
DESIGN AND STRATEGY
FOR DISTRIBUTED
DATA PROCESSING

COMPUTER
DATA-BASE
ORGANIZATION
(second edition)

INTRODUCTION
TO COMPUTER
NETWORKS
↔
COMPUTER NETWORKS
AND DISTRIBUTED
PROCESSING

PRINCIPLES
OF DATA-BASE
MANAGEMENT

INTRODUCTION
TO
TELEPROCESSING

PRINCIPLES OF
DISTRIBUTED
PROCESSING

AN END-USER'S
GUIDE TO
DATA BASE

Books On   Books On   Books On

SOFTWARE MAINTENANCE

A ——————— BOOK

SOFTWARE

MAINTENANCE
The Problem
and Its Solutions

JAMES MARTIN
CARMA MCCLURE

PRENTICE-HALL, INC., Englewood Cliffs, New Jersey 07632

Library of Congress Cataloging in Publication Data

Martin, James
  Software maintenance.

  Includes bibliographical references and index.
  1. Software maintenance. I. McClure, Carma L.
II. Title.
QA76.9.S65M37 1983   001.64′2   82-25180
ISBN 0-13-822361-0

TO
CORINTHIA
AND
CONSTANCE

Editorial/production supervision by *Linda Mihatov*
Jacket design by *Diane Saxe*
Manufacturing buyer: *Gordon Osbourne*

Software Maintenance: The Problem and Its Solutions
James Martin and Carma McClure

Printed in the United States of America

10 9 8 7 6 5 4 3 2

ISBN 0-13-822361-0

PRENTICE-HALL INTERNATIONAL, INC., *London*
PRENTICE-HALL OF AUSTRALIA PTY. LIMITED, *Sydney*
EDITORA PRENTICE-HALL DO BRASIL, LTDA., *Rio de Janeiro*
PRENTICE-HALL CANADA INC., *Toronto*
PRENTICE-HALL OF INDIA PRIVATE LIMITED, *New Delhi*
PRENTICE-HALL OF JAPAN, INC., *Tokyo*
PRENTICE-HALL OF SOUTHEAST ASIA PTE. LTD., *Singapore*
WHITEHALL BOOKS LIMITED, *Wellington, New Zealand*

Over $20 billion per year are being spent worldwide on mainte-
nance. If the techniques in this book had been employed everywhere they were appropriate, at least half of the $20 billion would
have been saved.

CONTENTS

PREFACE

Software maintenance claims an extremely large share of the software dollar and is becoming the most expensive part of the software life cycle. Yet, although there are countless books and courses on systems analysis and design, the very important subject of software maintenance has been almost totally neglected. There is little understanding of what can be done to lessen the crippling maintenance problem.

In fact much can be done. Widespread use of the techniques described in this book would cut the maintenance costs in most organizations to a fraction of what they are today.

To solve the software crisis the tasks of developing, using, and maintaining software must be simplified and automated. Software technologies typically have focused on the development phases of the software life cycle—in short, programming methods and tools. Following the development of high-level programming languages in the early 1960s, the predominant software advance has been the introduction of software engineering, and in particular structured techniques. Unfortunately, we have grossly underestimated the need to change programs and the difficulties of doing so.

The cost of failing to design systems for maintenance is very high. Often this is calculated to be the overt cost of doing the maintenance. There is, however, a hidden cost which is often higher. The system becomes so fragile that programmers and their managers are reluctant to change it. Any change has unforeseen consequences which often cause problems in other parts of the system, annoy users, and consume precious software personnel time.

A fundamental problem with software maintenance is that when a change is made it often introduces unforeseen side effects. Fixing a bug has a great chance of introducing a new bug.

While the worst maintenance stories are nightmares, we should also observe that maintenance has been brought under control in some systems, including complex systems. To control maintenance a diversity of development and maintenance actions are needed, most of which must begin when the system is initially designed.

To bring maintenance under control we believe that all DP staff—programmers, analysts, systems designers, and managers—should understand and apply the diversity of solutions and tools to the problems discussed in this book. It is essential for system developers to understand all of them and apply those which are relevant when building any system.

In consequence this is an amazingly wide-ranging report. It covers almost every aspect of DP from coding techniques to strategic planning, from the programmer to the president!

We would like to thank the following organizations and individuals for providing us with research data: Amdahl and Sally Warren, Bell Laboratories and G. Dave Bergland, Illinois Bell Telephone and Jeanne Follman, National C.S.S. and William Clark, and SAMI and Gloria Gleave. We would also like to thank Richard Murch for assisting with the compilation of this material, and Mr. and Mrs. John Collins and the Savant Institute for their assistance in publishing this material.

James Martin

Carma McClure

PART **I** INTRODUCTION

1 THE MAINTENANCE MESS

INTRODUCTION   We are accelerating into the computer age. Articles about computerization appear everywhere, from business journals to fashion magazines. By the end of the decade executives, secretaries, and consumers will all use computers as part of their daily activities, with an explosion of new applications such as electronic funds transfer, power facilities maintenance, exotic new weapons systems, automated design engineering, and robot production lines.

Yet when top business managers ask for information they know to be in their computers, they frequently cannot obtain it. When executives want to change procedures, they are told they cannot do that because the computer cannot make the change. Giant insurance companies have to resort to processing claims by hand after a change in government regulations. What is wrong?

The problem is that we have created computer programs that are very difficult to maintain.

WHAT IS MAINTENANCE?   We use the term *maintenance* to refer to changes that have to be made to computer programs after they have been delivered to the customer or user. We perform maintenance for a variety of reasons:

- To correct errors and design defects
- To improve the design
- To convert the programs so that different hardware, software, system features, telecommunications facilities, and so on, can be used
- To interface the programs to other programs

● To make changes in files or data bases

● To make enhancements or necessary changes to the applications

Program maintenance is different from hardware maintenance. Hardware maintenance for a computer consists of replacing deteriorated components, putting in engineering changes that correct defects and make design enhancements, and lubricating and cleaning mechanical parts. This does not affect how the computer is supposed to behave, so the user usually sees no change.

Program maintenance not only corrects defects and makes design enhancements; it also makes enhancements that change how the program behaves. Users constantly want to make adjustments in program behavior. Most maintenance work is caused by changing requirements rather than by reliability problems [1] (see Fig. 1.1).

Software systems used in industry are continually modified to adapt to changing data, and to meet changing user needs. Even a system that is totally reliable, completely meets user requirements, and is well structured will frequently be changed during the maintenance phase. Unless software systems of the future are designed to be changed more easily without jeopardizing their quality, maintenance of these systems will continue to be a time-consuming and costly activity.

If we push the analogy with hardware maintenance, the term "maintenance" seems inappropriate when referring to enhancements in program function. It might be better to use a different word. However, the word "maintenance" is now firmly embedded in common usage to mean all forms of software enhancement. Designing software for ease of maintenance

SOFTWARE MAINTENANCE ACTIVITIES

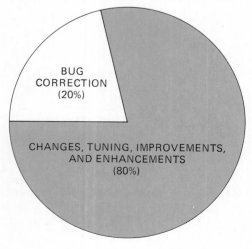

Figure 1.1 The major portion of maintenance work performed in most organizations is spent enhancing and improving software systems.

is the same problem whether we are talking about "engineering changes" or application enhancement.

INABILITY TO MEET APPLICATION NEEDS
Computers have plunged in cost dramatically. It is clear that the spectacular cost reductions will continue, accompanied by mass production of computers used in all walks of life. Can anything slow the momentum of the computer revolution? Certainly: ill-designed software.

Software has become the dominant factor in computerization. The success of computerization in many organizations hinges on the supply of software. The gap between the supply and demand of programs is rapidly growing. Most companies currently have a three- to four-year *backlog* of computer applications waiting to be programmed.

In addition, there is an *invisible backlog* of user needs which have not formally entered the queue of pending applications. A study by the Sloan School Center for Information Systems Research found that the invisible backlog of major enterprises studied averaged 164% of the declared backlog. The total backlog measured in this study represented 179% of the entire base of installed applications [2].

Programming accounts for an ever-increasing proportion of computer costs. Most software efforts of any magnitude are fraught with problems and failure. Programming projects take longer to complete and cost more than planned. As shown in Fig. 1.2, instances of actual costs running 300%

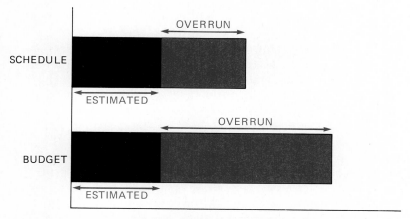

Figure 1.2 Instances of actual schedules running 200% over estimates and actual costs running 300% over budgeted costs are the rule rather than the exception in software projects.

over budget and actual schedules running 200% over estimates are the rule rather than the exception [3]. Managers are bewildered by their inability to apply normal management practices to the data-processing function. Users are frustrated and antagonized by applications that are difficult to change and do not work as expected. Software professionals are at a loss to understand why one project succeeds and the next one fails.

The economic stability of many nations is now being threatened by productivity lags. Computerization is seen as perhaps the best way to decrease production and office costs. Computer-aided design and manufacturing are rapidly being introduced. Major changes in paperwork procedures are needed. But the necessary changes need rapid increases in program production at the same time that there is an increasing shortage of analysts and programmers. A front-page *Wall Street Journal* article stated that "Oil and software are the two principal obstacles to economic progress" [4].

Advances in software technology have not kept pace with those in hardware technology. Installations that buy the latest computers often program in 20-year-old languages with ad hoc methods far removed from engineering discipline.

CLOSING THE SOFTWARE SUPPLY AND DEMAND GAP

Fundamental to the future of computerization is closing the supply and demand gap in programs. To solve the software crisis the tasks of developing, using, and maintaining programs must be simplified and automated.

Software technologies typically have focused on the *development* phases of the software life cycle—in short, programming methods and tools. Following the development of high-level programming languages in the early 1960s, the predominant software advance has been the introduction of software engineering, in particular structured techniques.

Like the software technologies of the 1960s and 1970s, those proposed for the 1980s mostly focus on the technical aspects of software development, for the most part ignoring the end user, management issues, and maintenance problems [5]. However, a closer look reveals that the latter problems overshadow the more technical problems of software development. Users are dissatisfied not only because of system bugs and failures but also because of poor documentation, inadequate training, and the inability of programs to be responsive to their changing requirements.

Past software failures and current cost trends explain the reason for doubting the effectiveness of software solutions that focus primarily on technical and development issues. Although valuable, they do not directly address a major cause of software crisis. Maintenance of existing software systems is diverting valuable and scarce resources away from new development efforts. It is a major contributor to the growing backlog of applications

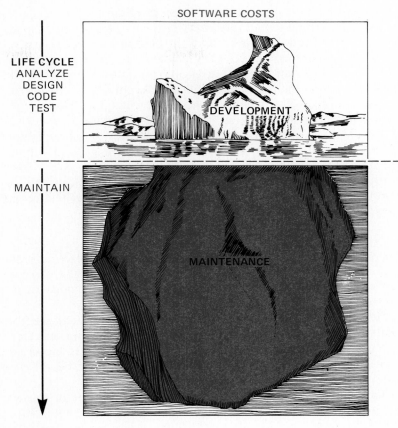

SOFTWARE COSTS

LIFE CYCLE
ANALYZE
DESIGN
CODE
TEST

DEVELOPMENT

MAINTAIN

MAINTENANCE

Figure 1.3 Software maintenance dominates the software life cycle. In many organizations, software maintenance activities consume three-fourths of the total life-cycle expenditures and over one-half of the data-processing personnel resources.

waiting to be programmed. Maintenance dominates the software life cycle in terms of effort and cost (Fig. 1.3).

We have grossly underestimated the need to change programs and the difficulties of doing so.

OPPORTUNITY COSTS   The cost of failing to design systems for maintenance is very high. Often this is calculated to be the overt cost of doing the maintenance. There is, however, a hidden cost which is often higher. The system becomes fragile so that data-processing managers are reluctant to change it. Any change has unforeseen consequences which often cause problems elsewhere, annoy users, and waste precious personnel resources.

So business executives are told that programs cannot be changed. "You cannot do that—the computer can't handle it." Even trivial changes are resisted. Executives cannot obtain the information they need for decision making. Improvements in procedures do not occur. Better forms of customer service are avoided. The business *should* be changing rapidly but the data-processing department is digging in its heels. Dynamic executives become frustrated. They constantly perceive changes they want to make but have increasing difficulty doing so. It is like swimming in slowly solidifying gelatin.

Computers offer the promise of enormous improvements in business efficiency. The promise will not be fulfilled unless the best techniques are used for achieving maintainability.

CHAIN REACTIONS

A fundamental problem with program maintenance is that when a change is made it often introduces unforeseen side effects. Fixing a bug has a substantial chance of introducing a new bug.

Often a change has system-wide ramifications which are not obvious. Attempts are made to affect a local change with minimum effort but this sets off a chain reaction of problems elsewhere. Unless the system is very well documented, these side effects will not be anticipated, or even known, until they cause problems in operation.

This situation is made worse because the maintainer or repairer is often not the person who wrote the original code. The change may affect the work of multiple coders.

Because of the side effects, maintenance needs far more program testing per line of code than other programming. When a change is made it may be necessary to run an entire bank of test cases to ensure that other areas still work correctly. Such *regression testing* to check for side effects can be costly. How costly depends on how convoluted the structure of the system is. In large entangled systems the chain-reaction effects can be very severe.

Maintenance changes tend to deteriorate the structure of programs, often making them more complex and more difficult to maintain next time. They are often done in an atmosphere of crisis. A quick patch is needed rather than any elegant restructuring. Patches accumulate. We get patches on top of patches on top of patches.

As flaw-fixing introduces new flaws, more and more time is spent on fixing these secondary problems rather than on correcting the structure that caused the original problem. The system steadily becomes less and less well ordered. Some complex systems reach a point where the maintainers cease to gain ground. Each fix introduces new problems. The system has become too unstable to be a base for progress.

Fred Brooks, philosophizing about his experience in managing the building of OS/360, wrote:

> Systems program building is an entropy-decreasing process, hence inherently metastable. Program maintenance is an entropy-increasing process, and even its most skillful execution only delays the subsidence of the system into unfixable obsolescence [6].

Lehman and Belady studied the history of successive releases of a large operating system [7]. It became steadily larger, the number of modules increasing linearly with the release number. However, the number of modules affected by maintenance changes grew *exponentially* with release number.

In corporate data processing (DP) the number of programs and files steadily grows. As this happens, the cost of maintenance tends to become a steadily larger part of the DP budget unless strong measures are taken to control it.

Figure 1.4 shows how maintenance has tended to grow in typical installations, becoming a larger portion of the DP budget. In many DP organizations, program maintenance activities consume nearly three-fourths of total life-cycle expenditures [8] and over half of the DP personnel resources [1]. Those organizations moving fastest into on-line and interactive systems are often spending as much as 80% of their time on maintenance. Using the types of techniques discussed in this book, this figure has been lowered to about 20% in some organizations.

A few organizations have reached a state where 100% of their effort is spent maintaining existing programs. No new applications are being

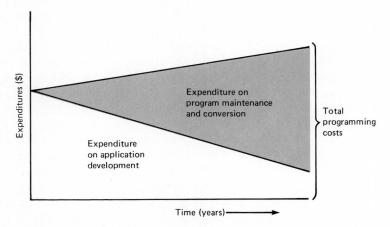

Figure 1.4 New application progress is often deferred by the rising cost of modifying existing programs and files. Some corporations spend more than 80% of their programming budget just keeping current and only 20% forging ahead.

written. One large government body froze all application development for $1\frac{1}{2}$ years while it tried to redesign its data structures. Such a situation is intolerable for end users, who often find means to bypass the DP organization.

FILE PROBLEMS   Many DP organizations have built up vast libraries of files on tape or disk. When the business needs change, programs are often modified in a way that causes a change in the structure of a record. Unfortunately, some other program also uses the same record, so, somewhat by surprise, that program also has to be modified. In an old installation *many* other programs use the file and they all have to be changed.

A seemingly trivial change in a file environment sets off a chain reaction of other changes that have to be made. This upheaval is expensive and the necessary programmers are doing other work. Sometimes the modifications are difficult to make because the applications were not adequately documented.

As time goes on this problem becomes worse because more and more programs are created. More programs have to be changed whenever a file is changed.

It is often thought by systems analysts and data-processing managers that existing programs which work well can be left alone. In reality, however, the data that they create or use are needed for other applications and almost always needed in a slightly different form. New data-item types are added. New record types are needed with data-item types from several previous records. The data must be indexed in a different way. The physical layout of data is improved. Data for different applications are merged, and so forth.

An old file environment is like a bowl of spaghetti. Every time you pull one piece of spaghetti it shakes all the others in the bowl. As time goes by it becomes steadily worse because the number of pieces of spaghetti increase and they become more interwoven. The maintenance difficulties of file systems grow geometrically with the number of applications produced.

As we discuss later, data-base technology was invented to deal with this problem. In well-managed data-base installations it has succeeded to a large extent. In badly managed ones it has made the problem worse.

The maintenance mess has become a nightmare for some organizations. It is alarming to reflect what it may be like in 20 years time as more and more applications and systems are developed. Microbes under appropriate conditions can multiply exponentially like today's computers. But if they multiply when shut in an enclosed laboratory dish they eventually drown in their own excrement. One top DP executive compared this to his maintenance problems. New growth, he said, was being stifled by the excrement of old COBOL and PL/1 systems. If new techniques were not widely accepted and used in the maintenance as well as the development environments, the programming staff would eventually drown in its own maintenance.

One recent DOD study showed that the cost of development of Air Force avionics software was $75 per instruction, while the cost of maintenance has ranged up to $4000 per instruction [9].

Fred Brooks cynically quotes C. S. Lewis [6]:

> That is the key to history. Terrific energy is expended—civilizations are built up—excellent institutions devised; but each time something goes wrong. Some fatal flaw always brings the selfish and cruel people to the top, and then it all slides back into misery and ruin. In fact, the machine conks. It seems to start up all right and runs a few yards, and then it breaks down. [10]

GAINING CONTROL While the worst maintenance stories are night-mares, we should also observe that maintenance *has* been brought under control on some systems, even complex systems. To control maintenance a diversity of design and management actions are needed, most of which must begin when the system is initially designed.

A large part of the problem is that in spite of its high costs and damaging effects, maintenance is treated completely inadequately in most organizations. In the first enthusiasm of new system conception the system is not designed so that it will be easily maintainable. Traditionally, maintenance has been handled separately and differently from new development. Usually, maintenance efforts are staffed by different and less-experienced personnel than development projects, with little interaction between the two groups. Within data-processing circles, there is a stigma attached to maintenance, which is viewed as a nonchallenging environment offering little opportunity to work with newer technologies. Modern software technologies are not thought appropriate or necessary for performing maintenance.

VAST PROGRAM INVESTMENT The computer programs on which governments and corporations depend represent hundreds of billions of dollars of human work. These systems cannot easily be replaced by newer technologies because the dollar investment is too great. Since they perform adequately and are not entirely unacceptable to users, it is not yet cost-effective to replace them. Furthermore, to avoid interruption in user service any replacement must be carefully planned and allowed to gradually evolve into newer systems. There are newer software technologies now with which better systems could be built, but these advancements will take a long time to fully penetrate. Programming productivity aids introduced in the early 1970s, such as structured techniques, test data generators, data-base design techniques, and data dictionaries, are still not widely used in many installations.

Existing programs will not cease to be a maintenance burden for many years. As the investment in programs grows still higher it is vital that we should not build up ever-increasing future costs in out-of-contol maintenance.

EVER-TIGHTENING PRESSURE   If a DP exectuvie does not take firm action to control maintenance it will become a worse problem in the future than it has been in the past. Unless deliberately brought under control, maintenance becomes worse. The cost of computers will continue to drop and the understanding of users about how to use them will continue to grow. The demand to create new applications at a more rapid rate will increase, and so will the pressures to modify old applications.

The DP executive will be caught in an ever-tightening squeeze between demands for new applications on cheaper machines and the maintenance pressures of old applications (Fig. 1.5).

To bring maintenance under control we believe that *all* DP staff—programmers, analysts, systems designers, and managers—should understand and apply the diversity of solutions to the problem discussed in this book.

SOLUTIONS TO MAINTENANCE   This book describes multiple types of approaches to the maintenance problem. It is desirable for system developers to understand all of them and apply those which are relevant when building any system.

Designing for ease of maintenance must begin when the system is originally conceived. Many actions can be taken when the system is being designed and programmed which will make it maintainable later. A system ill designed for maintenance cannot have maintainability retrofitted to it later. Too many organizations do not fully consider maintenance at the design stages.

We need to distinguish between the creation of complex software such as operating systems and the development of commercial data processing. In the latter it is easier to reduce complexity and many powerful actions may be taken to minimize future maintenance costs.

Among the types of approaches are the following:

- Conduct the system design and programming from the start with the intention of minimizing maintenance. Adopt management practices that are sound for maintainability.

DP EXECUTIVE

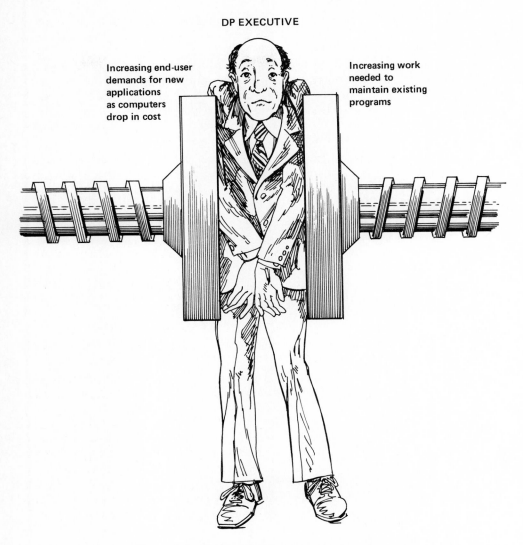

Increasing end-user
demands for new
applications
as computers
drop in cost

Increasing work
needed to
maintain existing
programs

Figure 1.5 Data-processing executive in a vice.

- Minimize the complexity of system and program structures.
- Select and enforce structured techniques that lead to ease of maintenance.
- Reduce the need for corrective maintenance by improving software reliability. Reduce the need for change maintenance by planning for and controlling user enhancements.
- Anticipate possible migration to new technologies or software, and plan to minimize the need for program rewriting.

- Ensure that the documentation and structure diagramming will be entirely clear for future maintainers.

The approaches listed above apply to all software development. Those listed below are particularly relevant for commercial data processing:

- Use that data-base software most suitable for minimizing future maintenance. Design and manage the data-base environment so that data bases are created which are as stable as possible.
- Use fourth-generation languages which make changes easy and quick to accomplish: for example, report generators, application generators, higher-level data-base languages, and fourth-generation programming languages. Use nonprocedural languages where possible.
- Use structured techniques which simplify the creation of data base procedures.
- Train users to generate their own reports and employ data management software, and ensure that they do enhancement maintenance of any applications which they create with such tools.
- Select application packages with careful attention to maintainability.
- Use external software suppliers and transfer maintenance responsibility to them.
- Encourage interaction among program developers, maintainers, and users.
- Employ tools that help with maintenance (e.g., prototyping tools, structure analyzers, data dictionaries).
- Identify those old systems with expensive maintenance and redevelop them with more modern techniques (data bases, fourth-generation languages, better structuring, software packages, etc.).

In the chapters that follow, these basic approaches are expanded into a range of solutions to minimize maintenance efforts and costs. Both long-term and short-term solutions are presented. Maintenance issues are discussed from both a management and technical perspective. Methods for improving the maintainability of new systems, existing systems, database systems and software packages are suggested.

SUMMARY

The most effective way to deal with maintenance is to design maintainability into systems from the start. We will discuss many diverse methods of doing this. The maintainer, however, is often confronted with programs written long ago that were not designed for maintenance. There are therefore two aspects to this book:

1. Maintaining existing programs which are often ill-designed, crudely patched, and poorly documented—the work, unfortunately, that most maintainers have to perform. Part I of the book concentrates on this work and other chapters refer to it.

2. Designing programs and systems for ease of maintainability. Part II discusses conventional methods of doing this. Part III discusses methods involving fundamental changes in software, or design philosophy. Part IV discusses purchased packages. Part VI looks at how future planning is needed to control maintenance costs.

At the time of writing, over $30 billion per year is being spent on maintenance, worldwide. If the techniques in this book had been employed everywhere they were appropriate, at least half of this $30 billion would have been saved.

REFERENCES

1. B. P. Lientz, E. B. Swanson, and G. E. Tompkins, "Characteristics of Application Software Maintenance," *Communications of the ACM,* Vol. 21, No. 6 (June 1978): 466–471.

2. R. B. Rosenberger, "The Information Center," SHARE Proceedings No. 56, Session M372, March 1981.

3. L. H. Putman, "A General Empirical Solution to the Macro Software Sizing and Estimation Problem," *IEEE Trans. on Software Engineering,* Vol. SE-4, No. 4 (July 1978): 335–361.

4. W. M. Bulkeley, "Computer Makers Feel Key to Sales Edge Lies in Better Programming," *Wall Street Journal,* Sept. 29, 1980, pp. 1, 18.

5. P. Isaacson and E. Juliussen, "Guest Editorial: Window on the 80's," *Computer,* Vol. 13, No. 1 (January 1980): 4–6.

6. F. Brooks, *The Mythical Man-Month* (Reading, MA: Addison-Wesley Publishing Co., Inc., 1975).

7. M. Lehman and L. Belady, "Programming System Dynamics," ACM SIGOPS Third Symposium on Operating System Principles, October 1971.

8. "Software Prototyping," *DCAS Newsletter,* Vol. 3, No. 2 (June 1981): 1.

9. B. deRose and T. Nyman, "The Software Life Cycle—A Management and Technological Challenge in the Department of Defense," *IEEE Trans. on Software Engineering,* Vol. SE-4, No. 4 (July 1978): 309–318.

10. C. S. Lewis, *Mere Christianity* (New York: Macmillan Publishing Co., Inc., 1960), p. 54.

2 STATE OF THE ART OF SOFTWARE MAINTENANCE

FOREMAN MANUFACTURING COMPANY

Foreman is a 50-year-old Chicago-based manufacturing company whose current annual sales are $60 million. Five years ago Foreman was purchased by an aggressive group of young executives whose plan was to quadruple Foreman's revenue within 10 years. Their ambitious goal was to be realized through the acquisition of other smaller companies.

Two years ago the Kolbe Plastics Company was selected as Foreman's first subsidiary. As part of determining the feasibility of acquiring Kolbe, Foreman's management consulted with its DP department. Foreman has one centralized DP department serving the entire company. It includes a DP manager, three programmer/analysts, three computer operators, a keypunching staff, and is supported by an in-house IBM 4331. Most of Foreman's computerized systems are batch systems such as a payroll system, accounting systems, a materials requirements planning (MRP) system, and a variety of engineering programs.

The DP department reported that the acquisition of Kolbe required one critical, immediate change to the existing Foreman programs. Because Kolbe used a nine-digit part number and Foreman's programs currently allowed only a six-digit part number, Foreman's programs would have to be changed to accommodate the larger part number.

Since Foreman is an inventory-sensitive business, it is extremely important to have an accurate accounting of inventory status. Being able to process the Kolbe part number was essential to inventory control and to ensuring the profitability of the new subsidiary. Although many programs were affected by the part-number change, the DP department was confident that this was a straightforward change which could easily be completed in three months.

With this assurance from the DP department and a favorable financial projection for Kolbe, Foreman acquired the new subsidiary. Unfortunately, all did not go as planned. A year later, the DP department was still struggling to complete the three-month part-number change. All new DP development efforts were suspended and the majority of the DP resources were devoted to the change. Not only was management confused about what had gone wrong, but they could not control inventory. The result was an unprofitable year for Kolbe and a substantial revenue loss for Foreman.

Foreman's management decided to abandon its ambitious acquisition plan. The blame was placed on the inability of Foreman's software to help Foreman realize its long-range corporate plan. Foreman's management complained that this was not the first time their software had proved too inflexible to meet changing company needs.

MIDWEST TELEPHONE COMPANY

TAS is a 20-year-old software system used by Midwest Telephone Company to assign telephone numbers in a major metropolitan area. TAS is a very large system consisting of over 600 programs and approximately 200,000 lines of code. The original TAS programs were written primarily in assembly languages, but new enhancements are being written in PL/1 whenever possible. As part of a plan to upgrade TAS to newer technologies, a conversion to IBM's data-base management system, IMS, was performed last year.

The annual DP budget to operate and maintain TAS is approximately $5 million. Most of this is used for maintenance. A staff of 50 programmers and analysts is employed to perform continuing development and demand maintenance work for TAS. In addition, a staff of 20 telephone service support personnel is employed to help track TAS program halts caused by invalid telephone number assignments. Each month about 10,000 program halts occur, but only a very small percentage of the halts are actually caused by program errors.

Recently, the number of TAS program halts decreased significantly and the backlog of unsolved program problems also decreased. Not more than 15 known errors remained unsolved at each month end throughout 1981. It was thought that the TAS system had finally stabilized. However, a closer investigation showed a quite different and alarming reason. The users, who were unhappy with the inability of TAS to provide reliable service, *were circumventing the system and had returned to manual assignment of telephone numbers.* The IMS data base drifted hopelessly out of date and the number of wrong numbers and uncompleted telephone calls was beginning to increase.

MARKETING RESEARCH INSTITUTE

SMCS is considered a high-quality, model software system at Marketing Research Institute (MRI). SMCS is a graphics system used to report sales trends in grocery products to the manufacturers. It is a 20,000-line ANS COBOL system developed in the mid-1970s using structured techniques. Not only was SMCS developed on schedule and within budget, but also SMCS has proved to be a very reliable system. Only a handful of errors have been detected in SMCS during its five-year period of use.

Based on its production history, it might be assumed that SMCS is a very maintainable system. When MRI DP management and programmers were asked about the quality of SMCS, they stated that it is well structured and easy to maintain. A closer look, however, showed a different reason for the low cost of maintenance. The application's logic is considered too complex to be understood by the typical MRI COBOL programmer. Its quality has been preserved by *discouraging any user requests for changes and enhancements.*

SOFTWARE FAILURES

The experiences of Foreman, the Midwest Telephone Company, and MRI are all too common. They illustrate the difficulty of providing adequate software for use in industry. But they are not examples of software development failures; they are examples of maintenance nightmares. For many organizations, the most serious and the most costly software problems occur during the maintenance phase.

Foreman's programs proved too difficult to change, forcing management to alter its corporate plan. Midwest Telephone's programs proved too error-prone to be dependable, convincing users to return to a manual system The SMCS system proved too complex to understand, discouraging programmers from any attempt to change it.

As at Foreman the consequences of maintenance problems often extend far beyond DP productivity concerns by affecting management and users throughout an organization.

What is the source of most maintenance work? What are the major difficulties in performing maintenance? What makes a software system easy or difficult to maintain?

A first step toward minimizing the maintenance burden is to understand what activities comprise the maintenance function and what factors contribute to the high cost and difficulty of maintaining software systems. With this understanding, more effective techniques and tools can be selected for controlling and reducing the maintenance burden. The purpose of this chapter is to provide that understanding by defining the term "maintenance" and by describing current maintenance activities and problems.

TYPES OF MAINTENANCE WORK

Swanson divides the causes for maintenance into three basic categories [6]:

1. Failures

2. Environmental changes

3. User and DP personnel requests

Failures are attributed to errors in programs, such as invalid output results, missing data edit checks, performance inefficiencies, or programming standard violations.

Environmental changes are a common occurrence in systems that are used by an organization over a period of time. Two types of changes are to be expected: changes in the data environment, such as a change in a transaction code or restructuring a data base; and changes in the processing environment, such as the installation of new hardware or a new operating system.

Users and maintainers themselves are a cause of maintenance. They request changes to a software system to improve the operating efficiency, to add new features, to change existing functions, and to improve maintainability.

Maintenance activities performed in response to these basic causes are defined by Swanson as [6]:

1. Corrective maintenance

2. Adaptive maintenance

3. Perfective maintenance

These categories are becoming the standard classification scheme to identify the basic types of maintenance. Box 2.1 gives examples of them. As shown in Box 2.2, Reutter uses a similar classification scheme but he further refines Swanson's three categories into seven categories [2]. One important addition by Reutter is the supportive maintenance category. Whereas Swanson includes support activities within each of his basic categories, Reutter separates support to emphasize the importance of communication between the user and the maintainer and the importance of planning for system support.

BOX 2.1   Examples of maintenance activities

Corrective Maintenance

- Correction of failure to reset a switch.
- Correction of failure to test for all possible conditions.
- Correction of failure to process the last record in a file.

Adaptive Maintenance

- Implementation of a data-base management system (DBMS) for an existing application system.
- Modification of designation codes from three characters to four characters.
- Tuning a system to reduce response times.
- Converting the MRP system from batch to on-line operation.
- Adjustment of two programs to make them use the same record structures.
- Modification of a program to make it use a different terminal.

Enhancement Maintenance

- Modification of the payroll program to incorporate a new union settlement.
- Addition of a new report in the sales analysis system.
- Improvement of a terminal dialogue to make it more user friendly.
- Addition of an extra column to a report.
- Adjustment of a program for printing bank statements to use a new design of preprinted stationery.
- Improvement of graphics output.
- Adding an on-line HELP command.
- Improvement of query processing capabilities to examine more types of data.
- Adding facilities required by auditors.

BOX 2.2   Types of maintenance work

Swanson's Categories	Reutter's Categories

Swanson's Categories

Corrective Maintenance

- Performed to identify and correct software failures, performance failures, and implementation failures

Adaptive Maintenance

- Performed to adapt software to changes in the data requirements or the processing environments

Perfective Maintenance

- Performed to enhance performance, improve cost-effectiveness, improve processing efficiency, or improve maintainability

Reutter's Categories

Emergency Repairs

- Performed when immediate repair is necessary to continue user service

Corrective Coding

- Performed to correctly reflect the specifications or to correctly utilize system resources

Upgrades

- Performed to adapt to changes in processing requirements

Changes in Conditions

- Performed to adapt to changes in business conditions due to regulatory situations or other situations beyond the control of the organization

Growth

- Performed to adapt to changes in data requirements or the addition of new programs, new users

Enhancements

- Performed in response to user requests for changes and additions to the system

Support

- Performed to explain system capabilities, to plan for future support, to measure performance

MAINTENANCE SURVEYS

Many opinions have been expressed concerning the basic issues and problems affecting application software maintenance. For example, maintenance is a necessary evil that no one likes. There is no pride or recognition in maintenance work. New software technologies are not applicable to maintenance.

Do these opinions reflect a realistic picture of maintenance? Recently, several surveys and studies have been conducted to clarify the software maintenance picture [9–12]. We shall use the findings from these surveys to gain insight into maintenance issues and problems currently faced by industry.

Problems such as maintenance staff morale, maintenance staff turnover, poor system reliability, and inadequate documentation often are cited as the major maintenance problems. At the 1981 National Computer Conference, Chapin cited the low esteem in which maintenance is held, poor documentation, and inexperienced maintainers as serious maintenance problems [10]; Reutter saw the lack of recognition of the importance of the maintenance function and poor management of the maintenance area as the real maintenance issues [2]; and Lyons pointed to the inability of software to be changed without destroying its structure and quality as the major cause of maintenance problems [4]. In general, continual requests from users are at the top of the maintenance problem list, with inflexible, fragile software running a close second.

Recommendations to ease the maintenance burden must include both managerial and technical solutions.

WHAT PORTION OF SYSTEMS AND PROGRAMMING RESOURCES ARE DEVOTED TO MAINTENANCE?

The business/industrial community is becoming alarmed by the amount of systems and programming resources needed to maintain software systems. It is feared that as more programs are developed and placed into the operations phase, maintenance needs will grow and will hinder new development efforts. This is a valid concern. The maintenance of existing systems receives priority over new development since their support is necessary for continued operation of the organization. As the number of systems to maintain increases, more resources are allocated to maintenance, so fewer are available for new development.

The proportion of systems and programming resources currently devoted to maintenance is estimated to lie in the range of 40 to 80% [13]. In 1976, deRose and Nyman reported that 60 to 70% of the DOD software dollar was spent on maintenance [14]. In 1976, Mills estimated that 75% of data-processing personnel time was allocated to maintenance [1]. In 1980, Cashman and Holt reported estimates as high as 80% [15]. Figures published by Zelkowitz are shown in Fig. 2.1.

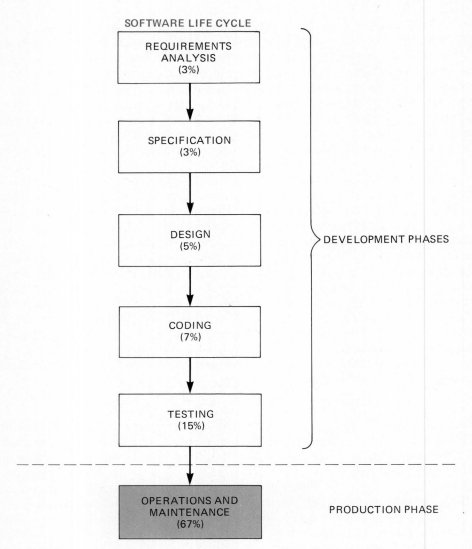

SOFTWARE LIFE CYCLE

Figure 2.1 For many large-scale software systems, only one-fourth to one-third of the entire life-cycle costs can be attributed to software development. Most effort is spent during the operations and maintenance phase of the software life cycle. The percentages above indicate relative costs. (Data from Ref. 16.)

From these reports it appears that the maintenance burden in existing installations is steadily increasing. Some sources report that the total maintenance effort relative to new development has neither increased nor decreased over the past decade [12]. This is probably because there are many new installations, often with minicomputers. These new installations initially have zero or low maintenance, but their maintenance burden rises, as elsewhere, when they grow older. What has changed is the *type* of maintenance work that is being performed. Newer systems appear to present fewer reliability and quality problems. For systems developed using newer software technologies, such as structured techniques and data-base management systems, more maintenance time is spent changing the system to meet user requests than to correct errors. For many organizations, the majority of the software maintenance work is now spent enhancing rather than correcting systems.

The results of the Lientz–Swanson surveys identified several variables that appear to affect the allocation of resources to maintenance. For example, *larger* and/or *older* data-processing departments tend to spend a larger portion of resources on maintenance than do smaller and/or younger departments. Department size is measured in terms of the hardware equipment budget and the number of analysts and programmers in the department. Older departments usually have more application systems to maintain, and larger departments probably support larger, more complex systems.

A third variable is *industry type.* Certain industries, such as banking, insurance, data-processing services, and the government, appear to spend a larger portion of their resources on maintenance activities. This is partially explained by the observation that larger, older data-processing departments are more characteristic of these industries.

One factor that may tend to reduce the relative effort devoted to maintenance is the organization of a separate maintenance staff. Less than 20% of the data-processing departments surveyed by Lientz and Swanson had a separate maintenance staff and those that did were usually the large data-processing departments. They claimed that programmer productivity was increased through programmer specialization and that management control of effort and costs was improved when maintenance activities were segregated from new development projects.

WHAT PROGRAM CHARACTERISTICS AFFECT MAINTENANCE EFFORT?

There has been a great deal of speculation about what makes a software system more difficult to maintain. Program factors frequently cited as affecting maintainability include (see Box 2.3):

- System size
- System age

- Number of input/output data items
- Application type
- Programming language
- Structuredness

On the whole, maintenance surveys and studies confirm these speculations, citing size, age, structuredness, and number of output reports as most influential. Today the move to new types of languages is having a major effect on maintenance, as we discuss later in the book.

Larger systems require more maintenance effort than do smaller systems. There is a greater learning curve associated with larger systems and

BOX 2.3 Program characteristics found to affect maintenance effort

Program Characteristics	Lientz	Chrylser	Chapin*
System age	√		
System size	√		√(C)
Number of output files		√	
Number of output fields		√	√(U)
Number of report control breaks		√	
Number of input files		√	√(U)
Number of input fields		√	
Number of input edits		√	
Number of predefined user reports	√	√	
Structuredness			
Modularity			√(C)
Hierarchical organization			√(C)
System documentation			√(C)
Naming conventions			√(C)
Complexity			√(C)
Application type			
Programming language			√(C)
Mathematics			√(U)
Difficulty of task			√(U)
Use of data-base techniques	√		
Switches and flags			√(C)
Levels of nested IFs			√(C)
Number of indexes and subscripts			√(C)
Use of numeric literals			√(C)

*C, controllable by system developer/maintainer; U, *not* controllable by system developer/maintainer.

larger systems are more complex in terms of the variety of functions they perform. Dijkstra identified the problem of system size when he first discussed structured programming at the 1969 NATO Conference on Software Engineering [17].

Older systems require more maintenance effort than do younger systems. Software systems tend to grow with age, to become less organized with change, and to become less understandable with staff turnover. Also, many older systems were developed with no understanding of how to use modularization and structured techniques to control complexity. One noteworthy observation is that software tends to be used longer than expected. There are many examples of "one-shot" programs that are still in use after several years. (There are also many examples of programs falling out of use rapidly due to not adapting to user requirements.)

System size is measured in terms of the number of source statements, the number of programs, the number of input/output files, the size of data base in bytes, and the number of predefined user reports. According to Lientz and Swanson, the number of programs and the number of predefined user reports appear to be good predictors of system size and hence of maintenance effort. In particular, systems possessing a larger number of predefined user reports appear to require a larger maintenance effort. Chrysler's study on program development effort lends support to the Lientz–Swanson findings. His study pointed out that the most significant variable affecting the development time of a data-processing application program was the number of output fields. The next most important variables were the number of control breaks and totals in output reports and the number of input files. This agrees with the Lientz–Swanson conclusion that the number of output reports is a valuable predictor of software effort in typical application software.

Program size can be controlled by using the most powerful (highest-level) language available. In general, the more powerful the language, the fewer instructions needed to create the program. Program age can be controlled by planning for program retirement and migration to newer technologies. Some DP managers suggest that a cost-effective solution to the growing maintenance burden for older systems is to plan for a redesign or replacement of an application system every five to seven years. Since the original system intent and state-of-the-art technologies will have changed so significantly during that time period, the original system design cannot and should not be preserved.

Besides controlling program size, data-base management systems can reduce the maintenance effort needed for application systems providing many user reports. Data-base tools make it easier to modify and enhance reports and allow end users to make many of their own modifications.

As shown in Box 2.3, Chapin divided program characteristics that affect maintenance productivity into two categories. The C category includes those characteristics normally controllable by the system developer and/or maintainer. The U category contains those characteristics not controllable by the developer or the maintainer but rather imposed from the outside. Chapin makes the interesting observation that the great majority of the program characteristics affecting maintenance effort fall into the C category and hence fall under the control of the system developers and maintainers. Chapin concludes that with the proper and diligent application of software technologies currently available, such as structured programming and documentation tools, the maintenance effort can be reduced. Lyons claims that normally when structured programming methodologies are used in development, maintenance efforts are reduced by a 3:1 ratio.

WHAT IS THE PREDOMINANT MAINTENANCE ACTIVITY?

As shown in Fig. 2.2, most maintenance work falls into the category of perfective maintenance. This is somewhat of a revelation for the data-processing community, challenging the common belief that most maintenance effort is expended in a "firefighting" mode reacting to emergency repairs. In reality, most maintenance work can be anticipated and planned much like new development activities. Furthermore, user enhancements dominate the perfective maintenance category. In fact, they dominate all maintenance work. As shown in Fig. 2.2, user enhancements account for almost half of all maintenance work. Most user enhancements involve giving the user more information rather than consolidating or reformatting existing information. Lientz and Swanson claim that DP application systems which provide a greater number of predefined output reports are likely to be systems requiring a greater maintenance effort to provide additional reports. Using data-base management systems and report generators can ease the maintenance burden for the systems and programming staff since these tools enable end users to perform much of their own enhancement maintenance.

Another interesting observation is that most corrective and adaptive maintenance work is considered obligatory while perfective maintenance is discretionary. Therefore, nearly half of all maintenance work is discretionary. From this it follows that one method of minimizing the cost of software maintenance is to eliminate perfective maintenance in the interest of redirecting system and programming resources to the speedier development of replacement systems better able to meet user needs. Another less radical method is to more carefully scrutinize perfective maintenance activities. Change-request logs, formal change procedures, and user charge-back schemes can result in fewer and more thoughtful change requests.

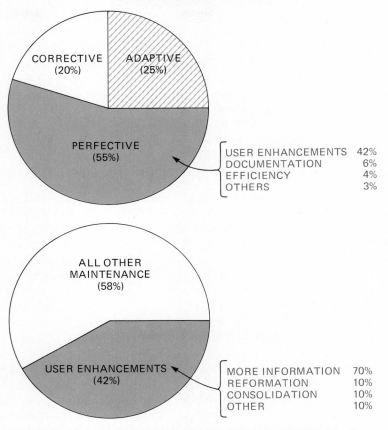

ALLOCATION OF SYSTEM AND PROGRAMMING RESOURCES
TO CORRECTIVE, ADAPTIVE, AND PERFECTIVE
MAINTENANCE ACTIVITIES

CORRECTIVE (20%) ADAPTIVE (25%) PERFECTIVE (55%)

USER ENHANCEMENTS   42%
DOCUMENTATION   6%
EFFICIENCY   4%
OTHERS   3%

ALL OTHER MAINTENANCE (58%) USER ENHANCEMENTS (42%)

MORE INFORMATION   70%
REFORMATION   10%
CONSOLIDATION   10%
OTHER   10%

Figure 2.2   Most maintenance work is performed to change or enhance, rather than correct, software. Perfective maintenance accounts for over half of all maintenance work, and responding to user enhancements alone accounts for almost half of all maintenance work. (Data from Lientz and Swanson surveys [9].)

MAINTENANCE STRATEGIES

Box 2.4 summarizes the state of the art of program maintenance. Based on these observations, here are some possible strategies to employ in controlling maintenance problems and costs.

1. *Corrective maintenance.* Ideally, we would like to completely elimi-

nate this type of maintenance by producing totally reliable systems. Although it is not yet cost-effective to produce 100% reliable software, use of newer technologies can substantially improve reliability and reduce the need to perform corrective maintenance. Some suggestions include:

- Data-base mangement systems
- Application development systems
- Program generators
- Very high-level (fourth-generation) languages
- Application packages
- Structured techniques
- Defensive programming
- Maintenance audits

The first four methods tend to produce more reliable code since much of the code is automatically generated. Application packages tend to have higher reliability than single-user systems since more users tend to find more errors. Programs developed using structured techniques tend to be easier to understand and to test since their control structure is standardized and the number of program paths is reduced by structuring restrictions. Defensive programming introduces self-checking capabilities into the program by checking for off-nominal situations, providing audit trails, and flagging unsafe programming practices. Finally, a periodic maintenance audit is a method that can help identify quality deficiencies before they cause maintenance problems.

2. *Adaptive maintenance.* This type of maintenance cannot be completely avoided, but it certainly can be controlled. For example, using configuration management to plan for computer hardware and operating system changes can reduce the need for some adaptive maintenance work. Also, isolating system-dependent features into special program modules can limit the portion of a program that must be modified to accommodate configuration changes. Finally, using internal program tables/arrays, external files, and packaged routines to handle special processing (e.g., government regulation) can make programs easier to modify when adaptive changes are necessary.

3. *Enhancement maintenance.* This can also be reduced by using the methods suggested for corrective and adaptive maintenance. Data-base management systems, generators, and packages can all be useful in reducing the maintenance support needed from the systems and programming staff. With these powerful yet easy-to-use tools, some enhancement work can be performed by the end users themselves or shifted to the software vendor.

In addition, building a prototype model of the system can reduce the need for future enhancements. Before the actual system is built, the users

BOX 2.4   Conclusions concerning program maintenance

1. Most organizations possess few historical data on maintenance. Data such as hours spent maintaining each application system categorized according to corrective, adaptive, perfective, and supportive activities, program and system error histories, and user enhancement requests should be recorded. Management will find such data invaluable in determining major maintenance problems and costs.

2. Maintenance problems encompass both technical and nontechnical issues. Approaches to solving maintenance problems that address only technical issues are valuable but insufficient. Approaches that address planning, project management, and user issues are at least equally important.

3. Although their use as development tools can improve software quality (especially reliability), current software development technologies do not address all facets of software maintainability. Technologies for designing software that is more amenable to change (such as data-base management systems, automatic generators) are also needed.

4. Because nearly one-half of all maintenance work is concerned with continuing development tasks, maintenance work is more similar to development projects than usually assumed, and software development technologies are more applicable to the maintenance environment than previously assumed. Techniques such as team programming concepts, structured walk-throughs, and quality audits should be used to improve the maintenance process.

5. Over one-half of all maintenance work falls into the enhancement maintenance category and is considered discretionary by the organization. Use of cost justification and user charge-back schemes may help curb this portion of maintenance effort.

6. Maintenance effort for a software system is dependent on variables such as system size, system age, system quality, and development experience of the maintainer. These variables can be measured by factors such as relative amount of routine debugging, number of predefined user reports, system complexity, and error-proneness. These factors can be used as predictors of maintenance effort (see Fig. 2.3).

7. Systems developed with newer technologies such as data-base management systems, automatic program generators, and structured techniques are more reliable and easier to modify and therefore easier to maintain.

8. Program quality often deteriorates with time since older systems tend to grow with age, to become less well organized with changes, and to become less understandable with staff turnover. Therefore, a system maintenance plan which includes a replacement/retirement plan, periodic quality audits, and a migration plan should be used to control system quality.

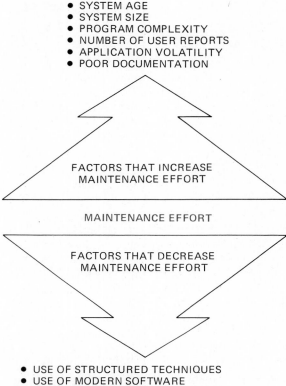

- SYSTEM AGE
- SYSTEM SIZE
- PROGRAM COMPLEXITY
- NUMBER OF USER REPORTS
- APPLICATION VOLATILITY
- POOR DOCUMENTATION

FACTORS THAT INCREASE
MAINTENANCE EFFORT

MAINTENANCE EFFORT

FACTORS THAT DECREASE
MAINTENANCE EFFORT

- USE OF STRUCTURED TECHNIQUES
- USE OF MODERN SOFTWARE
- USE OF AUTOMATED TOOLS
- USE OF DATA-BASE TECHNIQUES
- GOOD DATA ADMINISTRATION
- USE OF FOURTH-GENERATION LANGUAGES, GENERATORS, ETC.
- EXPERIENCE OF MAINTAINERS

Figure 2.3 Factors that affect maintenance effort.

are given a prototype model of the system. As users experiment with the prototype, they can more completely define system requirements. When users have a clearer understanding of how their system should behave and what functions it should provide, the actual system can be built.

4. *Supportive maintenance.* This type of maintenance can be reduced with the following:

- Up-to-date user documentation
- On-line user documentation
- Adequate user training
- Separate maintenance staff

BOX 2.5   Actions to take to minimize maintenance costs and delays

1. General

- Distinguish clearly between *prespecified* and *user-driven* incrementally changing applications. Understand that quite different techniques are needed for incrementally changing applications.
- Understand the importance of data-base techniques, especially Class IV data systems.
- Understand the impact of fourth-generation languages on the maintenance process.
- Estimate the costs of long-term maintenance when systems are being planned, and select techniques that minimize this.
- Evaluate the potential roles of the users in enhancement maintenance.
- Use prototyping tools to ensure that systems fit the users' requirements as well as possible before final programming.

2. Software Selection

- Use nonprocedural languages whenever possible.
- Use the most powerful languages—fourth-generation languages—rather than COBOL, PL/1, Ada, and so on.
- Select languages that are easy to maintain, and with which another person's code tends to be easy to understand.
- Use report generators (or graphics generators) for all reports.
- Use application generators for all applications that permit this approach.
- Use Class IV data systems wherever appropriate.
- Assess carefully the human factoring of software intended to be employed by users.
- Use application packages where these are suitable for future maintenance.
- Check the maintainability characteristics of packages carefully before purchase and evaluate the long-term maintenance costs.
- Build maintainability into the contract when purchasing or leasing packages.

3. Programming for Maintainability

- Use the highest-level languages that are practical.

(Continued)

BOX 2.5 (*Continued*)

- Use structured techniques designed to improve program quality and thereby minimize future maintenance.

- When programs are maintained, use the same structuring techniques and standards as originally used during development.

- Design systems that are easily modifiable and test this requirement (e.g., with inspections, change exercises).

- Define quality objectives and priorities in terms of measurable qualities, quality standards, and audit checks.

- Apply quantitative quality control measures (e.g., complexity analysis, 90–10 test, reliability models).

- Use modularization to divide the program into functionally and operationally independent components.

- Use a worst-first maintenance approach to uncover and replace systems or programs that are error-prone as soon as possible.

- Use data-base techniques fully for commercial DP.

- Ensure that the documentation is clear and comprehensive enough for future maintenance by emphasizing "what" and "why" type high-level commentary rather than "how" type low-level line-by-line comments.

- Structure the maintenance process by using team programming, structured techniques, scheduled maintenance, and maintenance reviews.

- Use defensive programming; that is, write programs that are self-checking.

- Opt for simplicity and clarity over machine efficiency and excessive generalization of function.

- Use data-base management systems, program generators, and application development systems that automatically generate reliable code and thereby decrease the need for corrective maintenance.

- Build a prototype before building the application, to reduce future enhancements requested by users.

- Use tools to improve the readability of systems (e.g., automated formatters, structuring engines, cross-reference generators, and documentation tools).

- Use state-of-the-art tools such as well-engineered operating systems, code auditors, structure display aids, optimizing compilers, documentation generators, test-data generators, on-line diagnostic programs, file compare utilities, source and file management systems, and on-line debuggers.

BOX 2.5 (*Continued*)

- When modifying an existing system, minimize the impact of the change by changing as little as possible, documenting the change, and preserving the original program style and integrity.
- Keep a maintenance journal describing maintenance objectives, plan, basic assumptions, change control philosophy, chronic problems, and so forth, for future maintainers.
- Strive for machine independence.
- Isolate specialized functions into separate modules and design module interfaces that are insensitive to internal module changes.

4. Data Considerations

- Control the design and definition of all data, except purely personal data, by good data administration techniques.
- Do not let programmers design their own data and embed them into programs. Generate all data definitions using a dictionary controlled by a data administrator.
- Model all data with a canonical modeling tool. Do not permit deviation from third-normal-form record structures (see Chapter 6) except in (very) exceptional cases with documented reasons.
- Apply stability analysis to all data structures before implementation.
- Endorse the principle of information engineering, enlist the support of top management to identify and build the information resources and data models that are needed, employ nonprocedural techniques for extracting information from those where possible, and use the same logical data representation to support program development.
- Use action diagrams with third-normal-form data models to create procedures that are directly translatable into program structures.

5. System Considerations

- Avoid software–hardware combinations that will lead to future maintenance difficulties (e.g., linking basically incompatible architectures, machines, operating systems, terminals, data bases, or networks).
- Do not modify complex systems software.
- Do not write your own data management facilities, network control programs, and so on.

(*Continued*)

BOX 2.5 (*Continued*)

- Understand the migration paths planned by your computer vendor(s) for future system evolution.
- Avoid becoming locked into data systems or network systems that will be expensive for future maintenance and need extensive future conversion.
- Use loose coupling rather than tight coupling between system modules unless the software is specifically designed for tight coupling.
- Plan what standards are necessary for the growth of distributed computing. Avoid distributing computers in ways that will lead to maintenance, compatibility, or conversion problems.
- Avoid proliferation of incompatible systems that will later have to be interconnected.
- Avoid proliferation of incompatible data on distributed systems where the data will later have to be exchanged or summarized.
- Avoid excessive system complexity by subdivision into largely autonomous modules designed to avoid maintenance problems.
- Establish configuration management policies to control hardware, operating system, and utility software changes.

6. End Users

- Make users develop and maintain user documentation and a user training program.
- Make users define system requirements and validation procedures.
- Encourage user participation in traditional software development by inviting users to attend development reviews and including users in development testing.
- Make users participate in the software package selection process.
- Encourage users to generate their own reports and graphics and to create their own applications where possible, with user-friendly languages.
- Make users document any systems they create (preferably with on-line documentation).
- Use information center management to encourage, support, and control user-driven computing and ensure that it employs the appropriate data modules and data dictionaries.
- Prevent skilled users from creating unmaintainable systems (e.g., in unstructured APL), except where these are purely personal tools.

BOX 2.5 (*Continued*)

7. Performing the Maintenance Function

- Establish a separate maintenance staff (in large installations) to improve control and increase productivity. Motivate the maintainers appropriately (to avoid low morale).

- Develop a system maintenance plan which includes a replacement/retirement plan and a new release plan.

- Employ powerful maintenance tools such as Amdahl's MAP (Chapter 19).

- Provide a program modification procedure that uses structured techniques.

- Improve documentation for existing systems.

- Emphasize careful and thorough retesting and revalidation when a program is modified.

- Cost-justify nonemergency changes and enhancements (to prespecified systems) and batch them into scheduled releases.

- Establish user charge-back schemes for discretionary maintenance work.

- Rotate development and maintenance staff to build experience in the development staff of what is required for maintenance.

- Use a "maintenance escort"—a development programmer who accompanies a system when it is transferred to the maintenance staff.

- Use fewer and better people to staff the maintenance function.

- Maintain clear accountability of each individual maintainer to enable each maintainer and his manager to measure performance.* Set up career paths, salary scales, and training opportunities to reward high performers.

- Justify modifications in terms of cost, time to implement, interruption to current user service, and risk of degrading software quality.

- Survey successful software project management approaches and adapt them to the maintenance environment.

- Use project management methods such as chief programmer team concepts and structured walk-throughs.

---

*The author has given much thought to the problem of avoiding words with a sexist connotation. It is possible to avoid words such as "man" and "manpower," but to avoid the use of "he," "his," and "him" makes sentences clumsy. In this book whenever these words appear, please assume that the meaning is "he or she," "his or her," and "him or her." They should be regarded as *neuter* words.

(*Continued*)

BOX 2.5   (*Continued*)

8. General Management Approaches

- Conduct periodic quality control audits of operational systems to ensure that quality remains at an acceptable level.

- Make sure that the data administrator reports at a high enough level and has enough clout to prevent deviation from his data models.

- Include experienced maintainers in the development process to ensure that software is developed with maintenance in mind.

- Establish and enforce programming and documentation standards.

- Identify those old systems with expensive maintenance and redevelop them with more modern techniques (data bases, fourth-generation languages, better structuring).

- Use an information center to maximize the use of user-developed, user-maintained systems (which link into the data administrator's data models).

- Motivate and educate all DP staff for good maintenance practices. Give all programmers, analysts, and DP managers a copy of this box.

The better end users understand the system, the less support they will require from the systems and programming staff. Often maintenance programmers spend a large portion of their time tracking reported program errors that are not actual errors but user misconceptions about how to use the system. Making user documentation more accessible and more understandable will alleviate much of this problem.

Establishing a separate maintenance staff allows better tracking of time allocated to the different types of maintenance work. If a substantial portion of time is spent on supportive maintenance, a buffer group can be created to act as an interface between system users and maintainers. The buffer group can relieve much of the maintainers' supportive maintenance burden by gathering problem reports and enhancement requests from the users and then passing them on to the maintainers. Also, the buffer group can improve user support by actually performing some maintenance tasks, such as documentation updates, error tracking, new release notification, and system revalidation. The buffer group should include some users and in some cases should be the responsibility of the users.

Box 2.5 provides a more comprehensive list of methods to minimize maintenance effort and costs. The methods are divided into seven categories:

1. General
2. Software selection
3. Programming for maintainability
4. Data considerations
5. System considerations
6. End users
7. Management approaches

In the chapters that follow, these methods will be presented and discussed in more detail.

REFERENCES

1. H. D. Mills, "Software Development," *IEEE Trans. on Software Engineering,* Vol. SE-2, No. 4 (December 1976): 265–273.

2. John Reutter, "Maintenance Is a Management Problem and a Programmer's Opportunity," AFIPS Conference Proceedings on 1981 National Computer Conference (Chicago), Vol. 50, May 4–7, 1981, pp. 343–347.

3. B. Boehm, J. Brown, and M. Lipow, "Quantitative Evaluation of Software Quality," 2nd International Conference on Software Engineering, Proceedings (San Francisco), October 13–15, 1976, pp. 592–605.

4. M. J. Lyons, "Salvaging Your Software Asset (Tools-Based Maintenance)," AFIPS Conference Proceedings on 1981 National Computer Conference (Chicago), Vol. 50, May 4–7, 1981, pp. 337–342.

5. C. Liu, "A Look at Software Maintenance," *Datamation,* Vol. 22, No. 11 (November 1976): 51–55.

6. E. Swanson, "The Dimensions of Maintenance," 2nd International Conference on Software Engineering, Proceedings (San Francisco), October 13–15, 1976, pp. 492–497.

7. B. Lientz, E. Swanson, and G. Tompkins, "Characteristics of Application Software Maintenance," *Communications of the ACM,* Vol. 21, No. 6 (June 1978): 466–471.

8. R. Riggs, "Computer System Maintenance," *Datamation,* Vol. 15, No. 11 (November 1969): 227–235.

9. B. Lientz and E. Swanson, *Software Maintenance Management* (Reading, MA: Addison-Wesley Publishing Co., Inc., 1980), pp. 151–157.

10. N. Chapin, "Productivity in Software Maintenance," AFIPS Conference Proceedings on 1981 National Computer Conference (Chicago), Vol. 50, May 4–7, 1981, pp. 349–352.

11. E. Chrysler, "Some Basic Determinants of Computer Programming Productivity," *Communications of the ACM,* Vol. 21, No. 6 (June 1978): 472–483.

12. "Easing the Software Maintenance Burden," *EDP Analyzer,* Vol. 19, No. 8 (August 1981).

13. B. Boehm, "The High Cost of Software," Proceedings of Symposium on High Cost of Software (Standford Research Institute), September 1973.

14. B. DeRose and T. Nyman, "The Software Life Cycle—A Management and Technological Challenge in the Department of Defense," *IEEE Trans. on Software Engineering,* Vol. SE-4, No. 4 (July 1978): 309–318.

15. P. M. Cashman and A. W. Holt, "A Communication-Oriented Approach to Structuring the Software Maintenance Environment," *Software Engineering Notes,* Vol. 5, No. 1 (January 1980): 4–17.

16. M. V. Zelkowitz, A. C. Shaw, and J. D. Gannon, *Principles of Software Engineering and Design* (Englewood Cliffs, N.J.: Prentice-Hall, Inc., 1979).

17. E. Dijkstra, "Structured Programming," in *Software Engineering Techniques* (New York: Petrocelli/Charter), 1976.

PART **DESIGNING FOR MAINTENANCE**

3 MEASURES OF PROGRAM MAINTAINABILITY

SOFTWARE
QUALITY

Maintainability is the ease with which a software system can be corrected when errors or deficiencies occur, and can be expanded or contracted to satisfy new requirements.

Maintainability is one of several characteristics sought in a high-quality software system. In general, a high-quality software system possesses such characteristics as usability, reliability, and understandability, in addition to maintainability. All these characteristics are desirable, but in practice they may not all be attainable. Emphasizing certain characteristics often leads to compromising others due to time, cost, and technological constraints.

Software developers and users have different notions of software quality. Software developers usually consider more technical characteristics, such as structuredness and completeness, as most important. On the other hand, end users probably consider ease of use and ability to respond to changing requirements as most important. When the user's, programmer's, and management's notions of software quality do not agree, an otherwise successful software effort may be doomed for failure. Even though a software system is delivered on schedule, within budget, and correctly performs all intended functions, it may not be capable of performing satisfactorily. The system may be reliable but difficult to understand and therefore difficult to modify. The system may be easy to use but also easy to misuse. It may be efficient but unnecessarily machine-dependent and therefore not portable.

The inability of users, managers, and programmers to understand one another's concept of software quality and the inability to define and measure quality are two major contributors to user disappointments and the high cost of software maintenance. The struggle to correct such quality discrepancies is often the underlying reason for the unexpected magnitude of many maintenance efforts.

How software quality is defined and how its importance is interpreted affects the resulting software product. A clear understanding of software quality and of the importance attached to the various software quality characteristics is essential to achieving success in any programming effort and to controlling software life-cycle costs. Too little quality translates into too much cost.

DEFINING MAINTAINABILITY

The definition of maintainability given earlier tells us the objective of maintainability but does not tell us how to achieve this objective. To quantify the concept of software quality Boehm et al. [1] defined software quality as a hierarchical set of quality characteristics (Fig. 3.1). Each characteristic represents an aspect of quality that is typically sought for most software systems. Each successive level in the hierarchy further expands the definition of quality. Higher levels relate to software usage needs and lower levels to metrics for evaluating quality. As shown in Fig. 3.1, general utility is at the root of quality hierarchy. Utility is the most general quality characteristic sought in all "real-world" software systems. If a system is not useful to or usable by its user community, it cannot be considered a high-quality system regardless of the elegance of its algorithm or its implementation.

The second level of the hierarchy explains that to possess the quality of general utility, a system must possess the qualities of as-is utility and maintainability as well as portability.

To be maintainable a software system must be testable, understandable, and modifiable. Testability is the ease with which we can demonstrate the correctness of software changes; understandability is the extent to which we

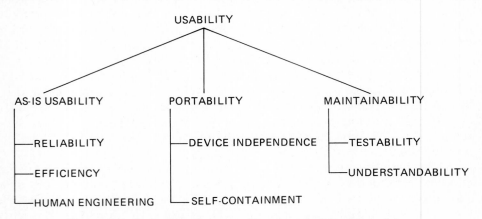

Figure 3.1 Boehm's software quality characteristics hierarchy.

can read and understand the software code and documentation; and modifiability is the ease with which we can modify the software code.

Do these three characteristics adequately define maintainability? To answer this question, recall (Chapter 2) Swanson's three basic categories of maintenance activities [2].

1. *Corrective maintenance:* performed to identify and correct software failures, performance failures, and implementation failures
2. *Adaptive maintenance:* performed to adapt software to changes in the data requirements or processing environments
3. *Perfective maintenance:* performed to enhance performance and improve cost-effectiveness, processing efficiency, and maintainability

First, consider corrective maintenance. Certainly, the characteristics of testability, understandability, and modifiability are essential to being able to perform corrective maintenance tasks efficiently and effectively. In addition, the characteristic of reliability is important. The more reliable a system, the less need to perform corrective maintenance. According to survey results shown in Fig. 3.2, making a system 100% reliable could result in a 20% maintenance savings [3].

Next, consider adaptive maintenance activities. Modifiability is perhaps the most essential characteristic needed to perform adaptive maintenance. However, portability is also extremely important since portability will improve a system's ability to respond to computing environment changes and thereby reduce the need to perform adaptive maintenance. As shown in

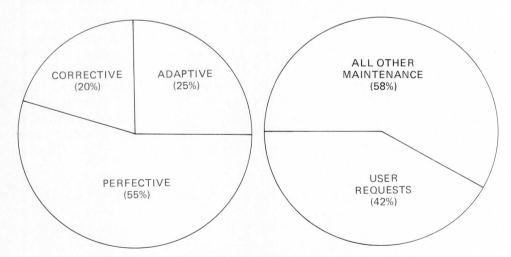

Figure 3.2 Maintenance effort according to the Leintz–Swanson surveys [3].

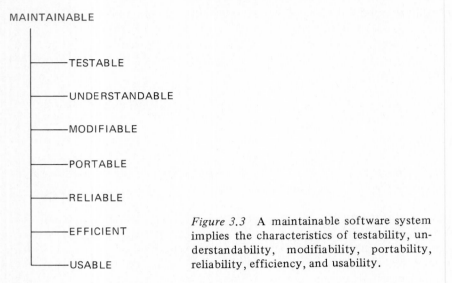

MAINTAINABLE

├──── TESTABLE

├──── UNDERSTANDABLE

├──── MODIFIABLE

├──── PORTABLE

├──── RELIABLE

├──── EFFICIENT

└──── USABLE

Figure 3.3 A maintainable software system implies the characteristics of testability, understandability, modifiability, portability, reliability, efficiency, and usability.

Fig. 3.2, adaptive maintenance activities on average account for 25% of the maintenance effort. Improving portability may translate into a significant maintenance savings.

Finally, consider perfective maintenance activities, which account for over half of the total maintenance effort. User requests for enhancements account for the majority of the perfective maintenance effort. By increasing the user's understanding of how to more effectively use a software system and by allowing the user to perform some types of software changes, this portion of the maintenance effort can be significantly reduced. In addition, perfective maintenance activities include changes made to improve software efficiency. Making software as efficient as possible will help reduce the need for this sort of maintenance.

An expanded view of maintainability is needed. Too narrow a view has led us to discount some very effective ways in which to reduce maintenance costs. As shown in Fig. 3.3, a high degree of maintainability in a software system should imply a high degree of reliability, portability, efficiency, and usability as well as testability, understandability, and modifiability.

MEASURING MAINTAINABILITY

Having defined a set of basic characteristics that a software system should possess to maximize its maintainability, the next step is to consider how to measure these characteristics. For example, how do we know whether or not a software program is understandable? We shall employ three methods:

1. Quality checklists

2. Quality tests

3. Quality metrics

Quality checklists are a list of questions testing for the presence of certain program properties considered essential in a high-quality software system. For example, one question testing for reliability is: Are procedures for recovery from errors and for restarts included? Each question is answered with a "yes" or "no" depending on the qualitative judgment of a human evaluator.

Quality tests and metrics provide a way of quantifying quality judgments. Several different tests and metrics have been proposed to measure objectively the degree to which certain quality characteristics are present in a software system. No claim can be made as to their completeness or universal applicability. However, many strong, convincing experiences in industry support their usefulness in quantifying the notion of software quality. Careful attention to quality has led to significant savings in software life-cycle costs. Long-term benefits include their ability to predict where errors and difficulties are likely to occur in a software system. No single test or metric has been developed thus far to measure overall software quality since many individual quality characteristics are in conflict. For example, efficiency may be obtained at the expense of portability, understandability, and accuracy. Therefore, we shall consider several different metrics. Some metrics will provide important insights into the limitations of existing software systems; others can help pinpoint potential problems in newly developed systems. In the sections that follow, each quality characteristic of maintainability shown in Fig. 3.3 will be defined and methods to measure it will be presented.

UNDERSTANDABILITY

Understandability is perhaps the most fundamental requirement for a maintainable program. If a program is not understandable, it is virtually impossible to maintain in any sort of efficient or effective manner. Unfortunately, in industry today there are countless examples of programs that are difficult to understand. This is a major factor in the high cost of maintenance and also a major factor in the distaste for performing maintenance tasks. Many programmer trainees have been discouraged from pursuing a programming career after a succession of frustrating and unsuccessful attempts to understand someone else's program.

Understandability is defined as the ease with which we can understand the function of a program and how it achieves this function by reading the program source code and its associated documentation. In an understandable program there is adequate information for a reader to determine the program objectives, assumptions, constraints, inputs, outputs, components, relationship to other programs, and status. Understandability also implies that we can easily understand the program at varying levels of detail and that the technical expertise required varies with the desired level of understanding. In an understandable program, a novice programmer (e.g., a user or manager) can easily obtain a cursory overview understanding of the program, or an experienced programmer can easily obtain a detailed understanding of each component in the program.

Several factors influence how easy or difficult it is to understand a particular program. These factors can be categorized into two groups: programmer ability and program form. The programmer's experience and fluency with a particular programming language greatly influences his ability to understand a program. Also, a programmer's familiarity with the application area can influence the ease with which a program is understood.

Understandable programs are typically characterized by certain properties such as:

1. Modularity
2. Consistency of style
3. Avoidance of "trick" or obscure code
4. Use of meaningful data and procedure names
5. Structuredness

Much of the work in structured programming was aimed at formalizing the notion of good program structure as the key to controlling program understandability and software costs. Structured programming attempts to improve understandability through a standardization of program form. This standardization imposes restrictions on program control constructs, modularization, and documentation. Automatic structure checkers are available to check the structuredness of a program.

Although helpful, good structure does not completely ensure all aspects of program understandability. Boehm suggests that in addition to being well-structured, an understandable program must also be concise, consistent, and complete [1].

A *concise* program is a program in which no excessive pieces are present. For example, in a concise program every program instruction must be reachable. This property is considered important because "unreachable" code can be a source of confusion to the program reader. Automatic flow-charting programs can be used to detect unreachable code.

A *consistent* program is a program that is written in a consistent coding style and follows a consistent design approach. Consistency of coding style implies that the program contains a uniform notation, terminology, and symbology. This aspect of consistency is included with the definition of a well-structured program. Consistency of a design approach is what Brooks

BOX 3.1 Understandability checklist*

Structuredness

1. Is the program modularized and well-structured? (See Chapter 4 for a list of general structuring rules.)

Documentation

2. Is the program documented? Minimal documentation for a well-structured program requires a comment block for each module, sub-routine, or subprogram that explains:

   (a) What the module does in one or two brief sentences.
   (b) A list of the program variables whose values may be modified in this module.
   (c) A list of the modules that invoke this module.
   (d) A list of the modules that this module invokes. (See Chapters 8 and and 9 for a detailed discusssion of documentation.)

3. Is other useful commentary material included in the program? This would include:

   (a) Inputs and outputs
   (b) Accuracy checks
   (c) Limitations and restrictions
   (d) Assumptions
   (e) Error recovery procedures for all foreseeable error exits
   (f) Modification history
   (g) Date written and date last changed

Consistency

4. Is a consistent indentation and spacing style used throughout the program?

5. Is there at most one executable statement per line of code?

6. Are all variable names and procedure names unique, descriptive, and in compliance to company standards?

7. Does each variable and each procedure have one and only one unique name in the program?

8. Is each variable used to represent one and only one quantity, and each procedure used to represent one and only one logical function?

9. Is the program a true representation of the design; that is, is the integrity of the design preserved throughout the entire program?

   (a) Does the program neither add to nor subtract from the design algorithm?
   (b) Is the design structure exactly and explicitly represented in the code?

(Continued)

BOX 3.1 *(Continued)*

10. Are all elements of an array/table functionally related?

11. Are parentheses used to clarify the evaluation order of complex arithmetic and logical expressions?

Completeness

12. Are cross-reference listings of variable names and a map of calling and called subroutines supplied?

13. Are all external references resolvable and all input/output descriptions available?

14. Does the program contain all referenced subprograms not available in the usual system library?

15. Are all unusual termination conditions described?

16. Are error recovery procedures included?

17. Are error messages descriptive and clearly displayed?

Conciseness

18. Is all code reachable?

19. Are all variables necessary?

20. Is redundant code avoided by creating common modules/subroutines?

21. Is there a transfer to all labels?

22. Is division of the program into an excessive number of modules, overlays, functions, or subroutines avoided?

23. Are expressions factored to avoid unnecessary repetition of common subexpressions?

24. Does the program avoid performing complementary operations on the same variable(s) such that removal of these operations leaves the program unchanged?

25. Does the program avoid poorly understood and nonstandard language features?

---

*Many of the questions have been adapted from Boehm's [1] checklists.

calls conceptual integrity [4]. Conceptual integrity is preserved when one basic design approach is carried through the entire program. Table-driven logic is an example of one possible design approach. In a program with conceptual integrity, the task of understanding the rationale behind the program logic is greatly simplified.

A *complete* program is a program for which all its components are present and each of its components is fully developed. This is an obvious requirement for understandability. If a reader cannot find the source code for some portion of the program, it will hamper his ability to understand the program—especially if he is seeking a detailed level of understanding— similarly if a reader cannot find overview documentation for the program and must resort to a tedious and time-consuming examination of the source code.

Box 3.1 contains a checklist of questions to measure program understandability. Each question requires a simple "yes" or "no" answer. The more "yes" responses for a program, the more understandable the program. For large programs this type of checklist evaluation may prove too time consuming. Instead of evaluating the entire program, a set of representative modules can be selected. At least 10% of the modules should be randomly selected. The understandability of the entire program is judged based on a checklist evaluation of these representative modules.

A major criticism of the checklist approach is that it is subjective and its validity depends on the knowledge of a human evaluator. To solve this problem more objective measures have been proposed.

90–10 TEST

Shneiderman suggests one test for measuring program understandability. He proposes that every program module should meet a 90–10 test; that is, a competent programmer should be able to functionally reconstruct from memory 90% of the module after 10 minutes of examining the source listing [5].

It is neither practical nor necessary to apply the 90–10 test to all modules in a program. Only a small, representative sample of modules need be tested to evaluate the overall understandability of the program.

PROGRAM COMPLEXITY METRICS

Program complexity is another measure of program understandability. The more complex a program, the more difficult it is to understand. Program complexity is introduced by the difficulty of the programming problem and the size of the program. It is a function of the number of possible execution paths in the program and the difficulty of determining the path for an arbitrary set of input data. As a simple example, a program that has only one execution path (regardless of its input data) has no complexity.

Several program complexity metrics have been proposed. Some may be applied to the program design; others examine the source code. Some evaluate the complexity of a module; others are used to evaluate the complexity of an entire program. Several uses for complexity metrics have been suggested:

1. *A design tool:* to evaluate the "goodness" of a modularization scheme so that the program is understandable, testable, and maintainable

2. *A testing tool:* to identify which modules will be most difficult to test

3. *A maintenance tool:* to predict which modules will be most difficult to modify and will be most error-prone.

In this chapter we look at four different complexity metrics:

1. Module size
2. Halstead's software science
3. McCabe's cyclomatic number
4. McClure's control variable complexity

These metrics have been selected because they are easy to use, they are generally applicable to a variety of programming languages, and they have been used in industry.

MODULE SIZE

The simplest complexity metric is module size. It is based on two assumptions:

1. Program complexity increases disproportionately as program size increases.
2. The best way to control size is to apply the divide-and-conquer rule. By dividing a program into understandable pieces, the whole program can be more easily understood.

For example, IBM advises that a program module not exceed 50 lines of code [6]. The reasoning is that confining a module to one page in a source listing allows the reader to understand the whole program by understanding each small piece.

This metric is probably too simplistic to measure complexity accurately since the length of a piece of code is usually not a good indicator of complexity. The logical tasks performed, the control constructs employed, and the program variables referenced also affect how easily the code can be understood. Module size is useful only as a rough "rule of thumb" guideline for restricting modules to a reasonable size.

SOFTWARE SCIENCE   During the 1970s there were several attempts to define and measure the complexity of a computer program. Halstead's theory, called *software science,* is among the most promising. Numerous studies and experiments from both the academic and the industrial communities have shown software science metrics to be amazingly accurate [7]. In addition to measuring complexity and overall quality of existing software, Halstead's metrics have been used to measure program reliability, to predict program length, and to estimate programming effort.

Perhaps what is most impressive about Halstead's theory is that it is based on a simple count of program operators and operands that can be automatically computed during compilation. Operators include arithmetic operators (e.g., +, −, *, |), logical operators (e.g., greater than, equal to), and keywords (e.g., FORTRAN DO, COBOL PERFORM), and delimiters. Operands include constants and variables. Software science metrics for any program can be derived from four basic counts:

n_1: number of distinct operators in program

n_2: number of distinct operands in program

N_1: total number of operators in program

N_2: total number of operands in program

In Fig. 3.4 the values of n_1, n_2, N_1, and N_2 are given for a section of COBOL code.

Several simple complexity theories have been developed to relate these counts to program properties, such as length, volume, and languages. For example, the length, N, of a program is computed by

$$N = N_1 + N_2$$

The vocabulary, n, of a program is computed by

$$n = n_1 + n_2$$

N is a simple measure of program size. The larger the value of N, the more difficult the program is to understand and the more effort required to maintain it. N is an alternative measure of program size preferred over counting lines of code in a module. Although it is almost as simple to compute, N is a more sensitive complexity measure than a line count because N does not assume that all instructions are equally easy or difficult to understand.

In a study of 154 PL/1 programs at General Motors Research Laboratories, Elshoff was able to predict the length of a program quite accurately

```
DE-LETE SECTION.
DE-LETE-ENTRY.
    MOVE SEQ-RESER-KEY TO RT-RESER-KEY.
    READ IS-FILE INTO RT-RESER-REC
        INVALID KEY MOVE 'NONEXIST RESERVATION' TO PRT-MES-SAGE
            PERFORM PRT-TRANS2
            GO TO DE-LETE-EXIT.
*TRY TO MATCH BETWEEN NAME TO BE DELETED AND NAMES ON RECORD.
    IF SEQ-NAME1 = RT-NAME1
        MOVE SPACES TO RT-NAME1
        MOVE 'RESERVATION DELETED' TO PRT-MES-SAGE
        PERFORM CHECK-NAME
    ELSE IF SEQ-NAME1 = RT-NAME2
        MOVE SPACES TO RT-NAME2
        MOVE 'RESERVATION DELETED' TO PRT-MES-SAGE
        PERFORM CHECK-NAME
    ELSE
        MOVE 'NONEXIST RESERVATION'  TO PRT-MES-SAGE
        PERFORM PRT-TRANS
        PERFORM PRT-TRANS2.
DE-LETE-EXIT.
    EXIT.
```

OPERATORS	COUNT	OPERANDS	COUNT
MOVE	7	SEQ-RESER-KEY	1
READ	1	RT-RESER-KEY	1
INVALID KEY	1	IS-FILE	1
PERFORM	5	RT-RESER-REC	1
GOTO	1	PRT-MES-SAGE	4
=	2	'NONEXIST RESERVATION'	2
IF	2	SEQ-NAME1	2
.	6	RT-NAME 1	2
	25	SPACES	2
		'RESERVATION DELETED'	2
		RT-NAME	2
			20

$n_1 = 8$ $n_2 = 11$
$N_1 = 25$ $N_2 = 20$

Figure 3.4 Software science metrics for any program can be derived from four basic counts: n_1, number of distinct operators in the program; n_2, number of distinct operands in the program; N_1, total number of operators in the program; N_2, total number of operands in the program. The values for n_1, n_2, N_1, and N_2 are shown for a section of COBOL program code.

(correlation between actual and predicted length was .98) by merely knowing the number of unique operators and operands in the program [8]. He calculated estimated length, $\hat{N}$, as follows:

$$\hat{N} = n_1 \log_2 n_1 + n_2 \log_2 n_2$$

In addition, Elshoff found that the estimated length, $\hat{N}$, more closely equaled the actual length, N, for well-structured programs. Based on this finding, he used a comparison of $\hat{N}$ and N as a simple check for structuredness.

Regardless of the programming language, any program has an integer number of unique operands, n_2. The simplest useful program has one input and one output, or $n_2 = 2$. The next simplest program has one input and two outputs or two inputs and one output; or $n_2 = 3$. Therefore, it has been proposed that n_2 is another measure of program complexity. Experiments have shown that as n_2 increases, programming difficulty also increases. For example, in an experiment which entailed converting ALGOL programs to FORTRAN and then expanding the number of outputs by 1, Woodfield observed that a 25% increase in n_2 doubled the programming effort [9]. Perhaps n_2 represents a simple way to quantify Dijkstra's premise that the difficulty of a program increases quadratically, not linearly, with its length [10].

Halstead's program volume and program level metrics represent ways to quantify the generally accepted intuitive notion that higher-level programming languages are easier to understand than lower-level programming languages. For example, consider the implementation of the sine function. In FORTRAN this requires one statement:

$$Y = SIN(X)$$

and involves two operands (X,Y) and two operators (=,SIN()). In COBOL or assembly language many instructions involving several operands and operators would be necessary. Program level, L, is a measure of the succinctness of the implementation of the program design. The highest, most succinct level at which a design can be implemented is with one instruction in which a single operator is capable of transforming input to output. (Of course, this implementation level does not always exist in practice.) Level, L, is defined as the ratio of potential volume to actual volume

$$L = V^*/V$$

where V^* is the volume of the most compact possible design implementation and $V = N \log_2 n$.

V measures the number of bits needed to provide a unique designator for each of the n items in the program vocabulary. If a given program is

BOX 3.2   Halstead's software science metrics

Basic Counts

- n_1:   number of distinct operators appearing in the program
- n_2:   number of distinct operands appearing in the program
- N_1:   total number of occurrences of operators in the program
- N_2:   total number of occurrences of operands in the program

Measures of Program Complexity

- Program length: $N = N_1 + N_2$
- Number of unique operands: n_2
- Program effort: $E = V/L$ where $V = N \log_2 n$
$$L = V^*/V$$
  V^* is volume of most compact design
     implementation
  $$n = n_1 + n_2$$

translated into another language, its volume and hence its complexity will change. As we would expect, the volume decreases as we go from lower-level to higher-level languages containing more powerful instruction sets.

According to several empirical studies, program effort, E, is an even better measure of program understandability than either N or n_2:

$$E = V/L$$

In several different programming experiments, the estimated programming effort calculated using software science metrics was found to closely match the actual programming effort. In a study involving FORTRAN, PL/l, and APL programs, Halstead predicted 22.51 hours for the experiment. Actual time was 20.15 hours [7].

When applied to individual programs, software science metrics may not always be accurate [11]. However, the great number of empirical results reported thus far provides significant indication that program understandability can be accurately assessed by a simple examination of a few elementary program factors such as those suggested by Halstead. Box 3.2 summarizes the software science metrics presented in this chapter.

The advantage of Halstead's software science as a measure of program understandability is threefold:

1. Software science metrics are easy to calculate and do not require resorting to analysis of programming features such as depth of statement nesting or detailed flow analysis.

2. Software science metrics are applicable to any program language and yet are programming language sensitive.

3. Many different statistical studies of programs from industry demonstrate their validity as predictors of programming effort and mean number of bugs in a program.

CYCLOMATIC NUMBER

McCabe suggest a graph-theoretic complexity measure [12]. His strategy is to measure program complexity by computing the number of linearly independent paths through a program. McCabe refers to this number as the *cyclomatic number.*

Complexity evaluation is applied at the module level in a program. McCabe uses the cyclomatic number to control the "size" of a program and hence its understandability by limiting the cyclomatic complexity of each module in the program to a maximum of 10. McCabe arrived at 10 as a reasonable limit for cyclomatic complexity after examining several FORTRAN programs. He found that modules (and indeed programs containing modules) whose cyclomatic complexity was greater than 10 were generally more troublesome and less reliable. McCabe suggests that modules with cyclomatic number greater than 10 should be redesigned and perhaps subdivided into a group of modules.

An automated tool, FLOW, was developed to compute the cyclomatic complexity of FORTRAN programs. It is used as a program design tool and a program test tool. During program design, the programmer computes the complexity of each module as it is designed. If its complexity is greater than the recommended limit, the module is redesigned before it is implemented in code. During the test phase, the programmer designs the test plan to concentrate on the more complex modules in the program.

For structured programs, cyclomatic complexity can be calculated simply by counting the number of compares:

$$\text{cyclomatic complexity} = \text{compares} + 1$$

Because calculation is so simple, an automatic tool is not even necessary for evaluating the complexity of structured programs.

Like Halstead's software science theory, McCabe's approach is appealing because it is so simple to apply. Although McCabe experimented primarily with FORTRAN programs, the cyclomatic complexity number can be computed for programs written in any programming language. For example, the COBOL code shown in Fig. 3.4 includes 2 compares, and therefore has a cyclomatic complexity value of 3.

CONTROL VARIABLE COMPLEXITY McClure suggests a complexity measure designed primarily for use with COBOL programs [13]. Although similar to McCabe's approach, McClure suggests that a more accurate measure of complexity must examine the complexity of the variables used in the compares as well as the number of compares. Consider the example shown in Fig. 3.5. Using McCabe's method of counting compares, the complexity of each segment of code is the same, 6. Intuitively, it can be argued that the code in segment B is more difficult to understand than the code in segment A because segment A references only one variable whereas segment B references five variables. But this difference is not detected by the cyclomatic complexity number.

McClure's method for calculating the complexity of a program includes three steps:

1. Compute the complexity value for each control variable. (A control variable is a variable whose value is used to direct path selection in a program, i.e., referenced in a compare.)
2. Compute the complexity value for each module in the program.
3. Compute the complexity value for a program by summing the complexity values for all its modules.

In a simplified version of McClure's complexity measure, the complexity $C(m)$ of a module m is calculated as follows:

$$C(m) = C + V$$

where C is the number of compares in the module and V is the number of control variables referenced in the modules. In Fig. 3.4, the COBOL DE-LETE section shown has two compares and three control variables, SEQ-NAME1, RT-NAME1, and RT-NAME2. Thus, $C(DE\text{-}LETE) = 2 + 3 = 5$. Note that constants are not counted.

In Fig. 3.5, $C(A) = 6$ and $C(B) = 10$. This agrees with our intuitive sense that segment B is more difficult to understand than segment A.

McClure's method can be used as a design tool or a testing tool. According to McClure, one objective of the design phase is to produce the best possible modularization scheme for the program—one that increases understandability, testability, and maintainability. Such a modularization scheme is one in which the complexity of each module is minimized and one in which complexity is evenly distributed throughout the program. Avoiding "pockets" of complexity will increase overall understandability. McClure does not suggest a complexity limit as does McCabe. Instead, she suggests computing an average complexity value for all modules in the program. Modules whose complexity is high or low relative to this average are ex-

```
IF TCODE = 1                    IF TCODE = 1 AND NAME = BLANKS
    PERFORM ADD                     PERFORM CREATE
ELSE IF TCODE = 2               ELSE IF TYPE = 2
    PERFORM DELETE                  PERFORM MODIFY
ELSE IF TCODE = 3                      WHILE FILEND = 1
    PERFORM MODIFY1             ELSE IF CFIELD = BLANKS
ELSE IF TCODE = 4                  MOVE 2 TO ERROR
    PERFORM MODIFY 2            ELSE
ELSE IF TCODE = 7                  MOVE 3 TO ERROR.
    PERFORM INSERT
ELSE
    MOVE 1 TO ERROR.



CODE FOR SEGMENT A              CODE FOR SEGMENT B




    No. of compares in Segment A:    5
    No. of compares in Segment B:    5
    Control variables in Segment A:  TCODE
    Control variables in Segment B:  TCODE, NAME,
                                     TYPE, FILEND, CFIELD
```

Figure 3.5 The code in segment B is more complex than the code in segment A because of the number of control variables referenced. Using McCabe's cyclomatic number to calculate complexity, the complexity of segment A and segment B is 6. But using McClure's control variable complexity to calculate complexity, the complexity of segment A is 6 and the complexity of segment B is 10.

amined. Since breaking a program into too many modules can be just as detrimental to understandability as breaking it into too few, both complexity extremes must be considered during redesign. Also, the complexity of control variables is examined and used to guide the redesign.

McClure also suggests that complexity considerations be used to guide the testing plan. A top-down testing approach stressing the need to test module interfaces is advocated. In addition, modules and variables which are the most complex are tested the most thoroughly since these portions of the program are more error-prone.

Box 3.3 summarizes McClure's control variable complexity metric.

RELIABILITY

Reliability is defined as the extent to which a program correctly performs its functions in a manner intended by the users as interpreted by its designers. A reliable program is correct, complete, and consistent.

BOX 3.3   McClure's control variable complexity

The complexity $C(m)$ of a program module m is calculated as follows:

$$C(m) = C + V$$

where C is the number of compares in module m and V is the number of control variables referenced in module m.

Total reliability remains a goal rather than an actuality in virtually all "real-world" software. There currently exists no means for guaranteeing 100% reliability or for measuring exactly how reliable a program is. Mathematical methods have been developed to establish program correctness through formal proofs. However, because of the difficulty of automating these methods, they have not yet become economically viable in practice.

The more practical and commonly accepted approach for showing correctness is program testing. *Testing* is defined as the controlled execution of a program in order to reveal errors [14]. Testing has several important limitations. Testing cannot prove a program correct; it can only show the presence of errors. Testing is not a means for introducing reliability; it is only a diagnostic exercise. Testing cannot address some reliability concerns. For example, will the program perform as intended for all possible input data—including valid and invalid data? What is the probability that incorrect output results will persist undetected? How many errors will be discovered during the operation/maintenance phase? Box 3.4 presents a checklist for measuring software reliability. The more "yes" responses to the questions, the more reliable the program.

BEBUGGING   Gilb suggests a method called *bebugging* to quantitatively measure reliability [15]. This method is based on the assumption that the number of errors removed from the program is related to the reliability of the program. Bebugging requires that a known number and type of artificial errors be inserted into the program and used to predict the number of actual errors remaining in the program. The program is seeded by someone other than the program testers. A seeding rate of four errors per 100 instructions is suggested. Then during testing, as both real and seeded errors are found, the number of seeded errors found is used to estimate the number of real errors remaining in the program:

BOX 3.4   Reliability checklist

1. Does the program contain checks for potentially undefined arithmetic operations (e.g., division by zero)?

2. Are loop termination and multiple transfer index parameter ranges tested before they are used?

3. Are subscript ranges tested before they are used?

4. Are error recovery and restart procedures included?

5. Are numerical methods sufficiently accurate?

6. Are input data validated?

7. Are test results satisfactory (i.e., do actual output results correspond exactly to expected results)?

8. Do tests show that most execution paths have been exercised during testing?

9. Do tests concentrate on most complex modules and most complex module interfaces?

10. Do tests cover the normal, extreme, and exceptional processing cases?

11. Was the program tested with real as well as contrived data?

12. Does the program make use of standard library routines rather than develop its own code to perform commonly used functions?

$$\text{no. of real errors remaining} = \frac{\text{no. of real errors found}}{\text{no. of seed errors found}} \times \frac{\text{total no. of}}{\text{seed errors}}$$

The percentage of real errors remaining in the program indicates program reliability.

Gilb also suggests that bebugging can be used to determine when a program has been tested enough. For example, if 95% reliability is considered sufficient, then testing stops when 95% of all seeded errors have been found.

RELIABILITY MODELS

Borrowing from hardware reliability terminology, Shneiderman defines software reliability as the probability that a program will operate successfully for at least some given period of time [5]. Shooman provides a similar but expanded definition in which software reliability is defined as the probability that a program will operate for some given period of time without software error on the computer system for which it was designed, provided that it is used within its intended limits [5]. These definitions suggest using software error statistics as a measure of software reliability. Consider the following three possibilities derived from hardware measures:

1. Mean time between errors (MTBE)
2. Mean time to repair errors (MTTR)
3. Percent uptime

Shooman created a software reliability model for predicting the mean time between errors (MTBE) based on the following assumptions:

1. The total number of errors in a program is fixed.
2. Most programs reach a reasonably debugged state.
3. The failure rate is proportional to the number of software errors remaining in the program after development testing.
4. The introduction of new errors when correcting detected errors has negligible impact on reliability.

Other software reliability models patterned after hardware reliability measures have been developed by Jelinksi and Moranda, and Hansen and Musa [5]. These models are criticized for their failure to distinguish between severity of errors, to consider program size and complexity, and to predict where errors are likely to occur in the program. Also, their basic assumptions are questionable.

ERROR STATISTICS

A *simpler* and perhaps more effective method for predicting software reliability is based on an evaluation of the program error statistics. The assumption is that programs (modules) that were difficult to test are difficult to maintain. Programs (modules) in which more errors were found during testing are the programs (modules) in which more are likely to occur during the operations/maintenance phase. A more detailed discussion of error statistics is presented in Chapters 8 and 18.

COMPLEXITY ANALYSIS

A *more* quantitative method for measuring software reliability is complexity analysis. The assumption is that reliability and complexity are related and that complexity can be used as a predictor of error-proneness. More specifically, program complexity metrics can be used to predict where errors are most likely to occur (i.e., in which modules) and the types of errors that are most likely to occur. Furthermore, knowing the type of errors and where they are likely to occur can lead to the detection and correction of more errors sooner and hence to improved reliability. For example, low complexity generally indicates smaller program (module) size, lower probability of errors, and clerical/coding type errors. On the other hand, high complexity indicates larger program (module) size, higher probability or errors, and specification/design type errors. The complexity metrics discussed as measures of program understandability are also appropriate measures of program reliability.

TESTABILITY   *Testability* is defined as the ease with which program correctness can be demonstrated. It is assumed that traditional program testing methods rather than formal program correctness proofs are used to demonstrate correctness. Testability is an extremely important program property in terms of building a high-quality software product and in terms of controlling software costs. For medium- to large-scale software systems, approximately half of the development budget is expended on testing [14]. In addition, a program that is difficult to test during development carries this property into the maintenance phase [16].

The process of testing a program involves the selection of a small sample of test cases and the execution of the program with each test case. Thoroughness of testing depends on a careful selection of test cases and is guided by the following rules:

1. Every program instruction and every path should be executed at least once.
2. The more heavily used parts of the program should be tested more thoroughly.
3. All modules should be tested individually before they are combined. Then the paths and intersections between the modules should be tested.
4. Testing should proceed from the simplest to the most complex test cases; that is, tests involving fewer loops and conditions should be performed before tests involving more complicated control constructs and more decisions.
5. Testing of a program should include normal processing cases, extremes, and exceptions.

Selection of test cases depends on a thorough understanding of the program. A testable program is understandable, reliable, and simple.

Whereas reliability is a measure of the absence of errors, testability is a measure of the ability to demonstrate this absence. The simpler the program, the easier to demonstrate its correctness. Simplicity in this sense means that the program is modular, is well-structured, and has minimal complexity.

Box 3.5 includes a checklist of questions to be used in measuring program testability.

In addition to being used as a quantitative measure of understandability

BOX 3.5   Testability checklist

1. Is the program modularized and well-structured?
2. Is the program understandable?
3. Is the program reliable?
4. Can the program display optional intermediate results?
5. Is program output identified in a clear, descriptive manner?
6. Can the program display all inputs upon request?
7. Does the program contain a capability for tracing and displaying logical flow of control?
8. Does the program contain a checkpoint-restart capability?
9. Does the program provide for display of descriptive error messages?

and reliability, complexity metrics can also be used to measure testability. For example, McCabe addresses the relationship between testability and cyclomatic complexity [12]. Cyclomatic complexity is an indicator of testability and also a helpful tool in preparing test cases. The larger the cyclomatic complexity number for a program, the more paths in the program and therefore the more difficult it will be to test the program thoroughly. According the McCabe, modules having greater cyclomatic complexity should be tested the most carefully.

MODIFIABILITY   A programmer has a relatively low probability of success when modifying a program. If the modification involves fewer than 10 program instructions, the probability of correctly changing the program on the first attempt is approximately 50%; but if the modification involves as many as 50 program instructions, the probability drops to 20% [18]. Van Tassel refers to a program that is difficult to modify as *fragile* [17]. A major contributor to the high cost of software maintenance is the abundance of fragile programs in industry today. Since change is the prevelant cause of most maintenance work, improving the modifiability of software is an extremely important factor in reducing maintenance costs.

Modifiability is defined as the ease with which a program can be changed. A modifiable program is understandable, general, flexible, and simple. Generality allows a program to be used for a variety of changing functions without making modifications, while flexibility allows a program to be modified easily. Box 3.6 provides a checklist of questions to measure modifiability.

BOX 3.6 Modifiability checklist

1. Is the program modular and well-structured?

2. Is the program understandable?

3. Does the program avoid using literal constants in arithmetic expressions, logical expressions, size of tables/arrays, and input/output device designators?

4. Is there additional memory capacity available to support program extensions?

5. Is information provided to evaluate the impact of a change and to identify which portions if the program must be modified to accommodate the change?

6. Is redundant code avoided by creating common modules/subroutines?

7. Does the program use standard library routines to provide commonly used functions?

8. Does the program possess the quality of generality in terms of its ability to:

    (a) Execute on different hardware configurations?
    (b) Operate on different input/output formats?
    (c) Function in subset mode performing a selected set of features?
    (d) Operate with different data structures or algorithms depending on resource availability?

9. Does the program posses the quality of flexibility in terms of its ability to:

    (a) Isolate specialized functions that are likely to change in separate modules?
    (b) Provide module interfaces that are insensitive to expected changes in individual functions?
    (c) Identify a subset of the system that can be made operational as part of contingency planning or for a smaller computer?
    (d) Permit each module function to perform one unique function?
    (e) Define module intercommunication based on the function the modules perform, not upon how the modules work internally?

10. Is the use of each variable localized as much as possible?

BOX 3.7   Measuring the difficulty of a program change

The difficulty, D, of making a program change is given by

$$D = \hat{A}/\hat{C}$$

where $\hat{A}$ is the average complexity of the modules to be changed;
$\hat{C}$ is the average complexity of all modules in the program.

If D is greater than 1 for simple changes, like adding a new report item, this is an indication that the program is difficult to modify.

CHANGE EXERCISES   Another method of measuring modifiability is with change exercises. The basic idea is to evaluate the difficulty of changing the program by making a few simple changes such as adding a new transaction type, changing an input/output device, or deleting an output report. What percentage of the program modules must be modified to make each change? If a large percentage of the modules (i.e., over 30%) must be modified to make even a simple change, this is an indication that the program is difficult to modify. In a variation of the change exercise, not only the percentage of modules to be modified but also the complexity of the modules involved is considered.

Suppose that $\hat{C}$ is the average complexity value for a module in the program, n is the number of modules that must be changed, and $\hat{A}$ is the average complexity of the modules to be changed (any of the complexity metrics discussed previously can be used to calculate $\hat{C}$ and $\hat{A}$). Then, as shown in Box 3.7, the difficulty, D, of making the change is given by

$$D = \hat{A}/\hat{C}$$

If D is greater than 1 for simple changes, this is an indication that the program is difficult to modify.

COHESIVENESS
AND COUPLING

Cohesiveness and coupling are two possible measures for program modifiability proposed by Stevens et al. [19]. A modifiable program is made up of modules that have high cohesiveness and low coupling.

Cohesiveness is a measure of an individual module's internal strength, that is, the strength of the interrelationship of its internal elements. The scale of cohesiveness from lowest to highest is coincidental, logical, temporal, communicative, sequential, and functional. Coincidental indicates that no meaningful relationship exists among the internal elements of a module, whereas functional indicates that all the elements in the module are related to the performance of a single function.

Coupling measures the degree of interdependence among modules. It depends on the type of intermodular connection and information that is passed among the modules. For example, coupling increases when modules are pathologically connected; that is, one module transfers control to labels within the boundary, rather than at the entry point of another module. High coupling is influenced by the amount of information, the accessibility of the information, the format of the information, and the types of information passed among modules.

Although cohesiveness and coupling normally are used to evaluate the "goodness" of a modularization scheme, they are also good measures of modifiability since both the internal structure of each module and the interrelationships among modules influences the ease with which a program can be changed.

PORTABILITY

If we wish to sell a program to many different users or if we wish to use a program over a long period of time, we must be concerned with the possibility of transferring it to a new computing environment. Portability measures this possibility. *Portability* is defined as the extent to which a program can be easily and effectively operated in a variety of computing environments. A portable program is well-structured, flexible, and independent of features peculiar to a particular computer and/or operating system.

Box 3.8 provides a checklist of questions useful in determining program portability.

EFFICIENCY

Efficiency is defined as the extent to which a program performs its intended functions without wasting machine resources such as memory, mass storage utilization, channel capacity, and execution time. Box 3.9 provides a checklist of questions for measuring efficiency.

Efficiency is important but should not be carried to an extreme. Many programmers are unnecessarily concerned with machine efficiency considerations. This obsession with tuning programs to achieve some optimal level of efficiency by playing off time and space requirements is a questionable maintenance expense. A better approach may be upgrading hardware rather than tuning software. This approach often is less expensive since hardware

BOX 3.8 Portability checklist

1. Is the program written in high-level, machine-independent language?

2. Is the program written in a widely used standardized programming language, and does the program use only a standard version and features of that language?

3. Does the program use only standard, universally available library functions and subroutines?

4. Does the program use operating system functions minimally or not at all?

5. Are program computations independent of word size for achievement of required precision or memory-size restrictions?

6. Does the program initialize memory prior to execution?

7. Does the program position input/output devices prior to execution?

8. Does the program isolate and document machine-dependent statements?

9. Is the program structured to allow phased (overlay) operation on a smaller computer?

10. Has dependency on internal bit representation of alphanumeric or special characters been avoided or documented in the program?

costs represent only a small portion of total computing costs. Also, it may be less risky since software changes are likely to introduce new errors.

Since emphasizing efficiency is often at the expense of other quality characteristics such as understandability and reliability, priorities must be considered and made explicit. Efficiency concerns depend on the type of program. Efficiency requirements are greater for highly used software systems such as operating systems, compilers, and airline reservation systems. But for many typical data-processing systems, programming resources are better spent on improving human efficiency usability rather than machine efficiency.

USABILITY   To control maintenance costs usability may be the single most important requirement for a maintainable software system. Responding to user requests for changes is a major cause for performing maintenance. In the Lientz–Swanson survey of over 500 data-processing departments, almost 50% of all maintenance work was attributed to user requests, while less than 20% was attributed to software errors [3]. Making a software system more usable from the user's perspective is a very effective way of reducing maintenance costs. For example, it is not

BOX 3.9 Efficiency checklist*

1. Is the program modularized and well-structured?

2. Does that program have a high degree of locality—that is, the program uses only a small subset of its pages at any point during execution—to aid efficient use of virtual memory?

3. Are unused labels and expressions eliminated to take full advantage of compiler optimization?

4. Are exception routines and error-handling routines isolated in separate modules?

5. Was the program compiled with the use of an optimizing compiler?

6. Was as much initialization (e.g., initializing arrays, variables, storage allocations) as possible done at compilation time?

7. Is all invariant code—that is, code which does not need to be processed within a loop—processed outside the loop?

8. Are fast mathematical operations substituted for slower ones? (For example, I + I is faster than 2*I.)

9. Is integer arithmetic instead of floating-point arithmetic used when possible?

10. Are mixed data types in arithmetic or logical operations avoided when possible to eliminate unnecessary conversions?

11. Are decimal points of operands used in arithmetic aligned when possible?

12. Are program variables aligned in storage?

13. Does the program avoid nonstandard subroutine or function calls?

14. In an *n*-way branch construct, is the most likely condition to be TRUE tested first?

15. In a complex logical condition, is the most likely TRUE expression tested first?

16. Is the most efficient data type used for subscripts?

17. Are input/output files blocked efficiently?

*Many of the questions are adapted from Van Tassel [17].

unusual for maintenance programmers to spend a substantial percentage of their time hunting for hypothetical errors reported by users who because of inadequate training and documentation could not understand how to use the system. Improving usability will eliminate much of this problem.

Besides being perhaps the most important quality characteristic, usabil-

BOX 3.10   Usability checklist*

1. Is the program self-descriptive from the user perspective?

   (a) Are explanations of how the program works and what the program does available in different levels of detail with examples included?
   (b) Is a HELP feature pertinent to any dialogue situation included?
   (c) Is a correct, complete explanation of each command and/or operating mode available on request?
   (d) Can the user become thoroughly acquainted with the program usage without human assistance?
   (e) Is current program status information readily available on request?

2. Does the program provide the user with a satisfying and appropriate degree of control over processing?

   (a) Does the program admit interruptions of a task to start or resume another task when operating in interactive mode?
   (b) Does the program admit process canceling without detrimental or unexpected side effects?
   (c) Does the program allow the user to make background processes visible?
   (d) Does the program have a command language that is easy to understand and allows clustering of commands to build "macros"?
   (e) Does the program provide detailed prompting when requested to help the user find his way through the system?
   (f) Does the program provide understandable, nonthreatening error messages?

3. Is the program easy to learn to use?

   (a) Is the program usable without special DP knowledge?
   (b) Are input formats, requirements, and restrictions completely and clearly explained?
   (c) Is user input supported by a menu technique in interactive systems?
   (d) Does the program offer error messages with correction hints?
   (e) For interactive systems, are manuals "on-line"? For batch systems, are manuals readily available?
   (f) Are manuals written using user terminology?

4. Does the program make use of a data management system to automatically perform clerical/housekeeping activities and manage formatting, addressing, and memory organization?

5. Does the program behave consistently in a manner that corresponds to user expectations?

   (a) Does the program have a syntactically homogeneous command language and error message format?
   (b) Does the program behave similarly in similar situations by minimizing variances in response times?

BOX 3.10 *(Continued)*

6. Is the program fault-tolerant?

  (a) Can the program tolerate typical typing errors?
  (b) Can the program accept reduced input when actions are to be repeated?
  (c) Can commands be abbreviated?
  (d) Does the program validate input data?

7. Is the program flexible?

  (a) Does the program allow for free-form input?
  (b) Does the program provide for repeated use without the need for redundant specification of input values?
  (c) Are a variety of output options available to the user?
  (d) Does the program provide for omission of unnecessary inputs, computations, and output for optional modes of operation?
  (e) Does the program allow the user to extend the command language?
  (f) Is the program portable?
  (g) Does the program allow the user to define his own set of functions and features?
  (h) Can the program be seen in a subset mode?
  (i) Does the program allow the experienced user to work with a faster version, allowing abbreviated commands, default values, and so on, and inexperienced users to work with a slower version, providing a help command, monitoring capabilities, and so on?

  *Many of the questions are adapted from Dzida et al. [20].

ity is also the most difficult to define and to measure in any sort of quantitative, objective fashion. There exists much more opinion than knowledge about how users perceive software quality. Different users perceive quality in different ways depending on their experience with computerized systems, how frequently they use the system, their perceptions of human factoring, how critical the system is to performing their job, and the mode of operation they use (batch versus interactive). Also, user-perceived quality varies with individual user needs, problems, and preferences.

Generally, a usable program is easy to use, is tolerant of user errors and changing needs, and minimizes user confusion. Taking the user perspective, we shall define *usability* as the extent to which a program is convenient, practical, and easy to use. A usable program is reliable, portable, and efficient. Box 3.10 contains a checklist of questions to be used in evaluating program usability.

REFERENCES

1. B. Boehm, J. Brown, H. Kaspar, M. Lipow, J. MacLeod, and M. Menit, *Characteristics of Software Quality* (New York: TRW/North-Holland Publishing Company, 1978), pp. 3-1 to 3-26.

2. E. Swanson, "The Dimensions of Maintenance," 2nd International Conference on Software Engineering, Proceedings (San Francisco), October 13-15, 1976, pp. 492-497.

3. B. Lientz and E. Swanson, *Software Maintenance Management* (Reading, MA: Addison-Wesley Publishing Co., Inc., 1980), pp. 67-96.

4. F. Brooks, *The Mythical Man-Month* (Reading, MA: Addison-Wesley Publishing Co., Inc., 1975), pp. 41-50.

5. B. Shneiderman, *Software Psychology: Human Factors in Computer and Information Systems* (Cambridge, MA: Winthrop Publishers, Inc., 1980), pp. 93-122.

6. L. E. Walston and C. P. Felix, "A Method of Program Measurement and Estimation," *IBM Systems Journal,* Vol. 16, No. 1, (1977), pp. 54-73.

7. A. Fitzsimmons and T. Love, "A Review and Evaluation of Software Science," *ACM Computing Surveys,* Vol. 10, No. 1 (March 1978), pp. 3-18.

8. J. Elshoff, "Measuring Commercial PL/1 Programs Using Halstead's Criteria," *ACM SIGPLAN Notices,* May 1976, pp. 38-46.

9. S. Woodfield, "An Experiment on Unit Increase in Problem Complexity," *IEEE Trans. on Software Engineering,* Vol. SE-5, No. 2 (March 1979), pp. 76-78.

10. E. Dijkstra, "Notes on Structured Programming," in *Structured Programming* (New York: Academic Press, Inc., 1972), pp. 175-220.

11. R. Gordon, "Measuring Improvements in Program Clarity," *IEEE Trans. on Software Engineering,* Vol. SE-5, No. 2 (March 1979), pp. 79-90.

12. T. McCabe, "A Complexity Measure," *IEEE Trans. on Software Engineering,* Vol. SE-2, No. 4 (December 1976), pp. 308-320.

13. C. McClure, *Reducing COBOL Complexity Through Structured Programming* (New York: Van Nostrand Reinhold Company, 1978), pp. 77-121.

14. R. Jensen and C. Tonies, *Software Engineering* (Englewood Cliffs, NJ: Prentice-Hall, Inc., 1979), pp. 329-408.

15. T. Gilb, *Software Metrics* (Cambridge, MA: Winthrop Publishers, Inc., 1977), pp. 26-49.

16. H. Mills, "Software Development," *IEEE Trans. on Software Engineering,* Vol. SE-2, No. 4 (December 1976): 265–273.

17. D. Van Tassel, *Program Style, Design, Efficiency, Debugging, and Testing* (Englewood Cliffs, NJ: Prentice-Hall, Inc., 1978), pp. 238–284.

18. B. Boehm, "Software and Its Impact: A Quantitative Assessment," *Datamation,* Vol. 19, No. 5 (May 1973), pp. 48–59.

19. W. Stevens, G. Myers, and L. Constantine, "Structured Design," *IBM Systems Journal,* Vol. 13, No. 2 (1974), pp. 115–139.

20. W. Dzida et al., "User-Perceived Quality of Interactive Systems," 3rd International Conference on Software Engineering, May 1975, pp. 188–195.

4 METHODS FOR BUILDING IN MAINTAINABILITY

INTRODUCTION   Box 4.1 summarizes the set of characteristics used to define the quality of maintainability and the measures proposed to determine the presence of these characteristics in a program. Now we turn our attention to building maintainability into software systems. How do we build maintainability into new systems and into existing systems? What are the special quality considerations for data-base systems, for software packages, and for different programming languages? The quality checklists presented in Chapter 3 offer numerous suggestions for building maintainability into programs. For example, a program should be modularized and well-structured. Also, a program should employ parameterization and be written in a standard version of widely used high-level language.

The checklists provide an understanding of the properties of a maintainable program, but they do not offer techniques and tools for developing such a program. The objective of this chapter is to present methods for building maintainability into programs. These methods are generally applicable to new systems, to existing systems, to data-base systems, and to software packages.

SIX METHODS   Six methods will be discussed:
FOR IMPROVING
MAINTAINABILITY

1. Setting explicit software quality objectives and priorities
2. Using quality-enhancing techniques and tools
3. Establishing explicit quality assurance activities

BOX 4.1 Software maintainability characteristics and measures

Characteristic	Properties	Measures	Measurement Tools
1. Understandability	Well-structured Concise Consistent Complete	90–10 test Complexity metrics	Structure checkers Automatic flow-charters Execution path Tracers Automatic complexity analyzers
2. Reliability	Correct Complete Consistent	Debugging Reliability models Error statistics Complexity metrics	Execution path tracers Automatic complexity analyzers
3. Testability	Understandable Reliable Simple Well-structured	Complexity metrics	Automatic flow-charters Execution path tracers Automatic complexity analyzers
4. Modifiability	Understandable General Flexible Simple	Change exercises Cohesiveness and coupling 20% test	Automatic complexity analyzers
5. Portability	Well-structured Flexible Machine independent	Test execute on different computers	Standard language version compiler Structure checker
6. Efficiency	Small Fast Well-structured	20% test	Structure checkers Performance monitors
7. Usability	Reliable General Portable Efficient	User acceptance tests	

4. Choosing a maintainable programming language

5. Improving program documentation

6. Contracting for maintainability

The first three methods are explored in this chapter and the last three in Chapters 5, 6, and 7.

SETTING
SOFTWARE
QUALITY
OBJECTIVES
AND PRIORITIES

One of the simplest ways to build maintainability into software is to ask for it. By clearly defining objectives and priorities it is possible to exert a strong influence of software quality, user satisfaction, and life-cycle costs [1].

The first step in building maintainability into a program is to tell the programmer what is expected. A maintainable program should be understandable, testable, modifiable, reliable, portable, efficient, and usable. In reality, the achievement of all these qualities may not be cost-effective or even feasible. While some qualities imply one another —understandability and testability or understandability and modifiability— other qualities may be in conflict with one another—efficiency and portability or efficiency and modifiability.

Although each quality should be present to some degree to ensure maintainability, its relative importance will vary depending on the program purpose and the computing environment. For example, in the case of a compiler, the qualities of efficiency, reliability, and portability might be emphasized, whereas in the case of a management information system, usability and modifiability might be emphasized.

Three experiments illustrate the importance of clearly defining programming objectives and priorities. In an experiment by Boehm, two programmers were assigned the same programming task but given different objectives [2]. One programmer was instructed to maximize machine efficiency, while the second programmer was instructed to emphasize simplicity. The result of this experiment was that although more efficient, *the program in which efficiency was stressed contained 10 times as many errors as the program in which simplicity was stressed.*

In an experiment by Weinberg, several groups of programmers were given the same programming assignment with a different top priority objective, such as understandability, efficiency, or reliability [3]. The result of this experiment was that *each group achieved its highest-priority goal.*

In an experiment by McClure, the same programming team was studied during two programming tasks [4]. For the first task, the programmers were told to minimize program complexity but were given no instructions for achieving this objective. For the second task, the programmers were again told to minimize program complexity but this time were given further instructions. They were instructed to minimize complexity be reducing the number of compares in the code. The result of this experiment was that the frequency of compares (frequency of compares = number of source lines excluding comments/number of compares) in the second program was half that of the first program.

These experiments point out that in the case of software, we can get what we ask for. According to Boehm:

> the degree of quality a person puts into a program correlates strongly with the software quality objectives and priorities he has been given. [1, p. 600]

Using explicit definitions and measures of quality such as those suggested in Chapter 3 will help us better convey our notions and expectations of program quality.

USING QUALITY-ENHANCING TECHNIQUES AND TOOLS

Using the appropriate programming techniques can greatly enhance software quality and reduce software costs. For example, experiences from industry indicate that the use of structured techniques can improve program understandability and thereby reduce software costs.

In a survey by McClure, programmers reported that the standardization of style introduced by structured programming conventions made programs easier to understand [5]. IBM reported an average of 40% productivity savings in real-time, business application, and systems application software projects employing structured techniques [6]. McDonnell-Douglas and Time-Life also reported dramatic productivity increases in projects employing structured techniques. Other organizations reported that maintenance costs for software developed with structured techniques are reduced by a ratio of 3:1 compared to maintenance costs for "unstructured" software [7]. Error rates in tested unstructured software average one error per every 200 lines of source code. But in many structured software systems, production error rates are averaging less than one error per 1000 lines of source code [8].

Structured techniques are a collection of programming methods whose common objective is to organize and streamline the entire software life cycle by following a structured approach (see Fig. 4.1). The structured approach can be described simply as the introduction of standardization and discipline into both the programming process and the program form. Structured techniques such as top-down programming, structured analysis, and the chief programmer team propose to improve program quality through the use of well-defined procedures, project controls, and communication mechanisms. They structure the software life cycle into a sequence of step-by-step procedures; they use standardization, review, and documentation to provide order

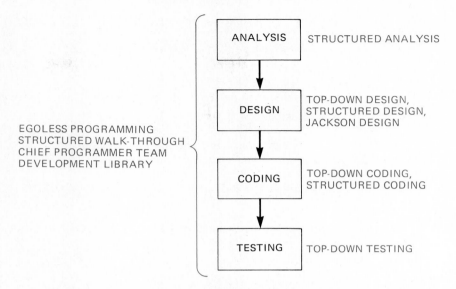

Figure 4.1   Use of structures techniques during the software life cycle.

and visibility; and they emphasize the early life-cycle phases as the most crucial to building high-quality, low-cost software. Other techniques, such as structured programming, HIPO diagrams, and structure charts, address the issue of program quality through a standardization of program form and program documentation.

Structured techniques evolved from a coding methodology (i.e., structured programming) to also include analysis, design, and testing methodologies as well as team programming concepts and documentation tools. Structured programming, in turn, evolved from the earlier programming concept of modularization.

MODULARIZATION

The traditional approach for enhancing program quality is modularization. The modularization philosophy is that constructing a program as a set of conceptually and operationally independent pieces (modules) will simplify program understandability and the programming task. The rules for modularizing a program are given in Box 4.2.

Modularization is a very effective technique for building maintainability into a program. It offers several advantages:

1. If a function performed by a module changes, only that module changes and the rest of the program is unaffected.

BOX 4.2   Rules for modularization

- Decompose the program into independent, discrete modules.
- Structure the program modules to reflect the design process.
- Construct each program module with the following properties:
  The module is closed.
  The module has one unique entry point and one unique exit point.
  The module represents one logical, self-contained function.

2. If a new program feature is added, a new module or hierarchy of modules to perform that feature can be added.

3. Program testing and retesting is easier.

4. Program errors are easier to locate and correct.

5. Program efficiency is easier to improve.

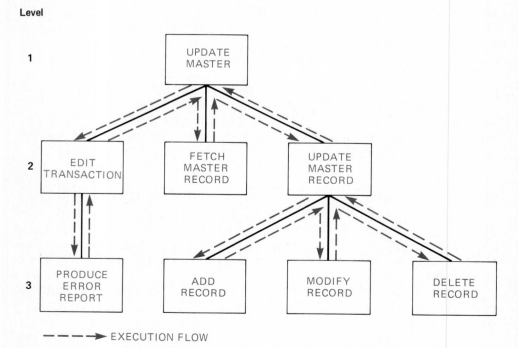

Figure 4.2 A structured program is divided into a set of modules arranged as a hierarchy defining their logical and execution-time relationships.

**STRUCTURED
PROGRAMMING**
Structured programming takes the modularization philosophy one step further by standardizing not only module construction but also module inter-action. The structured programming approach is to:

1. Reduce the number of program paths by imposing a simple program control structure.

2. Clarify program path meaning by requiring the flow of program control to return to the invoking module.

3. Limit program path patterns by restricting the set of allowable control constructs.

A program that follows the structured programming approach is called *well-structured* (see Fig. 4.2) and is characterized by the six properties defined in Box 4.3.

Many organizations now require that programs conform to a set of structured programming coding conventions. A list of structuring rules that are representative of those typically suggested for high-level, procedure-

BOX 4.3 Properties of a well-structured program

- *Property 1:* The program is divided into a set of modules arranged in a hierarchy defining their logical and execution-time relation-ships.

- *Property 2:* The execution flow from module to module is restricted to a simple, easily understood scheme in which control must enter the module at its entry point, must leave the module from its exit point, and must always be passed back to the invoking module.

- *Property 3:* Module construction is standardized according to the tradi-tional modularization rules (see Chapter 6), and legal program control constructs are restricted to concatenation, selection, repetition, and a "well-behaved" branch.

- *Property 4:* Each program variable serves only one program purpose, and the scope of a variable (i.e., the set of modules in which the variable is accessed) is apparent and limited.

- *Property 5:* Error processing follows normal control flow except in the case of unrecoverable errors where normal processing cannot continue.

- *Property 6:* Documentation is required in the source code to introduce each module by explaining its function, its data requirements, and its invocation relationship to other modules in the program.

BOX 4.4 Structured programming coding standards

1. The program is divided into independent pieces called modules.

2. A module is a self-contained unit whose code is physically and logically separate from the code of any other module in the program.

   A module represents one unique logical program function (e.g., Fetch a transaction.)

   The size of a module should not exceed 100 instructions.

   A module is bounded by one entry point and one exit point. During execution, program control can enter a module only at its entry point and can leave the module only from its exit point.

3. Modules are related to one another in a hierarchical control structure. Each level in the control structure represents a more detailed functional description of what the program does. It also dictates the transfer of program control from module to module during execution (see Fig. 4.2).

   Level 1 (top of the hierarchy) contains one and only one program module. Logically, this module represents the overall program structure and contains the "mainline" code for the program. Program execution always begins with this module.

   Level 2 contains modules that are performed to execute the overall program function. The modules at level 2 can be executed only by transferring control to them from the mainline module. Execution cannot cause control to "fall" into a module.

   Level 3 modules represent functions required to further define the functions at level 2. Control is transferred to level 3 modules only from level 2 modules. This scheme continues from level to level down the entire hierarchical structure.

   Program control is always transferred from a module at one level to a module at the next successive lower level (e.g., from level 3 to level 4). When a module completes executing its code, control is always returned to the module that "called" it. (e.g., UPDATE MASTER RECORD transfers control to MODIFY RECORD; when MODIFY RECORD completes executing its code, it returns control to UPDATE MASTER RECORD).

   No loops are allowed in the control structure. This means that a module cannot call itself, nor can it call any module that has called it.

4. Each module should begin with a comment block explaining the function that the module performs, the values passed to the module, the values returned, the modules that call this module, and the modules that this module calls.

5. Comments embedded in the module code should be separated from instructions by one blank line.

6. All comments should be meaningful (e.g., a meaningful comment does not state that this is an add instruction).

BOX 4.4 *(Continued)*

7. Avoid unnecessary labels; do not use labels as comments.

8. All variable and module names should be meaningful. Module names should suggest the logical function they perform (e.g., EDIT) and variable names should suggest their purpose in the program (e.g., ERRORSW).

9. Names of variables that belong to the same table or that are local (i.e., used only in one module) should begin with the same prefix.

10. The only allowable control constructs are concatenation, selection, repetition, and branch.

11. At most, one instruction is coded on a line. If an instruction requires more than one line, successive lines are indented.

12. IF statements should not be nested more than three levels.

13. The scope of a GO TO statement (branch instruction) should be limited to the module in which it occurs. This means that the GO TO should not be used to transfer control from one module to another; it is used only to branch to the entry point or the exit point of the module in which it occurs.

14. Nonstandard language features should not be used as a general rule.

15. Obscure (trick) code should be avoided.

oriented languages such as FORTRAN, COBOL, and PL/1 is shown in Box 4.4. Program compliance to such structuring rules can be checked at compilation time with the use of automated structure checkers.

STRUCTURED TECHNIQUES, PROGRAM EFFICIENCY, AND PROGRAM USABILITY

Structured techniques can be shown to improve program understandability, reliability, and modifiability, but there has been some question concerning their effect on program efficiency and usability.

In the case of efficiency, there has been concern that imposing a standardization of form on the program structure will have a detrimental effect on machine efficiency. Certainly, there are many examples of well-structured programs that are less efficient than comparable unstructured programs performing the identical function. However, in most of these instances, rewriting only a small portion of the well-structured programs can substantially improve their efficiency.

As a matter of fact, performance tuning is more easily accomplished when a program is well-structured because it is easier to isolate the critical code. Typically, only about 5% of the code really affects efficiency.

When efficiency is a real concern, there are automated tools such as optimizing compilers and profilers that can be used to improve program efficiency. Optimizing compilers (e.g., IBM's PL/1 Optimizer) can be used to produce more efficient object code. Some compilers allow the programmer to select the resource (e.g., execution storage or execution time) to be optimized since optimization of one resource may be achieved at the expense of other resources. Profilers (e.g., CAPEX's COTUNE or CACI's PROFILE) can be used to pinpoint the critical code to be rewritten.

Perhaps more important to efficiency is the choice of design algorithm. In some cases because of the algorithm, no amount of automatic or manual optimization will provide the needed efficiency improvements. In such cases it is more cost-effective to replace the program with another in which a more efficient design algorithm is used.

In the case of usability, structured techniques cannot be shown to have a direct effect other than by improving quality in general. However, because they emphasize the importance of communication and encourage user involvement in the software development process, structured techniques provide a means for increasing user knowledge of the capabilities and limitations of software. The structured walk-through is an excellent forum in which users can learn about software as well as review its quality. Documentation tools such as HIPO diagrams, Warnier diagrams, and structure charts provide the user with an overview understanding of what the software does and how it works.

STRUCTURED TECHNIQUES AND NEW SYSTEMS

Structured techniques were designed primarily for use in the development of new software systems written in third-generation procedural languages such as COBOL, PL/1, and Pascal. They have proven particularly useful and often essential in large-scale software development efforts requiring many person-years and large programming teams to complete. However, they are also very useful in medium- and small-scale development efforts because of their emphasis on standardization. Even in small efforts requiring only one individual it is not unusual for more than one individual to work on a program. Frequently, before a program is completed it must be reassigned to another individual because of personnel turnover, a promotion, or a transfer; and even more frequently, after the program is completed, many different individuals will be assigned to maintain it. The standardization of programming procedures and program style introduced by structured techniques greatly improves our ability to understand programs developed and maintained by many different individuals.

STRUCTURED TECHNIQUES AND EXISTING SYSTEMS

There are two schools of thought on the feasibility of applying structured techniques to existing software systems:

1. Structured techniques are adoptable to the maintenance of existing systems.
2. Structured techniques are *not* adoptable to the maintenance of existing systems.

Consider the negative viewpoint first. The basic, underlying assumption is that the majority of existing software systems were developed prior to the introduction of structured techniques and therefore are unstructured. Since structured techniques are just beginning to have widespread impact in industry, this assumption appears to be valid.

The argument against using structured techniques in an unstructured environment is that forcing structure may have serious consequences. Since many maintenance tasks involve changing a few lines of code here and there in a program, it is impossible to introduce structure without expanding the scope of the change to include larger sections of code. This increases the risk of introducing new errors and violates the very fundamental maintenance rule: Do not change any more than necessary. Not only does changing more code than necessary threaten program reliability, but it also requires more programming resources and increases the maintenance burden.

An even more serious consequence is that introducing structure into an existing program may threaten its conceptual integrity. Just as structure cannot guarantee maintainability, a lack of structure (in the structured programming sense) does not necessarily indicate poor quality.

An all-or-nothing approach is best. If a program is not maintainable, replace it in its entirety. If a program is maintainable, preserve its style (whatever it may be) by carefully making only necessary changes and then updating the program documentation accordingly. Certainly, there is merit in this position.

BOX 4.5 Guidelines for improving the maintainability of existing systems

- Use a spare-parts approach.
- Use automatic restructuring and reformatting tools.
- Improve program documentation.
- Use structured programming methodologies to implement new subsystems.
- Use structured team programming concepts and structured documentation tools to perform maintenance activities.

The basic argument in favor of introducing structured techniques to the maintenance of existing systems is that they are an effective and much needed method for reducing maintenance costs in the short term (over the next decade). It is neither feasible to immediately replace all existing software systems of questionable maintainability, nor realistic to ignore the enormous and growing burden of maintaining existing systems. Gradually improving the maintainability of existing systems with the aid of structured techniques as part of normal maintenance work is a reasonable approach. Some guidelines for improving the maintainability of existing systems are suggested in Box 4.5.

SPARE-PARTS APPROACH

Gilb suggests using the "spare-parts" approach to maintain a program [9]. When a program module is changed, the whole module is replaced with a new module. This approach requires understanding the interface specifications for the module but not the inner workings. It may reduce the possibility of introducing new errors since the programmer will better understand his own code than that written by someone else. Also, it offers the opportunity of replacing the module with a well-structured module as a way of gradually improving maintainability. Of course, the spare-parts approach is applicable only to modularized programs or to major enhancements involving the addition of a new subsystem.

STRUCTURED RETROFIT

Lyons and deBalbine propose "structured retrofit" as a method for introducing structured techniques and their benefits to existing software systems *after the fact* [7]. The objective is to improve the understandability of existing software and thereby improve their maintainability and extend their useful life.

The approach is to transform unstructured source code into well-structured code with the aid of automatic software tools such as code evaluators, reformatters, and structuring engines. The resulting structured program is executionally equivalent to the prestructured program since both programs perform the same sequence of operations on the same data. Of course, any logic errors contained in the prestructured program will be transferred to the newly structured version. Structuring engines are currently available for FORTRAN and COBOL (e.g., Caine, Farber & Gordon FORTRAN Engine, and Catalyst Corp. COBOL Engine).

The advantage of the structured retrofit approach is that it is an automatic procedure requiring little programmer assistance. The restructuring process consists of four steps. First, the program is compiled to assure that there are no compilation errors. Next, the program source code is restructured with the aid of a structuring engine. Then, a reformatter is used to introduce indentation and paragraphing. Finally, the source code is recompiled with the aid of an optimizing compiler to enhance its efficiency.

The disadvantages of the approach are:

1. There is a learning curve associated with becoming familiar with the program in its new form.
2. There is no guarantee that the result of the restructuring will be more than a translation of poor, unstructured code into poor, structured code.
3. The new structured version may be less efficient than the old unstructured version of the program.

It is recommended that restructuring be performed only on carefully selected programs. Programs that execute correctly and are changed only infrequently should be not restructured regardless of their style. Programs that are complex, error-prone, and changed frequently are top-priority candidates for restructuring.

REFORMATTING

Gilb argues that simply reformatting the code is just as effective and much less risky than restructuring the code to improve its maintainability [10]. Reformatting can be performed during program compilation to indent the code, to introduce standard labeling conventions, to limit one instruction to a line, to standardize use of keywords, and so forth (e.g., ADR'S MetaCOBOL).

In programming experiments at the University of Toronto, Weismann found that simple indentation may have more impact on improving understandability than would more complicated structuring conventions [10]. Also, reformatting avoids the problems of introducing new errors as a by-product of the restructuring process and the relearning time needed for the programmers to familiarize themselves with the code in its new form.

STRUCTURED DOCUMENTATION TOOLS AND TEAM PROGRAMMING CONCEPTS

Although it can be argued that structured programming is of limited use in improving the maintainability of existing software systems (with the exception of major, stand-alone enhancements), other structured techniques such as team programming concepts and structured documentation tools can be very helpful. Since poor documentation is frequently cited as a major maintenance problem, improving the program documentation for existing software systems is an effective way of improving maintainability and controlling maintenance costs. Program documentation tools such as HIPO diagrams, Warnier diagrams, action diagrams, and data flow diagrams combine graphic and narrative techniques, making both the maintenance process and the software itself easier to understand. Program documentation is discussed in detail in Chapters 8 and 9.

Rather than trying to restructure existing systems to improve their maintainability, a better approach may be to structure the maintenance process. Structured techniques such as the chief programmer team and the structured walk-through are people-organization tools designed to improve communication, programmer productivity, and program understandability. These techniques are applicable to the program maintenance process as well as to the program development process. Structuring the maintenance process is discussed in Part V.

CONDUCTING QUALITY ASSURANCE AUDITS

Another method for building in software maintainability is to audit for it. Quality assurance audits are a powerful technique for introducing and preserving software quality. In addition to ensuring that quality is properly introduced into software, audits can be used to detect changes in quality during the software development and maintenance phases. Once detected, steps can be taken to correct the problem, to control rising maintenance costs, and to extend the useful life of a software system.

Although frequently recommended in the literature, quality control audits are infrequently used in practice, especially in the maintenance environment. In a maintenance survey of over 500 data-processing departments, Lientz and Swanson found that less than one-third of the departments performed periodic audits of application software systems [11]. One reason audits are not more frequently used is an uncertainty about what and how to audit. With only an intuitive notion of quality, how can audits be useful in practice? The software quality definitions and measures presented in Chapter 3 address this concern by providing a more quantitative, objective basis for evaluating software quality.

Another reason audits are not more frequently used is a concern for the additional cost. How can the overhead for performing software audits be cost-justified? Furthermore, with such a large backlog of software applications waiting to be programmed, how can the allocation of systems and programming personnel needed for performing audits be justified?

Many organizations have found that software audits do not increase but rather decrease software costs. For example, Fagan reported that IBM found audits to be powerful tools for increasing programmer productivity. In one IBM project in which design and code audit inspections were used, 80% of the total errors found during development were found before the testing phase began [12]. This resulted in a 30% productivity savings. Also, Lientz and Swanson claim that audits are an effective method for controlling soft-

BOX 4.6　Software audit guidelines

- Audits should be simple and straightforward to apply. Ideally, the audit procedure should be standardized and should employ a checklist format.

- There should be a commitment from management recognizing the personnel and computing resources needed to perform audits.

- Audits should *not* be performed at every possible life-cycle checkpoint but instead selectively performed at those points where quality concerns have proven to be the most serious for an organization.

- Decisions concerning what audit checks will be performed, when audits will be conducted, and who will participate in the audit should be made as early as possible in the software life cycle.

- Follow-up action to investigate and to correct quality deficiencies uncovered during audits should be required and enforced.

- Automated tools should be used whenever possible to reduce the staff needed to apply quality measures.

ware costs. In their survey they found that when software audits were used during the maintenance phase, less maintenance effort was spent on emergency error repairs, thus allowing more time for providing user enhancements [11].

Software audits will not be effective tools unless they are properly managed and applied. Box 4.6. lists some general guidelines.

Four types of software audits are useful for ensuring maintainability:

1. Checkpoint reviews for developing new software
2. Acceptance audits for moving software from the development stage to the operations and maintenance stages
3. Periodic maintenance audits for operational software
4. Benchmark audits for software packages

CHECKPOINT REVIEWS

Perhaps the best way to ensure software quality is to build it into the software originally and to audit for it as the software is developed. The approach of checking our work as we go is fundamental to the structured techniques philosophy. Developing software in phases will help us find more errors and deficiencies sooner, resulting in a better software product and in lower software costs. This claim is supported by empirical evidence from several experiences.

For example, the Air Force CCIP-85 study performed by TRW showed that early checks for program completeness and consistency lead to significant improvements in software reliability [13]. An IBM study of the error distribution in several commercial programs (see Fig. 4.3) showed that over half the errors were design errors and that error costs were 10 to 100 times greater the later in the life-cycle process errors were corrected [14].

Checkpoint reviews can be conducted at the end of each software development life-cycle phase (see Fig. 4.4) to demonstrate that required development procedures have been performed and that required software deliverables have been produced (see Box 4.6). They are a means of incorporating explicit audit steps into the development process to assess software quality. During a checkpoint review, software is audited for compliance to standards and quality control criteria. For example, during the coding-phase checkpoint review, program source code is evaluated in terms of its

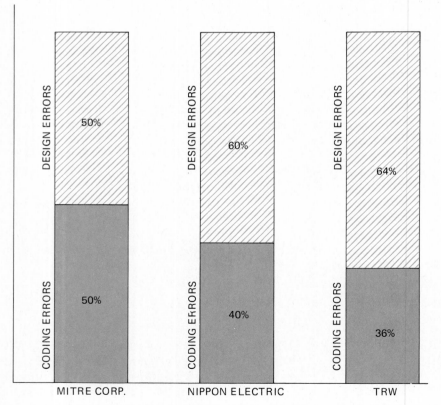

Figure 4.3 Software error distribution comparisons. (From B. M. Knight, "On Software Quality and Productivity," *IBM Technical Directions,* Federal Systems Division, July 1978.)

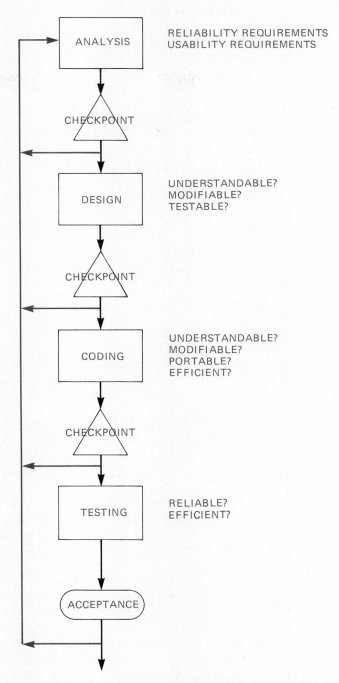

Figure 4.4 Checkpoint reviews to audit the maintainability of new systems during development.

ability to conform to structuring guidelines. The output of an automatic structure checker may be used to demonstrate this ability.

A checkpoint review is conducted as a structured walk-through by the person responsible for that development phase. It is attended by those persons responsible for all other life-cycle phases (including the operations and maintenance phase) as well as by a user representative and a quality assurance group representative. During the review the following activities occur:

- The completeness and quality of the software deliverables produced by the development phase are evaluated.
- Possible problems and deficiencies are identified and assigned for further investigation.
- Possible project schedule impacts are identified.
- Each reviewer attending the meeting signs a checkpoint review document signifying his approval of the completeness of the review and the quality of the material reviewed (with any exceptions noted).

A variation of the approach of conducting checkpoint reviews is to substitute inspections performed by a separate inspection team. This variation has been successfully used by Fagan in IBM projects [12]. Another variation is to conduct a checkpoint review only for those development phases that have proven in past projects to be the most difficult to control, have been the most costly to perform, and/or have had the most impact on the total project outcome.

During the checkpoint review maintainability can be audited by applying the quality checklists and measures presented in Chapter 3. As part of the requirements analysis phase, management, users, software developers, and software maintainers should agree on a definition of maintainability and a set of measures for maintainability. For example, a common requirement for a usable interactive system is adequate response time, where adequate response time is precisely defined as a mean of m seconds and a standard deviation of n seconds. Or a requirement for an efficient system may be defined as an x percent reserve for memory space and processor time on the computer system(s) on which the program is designed to run.

Defining maintainability in quantitative terms at the beginning of the development process makes auditing possible during each subsequent development phase. Different characteristics of maintainability are examined and different measures for maintainability are applied depending on the phase. For example, during the design phase, the characteristics of understandability, modifiability, and testability are evaluated. Understandability is measured by examining the complexity of the design. McCabe's cyclomatic number can be calculated for each module. The checkpoint review recommendation will be that those modules with a cyclomatic number greater than

10 are not coded until their complexity can be justified or until they are redesigned and the complexity is sufficiently reduced.

Modifiability is evaluated by performing some simple change exercises to the baseline design and then evaluating the coupling and cohesiveness of the most complex modules. Change exercises are chosen from the user's "wish list" for future program features. The checkpoint review will recommend that the program should be redesigned before development continues if over 30% of the program modules must be modified to implement the change. In particular, modules with high complexity, high coupling, and low cohesiveness that are affected by the change should be redesigned.

Testability is reviewed by applying the testability checklist (Box 3.5) to the design. "No" answers to checklist questions indicate possible deficiences in meeting testability requirements. The checkpoint review recommendation will be that all possible deficiencies are investigated further to ensure maintainability.

During the coding phase checkpoint review, the characteristics of understandability and modifiability are again evaluated. However, this time the program source code instead of the program design is reviewed. Besides using complexity metrics as in the design phase, the 90–10 test may be applied to measure understandability. Recall from Chapter 3 that in the 90–10 test a programmer is expected to reconstruct from memory 90% of a program module after a 10-minute study of the source code. If a maintenance programmer cannot successfully "pass" the 90–10 test for a sample of randomly selected modules, the checkpoint review recommendation will be to investigate the complexity of the program and perhaps redesign the most complex modules before development continues.

How exhaustive checkpoint reviews are depends on the software requirements, project scheduling, project budget, and personnel availability. Applying certain measures such as the 90–10 test or change exercises and even answering many of the checklist questions requires a certain level of programming expertise and, of course, personnel time. Some personnel time can be justified as a means of familiarizing maintenance programmers with a new software system that they will soon be expected to support. Also, audits serve as incentives for programmers to produce higher-quality products— especially when their work is being judged by their peers. Not all measures must be applied and not all modules must be examined to make quality judgments. Shneiderman suggests that randomly selecting 10% of the modules to which the 90–10 test is applied will provide a good indication of understandability [15].

Box 4.7 lists the characteristics of maintainability to be examined at the completion of each development phase and some possible measures to be applied. By no means does Box 4.7 represent a complete list of all possible quality checks and measures to be applied. It is merely one example of auditing for maintainability as part of the software development process.

BOX 4.7 Checkpoint maintainability evaluation

DEVELOPMENT PHASE CHECKPOINT

I. Requirements/Specification Phase

1. What are the maintainability requirements for the program?
   Example—define usability: response time for interactive system
   Example—define reliability: 95% reliable

Requirements to be Reviewed

1. Requirements and specifications
2. Schedule
3. Constraints, priorities
4. Test plan

Measures Applied to the Specification Phase

1. Usability checklist

II. Design Phase

1. Is the program understandable?
2. Is the program modifiable?
3. Is the program testable?

Design Material to be Reviewed

1. Design approach
2. Design
3. Schedule
4. Operation and maintenance support plan

Measures Applied to the Design Phase

1. Complexity metrics
2. Change exercise; coupling/ cohesiveness evaluation
3. Testability checklist; complexity metrics

III. Coding Phase

1. Is the program understandable?
2. Is the program modifiable?
3. Is the program portable?
4. Is the program efficient?

Coding Material to be Reviewed

1. Source code
2. Documentation
3. Program complexity
4. Unit test results

Measure Applied to the Compiled Source Code

1. Complexity metrics; 90–10 test; automated structure checker
2. Change exercise; modifiability checklist
3. Compilation results using compiler for standard version of language
4. Efficiency checklist; compilation time and space requirements

IV. Testing Phase

1. Is the program reliable?
2. Is the program efficient?
3. Is the program portable?
4. Is the program usable?

Testing Material to be Reviewed

1. Test results
2. User documentation
3. Program and data documentation
4. Operations documentation

Measures Used in Examining Test Results

1. Debugging; error statistics; reliability models
2. Efficiency checklist; 20% test
3. Comparison results from execution on different computer systems
4. User acceptance tests results; usability checklist

To make the checkpoint review as efficient as possible, quality measures should be applied before the review meeting. Only the results are discussed during the review meeting. The purpose of the checkpoint review meeting is to discuss quality evaluation results, to identify problems, and to make assignments; the purpose is *not* to perform evaluations or to correct deficiencies. Quality measures should be automated when possible (e.g., calculating complexity at compilation time). The technical expertise needed to apply or interpret the evaluation results depends on which measures are used. A good approach is to begin with a few simple measures and test their validity in a particular organization. Assigning some measurement tasks to junior programmers will lessen the drain on more senior personnel time and will help junior programmers gain a better understanding of good programming practices and program quality.

ACCEPTANCE REVIEW

The acceptance review is a special checkpoint review marking the end of a software development effort. It is sometimes called project cutover or turnover—the point at which the development portion of the software life cycle is concluded and the operations and maintenance phase begins. This is an important audit for controlling maintenance costs since it is the last opportunity to ensure maintainability before the software becomes an operational system. The purpose of this audit is to ensure maintainability and to formalize the transfer of system responsibility from the development group to the maintenance group. If the software does not pass the acceptance audit, it remains the responsibility of the development group until the noted deficiencies are rectified; if the software passes the acceptance audit, its support becomes the responsibility of the maintenance group.

To be effective the audit must be taken seriously by developers, maintainers, users, and management. Acceptance criteria must be clearly defined and clearly explained to all parties involved in advance of the acceptance review to allow for adequate preparation. To avoid bias, an independant inspection group can conduct the audit. To be practical audit tests should be kept simple and chosen to measure the characteristics of maintainability that are most important for this particular software system. Defining acceptance criteria in a checklist format will simplify the audit. Box 4.8 shows an example of a maintenance acceptance checklist. Note the use of maintainability tests to evaluate quality.

Gilb suggests bebugging as a practical maintainability test. He defines maintainability as the probability of repairing the software within a specified time under specified conditions. In Gilb's acceptance test the assigned and trained maintenance programmer must find 9 of 10 seeded errors in 5 hours. Seeded errors represent the type of errors that are likely to occur based on historical data from operational software. Gilb claims to have successfully

BOX 4.8   Maintenance acceptance checklist

APPLICATION _____   PROGRAM _____

CHECKLIST DELIVERABLES ITEMS

_____   1. SYSTEM REQUIREMENTS
_____   2. FUNCTIONAL SPECIFICATIONS
_____   3. DESIGN DOCUMENTS
_____   4. SOURCE CODE
_____   5. PROJECT PLAN (INCLUDING TEST PLAN)
_____   6. SYSTEM DOCUMENTATION
_____   7. SYSTEM DEVELOPMENT JOURNAL
_____   8. SYSTEM COMPLEXITY PROFILE
_____   9. SYSTEM TEST HISTORY
_____   10. SYSTEM OPERATION INSTRUCTIONS
_____   11. SYSTEM USER INSTRUCTIONS

MAINTAINABILITY TESTS

	PASS	NO PASS	COMMENTS
CHANGE EXERCISES	___	_____	_____
DEBUGGING EXERCISES	___	_____	_____
COMPLEXITY ANALYSIS	___	_____	_____
WARRANTY PERIOD	___	_____	_____

PASS NO PASS

SYSTEM ACCEPTED: ___   _____
COMMENTS: _____
_____

MAINTENANCE REVIEWER: _____ DATE: _____
SYSTEM DEVELOPER: _____ DATE: _____

applied this acceptance test in the development of several software systems, including a Scandinavian bank on-line system [16].

Also note the use of a warranty period as another maintainability test. One possible variation of project cutover is not to go directly from software development to the software operations and maintenance phase. Instead, a transition or warranty period is included as a sort of extended acceptance test. During this period (e.g., 90 days) the software is used as an operational system but remains the responsibility of the development group. Any errors that occur during the warranty period are corrected by the maintenance group with the assistance of the development group, and information about error type, modules in which errors occurred, and time to detect and correct errors is recorded. At the end of the warranty period the error data are evaluated. A form of mean time to repair (MTTR) is used to measure system reliability against system reliability acceptance criteria. For example, reliability acceptance may require that 90% of all errors discovered during the warranty period are correctable within 2 hours by the maintenance programmers. If all acceptance criteria are met, the software becomes the responsibility of the maintenance group. If not, the warranty period is repeated and the maintenance and development groups continue to share software support responsibility.

The use of a warranty period is particularly useful for software systems that are custom-developed by an outside consulting organization or for standardized software packages supplied by an outside software vendor. This is discussed further in Chapter 16.

The larger and more critical the software system, the more comprehensive the audit should be. Each organization should standardize a set of standards and acceptance criteria specifying a minimal subset that all software must meet. Box 4.9 provides a set of general maintainability standards.

PERIODIC MAINTENANCE AUDITS

Checkpoint reviews and acceptance reviews are used for ensuring the maintainability of new software systems. But the need for quality audits does not end with the completion of the development phase of the software life cycle. Software quality cannot be built permanently into software because of change. If software were not changed during the maintenance phase, its quality would remain intact. But in practice this is almost never the case. Software must be changed to continue to be useful. Software is changed to correct latent errors and deficiencies not detected during development, to adapt to changing computing environments, and to respond to changing user needs.

As software is changed its quality is threatened. New errors are introduced and the conceptual integrity is destroyed. There are countless examples among large and small software systems where the act of maintaining software resulted in degrading its future maintainability. For example, IBM studies of OS showed that over its lifetime OS became impractical to maintain and therefore uneconomical to use [17].

Performing periodic audits of operational software is a way of tracking changes in software quality. If deterioration of quality can be detected, measures can be taken to remedy the problem or to replace the software with a new, more cost-effective system.

Periodic maintenance audits are really just a continuation of develop-

BOX 4.9 Maintainability standards

1. Requirements and Specifications Standards

Requirements should be written, prioritized, and defined in testable terms.

Required, optimal, and future requirements should be differentiated.

Requirements should include computing facility requirements for operations and maintenance testing, operational and maintenance personnel requirements, and test tools.

2. Design Standards

Program design should be expressed as a hierarchy of modules such that each module represents one unique functional task and such that high cohesiveness and low coupling is achieved.

Extensibility, contractability, and adaptability capabilities of the design should be explained with examples of expected changes.

3. Source Code Standards

The highest-level programming language possible should be used.

Only standard versions and standard features of programming languages should be allowed.

All code should be well-structured.

All code should be documented to explain its purpose, its inputs, its outputs, and any special idiosyncrasies to facilitate testing/retesting efforts.

4. Documentation Standards

Documentation should explain program inputs and outputs, methods/algorithms used, error recovery procedures, all parameter ranges, and default conditions. (For a detailed discussion of program documentation, the reader is referred to Chapters 8 and 9.)

ment phase checkpoint reviews. The same quality measures and the same audit check can be performed during the maintenance audit as were performed during the checkpoint reviews. Results from the maintenance audits can be compared with results from previous maintenance audits and checkpoint reviews. Any changes indicate possible changes in software quality and/or some other types of problems (e.g., a decline in the expertise of the software maintainer, insufficient maintenance support tools).

The causes for change should be investigated. For example, if complexity metrics are used, then as part of a periodic audit the complexity of a small number of randomly selected modules is remeasured. If their new complexity values are greater than their previous values, this may be an early indication of a decrease in software maintainability and a prediction that more maintenance effort will be required to maintain the system in the future. Furthermore, it may indicate that modifications were made too hastily without thought to preserving system integrity, or that software documentation, technical tools, or programmer expertise are inadequate. On the other hand, decreases in complexity values may indicate stability in software quality.

As a general guideline, each application program should be audited annually. Auditing can be performed by a separate inspection team or by new maintenance programmers to familiarize them with the software they will soon maintain.

SOFTWARE BENCHMARKS

Checkpoint audits are methods for ensuring the quality of custom-designed software built by an internal data processing staff or an outside consulting organization. In the case of custom-designed software, the organization that both owns and uses the software normally has a great deal of control over its quality. There is a second type of software which is standardized for use by many different users in many different organizations and which is commonly referred to as *packaged software*. Packages are discussed further in Chapter 15.

How do we judge the maintainability of a software package? A reasonable answer would seem to be the same way we judge the maintainability of custom-built software. To be maintainable a software package should possess the quality characteristics of understandability, testability, modifiability, reliability, portability, efficiency, and usability. The same quality checklists, tests, and metrics used to evaluate custom-built software should be used to evaluate the quality of a software package, with the major emphasis placed on the quality of modifiability. For example, how easily can the package be customized to fit the needs of a particular organization or changed to meet new requirements in the future? What hooks and exits are available? Is it parameterized?

If the customer has access to the source code and program documentation, this approach is reasonable. But this is not usually the case for software packages that are sold or leased since the software vendor considers the software package proprietary. This means that many quality measures are no longer feasible. For example, the 90–10 test, change exercises, and complexity metrics requiring an examination of the program design or the program source code cannot be applied. However, the customer can examine user manuals, operations manuals, training courses, new release policy, computer environment requirements, future features lists, and vendor-supplied acceptance tests. Also, he can interview current users, consult software product directories (e.g, DATAPRO Directories, IPC Directories), examine user surveys (e.g., Datamation annual software package evaluations), and conduct software benchmarks.

A *software benchmark* is a program test conducted to ensure that a software package performs according to the customer's expectations. It is performed as part of the package selection process. The benchmark test should be designed by the customer to test the requirements that are most critical to his organization. To construct the most comprehensive benchmark tests the customer should prepare a meaningful set of tests using the organization's data on the customer's computer system. It may be difficult to convince the package vendor to allow a test on the customer's computer system since this increases the vendor's risk of having the software copied. Instead, the vendor may prefer to use his own test site, which is probably acceptable if the computing environment is similar to the customer's. It should *not*, however, be difficult to convince the package vendor to permit a customer-designed benchmark test as part of the selection process. If the vendor refuses, the customer is best advised to consider another vendor.

CHOOSING A MAINTAINABLE PROGRAMMING LANGUAGE

Choice of a programming language can greatly affect program maintainability. Low-level languages (machine-code and assembly languages) are difficult to learn and to understand and for this reason are difficult to maintain. Although generally considered more understandable than low-level languages, some high-level languages are more understandable than others. For example, because it more closely resembles English and offers more flexibility in assigning meaningful variable names, COBOL is considered more understandable than FORTRAN. Because it has a richer, more powerful instruction set, PL/1 is considered more understandable than COBOL. On the other hand, because of the subtleties of its very high-level instruction set, APL programs are considered among the most difficult to understand.

The difficulty of creating well-structured programs is also language dependent. Many languages simply do not have adequate constructs to create well-structured programs. For example, FORTRAN limits variable names to six characters, making it difficult to create meaningful variable names. The FORTRAN logical IF statement does not allow the construction of nested IFs or the creation of in-line procedures for the true part or false part of the IF construct. COBOL also has many limitations. Although COBOL allows variable names containing up to 30 characters, it has no provision for local variables. Also, there is no block structuring capability in COBOL.

To compensate partially for such inherent deficiencies in the language, preprocessors have been developed. The programmer reads and writes a "structured" version of the language, which is then automatically translated by the preprocessor before compilation or assembly. There are two problems with this approach.

1. It requires that the programmer learn and understand another version of the programming language.

2. The extra step needed to translate the structured code into compilable code reduces efficiency and increases the risk of introducing errors.

The structuring deficiencies present in the most widely used programming languages today (e.g., FORTRAN, COBOL, assembly languages) provide a strong argument for moving from first-generation, second-generation, and even some third-generation languages to fourth-generation languages, which are inherently more understandable, more powerful, and therefore more maintainable (see Fig. 4.5). Attempting to build maintainability into programs written in inadequate languages can provide only a very limited, short-term remedy to maintenance problems. As the number of programs to be maintained increases, this approach will prove hopelessly inadequate. If we do not begin using the most powerful software tools, techniques, and languages available, we will not simply be facing the same software crisis 10 years from now as we do today; we will be facing a much worse one.

Fourth-generation languages (discussed in Chapter 11) offer a powerful, long-term solution to controlling maintenance costs. They are easy to use, to understand, and to modify. Fourth-generation languages permit users or analysts to develop business application programs many times more quickly than do second- and third-generation languages traditionally used for business applications software. Some fourth-generation languages are procedural, others are not. For both types, many business applications can be programmed with an order of magnitude fewer instructions than with COBOL or PL/1. Reducing program size helps control complexity and improve maintainability.

With some fourth-generation languages, the user does not have to

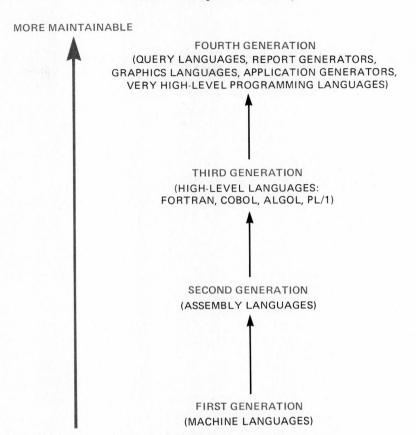

Figure 4.5 To ensure maintainability, use the highest-level programming language possible. Fourth-generation languages are easy to learn to understand and modify.

specify how to implement the algorithm. Instead, the compiler or interpreter makes intelligent assumptions about how to implement what the user needs. For example, it may automatically select a report format, number report pages, and select character types for graphics display, all in a "user-friendly" manner. Automatically generating instructions improves reliability.

Fourth-generation languages are easy to learn. Users can satisfy many of their needs with some languages after a two-day training course. Because they are simpler to understand, not only is it easy to create fourth-generation language programs, but also to modify and maintain them. Fourth-generation languages are discussed in more detail later in the book.

REFERENCES

1. B. Boehm, "Quantitative Evaluation of Software Quality," 2nd International Conference on Software Engineering, Proceedings (San Francisco), October 13–15, 1976, pp. 592–605.

2. J. Brown and M. Lipow, "The Quantitative Measurement of Software Safety and Reliability," revised from TRW Report SDP-1776 (August 1973), TRW Software Series.

3. G. Weinberg, "The Psychology of Improved Programmer Performance," *Datamation,* November 1972, pp. 82–85.

4. C. McClure, "A Model for Program Complexity Analysis," 3rd International Conference on Software Engineering, Proceedings (Atlanta), May 10–12, 1978, pp. 149–157.

5. C. McClure, "Formalization and Application of Structured Programming and Program Complexity," Ph.D. dissertation, Illinois Institute of Technology, 1976.

6. B. Boehm, "Seven Basic Principles of Software Engineering," in *Infotech State of the Art Reports: Software Engineering Techniques* (Maidenhead, England: Infotech International, 1977), pp. 77–113.

7. M. J. Lyons, "Salvaging Your Software Asset (Tools-Based Maintenance)," AFIPS Conference Proceedings on 1981 National Computer Conference (Chicago), Vol. 50, May 4–7, 1981, pp. 337–342.

8. C. McClure, *Reducing COBOL Complexity Through Structured Programming* (New York: Van Nostrand Reinhold Company, 1978), pp. 1–7.

9. T. Gilb, "Maintainability Is More than Structured Coding," in *Techniques of Programs and System Maintenance* (Lincoln, NE: Ethnotech, 1980), pp. 201–203.

10. T. Gilb, "Structured Program Coding: Does It Really Increase Program Maintainability?" in *Techniques of Program and System Maintenance* (Lincoln, NE: Ethnotech, 1980), pp. 197–199.

11. B. Lientz and E. Swanson, *Software Maintenance Management* (Reading, MA: Addison-Wesley Publishing Co., Inc., 1980), pp. 97–114.

12. T. Gilb, *Software Metrics* (Cambridge, MA: Winthrop Publishers, Inc., 1977), pp. 60–64.

13. B. Boehm et al., *Characteristics of Software Quality* (Amsterdam, North-Holland Publishing Company, 1978), pp. 5-1 to 5–42.

14. B. Knight, "On Software Quality and Productivity," IBM Technical Directions, Federal Systems Division, July 1978.

15. B. Shneiderman, *Software Psychology* (Cambridge, MA: Winthrop Publishers, Inc., 1980), pp. 93–120.

16. T. Gilb, "Guaranteeing Program Maintainability," in *Techniques of Program and System Maintenance* (Lincoln, NE: Ethnotech, 1980), pp. 215–216.

17. J. Munson, "Software Maintainability: A Practical Concern for Life-Cycle Costs," IEEE 2nd International Computer Software and Application Conference, Proceedings (Chicago), November 13–16, 1978, pp. 54–59.

5 THE SIGNIFICANCE OF DATA BASE

There is one story after another of management not being able to obtain the information they need from their computer system.

One story in the *Harvard Business Review* [1] describes a marketing vice-president confronted with sales forecasts for a new line of industrial products, similar to the company's existing line. The new line was intended to complement the existing line where competition had been making serious inroads. The forecasts for the new line were more promising than the marketing vice-president had dared to hope, and the forecasting team had shown good reason to take them seriously.

To gain the much-needed profits from the increased sales it was necessary to ensure that the higher sales volume could be manufactured and distributed. Data were needed about plant capacity, personnel, and warehouses. A preliminary examination indicated that the regional warehousing facilities might impose a severe constraint on sales, both in physical space and personnel. The forecasts, however, did not show regional variations in such a way as to make it clear which warehouses would be worst hit and which ones nearby might have excess capacity.

The marketing vice-president had planned an aggressive promotion campaign, and he suspected that if it were successful some regions would need four times their normal warehousing capacity for at least three months. The chief executive officer concluded that it was essential to compute in more detail the impact of the projected marketing campaign on inventory turnover and warehouse crowding. He assumed that this could be computed because the computer already had:

1. Inventory simulation programs and several years' data on inventory turnover.

2. Forecasting programs designed to produce forecast sales reports by region and product.

3. A model for market penetration of the new line based on the sales of the old line which it would supplement.

The chief executive officer presented his requirement to the data-processing manager. The results, he said, were needed quickly because the new product line was only a few months from announcement. The DP manager pointed out that, unfortunately, although the data needed did exist, they were not in a form that could be used for the required simulation. The programs for forecasting sales did provide regional projections, but the resulting records did not contain the data necessary for regional inventory simulations. Further, the data about past years' sales were specially coded for the programs with which they had been used in the past and could not be used by the regional inventory simulations without a massive reorganization.

> The Chief Executive Officer looked glum: "How long will it take you to clean up the data and write a simulation program that will give us some answers?"
> "Nine months, maybe a year," said the DP manager.
> "Because all our data are frozen into these other programs?" the CEO asked.
> "That's the main reason," the DP manager replied.
> "That's a hell of a reason," the CEO said and stalked toward the door.
> "Of course, we could have done it the other way," the DP man called after him, "but now what we'd have to do is. . . ."
> But the CEO was gone. [1]

"The other way" would have used *data-base techniques* instead of letting each department use files designed solely for its own purposes—but it was too late.

THE DATA-BASE ENVIRONMENT

Data-base management systems were originally devised to deal with the expensive maintenance problems associated with data on files. When well managed, the data-base environment has greatly reduced maintenance costs. When poorly managed, however, it has made maintenance worse.

It has become clear that the data-base environment represents not just a change in software, but a change in DP management. An objective should be a major reduction in long-term maintenance costs. To achieve that, strongly enforced management of sound data representation is needed.

MULTIPLE USAGE OF DATA

Figure 5.1 illustrates the way data are organized for computers that do not use data-base techniques. There are many files of records, some on tape and some on quickly accessible media such as disk. The records contain data items, shown as circles in Fig. 5.1. When a program is written for a new application or a variation of an old application, there may be a file which contains the required set of data items. Often, however, there is not, and a new file has to be created.

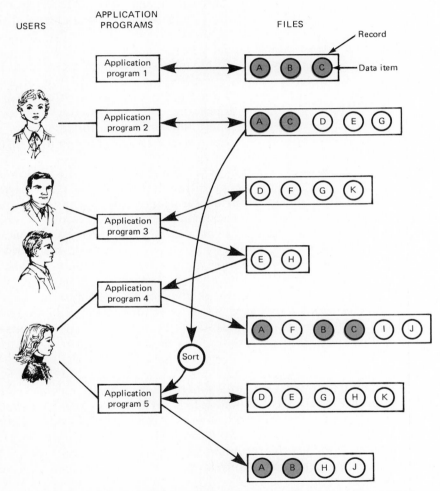

Figure 5.1 File environment. For each new application a programmer or analyst creates a new file. A large installation has hundreds or thousands of such files with much redundancy of data.

Suppose that a new user request needs a file with data items A, F, and H. These data items do not appear together in the existing files in Fig. 5.1. Other files must be sorted and merged to obtain the new file, but this will not be straightforward if, as with the marketing problem above, the existing files do not have the required sets of keys. There may not be an H data item for every pair of A and F data items.

PROBLEMS WITH FILE SYSTEMS

There are three problems about the organization of data in *files* as in Fig. 5.1. To understand them the reader should imagine hundreds or thousands of files rather than the seven in Fig. 5.1.

First, there is a high level of redundancy. The same type of data item is stored in many different places. The different versions of the same data items may be in different stages of update. In other words, they have different values. This may give the appearance of inconsistency to users. A manager obtains a report saying one thing and a terminal inquiry says something different. With multiple copies of the same data item it is difficult to maintain consistency or to ensure integrity of the data items.

Second, a file system is *inflexible*. Requests for information that require data items to be grouped in different ways cannot be answered quickly. Most ad hoc queries from a user employing a generalized query language cannot be answered. Although the data exits, information cannot be provided relating to that data. The data cannot be processed in new ways without restructuring. One sometimes hears the protest from management: "We paid millions for that computer system and we cannot obtain the information we want from it."

Third, it can be expensive to make changes to a file system. Suppose that application program 3 in Fig. 5.1 has to be changed in such a way that its record $\boxed{\text{E} \qquad \text{H}}$ has to be modified. Unfortunately, application program 4 uses this same record; therefore, application program 4 has to be modified. Many other application programs may also use the same record (Fig. 5.2) and all have to be changed.

A seemingly trivial change in a file environment sets off a chain reaction of other changes that have to be made. This upheaval is expensive and the necessary programmers are doing other work. Sometimes the modifications are difficult to make because the applications were not adequately documented. As time goes on this problem becomes worse because more and more programs are created. More programs have to be changed whenever a file is changed.

MAINTENANCE

Computer data in an organization are no more a static entity than are the contents of the organiza-

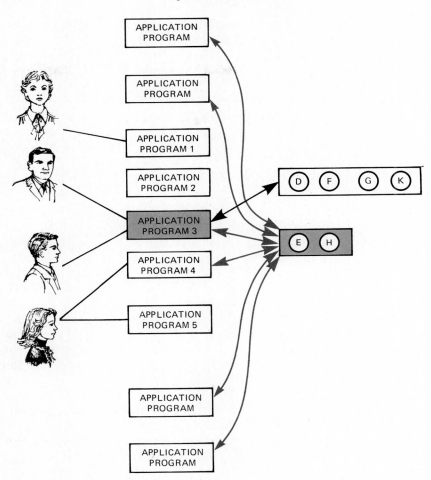

Figure 5.2   One file becomes used by multiple applications. When an application is changed (application program 3 above) and its file has to be restructured, all the programs which use that file have to be changed. A seemingly trivial change in a file environment can set off a chain reaction of other changes that have to be made.

tion's filing cabinets. The details of data stored, and the way they are used, change continuously. If a computer system attempts to impose an unchangeable file structure on an organization, it is doomed to the types of pressure that will result in most of the programming efforts being spent on modifying existing programs rather than developing new applications.

It is often thought by systems analysts that existing programs which work well can be left alone. In reality, however, the data which they create

BOX 5.1 Typical problems in old, established file installations

- High proportion of DP professionals devoted to maintenance activities.
- High cost and slow speed in developing new systems.
- Inability to respond quickly to necessary changes.
- Inability to provide ad hoc management information.
- Inconsistent definition of similar data items across applications.
- Steadily worsening proliferation of separate files.
- Increasing proliferation of inconsistent values of redundant data.
- The greater the number of programs, the worse the problem of converting them when data changes, and so the greater the reluctance to respond to requests for such change by end users.
- Difficulty in maintaining inventory and control of data.
- Cost of redundant storage.
- Cost of repetitive data entry.
- Lack of overall management of the data resource.

or use are needed for other applications and almost always needed in a slightly different form. New data-item types are added. New record types are needed with data-item types from several previous records. The data must be indexed in a different way. The physical layout of data is improved. Data bases for different applications are merged, and so forth.

Box 5.1 summarizes the problems that develop in an old file environment.

THE NEED FOR DATA INDEPENDENCE Data-base management software was invented to help solve these problems. One of the main objectives of a data-base system is that the data should be usable in new ways without setting off a chain reaction of difficult modifications to other programs. A program may be modified, changing in some way the data it uses, without disturbing other programs that use the same data.

We commented earlier that an old file environment is like a bowl of spaghetti. Every time you pull one piece of spaghetti it shakes all the others in the bowl. As time goes by it becomes steadily worse because the number

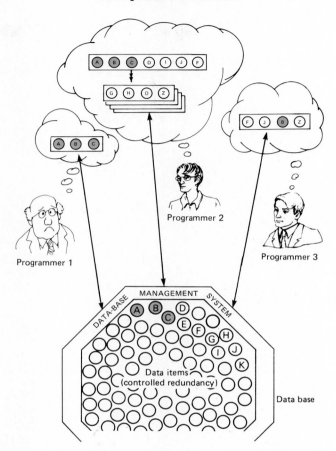

Figure 5.3 With data-base management systems, programmers users can live in blissful ignorance of how the data are really stored.

of pieces of spaghetti increases and they become more interwoven. The maintenance difficulties of file systems grow geometrically with the number of applications produced.

The intent of a data-base environment is to *insulate each program* from the effects of changes to other programs. And all programs should be insulated from the effects of reorganizing the data.

Data-base systems attempt to lower the maintenance costs by separating the records that the programmers perceive from the records that are physically stored. You might think of the programmer as perceiving a *make-believe* record—a record that does not exist in physical reality. The data-base management software derives this record for the programmer from the collection of data that are physically stored.

Figure 5.3 illustrates this. In Fig. 5.3, when programmer 2 changes his record structure, his new record structure is derived from the data base by the data-base management system. The change made by programmer 1 does not force programmers 2 or 3 to change *their* records.

Of course, we do not call them anything as unrespectable as "make-believe records." The records shown in Fig. 5.3 are called *logical* records. Each program refers to logical records, not the physical records, which are stored in magnetic pulses on the disks or other storage media.

DATA-BASE MANAGEMENT SYSTEMS

The data-base management system is the entity that provides programmers or end users with the data they ask for. Like a conjurer pulling different colored handkerchiefs out of a hat, it derives its users' *make-believe* records from its store of data. It finds out what *physical* records contain the data in a given request, has a means of locating those records, and from them derives the logical records that were asked for.

All of the major computer manufacturers provide data-base management systems, with names such as IMS, IDS, DMS, and IDMS (I in these names stands for information or integrated, D for data, M for management, and S for system). Independent software companies have also provided data-base management systems, with names such as TOTAL, ADABAS, IDMS, and SYSTEM 2000.

ARE YOUR DATA INDEPENDENT?

A data base is intended to make data independent of the programs that use them. Either data or programs can be changed without causing the other to have to be changed. The data can be easily reorganized or their content added to. Old application programs do not have to be rewritten when changes are made to data structures, data layout, or the physical devices on which data are stored.

This independence of data is essential if data are to become a general-purpose corporate resource. In the past data structures have been devised by a programmer for his own use. He writes a program to create a file of data. Usually, when another programmer needs the data for another purpose, it is not structured in the way he wants, so he creates another file—hence the duplication in Fig. 5.1.

Data independence is one of the most important differences between the way data are organized in data bases and the way they are organized in the file systems of computers that do not use data-base management software. The programmers can each have their own logical data structure, as shown in Fig. 5.3, and can program in blissful ignorance of how the data are really organized. When the data organization is changed, *the old programs still work.*

This facility makes the data-base software complex. However, without it, new application development can be immensely time consuming and prohibitively expensive because it makes it necessary to rewrite existing programs or convert existing data. The total number of person-years that a corporation has invested in application programs grows steadily. The programmers are gone long since, and it is too late to complain that their documentation is inadequate.

The greater the number of programs, the more horrifying the thought of having to convert them or their data, so there is reluctance in the DP department to respond to the latest needs of the end users.

DATA-BASE LANGUAGES

One aspect of data-base technology was not present in the early data-base systems, but it is now becoming so important that it is a tail which is wagging the whole dog.

Data-base languages exist, and are rapidly improving, which allow data bases to be interrogated, reports generated from them, data displayed in graphics form, data entered with integrity controls, and complete applications generated. Figure 5.4 illustrates the important high-level data-base software which makes this possible.

New, unanticipated requests for information, such as that in the story at the start of this chapter, are increasing. As end-user management realize the potential value to them of the data that are stored, their requests for information increase. Much future growth can be expected in the data requests from users as they better comprehend the potential of computers. However, to the data-processing manager without appropriate data bases, these requests can be a menace. He does not have the programmers to deal with the requests. Many end users in a file environment are finding that important requests for data or reports are not met.

The concept of data base, shown in Fig. 5.4, if it works as intended, should enable the DP department to be more responsive to such requests. However, for this to happen, the right *logical* data structures must be created, and this requires close cooporation between the data-base designer and the end users. The data items are usually not stored entirely independently of one another but in groups of related data items, sometimes called *records*, sometimes *segments*. The software must be able to extract segments and combine them to form the records that an application or report uses.

Data-base dialogues for end users are becoming increasingly important. They enable information to be extracted from computers, and reports and listings generated *without* programming. Increasingly, end users will interact directly with the data-base systems.

Figure 5.4 suggests that a corporation's data are stored in a large reservoir in which the users can go fishing. Although this figure forms a

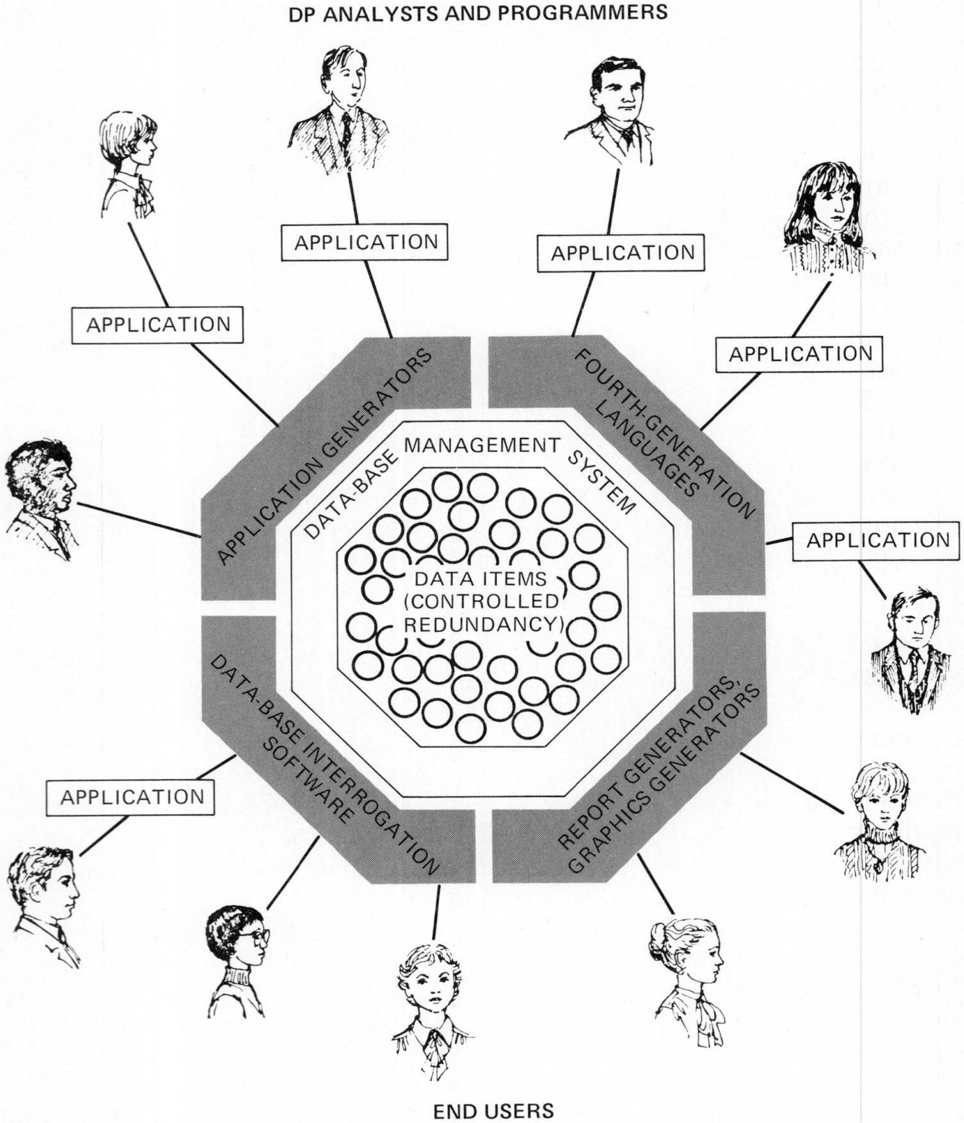

DP ANALYSTS AND PROGRAMMERS

Figure 5.4 High-level data-base languages speed up the application development process and alleviate the maintenance tasks.

useful way to explain data-base concepts to management, it is nevertheless a naive view of a data base—in some cases dangerously naive, as we shall see. The data items inside the octagon of Fig. 5.4 have to be organized in such a way that they can be found and accessed with sufficient speed. The organizing introduces many complexities into data-base design. The structuring problems can be sufficiently great that a designer may sometimes elect to employ separate data-base systems, even though they contain much of the same information.

The striving for flexibility, however, is vital. In many corporations, systems (of accounts, organization, methods, responsibilities, and procedures) have been more of a hindrance to change than physical plant and unamortized capital investments. For some, retraining the whole labor force would be easier than changing the system. Quite frequently, the computer has contributed to the inflexibility by dressing hallowed procedures in a rigid electronic framework. The computer has been hailed as one of the most versatile and flexible machines ever built, but in many corporations, because of the difficulty and cost of changing their programs and data bases, it becomes a straitjacket which precludes change and even constrains corporate policy. The comment is often heard: "We cannot do that because change is too difficult with our computer system."

One of the most difficult tricks that we have to learn is how to introduce automation without introducing rigidity. The computer industry is only now beginning to glimpse how that can be done. Data-base techniques are an important part of the answer.

FOUR CLASSES OF DATA SYSTEM

There are four types of environments of computer data. It is important to distinguish clearly between them. Box 5.2 summarizes the four types of environment.

They have a major effect on management at all levels in an enterprise, including top management. An efficient enterprise ought to have a substantial foundation of Class III and Class IV data. These, however, are only likely to be pervasive and successful if there is top management support for them, as we shall see.

FILES

A Class I environment is that of *files*. A separate file is designed for each, or most, applications. Often a direct result of structured analysis, the data are embedded in the function.

It is important to distinguish between file systems and data-base systems. In a data base the data are not embedded in the function. They are made independent and many different types of processes may employ the same data.

A data base may be defined as follows:

A *data base* is a shared collection of interrelated data designed to meet the needs of multiple types of end users. It can be defined as a collection of data from which many different end-user views can be derived. The data are stored so that they are independent of the programs that use them. Adding

BOX 5.2   The four types of data environment

Class I Environment: Files

A data-base management system is not used. Separate files of data are used for most applications, designed by the analysts and programmers when the application is created.

Examples of software: VSAM, BDAM, RMS.

Characteristics:

Simple. Relatively easy to implement.

A large proliferation of files grow up with high redundancy, leading to high maintenance costs.

Seemingly trivial changes to applications trigger a chain reaction of other changes and hence change becomes slow, expensive, and is resisted.

Class II Environment: Application Data-Bases

A data-base management system is used but without the degree of sharing in a Class III environment. Separate data bases are designed for separate applications.

Examples of software: TOTAL, IMS, IDMS, IDS, ADABAS.

Characteristics:

Easier to implement than a Class III environment in that the management problems of integrating data across function areas are avoided.

A large proliferation of data bases grow up with high redundancy, as in a file environment.

High maintenance costs.

Results from the application of process-oriented analysis methods rather than information engineering.

Sometimes more expensive than a Class I environment.

Does not achieve the major advantages of data-base operation.

Class III Environment: Subject Data Bases

Data bases are created which are largely independent of specific applications. Data are designed and stored independently of the function for which they are used. Data for business subjects such as customers, products, or personnel are associated and represented in shared data bases.

Box 5.2 *(Continued)*

Examples of software: IMS, IDMS, IDS, ADABAS, SYSTEM 2000.

Characteristics:

Thorough data analysis and modeling needed, which takes time. Much lower maintenance costs.

Leads eventually (but not immediately) to faster application development and direct user interaction with the data bases.

Requires a change in traditional systems analysis methods and in overall DP management.

If not managed well, it tends to disintegrate into a Class II (or sometimes Class I) environment.

Class IV Environment: Information Systems

Data bases organized for searching and fast information retrieval rather than for high-volume production runs. Employs software designed around inverted files, inverted lists, or secondary key search methods. Good end-user query facilities. Most user-driven computing employs Class IV data bases.

Examples of software: IBM STAIRS, STATUS, the relational data bases of MAPPER, SEQUEL, NOMAD, and some other non-procedural languages, ICL CAFS.

Characteristics:

Often easy to implement.

More flexible than Class III but often does not handle high throughputs of routine transactions with high machine efficiency.

Should often coexist with a Class III environment.

The data system software and the language that uses it are sometimes packaged together (but not always).

Low maintenance.

new data and modifying and retrieving existing data is carefully controlled. Retrieving data may be carried out by multiple users in different ways with appropriate privacy controls. The data are structured so as to provide a foundation for future application development.

One system is said to contain a collection of data bases if they are entirely separate in structure.

Figure 5.5 illustrates the definition of data base. For a detailed dis-

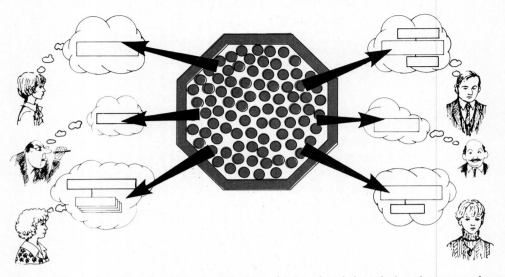

Figure 5.5 A data base is a shared collection of interrelated data designed to meet the needs of many types of end users. It can be defined as a collection of data from which many different end-user views can be derived. The data are stored so that they are independent of the programs that use them. Adding new data and modifying and retrieving existing data are carefully controlled. Retrieving data may be carried out by multiple users in different ways with appropriate privacy controls. The data are structured so as to provide a foundation for future application development. One system is said to contain a collection of data bases if they are entirely separate in structure.

cussion of data-base systems and management, the reader is referred to other Martin books on the subject [2–5].

SUBJECT DATA BASES VERSUS APPLICATION DATA BASES

As we look back now on years of data-base case histories we can observe two types of approach: *application data bases* and *subject data bases*. It is quite clear which has given the best results *in the long term:* subject data bases.

Subject data bases relate to organizational *subjects* rather than to conventional computer *applications*. There should, for example, be a *product* data base rather than separate *inventory, order* entry, and *quality control* data bases relating to that product. Many applications may then use the same data base. The development of new applications relating to that data base becomes easier than if application-oriented data bases had been built.

By using *subject* data bases rather than *applications* data bases the eventual number of data bases is far lower. A corporation builds up a very large number of applications but does not have a large number of operational *subjects.* If *files* are designed for specific applications, the number of files grows almost as rapidly as the number of applications, and results in the great proliferation of redundant data found in a typical tape and disk library today. Application-oriented data bases can also proliferate rapidly. Using *subject* data bases, however, the number of applications grows much faster than the number of data bases.

Sometimes the term *integrated data base* is used rather than *subject data base.* This implies that data throughout an organization are integrated and shared. If this were done, it would result in a data base of great complexity. The *subject-data-base* approach is an attempt to divide this complexity into more manageable slices. In some installations the term *integrated data base* is more appropriate. Again, it is designed independently of specific applications with the intention of creating a stable foundation stone on which many applications can be built.

CLASS II
ENVIRONMENT
A Class II environment is one of application data bases rather than subject data bases. The systems analysts tend to create a separate data base for each new application, as they do with file systems. Because data-base management systems are used there is some degree of data independence, but redundant data grows, as with file systems, and has most of the problems listed in Box 5.1.

It is sometimes said that a data-base management system is used *like a file access method* rather than as a true data-base system. This is the Class II environment.

CLASS III
ENVIRONMENT
A Class III environment is one of *subject* or *integrated* data bases. When a collection of such data bases has been built they represent the data resource we discussed—data independent from specific applications.

The types of data represented do not change very frequently, whereas the functions that use the data do. Therefore, it makes sense not to embed the data in the functions, as in a Class I environment.

INADEQUACY OF
THE CLASS II DATA
ENVIRONMENT
Although the intention of data-base management systems was to *reduce maintenance* and to create *flexible derivation of information* when it is needed, the application-oriented data-base systems that were built often failed to achieve these objectives. The DP world is full of horror stories of management wanting information urgently, the data from which that information can be derived being on disks, a data-base

management system being in use, but the DP department are unable to derive the information without lengthy reprogramming.

In one chemical company it was discovered that certain employees had a strange illness. It became suspected that the illness was caused by an earlier exposure to an exotic chemical. It became urgent to list all those employees throughout the organization who had been exposed to this chemical. All the necessary data existed. Data-base management software was in use. But for a long time the DP organization was unable to produce a complete list.

In a large bank the top management compiled a set of information requests which they wanted answered urgently because a competing bank had gone bankrupt. Could conditions like those leading to the bankruptcy exist in *this* organization? Again the data were on-line. But the questions could not be answered without major restructuring of data and new programming, which would take too long.

The application of data-base and data communication techniques *ought* to bring a fundamental change in the *use* of data processing. Employed properly, data-base systems make all data available to all users who can put them to valuable use. However, this needs a substantial amount of planning and DP control.

The necessary consolidation of data and effective use of enterprise data bases demands an organizational understanding of the meaning and use of the different functional versions of data. Organizations have grown, and the data resource has been dissipated across many functional areas. In an endeavor to maintain current and up-to-date all versions of these dissipated data, changes in one data version have had to be communicated (generally by paper) to other functional areas that need to be aware of that change.

The complexity of data base and its demand for computer understanding has seen the establishment of the position of Data Administrator. It has fallen to this individual to identify and consolidate the redundant versions of data throughout the organization. Once identified, data are structured for implementation and management using data-base management system (DBMS) software products.

These products of *themselves* are unable to *identify* redundant data. Of themselves they are unable to bring order into the real-life data chaos which exists.

DISINTEGRATION   Many data-base installations have set out to create a Class III environment and have had problems. A new application comes along and for some reason a new data base is created for it rather than using the existing subject data bases.

It requires less management organization to create *application* data bases than to do the overall design that is needed for *subject* data bases. However, as the years go by installations that do this end up with almost as many separate data bases as they would have had *files* if they had not used data-base management. They do not then achieve the full advantages of data base. The use of data-base management in such installations has not reduced the program maintenance cost as it should.

Too often the attempt to create a Class III environment disintegrates into Class II. This may be due to poor management or to poor subject data-base design.

Sometimes end users or analysts want their own data base for reasons of pride, politics, or because it is easier. Management is not strong enough to enforce the principles of the Class III environment, or possibly does not understand them or their significance. The results are sometimes tragic; excellent work by a data administrator falls into disuse because management does not resist the counterpressures, and the major long-term payoffs of data-base operation are lost.

Sometimes the analyst needs a new view of data that cannot be derived from the existing data bases. Consequently, a new data base is created. This happens over and over again until there is a proliferation of data bases. The cause of this is usually inadequate design in the first place. The principles of information analysis, data modeling, and stability analysis described later in this book have not been followed.

It is extremely important that management understand the difference between a Class II and Class III data-base environment, and understand how the Class III environment should be designed and managed so that it does not disintegrate into a Class II environment (or worse, Class I) [2].

It is important to understand this at the start, not when it is too late.

CLASS IV ENVIRONMENT   As data-base technology spread, many good query languages were created. The query languages increased in flexibility and grew into more complete languages which could generate reports, generate graphic representations of data, manipulate the data with arithmetic and logic, and generate complete applications.

Some of these languages were well-human-factored and user-friendly. Some were nonprocedural. They made possible *application development without programmers,* which needed new forms of DP management [6]. User-driven computing, in different forms, swept through some organizations, as is discussed in this book.

To make good use of these languages it became necessary to have data systems in which the data were accessible in a more flexible fashion than with traditional data-base management systems. We saw the growth of *relational* data systems [3], some created specifically to support the new languages, and *information retrieval* systems, which made possible the searching of large bodies of data.

For some types of uses of information, the users would like a large reservoir of data in which they can go fishing. In other cases they would like the freedom to sort, merge, and search their own logical files, using a simple language at terminal, to analyze the data, to ask "What if?" questions using them, and to generally employ the data to assist in decision making.

To support such languages and use of data, the data have to be organized in such a way that they can be found and accessed with sufficient speed. The organizing introduces many complexities into data-base design. The structuring problems can be sufficiently great that a designer may sometimes elect to employ separate data-base systems, even though they contain much of the same information.

The fields in a data base are arranged into groups which are called records or segments, and a single READ instruction results in one such record or segment being read into the computer's main memory. Many data-base inquiries refer to *one* record: for example, "Display purchase order 29986," or for a small number of records "Display the account of R. V. ASTON," or "Display details of the armaments on the ship INTREPID." Others, however, require the data base to be searched: for example, "Display all U.S. ships within 200 miles of the Straits of Hormuz carrying torpedoes with a range greater than 20 miles."

Queries that cause searching can take much more machine time. If there are too many of them, they take too much machine time, slow down the main work of the system, and give unacceptable response times. Some of the powerful data-base languages encourage end users to take actions, often unwittingly, that cause expensive searching of data bases.

Some data-base software is specifically designed to permit the data bases to be searched efficiently. Spontaneous queries of a diversity of types can be handled quickly. The software employs data structures that are appropriate for this, such as inverted files, inverted lists, or multiple efficiently designed secondary indices [3]. In some cases special hardware is used to make the data searching fast. We describe this as a Class IV environment—a system designed for general information retrieval and flexible data searching.

Information retrieval systems are often separate from the production data-base systems that produce the daily paperwork and do the routine data processing. They are often easier to install and easier to manage. They use different software. A Class II or III environment uses software such as IMS, IDMS, TOTAL, and IDS. A Class IV environment uses software such as STAIRS, STATUS, and other information retrieval software, or flexible data systems linked to fourth-generation languages, such as Univac's MAPPER, IBM's SQL (pronounced "Sequel" and obtainable with the ORACLE data base of Relational Systems Inc.), and National CSS's NOMAD. All of the latter data systems employ *relational* data bases. They permit a search index to be built on any field, and permit logical files (relations) to be merged or jointly manipulated with *relational join* operations.

Sometimes special hardware is used for the Class IV environment, such as ICL's CAFS (Content Addressable File System) or the Britton–Lee Intelligent Data Base Machine.

The end-user language for interrogating the data base is often closely interrelated to the data structures. Some software can handle either a Class III or Class IV environment, or both at the same time, but one or the other is handled without the highest efficiency.

An information retrieval system often contains some of the same data as a related production system. Why should they be separate? Primarily for reasons of efficiency. An information system needs its data to be organized differently from a production system's. Often it contains only a subset of the data. An information system could be highly inefficient if it contained and had to search the vast mass of data kept in a production system. On the other hand, the production processes could be disrupted by many end users entering queries that trigger searching operations.

ACCESS MODULES　　　Searching and joining mechanisms have been created by means of [2] :

- Secondary indices
- Ring structures
- Multilist structures
- Inverted lists
- Inverted files
- Bit maps designed to direct searches
- Associative storage

In some systems, *access modules* are created for searching on particular fields. When a statement from a user triggers such a search the system will find whether a suitable access module exists. If it does not, every record may have to be searched in a time-consuming fashion. Some Class IV systems analyze the usage patterns and indicate to a system administrator what access modules should be created. Some systems permit the access modules to be created *dynamically,* while other users are employing the system.

A problem with all of these mechanisms that give efficient searching or efficient relational joins is that *they degrade the performance of simple updating of the data.* Consider what must happen when a field is updated. If there is a secondary index on that field the index entry relating to the field value must be changed. If there was no index entry for that value, one must be inserted. The index entry relating to the old field value must also be changed. If a ring or multilist structure is used, the pointers must be re-threaded to represent the new value and the deletion of the old value. If an inverted list or associative structure is used, it must similarly be changed to reflect the new value and absence of the old value.

The secondary indices, inverted lists, and so on, take up much storage space—sometimes more than the original data. Long accesses are therefore needed to update the indices or lists.

If the *update* transaction rate is low, as it usually is in information retrieval and decision support systems, the work needed to update the access modules is not a major concern. However, on a heavy-duty system, with a high rate of updates or data entry, it is a major concern. A system that is processing 100,000 bank transactions a day from terminals would be heavily burdened if it also had to change access modules each time it changed a record. It therefore makes sense to separate the heavy-duty production system from any associated Class IV systems, even though they might use some of the same data.

It is important in discussing data-base management to distinguish between Class III and IV environments. They have different problems and are managed differently. Class IV systems have more flexibility and tend to support user-friendly languages which permit changes to be made without high maintenance costs. Both need to fit into the overall planning of a corporation's data resources.

MIXTURES   An ideal situation is a mixture of Class III and Class IV. However, most corporations have substantial existing Class I and Class II environments. It is almost always necessary that these coexist with the Class III and Class IV environments. Conversion of Class I, and sometimes Class II, to Class III environments is often necessary [2].

In a few systems there are good reasons in certain cases for using files rather than a shared data base. These include the following:

- A *very* high transaction volume is to be processed with fast response times (as on airline reservation systems). Data-base systems do not give good enough machine performance in some such cases.

- *Very* large files must be processed in different ways using different keys. Sorts are necessary in a file system to accomplish this. It would be too inefficient with existing data-base management systems.

- The data are *highly* volatile with a *very* rapid rate of creating new records and deleting old ones. Again, data-base systems have efficiency problems.

- Application software has been purchased that uses files rather than data bases.

Although there are a few cases where files are desirable rather than data base, usually an analyst's determination to use files has not been based on sound technical judgment but on lack of understanding of the long-range objectives of data base, or resistance to a data-base environment for personal reasons.

In some cases departmental minicomputers or personal computers are used. It is often easier to obtain results from these than from large complex systems.

Such local computers may use their own files or may use Class IV data systems. Sometimes data are extracted from large systems and moved to the distributed departmental systems. Sometimes users employ the departmental systems for data entry and the files of data created are moved to larger systems. In either case the data structures in the departmental computers need to conform to the overall data models, unless their data are *purely* personal (i.e., only one person uses them).

DIFFERENT SYSTEMS FROM COMMON DATA MODELS	It is necessary to recognize the advantages and disadvantages of the four classes of data system and choose them knowledgeably. A particularly important concept is that the data in the separate systems are derived from *common logical data*

models, as will be described later. Only in this way can data be extracted to support the changing requirements of management.

All or part of the data in the Class IV data bases may be spun off from the Class III data bases or other routine computing systems. For this purpose an *extractor* program is used. Figure 5.6 illustrates this. It transfers specified data to the Class IV data bases which serve the user-driven applications—the information retrieval systems, report processing systems, and decision support systems. As the data are transferred they are rebuilt in the Class IV structures with inverted lists, secondary indices, or whatever is used.

The extractor program can work with several possible forms of timing:

- *Off-line, periodic.* For example, data are extracted at night and passed to the Class IV environment.
- *On-line, periodic.* For example, data are extracted every half-hour while the pre-scheduled system is on-line.
- *Trigger.* A preassigned condition triggers the extraction of certain data.
- *Ad hoc.* A human request may initiate the extraction of certain data.
- *Real-time.* Data of certain types are passed to the Class IV environment as soon as any change is made to them.

Inquiries can, of course, be made to the Class III data bases (or Class I or II data). These data bases may contain details of customers, transactions, or other entities, which are not passed to the Class IV environment. The user may be able to make queries on either from the same terminal.

Sometimes the software permits *simple* queries to the Class III (I or II) data and *complex* queries to the Class IV data. The former may be primary-key queries, such as "Show me the details of patient X's records." The latter may have multiple secondary-key queries, such as "Which patients in the quarantine ward have been hospitalized before for infectious diseases?"

Sometimes data are extracted from public data banks and placed in the Class IV environment, where they may be searched, matched with internal data, graphed, or processed.

REDUNDANCY

Data base has been sold in many organizations as a means of avoiding *redundant* data. The type of configuration in Fig. 5.6 introduces redundant data. Because of this, some DP staff argue against configurations like Fig. 5.6.

There is no merit in avoiding redundancy for its own sake. Data base *should* be defined as using a data organization which avoids *harmful* redundancy. It would be harmful to have multiple copies of the same data being updated without coordination. The end-user data bases may use data without updating it. They may update and maintain data for a given set of user-driven applications. Summaries of this end-user data may be passed to a routine-processing (Class I, II, or III) system. The introduction of redundant data in Fig. 5.6 relieves maintenance pressures on the Class III system and can permit changes in data reporting and use without maintenance costs.

Data redundancy is also deliberately introduced in certain types of distributed system in order to use low-cost computers, improve availability, improve response times, or avoid expensive telecommunications links.

Although the data may be *physically* redundant, they should be represented in *nonredundant* data models, as discussed in Chapter 7. The design process should establish the logical representation of data at first without examining physical considerations. Usage analysis and examination of distribution considerations may lead to physical separation of the data with possible introduction of redundancy. Where this has not been done, data vital for decision making have usually been inaccessible to the managers who need them.

INFRASTRUCTURE

A better way to think of data-base systems is that they form an infrastructure which will allow better use of data processing in the future. A clearly defined representation of the corporate data, modeled in a relatively stable form, will steadily grow. This data modeling should keep well ahead of the implementation of specific data bases. The implementation will be such that the data representation can change and grow without usually forcing the rewriting of application pro-

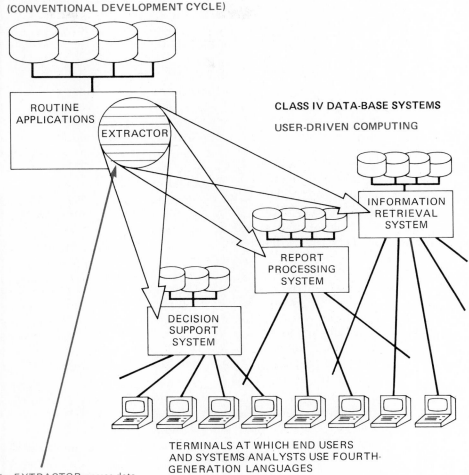

CLASS III DATA-BASE SYSTEM (or Class I or II)

PRESPECIFIED COMPUTING
(CONVENTIONAL DEVELOPMENT CYCLE)

ROUTINE
APPLICATIONS

EXTRACTOR

CLASS IV DATA-BASE SYSTEMS

USER-DRIVEN COMPUTING

INFORMATION
RETRIEVAL
SYSTEM

REPORT
PROCESSING
SYSTEM

DECISION
SUPPORT
SYSTEM

TERMINALS AT WHICH END USERS
AND SYSTEMS ANALYSTS USE FOURTH-
GENERATION LANGUAGES

The EXTRACTOR passes data
to the Class IV data bases.
  It works in one of the
following ways:
  1. Periodic, off-line (e.g., at night)
  2. Periodic, on-line (e.g., every hour)
  3. Operated by a trigger condition
  4. Ad hoc, or on demand
  5. Real-time

Figure 5.6 Certain data are extracted from a Class III (or I or II) system and transferred to Class IV systems.

grams. The programs will not have to be rewritten when better hardware is installed.

At today's state of the art, then, most corporations should not talk about a corporate-wide data base but rather a *corporate-wide organizing principle* which forms the structure for data-base development. An essential of this principle is that the data descriptions be standardized throughout the corporation.

As the data in a corporation are defined and modeled (as described later) more separate data bases come into existence. When more data bases exist, more projects are undertaken using these data bases. Many such projects may go on at the same time. Most projects using the data bases will be relatively short in duration—not more than a few months. Many of the incremental steps will be very short to implement, such as the production of a new type of report from an existing data base.

After several years of stage-by-stage buildup the overall data-base systems will begin to look impressive if they were appropriately directed toward overall goals. To be successful the data-base management system used must provide a high level of data independence, so that schema growth can continue without rewriting programs.

DELUSIONS

There are several common misconceptions about data-base systems which need clarifying.

First, a data base, or data-base management system, does not necessarily imply a "management information system." There is no direct relationship between the terms. In their initial use, most data bases should be thought of merely as a way of storing data for conventional applications and making those data more easily accessible to end users. Data-base techniques are justified by giving faster application development, lowering the cost of maintenance, and enabling much end-user data to be obtained without programming. They permit the data-processing department to be responsive.

A second delusion is that a data-base system is sometimes described as containing all the data items in a corporation or a division. Typical comments on the subject from journals such as the *Harvard Business Review* include the following misconception: "If the company had maintained all its computer-readable data in a single pool or bank—in a so-called 'data base'—and if the company had structured this base of data so that a program for virtually any feasible use could have been run from this data base, then it would have been a matter of sheer expertise and flair for a good, experienced programmer to concoct a program that pulled the desired information together" [1]. And "The data-base concept structures EDP activity in such a way that all of a company's computer-readable data are merged in a single pool, which is used to run both routine programs and programs written in response to ad hoc requests" [1].

Any attempt to implement so grand a notion is doomed to disaster before it begins. One of the reasons for data-base techniques is that files or data bases that were separate can later be combined. In this way larger collections of data can be built up with a subsequent drop in data redundancy and increase in data-base interrogation capability. However, to begin with the notion that the data base will serve everyone who uses data is asking for trouble.

Related to the foregoing delusion is the notion that an organization will have *one* data base. In reality it is likely to have many data bases, eventually perhaps hundreds. Many different data bases may be used on the same data-base system, but they will be both physically and logically separate. They should be built with a common schema language and common design policies because linkages between them will be forged in the future. The data-base management system should be common to all, but the data bases themselves entirely separate.

THE ARGUMENT AGAINST DATA BASE

Some authorities on structured design have argued strongly against data-base operation. Their argument is that a principle of good structured design is "divide and conquer"—divide complex systems into largely autonomous modules. The data-base approach, they say, ties together modules that could be otherwise separate. The fallacy in this is that the separate modules are not really separate. Data used in one are also used in another. If they are represented incompatibly in each, that will cause the type of problems described early in this chapter. If the data in different areas are different, then these areas can use separate disjoint data bases.

To lower maintenance costs and complexity, we need to lessen the entanglements between different portions of systems. If data-base operation

PROCESSES WHICH USE THE DATA

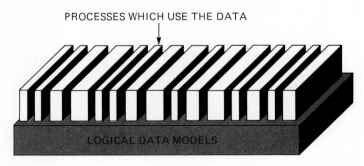

LOGICAL DATA MODELS

Figure 5.7 Once logical data models have been designed, the processes that use the data models can be created largely autonomously, often by one person each. The key to success in data base is designing the data models so that they are stable.

increases the entanglements, it will make maintenance worse. In practice the entanglements are already there, often hidden or ignored. *Unrecognized* entanglements cause *severe* maintenance problems.

Data-base operation, when well managed, leads to a high level of modularization. Once the foundation stone of data is built, separate processes can be created and changed independently of one another. Figure 5.7 illustrates this. The key to success is to design the logical data structures so as to be as stable as possible. This is the subject of the following two chapters.

Once the data-base structures have been created, high-level data-base languages can be used. These make the creation of many of the applications that employ the data base fast and simple. *One person can usually be assigned to each procedure which employs the data bases.* This greatly lessens communication requirements among developers (and maintainers). It speeds up the development and maintenance processes.

Once the logical data structures exist, techniques can be used which make the structuring of procedures clean and easy (Chapter 14) and make these procedures relatively easy to change.

Figure 5.7 might be contrasted with Fig. 5.8, which shows the same modules with separately designed data embedded into the application programs. The red lines in Fig. 5.8 are the data that pass among the programs. The system in Fig. 5.8 causes far more maintenance problems.

In practice, in some installations the move from file management to data-base management has *not* decreased the maintenance costs. The reason is that the data-base usage was managed like Fig. 5.8 rather than like Fig. 5.7. The data-base management system was used like an access method and little attention was paid to the logical design of data as a resource which is independent of the programs that use it.

The difference between Figs. 5.8 and 5.7 represents a change in DP management. A data administration function has to be created to design and manage the logical data structures and ensure that programmers employ them. This needs appropriate tools and techniques, good communication with the end users, and strong management support.

Designing the foundation stone of Fig. 5.7 takes some time and skill. It is time well spent because it greatly lowers future maintenance costs.

REFERENCES

1. R. L. Nolan, "Computer Data Bases: The Future Is Now," *Harvard Business Review,* September–October 1973. (The rest of Mr. Nolan's article is, like everything Nolan writes, excellent!)

2. J. Martin, *Managing the Data-Base Environment* (Englewood Cliffs, NJ: Prentice-Hall, Inc., 1983).

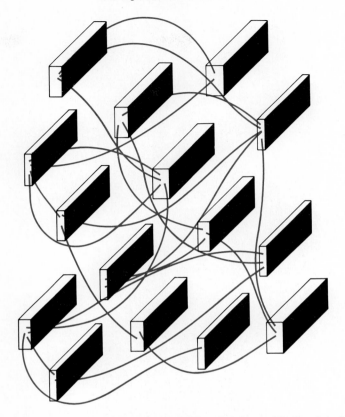

Figure 5.8 The same processes as in Fig. 5.7 but with the data base embedded into the application programs rather than being separately managed as a separate resource. There are now complex interractions between the programs which cause severe maintenance difficulties.

3. J. Martin, *Computer Data-Base Organization,* 2nd ed. (Englewood Cliffs, NJ: Prentice-Hall, Inc., 1977).

4. J. Martin, *Principles of Data-Base Management* (Englewood Cliffs, NJ: Prentice-Hall, Inc., 1976).

5. J. Martin, *End User's Guide to Data Base* (Englewood Cliffs, NJ: Prentice-Hall, Inc., 1981).

6. J. Martin, *Application Development Without Programmers* (Englewood Cliffs, NJ: Prentice-Hall, Inc., 1982).

6 NORMALIZATION OF DATA

STABILITY
If future maintenance costs are to be minimized, a data base needs to be as *stable* as possible. By "stable" we do not mean that its structure will never change. We mean that *when changes in structure occur they can be made without having to modify applications that use the data base.*

This property of *stability* is the single most important requirement in data-base design if the data base is to meet its objectives of minimizing maintenance costs. Chapter 7 discusses various approaches to making the data base as stable as possible. One of these approaches is to put the data into *third normal form.* That is the subject of this chapter.

NORMALIZATION
OF DATA
The data administrator (or data-base designer) needs to be concerned with what data items should be grouped together into records. (We will use the term "record" to mean one logical grouping of data items which is read with one machine operation. With some DBMSs this is referred to as a segment or tuple.)

There are many different ways in which the hundreds or thousands of data items can be grouped, and some ways are better than others. Some will lead to subtle problems in the future.

As we have stressed, most data bases constantly change. New data items and new associations between data items are added frequently and new usage patterns occur. As we change the data base, we must preserve the old user views of data so as to avoid having to rewrite programs. There are, however, certain changes in data associations or usage which could force modification of programs. For example, we may have to split a record (segment) into two, or change the key that is used for certain data items. Such changes can be extremely disruptive. If the grouping of data items and keys is well thought out originally, we can make such disruption unlikely.

This chapter is concerned with the best grouping of data items into records (segments or tuples). The ideas in this chapter are a fundamental part of a systems analyst's understanding of the data. They are important for the design of stable data structures that will minimize future maintenance work. They may be tedious for some readers to grasp but fortunately can be automated in the design process.

ENTITIES

An *entity* is something about which we store data. It may be a tangible object, such as an employee, a part, a customer, a machine tool, or an office. It may be nontangible, such as a job title, a profit center, an association, a financial allowance, a purchase, an estimate, or an insurance claim.

In doing information analysis we study the entities of the enterprise in question. A typical corporation has several hundred entities. Its set of entities do not change much as time goes by unless it moves into a fundamentally different type of business.

An entity has various *attributes* which we wish to record, such as size, value, date, color, usage code, address, quality, performance code, and so on. Often in data processing we are concerned with a collection of similar entities, such as employees, and we wish to record information about the same attributes of each of them. A programmer commonly maintains a *record* about each entity, and a data item in each record relates to each attribute. Similar records are grouped into *files.* The result, shown in Fig. 6.1, is a two-dimensional array.

Inside the box in Fig. 6.1 is a set of data items. The value of each data item is shown. Each row of data items relates to a particular entity. Each column contains a particular type of data item, relating to a particular type of attribute. At the top of the diagram, outside the box, the names of the attributes are written. The leftmost column in the box contains the data items that *identify* the entity. The entity in this example is a person, an employee. The attribute referred to as the entity identifier in this case is EMPLOYEE NUMBER.

Such a two-dimensional array is sometime referred to as a *flat file.* The use of flat files dates back to the earliest days of data processing when the file might have been on punched cards. Each card in a file or deck of cards such as that shown in Fig. 6.2 might contain one record, relating to one entity. Certain card columns were allocated to each data-item type, or attribute, and were called a *field.* When magnetic tapes replaced decks of cards and disks replaced magnetic tapes, many programmers retained their view of data as being organized into flat files.

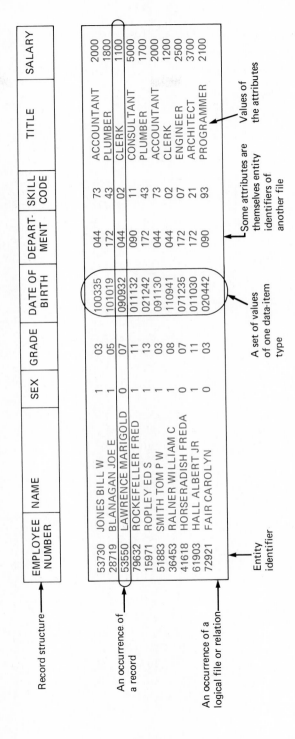

EMPLOYEE NUMBER	NAME	SEX	GRADE	DATE OF BIRTH	DEPART-MENT	SKILL CODE	TITLE	SALARY
53730	JONES BILL W	1	03	100335	044	73	ACCOUNTANT	2000
28719	BLANAGAN JOE E	1	05	101019	172	43	PLUMBER	1800
53550	LAWRENCE MARIGOLD	0	07	090932	044	02	CLERK	1100
79632	ROCKEFELLER FRED	1	11	011132	090	11	CONSULTANT	5000
15971	ROPLEY ED S	1	13	021242	172	43	PLUMBER	1700
51883	SMITH TOM P W	1	03	091130	044	73	ACCOUNTANT	2000
36453	RALNER WILLIAM C	1	08	110941	044	02	CLERK	1200
41618	HORSERADISH FREDA	0	07	071235	172	07	ENGINEER	2500
61903	HALL ALBERT JR	1	11	011030	172	21	ARCHITECT	3700
72921	FAIR CAROLYN	0	03	020442	090	93	PROGRAMMER	2100

Record structure

An occurrence of a record

Entity identifier

An occurrence of a logical file or relation

A set of values of one data-item type

Some attributes are themselves entity identifiers of another file

Values of the attributes

Figure 6.1 An example of a two-dimensional array.

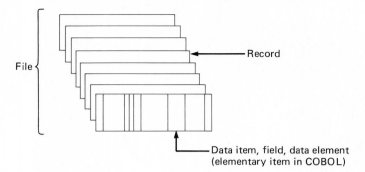

File { Record

Data item, field, data element
(elementary item in COBOL)

Figure 6.2   Flat file; a programmer's or user's view of the data.

NORMALIZED RECORDS

In examining the data that need to be stored in a corporation we will think of them initially as a collection of flat files such as those shown in Fig. 6.1 or 6.2. Each flat file contains information about one type of entity. A record in that file contains information about one occurrence of that entity. For example, a CUSTOMER record contains information about one CUSTOMER. This is sometimes referred to as an *entity record.*

The entity record is a *logical* view of the data. The data may be stored in a different form *physically* in a data base. The entity record contains data about *one and only one* type of entity. It contains *all* the attributes of that entity that are stored.

Often, data are stored about combinations of entity types. For example, we store a quotation record with a combined key SUPPLIER# + PART#. This record shows the price a given supplier has quoted for a given part, quoted delivery time, or other item. Sometimes the quoted price and delivery time vary with the quantity ordered. Then we have a record type with the key SUPPLIER# + PART# + ORDER-QUANTITY.

Because some records refer to more than one entity type, we prefer to use the term *normalized record* rather than *entity record.* Box 6.1 summarizes the properties of a *normalized record.*

THE REASON FOR NORMALIZATION

Normalization is a formal approach that examines data and groups the data items together in a form that is better able to accommodate future business change and to minimize the impact of that change on application systems.

Data exist in real-life as groups of data items. They exist on invoices, weighbills, tax forms, driving licences, and so on. These groupings are often not in a normalized form. Not surprisingly, systems analysts have often implemented computer records that are also not normalized. However, data that are not normalized can lead to various subtle problems in the future.

BOX 6.1   What is a normalized record?

The term *normalized record* implies the following properties:

1. It is a logical record.
2. The data in it contain no repeating groups.
3. It is in third normal form (discussed in this chapter).
4. It often relates to one entity but sometimes relates to multiple entities when all the attributes in it are functionally dependent on a concatenated key (e.g., a quoted price is functionally dependent on SUPPLIER + PRODUCT).

Sometimes the term *entity record* is used to refer to a normalized record relating one entity type.

In this chapter we are concerned with what data items should be grouped together into records in data bases at least in the logical design. There are many different ways in which the hundreds or thousands of data items can be grouped. Using one of these ways, third normal form, will preclude many of the problems that occur with computerized data.

Experience has shown that when computer data are organized as described in this chapter (i.e., in "third normal form") the resulting data structures are more stable and able to accommodate change. Each attribute relates to its own entity and is not mixed up with attributes relating to different entities. The actions that create and update data can then be applied with simple structured design to one normalized record at a time.

FIRST, SECOND, AND THIRD NORMAL FORM
Third normal form is a simple, relatively stable grouping of data items into records (segments, tuples). Its purpose is to find those groupings of data items least likely to give maintenance problems —least likely to change in ways that force application program rewriting.

The basic simplicity of data in third normal form makes the records easy to understand, and easier to change, than other ways of organizing a data base. It avoids some of the anomalies that arise with other data structures.

At the time of writing only a small proportion of existing data bases are in third normal form. Some corporations have several years of experience of operation of third-normal-form data structures. There is no question that they have greatly reduced their maintenance costs by using this type of design.

Reacting to the perceived benefits, some corporations have incorporated into their data-base standards manuals the requirement that all data-base structures be in third normal form. Usually, this form of design is better in terms of *machine* requirements as well as in logical structuring, but this is not always the case. Sometimes the physical designer finds it desirable to deviate from third normal form. A compromise is then needed. Which is preferable: somewhat better machine performance or better protection from maintenance costs? Usually, the potential maintenance costs are much more expensive than somewhat reduced machine performance.

We suggest that the data-base standards manual should say that all data will be *designed* in third normal form, but that the physical implementation may occasionally deviate from third normal form if the trade-off is fully explored and documented.

To put data into third normal form, three steps may be used (first described mathematically by E. F. Codd [1]). They are put into *first normal form,* then *second normal form,* then *third normal form.* Box 6.2 summarizes these steps.

The basic ideas of this normalization of data are simple, but the ramifications are many and subtle, and vary from one type of data-base usage to another. It is important to note that normalization describes the *logical,* not the physical, representation of data. There are many ways of implementing data physically.

FIRST NORMAL FORM

First normal form refers to a collection of data organized into records which have no repeating groups of data items within a record. In other words, they are flat files, two-dimensional matrices of data items such as those shown in Figs. 6.1 and 6.2. Such a flat file may be thought of as a simple two-dimensional table. It may, however, contain many thousands of records.

Most programming languages give programmers the ability to create and refer to records which are not *flat*; that is, they contain repeating groups of data items within a record. In COBOL these are called *data aggregates.* There can be data aggregates within data aggregates—repeating groups within repeating groups.

The following COBOL record contains two data aggregates, called BIRTH and SKILLS.

```
                  RECORD NAME IS PERSON

        01           EMPLOYEE# PICTURE "9(5)"
        01           EMPNAME TYPE CHARACTER 20
        01           SEX PICTURE "A"
```

BOX 6.2   Conversion to third normal form

UNNORMALIZED DATA
(Records with repeating groups)

1. Decompose all non-flat
   data structures into
   two-dimensional records.

FIRST NORMAL FORM
(Records with no repeating groups)

2. For records whose keys
   have more than one
   data item, ensure that
   all other data items
   are dependent on the
   whole key. Split the
   records, if necessary,
   to achieve this.

SECOND NORMAL FORM
(All nonkey data items *fully*
functionally dependent on the
primary key)

3. Remove all
   transitive dependencies
   splitting the record, if
   necessary, to achieve
   this.

THIRD NORMAL FORM
(All nonkey data items fully
functionally dependent on the
primary key and *independent of each
other*)

```
01              EMPJCODE PICTURE "9999"
01              SALARY PICTURE "9(5)V99"
01              BIRTH
     02           MONTH PICTURE "99"
     02           DAY
     02           YEAR PICTURE "99"
01              SKILLS OCCURS NOSKILLS TIMES
     02           SKILLCODE PICTURE "9999"
     02           SKILLYEARS PICTURE "99"
```

PERSON

EMPLOYEE#	EMPNAME	SEX	EMPJCODE	SALARY	BIRTH			SKILLS	
					MONTH	DAY	YEAR	SKILLCODE	SKILLYEARS

BIRTH causes no problems because it occurs only once in each record. SKILLS can occur several times in one record, so that record is not in first normal form. It is not a *flat*, two-dimensional record. To *normalize* it, the repeating group SKILLS must be removed and put into a separate record, thus:

PERSON

EMPLOYEE#	EMPNAME	SEX	EMPJCODE	SALARY	BIRTH		
					MONTH	DAY	YEAR

SKILLS

EMPLOYEE# + SKILLCODE	SKILLYEARS

The lower record has a concatenated key EMPLOYEE# + SKILLCODE. We cannot know SKILLYEARS (the number of years of experience an employee has had with a given skill) unless we know EMPLOYEE# (the employee number whom this refers to) and SKILLCODE (the skill in question). In general, a nonflat record is normalized by converting it into two or more flat records.

If the normalized records illustrated above were implemented in a CODASYL, DL/1, or other nonrelational data-base management system, we would not repeat the field EMPLOYEE# in the lower record. A linkage to the upper record would imply this key:

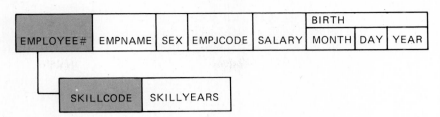

A relational data base *would* employ a separate SKILLS record (relation) with a key EMPLOYEE + SKILLCODE; it thus avoids pointer mechanisms in the logical representation of data.

In the initial modeling of data we are concerned, not with how the physical implementation is done, but with the overall *logical* representation of data. We need to analyze and chart an enterprise's information resources and how they are used. We draw the lower record with its complete concatenated key so that it can stand alone—so the key uniquely identifies the data in the record.

CONCATENATED KEYS

Employee number and skillcode in the example above are both entities. To identify the number of years an employee has had a skill, we need to refer to both entities and use a key that combined the two entity identifiers. The same is true with a line item on an order. We need both ORDER NUMBER and PRODUCT NUMBER to identify it. Some records need more than two entity keys to identify them.

We use the term *normalized record* to refer to records with concatenated keys as well as to records with a single data-item key. The attributes that we store in them should be dependent on the complete concatenated key, just as SKILLYEARS is dependent on EMPLOYEE# and SKILLCODE.

FUNCTIONAL DEPENDENCE

In attempting to lay out the relationships between data items, the designer must concern himself with which data items are dependent on which other. The phrase "functionally dependent" is defined as follows:

> Data item B of a record R is functionally dependent on data item A of R if, at every instant of time, each value in A has no more than one value in B associated with it in record R. [1]

Saying that *B* is functionally dependent on *A* is equivalent to saying that *A identifies B.* In other words, if we know the value of *A,* we can find the value of *B* that is associated with it.

For example, in an employee record, the SALARY data item is functionally dependent upon EMPLOYEE#. For one EMPLOYEE# there is one SALARY. To find the value of SALARY in a data base you would normally go via EMPLOYEE#. The latter is a key that identifies the attribute SALARY.

We will draw a functional dependency with an arrow that has a single barb, thus:

EMPLOYEE# _____ SALARY

(A distinctive form of arrow is drawn for a functional dependency to distinguish it from arrows that indicate flows or pointers.)

Consider the record for the entity EMPLOYEE.

EMPLOYEE#	EMPLOYEE-NAME	SALARY	PROJECT#	COMPLETION-DATE

The functional dependencies in this record are as follows:

EMPLOYEE#	is dependent on EMPLOYEE-NAME
EMPLOYEE-NAME	is dependent on EMPLOYEE#
SALARY	is dependent on either EMPLOYEE-NAME or EMPLOYEE#
PROJECT#	is dependent on either EMPLOYEE-NAME or EMPLOYEE#
COMPLETION-DATE	is dependent on EMPLOYEE-NAME, EMPLOYEE#, or PROJECT#

EMPLOYEE# is not functionally dependent on SALARY because more than one employee could have the same salary. Similarly, EMPLOYEE# is not functionally dependent on PROJECT#, but COMPLETION-DATE is. No other data item in the record is fully dependent on PROJECT#.

We can draw these functional dependencies as follows:

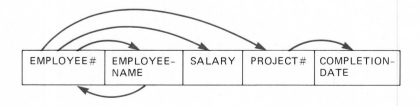

A data item can be functionally dependent on a *group* of data items rather than on a single data item. Consider, for example, the following record, which shows how programmers spent their time:

PROGRAMMER-ACTIVITY

PROGRAMMER#	PACKAGE#	PROGRAMMER-NAME	PACKAGE-NAME	TOTAL-HOURS-WORKED

TOTAL-HOURS-WORKED is functionally dependent on the concatenated key (PROGRAMMER#, PACKAGE#).

The functional dependencies in this record can be drawn as follows:

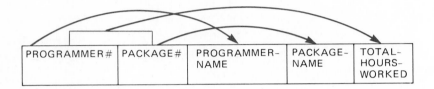

FULL FUNCTIONAL DEPENDENCY

A data item or a collection of data items, B, of a record R can be said to be *fully functionally dependent* on another collection of data items, A, of record R if B is functionally dependent on the whole of A but not on any subset of A.

For example, in the record above, TOTAL-HOURS-WORKED is fully functionally dependent on the concatenated key (PROGRAMMER#, PACK-AGE#) because it refers to how many hours a given programmer has worked on a given package. Neither PROGRAMMER# alone nor PACKAGE# alone identifies TOTAL-HOURS-WORKED.

TOTAL-HOURS-WORKED, however, is the *only* data item that is fully functionally dependent on the concatenated key. PROGRAMMER-NAME is fully functionally dependent on PROGRAMMER# alone, and PACKAGE-NAME is fully functionally dependent on PACKAGE# alone. The arrows above make these dependencies clear.

SECOND NORMAL FORM

We are now in a position to define second normal form. First a simple definition:

Each attribute in a record is functionally dependent on the whole key of that record.

Where the key consists of more than one data item the record may not be in second normal form. The record above with the key PROGRAMMER#

+ PACKAGE# is not in second normal form because TOTAL-HOURS-WORKED depends on the whole key, whereas PROGRAMMER-NAME and PACKAGE-NAME each depend on only one data item in the key. Similarly, the following record is not in second normal form:

PART#	SUPPLIER#	SUPPLIER-NAME	SUPPLIER-DETAILS	PRICE

There are a few problems that can result from this record not being in second normal form:

1. We cannot enter details about a supplier until that supplier supplies a part. If the supplier does not supply a part, there is no key.
2. If a supplier should temporarily cease to supply any part, then deletion of the last record containing that SUPPLIER# will also delete the details of the supplier. It would normally be desirable that SUPPLIER-DETAILS be preserved.
3. We have problems when we attempt to update the supplier details. We must search for every record which contains that supplier as part of the key. If a supplier supplies many parts, much redundant updating of supplier details will be needed.

These types of irregularities can be removed by splitting the record into two records in second normal form, as shown in Fig. 6.3. Only PRICE is fully functionally dependent on the concatenated key, so all other attributes are removed to the separate record on the left, which has SUPPLIER-NUMBER only as its key.

Splitting to second normal form is the type of splitting that natural data-base growth tends to force, so it might as well be anticipated when the data base is first set up. In general, every data item in a record should be dependent on the *entire* key; otherwise, it should be removed to a separate record. Figure 6.3 illustrates the splitting of the record above into second-normal-form *normalized records.*

CANDIDATE KEYS

The *key* of a normalized record must have the following properties.

1. *Unique identification.* For every record occurrence the key must uniquely identify the record.
2. *Nonredundancy.* No data item in the key can be discarded without destroying the property of unique identification.

It sometimes happens that more than one data item or set of data items *could* be the key of a record. Such alternative choices are referred to as *candidate keys.*

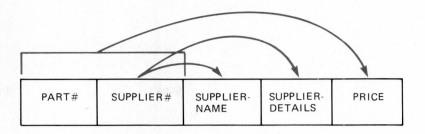

| PART# | SUPPLIER# | SUPPLIER-NAME | SUPPLIER-DETAILS | PRICE |

An instance of this record:

PART#	SUPPLIER#	SUPPLIER-NAME	SUPPLIER-DETAILS	PRICE
1	1000	JONES	x	20
1	1500	ABC	x	28
1	2050	XYZ	y	22
1	1900	P—H	z	30
2	3100	ALLEN	z	520
2	1000	JONES	x	500
2	2050	XYZ	y	590
3	2050	XYZ	y	1000
4	1000	JONES	x	80
4	3100	ALLEN	z	90
4	1900	P—H	z	95
5	1500	ABC	x	160
5	1000	JONES	x	140

To convert the records above into second normal form, we split it into two records, thus:

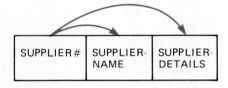

| SUPPLIER# | SUPPLIER-NAME | SUPPLIER-DETAILS |

| PART# | SUPPLIER# | PRICE |

An instance of the above pair of records:

SUPPLIER#	SUPPLIER-NAME	SUPPLIER-DETAILS
1000	JONES	x
1500	ABC	x
2050	XYZ	y
1900	P—H	z
3100	ALLEN	z

PART#	SUPPLIER#	PRICE
1	1000	20
1	1500	28
1	2050	22
1	1900	30
2	3100	520
2	1000	500
2	2050	590
3	2050	1000
4	1000	80
4	3100	90
4	1900	95
5	1500	160
5	1000	140

Figure 6.3 Conversions to second normal form.

One candidate key must be designated the *primary key.* We will draw the functional dependencies for candidate keys which are not the primary key *underneath* the record, thus:

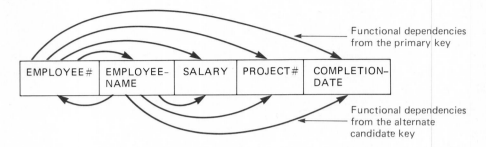

In this illustration EMPLOYEE-NAME is regarded as a candidate key—an alternative to EMPLOYEE#. This is not generally done in practice because two employees *might* have the same name. Only EMPLOYEE# is truly unique. The possible existence of candidate keys complicates the definitions of second and third normal form.

A more comprehensive definition of second normal form is:

> A record R is in second normal form if it is in first normal form and every nonprime data item of R is fully functionally dependent on each candidate key of R. [1]

In the EMPLOYEE record above, the candidate keys have only one data item, and hence the record is always in second normal form because the nonprime data items must be fully dependent on the candidate keys. When the candidate keys consist of more than one data item, a first-normal-form record may not be in second normal form.

THIRD NORMAL FORM

A record that *is* in second normal form can have another type of anomoly. It may have a data item which is not a key but which itself identifies other data items. This is referred to as a *transitive dependence.* Transitive dependencies can cause problems. The step of putting data into *third normal form* removes transitive dependencies.

Suppose that A, B, and C are three data items or distinct collections of data items of a record R. If C is functionally dependent on B and B is functionally dependent on A, then C is functionally dependent on A. If the inverse mapping is nonsimple (i.e., if A is not functionally dependent on B or B is not functionally dependent on C), then C is said to be *transitively* dependent on A.

In a diagram C is transitively dependent on A if

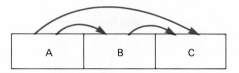

Conversion to third normal form removes this transitive dependence by splitting the record into two, thus:

The following record is not in third normal form because COMPLETION-DATE is dependent on PROJECT#.

EMPLOYEE

EMPLOYEE#	EMPLOYEE-NAME	SALARY	PROJECT#	COMPLETION-DATE

A few problems might result from this record not being in third normal form.

1. Before any employees are recruited for a project the completion date of the project cannot be recorded because there is no EMPLOYEE record.

2. If all the employees should leave the project so that the project has no employees until others are recruited, all records containing the completion date would be deleted. This may be thought an unlikely occurrence, but on other types of files a similar danger of loss of information can be less improbable.

3. If the completion date is changed, it will be necessary to search for all records containing that completion date, and update them.

A simple definition of third normal form is: A record is in second normal form and each attribute is functionally dependent on the key and *nothing but the key*. A more formal definition that incorporates candidate keys is as follows:

A record R is in third normal form if it is in second normal form and every nonprime data item of R is nontransitively dependent on each candidate key of R. [1]

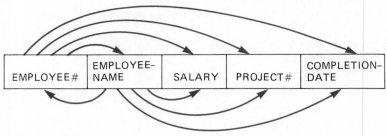

An instance of this record:

EMPLOYEE#	EMPLOYEE-NAME	SALARY	PROJECT#	COMPLETION-DATE
120	JONES	2000	x	17.7.84
121	HARPO	1700	x	17.7.84
270	GARFUNKAL	1800	y	12.1.87
273	SELSI	3600	x	17.7.84
274	ABRAHMS	3000	z	21.3.86
279	HIGGINS	2400	y	12.1.87
301	FLANNEL	1800	z	21.3.86
306	MCGRAW	2100	x	17.7.84
310	ENSON	3000	z	21.3.86
315	GOLDSTEIN	3100	x	17.7.84
317	PUORRO	2700	y	12.1.87
320	MANSINI	1700	y	12.1.87
321	SPOTO	2900	x	17.7.84
340	SCHAFT	3100	x	17.7.84
349	GOLD	1900	z	21.3.86

To convert the above record into third normal form we split it into two records, thus:

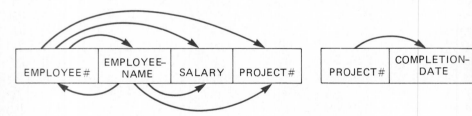

An instance of the above pair of records:

EMPLOYEE#	EMPLOYEE-NAME	SALARY	PROJECT#
120	JONES	2000	x
121	HARPO	1700	x
270	GARFUNKAL	1800	y
273	SELSI	3600	x
274	ABRAHMS	3000	z
279	HIGGINS	2400	y
301	FLANNEL	1800	z
306	MCGRAW	2100	x
310	ENSON	3000	z
315	GOLDSTEIN	3100	x
317	PUORRO	2700	y
320	MANSINI	1700	y
321	SPOTO	2900	x
340	SCHAFT	3100	x

PROJECT#	COMPLETION-DATE
x	17.7.84
y	12.1.87
z	21.3.86

Figure 6.4   Conversion to third normal form.

Figure 6.4 shows the conversion of the EMPLOYEE record above to third normal form.

The conversion to third normal form produces a separate record for each entity—a normalized record. For example, Fig. 6.4 produced a separate record for the entity PROJECT. Usually, this normalized record would be needed anyway. We need data separately stored for each entity.

STORAGE AND PERFORMANCE

The concept of third normal form applies to all data bases. Experience has shown that the records of a CODASYL system, the segments of a DL/1 system, or the group of data items in other systems can benefit from being in third normal form.

Objections to third normal form are occasionally heard on the grounds that it requires more storage or more machine time. A third-normal-form structure usually has more records after the splitting described above. Isn't that worse from the hardware point of view?

Not necessarily. In fact, *although there are more records, they almost always take less storage.* The reason is that non-third-normal-form records usually have much *value* redundancy.

Compare the records shown in Fig. 6.3. Here records not in second normal form are converted to second normal form by splitting. It will be seen that the lower red part of Fig. 6.3 has fewer *values* of data written down than the red part at the top. There are fewer values of SUPPLIER-NAME and SUPPLIER-DETAILS. This shrinkage does not look very dramatic on such a small illustration. If there had been thousands of suppliers and thousands of parts, and many attributes of both, the shrinkage would have been spectacular.

Again, compare the red parts of Fig. 6.4. Here a record is converted to third normal form by splitting. The number of *values* of data shrinks. There are fewer values of COMPLETION-DATE recorded after the split. Once more, if there had been many employees, many projects, and many attributes of those projects, the shrinkage would have been dramatic.

Conversion to third normal form almost always reduces the amount of storage used, often dramatically. What about machine time and accesses? Often this is less after normalization. Before normalization many aspects of the data are tangled together and must all be read at once. After normalization they are separated, so a small record is read.

Also, because there is less value redundancy in third normal form, there is less duplicated updating of the redundant values. Suppose that project x slips its completion date (which it does every week!). In the record at the top of Fig. 6.4 the completion date has to be changed seven times; in the third-normal-form version it has to be changed only once. A similar argument applies to SUPPLIER-NAME and SUPPLIER-DETAILS in Fig. 6.3. The

argument would have more force if the examples had hundreds of employees, thousands of suppliers, and many attributes that have to be updated.

There are, however, exceptions to this. On rare occasions a designer
may consciously design non-third-normal-form records for performance
reasons. He should calculate the possible future maintenance costs of deviating from third normal form.

SEMANTIC   A further reason for using third normal form is
DISINTEGRITY   that certain data-base queries can run into prob-
                          lems when data are not cleanly structured. A query,
perhaps entered with a data-base query language, can appear to be valid but
in fact have subtle illogical aspects sometimes referred to as *semantic disintegrity*. When the data are in third normal form, rules can be devised for
preventing semantic disintegrity or warning the user about his query. These
rules are given in Martin's book *Computer Data-Base Organization* [2].

CLEAR THINKING   Third normal form is an aid to clear thinking about
ABOUT DATA   data. It is a formal method of separating the data
                          items that relate to different entities.
A record in third normal form has the following clean, simple structure:

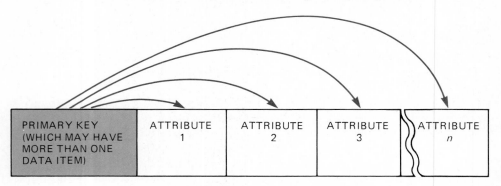

The functional dependency lines all come from the primary key. There
are no hidden dependencies not relating to the key. If the key is concatenated, all data items are dependent on the entire key.

We can give a loose definition of third normal form, which has the
advantage of being easy to remember:

> Every data item in a record is dependent on the key, the whole key, and
> nothing but the key.

If a systems analyst remembers this definition (understanding that it is
not rigorous like those earlier in the chapter), he can quickly spot and modify

records that are not in third normal form. He should be familiar enough with this that alarm bells go off in his head whenever he sees records that are not in third normal form.

This clean, simple, data grouping is easy to implement and to use. There may be complications in store in the future if more complex record structures are used.

For the data-base administrator, third normal form is an aid to precision. A data base in third normal form can grow and evolve naturally. The updating rules are straightforward. A third-normal-form record type can have records added to it or can have records deleted without the problems that could occur with non-third-normal-form record types. Third-normal-form structuring gives a simple view of data to the programmers and users, and makes them less likely to perform invalid operations.

Figure 6.5 gives a simplified illustration of the three steps in achieving third-normal-form structures.

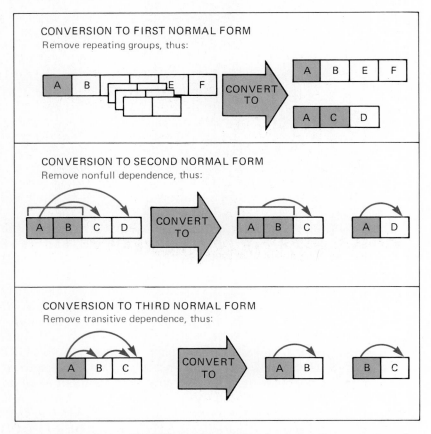

Figure 6.5   A simplified illustration of the three steps in conversion of data to third normal form. Figure 6.6 gives an illustration with real data.

A SUGGESTED EXERCISE	Probably they best way for a data-processing user to become convinced of the value (or otherwise) of normalization is to take a section of his files and

write down what third-normal-form records would be used to represent them. A group of systems analysts should then list all the plausible changes that might occur to the files as data processing evolves in the years ahead, and see how many of these changes would necessitate restructuring the records in such a way that previously written application programs would have to be changed. Compare this with what reprogramming would be needed if the same changes were applied to the existing records.

In examining existing data bases it has been our experience that time and time again they are not in third normal form. This spells trouble for the future. Unless it was the conscious policy of management to create third-normal-form structures the design has been far from these principles.

We have found many examples of systems analysts consciously deviating from third normal form. Time and time again this has proved to be a mistake in the long run. Experience of long-term data-base operation suggests that in practice it rarely pays to deviate from third normal form.

AN EXAMPLE OF NORMALIZATION	The following shows details of a typical ORDER record with an unnormalized structure:

ORDER   (*Order#*, order-date, customer#, customer-name, customer-address ((product-number, product-name, quantity-ordered, product-price, product-total)), order-total.)

The primary key of this record is Order#.

The application of the three normalization steps to this example is illustrated in Fig. 6.6.

Application of the *first normal form* rule (remove repeating groups) creates two records: ORDER and ORDER-PRODUCT. The primary key is made up of Order# and Product#. (ORDER-PRODUCT might be called the ORDER LINE ITEM record.)

Second normal form removes the product name from the ORDER-PRODUCT record into a new record: PRODUCT. Product name is wholly dependent on product number; it is only partially dependent on the primary (combined or compound) key of ORDER-PRODUCT: Order# + Product#.

Third normal form removes the customer details from the ORDER record to a separate CUSTOMER record. Customer name and address are wholly dependent on customer number; they are not dependent at all on the primary key of ORDER (i.e., Order#). (A customer will not change his name and address with each new order . . . unless he doesn't intend to pay for it!)

The four resulting records—ORDER, CUSTOMER, ORDER-PRODUCT,

UNNORMALIZED RECORD:

Order

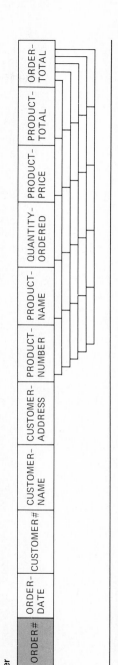

| ORDER# | ORDER- DATE | CUSTOMER# | CUSTOMER- NAME | CUSTOMER- ADDRESS | PRODUCT- NUMBER | PRODUCT- NAME | QUANTITY- ORDERED | PRODUCT- PRICE | PRODUCT- TOTAL | ORDER- TOTAL |

FIRST NORMAL FORM: Remove the repeating group.

Order

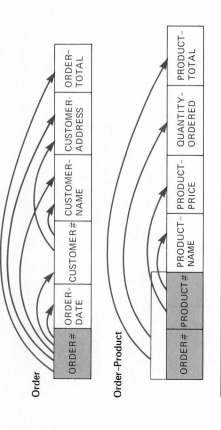

| ORDER# | ORDER- DATE | CUSTOMER# | CUSTOMER- NAME | CUSTOMER- ADDRESS | ORDER- TOTAL |

Order-Product

| ORDER# | PRODUCT# | PRODUCT- NAME | PRODUCT- PRICE | QUANTITY- ORDERED | PRODUCT- TOTAL |

Figure 6.6 Illustration of the three stages of normalization.

(Continued)

155

SECOND NORMAL FORM: Remove attributes not dependent on the whole of a (concatenated) primary key, as in the ORDER-PRODUCT record above.

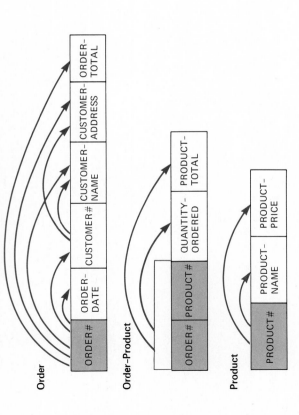

THIRD NORMAL FORM: Remove attributes dependent on data item(s) other than the primary key, as in the ORDER record above.

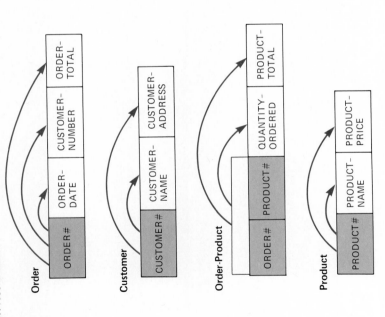

Figure 6.6   (Continued)

and PRODUCT—in Fig. 6.6 are in third normal form. The CUSTOMER and PRODUCT normalized records would be needed for other purposes and created by other analysts. We need to synthesize the data used for multiple purposes into third-normal-form records relating to each specific type of entity.

REFERENCES

1. E. F. Codd, "Further Normalization of the Data Base Relational Model," in Courant Computer Science Symposia, 6: *Data-Base Systems,* R. Rustin, ed. (Englewood Cliffs, NJ: Prentice-Hall, Inc., 1972).

2. J. Martin, *Computer Data-Base Organization,* 2nd ed. (Englewood Cliffs, NJ: Prentice-Hall, Inc., 1977).

7 CREATING STABLE DATA STRUCTURES

ACHIEVING
STABILITY IN DATA
We have stressed that modern data processing should be built on a foundation stone of data. The data required to run an organization are identified and stored in data systems. To design a data structure without stability is like building one's house upon the sand; sooner or later the maintenance costs will be great.

How can stability be achieved? In several ways:

1. The choice of data management software has a major effect.

2. Data should be in third normal form, as discussed in Chapter 6.

3. Models can be built of data *which represent the inherent properties of the data* independently of any applications. Data with these structures tend to be stable. The application can change without the data changing.

4. To understand fully the properties and definitions of data, the knowledge of experienced users who work with the data needs to be harnessed.

5. The data administrator who designs and ensures the use of the stable data structures needs to report at a high enough level to ensure that powerful user groups do not ignore or violate his data models.

6. A set of steps called *stability analysis* can be applied to the data structures *before* they are implemented in a data-base management system, to ensure that they are as stable as possible.

7. Strategic planning and analysis is needed to identify the information resources which an organization needs.

DBMS PROPERTIES
Certain properties are desirable in data-base management systems if maintenance is to be minimized. These are listed in Box 7.1.

BOX 7.1   Properties of data-base management software that minimize application maintenance costs

- *Field sensitivity.* New data items (fields) can be added to data-base record structures without necessitating change in the logical record structures which an application program uses. In other words, the record structure seen by the application program can include *some* but not necessarily *all* of the data items in a data-base record.

- *Ability to represent all data structures.* All patterns of associations between records should be representable [i.e., all plex (network) structures as well as hierarchical structures].

- *Ability to dynamically create new access paths.* It is sometimes necessary to build a secondary index on an existing data item, or to otherwise create new access paths, without affecting programs that already use the data base.

- *Automatic generation of programmers' data from a dictionary.* The programmers can be prevented from inventing their own data descriptions if all the data descriptions they need are automatically generated from the data base. This lessens incompatibility problems which result in future maintenance costs.

- *Ability to dynamically change associations among records.* In some data bases the associations between records are rigidly set up when the system is created. That is, there are pointer linkages between records which represent hierarchical structures, CODASYL set structures, and so on, and these cannot be changed without changing the application programs that use them.

    It is desirable to be able to add new associations between records without disrupting old programs.

- *Flexible query facilities and report generators.* The ability to extract and associate data is needed so that the data can be displayed or correlated in the ways most valuable to end users. This requires a user-friendly language.

- *Application generators.* A language is needed with which applications can be generated from the data base, preferably without programmers, and easily modified, as required.

- *Automatic navigation.* The high-level data-base languages should be able to navigate through the data base automatically to produce the required results without a program which states how to progress a step at a time from one record to another. The commands of a relational algebra offer this capability. It is desirable that the data-base system be able to execute such commands automatically.

- *Hardware/software independence.* It is desirable that the data-base applica-

Box 7.1 *(Continued)*

tion programs still work when the computer, storage units, operating system, or other hardware or software components are changed.

- *Distribution independence.* It is desirable that if the data are distributed on distant machines in a different fashion the old applications using the data still function correctly.

- *Data-base-management-system independence.* It is desirable that if a change is made to a different data-base management system the old applications still function correctly. This property often does not exist in a complete form, although migration to improved versions of the same data-base management system is made possible.

Many data-base management systems have some but not all of these properties. Some have the first four properties but not the ability to dynamically create new associations among data, do automatic navigation, or perform relational algebra operations.

Some of the properties in Box 7.1 are expensive in machine cycles. They are desirable for low-traffic applications but too expensive for high-traffic applications. Some are desirable for small data bases but not for very large data bases.

In Chapter 5 we distinguished between classes of data environment. A Class IV environment may employ a data management system which has all the properties listed in Box 7.1 except perhaps the last two. Such an environment is better for maintenance than the other classes. Why are the other classes still used? For two reasons: first, machine performance—machine cost or response-time considerations; and second, to protect the large investment in existing programs which employ a given data base or file management system.

TRAPPED IN A DBMS   In practice, organizations become trapped into continuing use of a data-base management system (DBMS) once they have made a major commitment to it. Often, they do not expect to be trapped. The reason for the entrapment is that it is too expensive to change; too many programs would have to be rewritten.

Not only do user organizations become trapped; manufacturers of the DBMS also become trapped. So many customers depend on an old DBMS that the manufacturer has to keep supporting and improving it rather than switch to a better but incompatible form of DBMS. More than $1 billion per year is being spend by IBM's customers, for example, on analysis and programming of applications that employ IMS. IMS cannot be replaced by a different form of DBMS unless intricate conversion aids are made to work fully. Because of this entrapment, new forms of DBMSs often come from new vendors. Most *relational* data bases that do have most of the properties in Box 7.1 come from organizations other than the major mainframe vendors. Some customers are reluctant to use them for fear of becoming locked into a product that is not from the old, established vendors.

The initial choice of DBMS is thus more critical to future maintenance problems than is often realized when that choice is made. Should organizations delay the difficult decision? Probably not, because the move to data base is a change in DP management which encourages the cleaning up of the data in the enterprise. The sooner this is done, the sooner the benefits will be felt, and the benefits of a well-designed data-base environment are great.

CANONICAL MODEL OF DATA   As we saw, third-normal-form design is concerned with the grouping of data items into stable records. We can extend the process further and talk about the association of data items to form an entire data base or model of data.

If we have a given collection of data items we can identify the *functional dependencies* among them. We can draw a graph of these functional dependencies in such a way that each data item is on the graph once only and redundant functional dependencies are removed. We produce a data graph with no redundancies either in the data items or in the functional dependencies among them. The graph is referred to as a *model* of the data. The minimal nonredundant graph is called a *canonical model.*

We will define a canonical model as a *graph of data which represents the inherent structure of that data and hence is independent of individual applications of the data and also of the software or hardware mechanisms which are employed in representing and using the data.*

The canonical model can be created by automated techniques [1]. If done correctly, the records of the model are *automatically in third normal form.* This provides the best method we know of creating stable foundation stones of data on which to build applications.

The input to a computer program which synthesizes data into a canonical model is a list of data items and their functional dependencies. The model can be built up a step at a time. As each new data item is added to the model we need to indicate what other data item(s) it is functionally dependent on: in other words, what key (concatenated or not) identified it.

A data administrator with no computer experience but much experience of the data and the enterprise, can conduct this synthesis process—given a computerized tool. The data models he creates need to reflect the enterprise as completely as possible. When the resulting third-normal-form canonical structure is used it minimizes the risk of having to rewrite application programs because of data-base changes.

The author has discussed canonical modeling of data in his data-base books and the reader wanting more detail is referred to these [1–4]. There is now much experience of this in practice. It has caused a major reduction in maintenance work. It needs a computerized tool because it is too tedious to do by hand. Hand-built data models of any complexity usually contain errors. With an appropriate tool the mechanics of the data modeling process become easy.

DOCUMENTATION   A vital function of the data administrator is to produce good documentation which the analysts, programmers, users, and maintainers can employ. This documentation should be created and maintained using appropriate software. A data dictionary and a data modeling tool are needed. Figure 7.1 shows graphic output of a data modeling tool. The records illustrated are in third normal form.

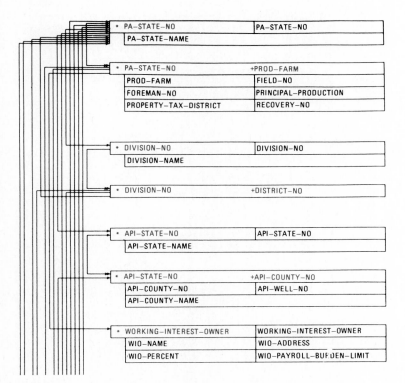

Figure 7.1 Example of the graphic output of a data modeling tool. (From Ref. 1.)

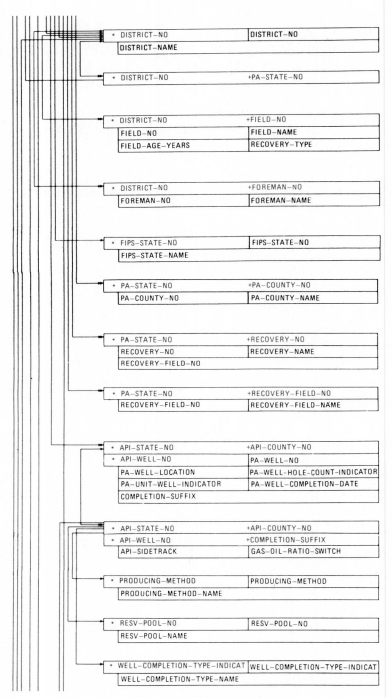

Figure 7.1   (Continued)

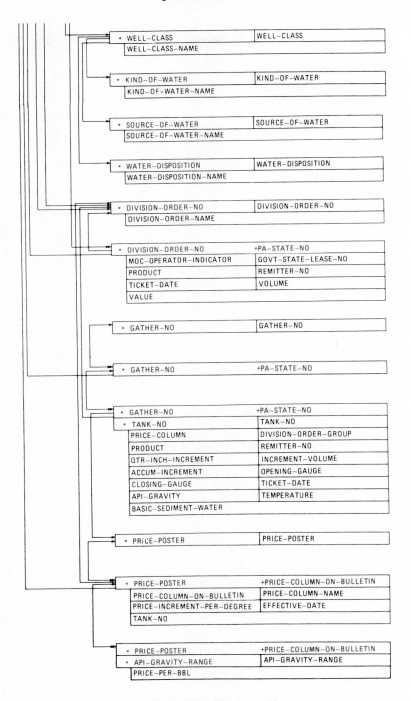

Figure 7.1   (Continued)

The documentation tools are often themselves a data-base system—a data base about data bases, which has good query and report generation facilities. The data administrator controls and updates this data base, and the analysts, programmers, and maintainers employ it.

The dictionary should *generate* the data descriptions which the programmers and maintainers use, so that there is no scope for misrepresentation. If the maintainers want to change the data structures, they communicate with the data administrator to achieve this. The administrator can find out from the dictionary where else the data in question are used. He can quickly add any proposed changes to the data model.

Data documentation is discussed further in Chapter 8.

END-USER PARTICIPATION   Perhaps the most important aspect of the data modeling process is participation of the end users.

Users know their own data instinctively, whereas DP analysts are much less familiar with the data. It is only too easy for analysts to assume that they understand the data when in fact there are subtleties which are not understood. There are many subtleties. Different accountants attach different meanings to the same word. One insurance company had six different definitions of what a "claim" was. "Prospect" meant one thing to the sales staff and another to the marketing department.

The successful data administrator thoroughly harnesses the knowledge of the subject-matter experts. These end users are employed to check the definitions in the data dictionary and the functional dependencies in the data model.

It has been found in practice that end users can be taught to understand the concept of functional dependencies—of one data item identifying others. They can be taught to create the input for and understand the output from the computerized data modeling process. They can understand that each attribute depends on "the key, the whole key, and nothing but the key."

They have difficulty and react against learning the software technicalities of data-base systems. The course given to end users on data base should be quite different from the course given to systems analysts or programmers [3].

The documentation created by the data administrator should be checked by the users. Probably the best way to do this is to form user teams who are highly knowledgeable about certain areas of data [4]. The data administrator takes the dictionary definitions and the data model for these data to the user teams for checking. Often, they argue strongly about some of the data definitions. This argument is part of the process of cleaning up the data representation, which is to be the foundation stone of a computerized corporation.

THINKING ABOUT THE FUTURE

When the output from the modeling process is reviewed, this is the time to think about the future.

If future requirements can be understood at this stage, a better logical design will result with a lower probability of expensive maintenance later.

The users, systems analysts, and data administrator should examine the output and ask themselves, "How might these data be used in the future?" Any potential future use should be incorporated provisionally in the model to see whether that use causes changes in the structure of the data-item groups.

Sometimes end users are better at thinking about the future than DP professionals because they know their possible applications better. This is not always the case. Sometimes imaginative systems analysts, or a data administrator, are best at thinking up future uses for the data.

Often the best way to do it is with a user group meeting, with the users, analysts, and data administrator all trying to brainstorm future users of the data.

One data administrator describes this process as follows:

"We try to anticipate certain types of changes. We sometimes place things in the model that take into account not precisely how we do business today, but how we might do business in the future.

Legal changes are a menace. Recent examples are federal maternity legislation and age discrimination legislation, which come down on us pretty rapidly. It doesn't allow us much time to expand and in many cases they're effective last month. We have to move quickly.

But even here the attempt to anticipate does help. Some of the legislative changes are anticipated. State-by-state changes follow a certain pattern—we can be responsive to that. We can look ahead and we can say: "We've had three states that have done this and we know some more will; let's plan for it."

INHERENT PROPERTIES OF DATA

The intent of the data model is to represent the *inherent* properties of the data. If it does this, it has a better chance of being stable.

There are two types of inherent characteristics of the links on the bubble chart—those which are *naturally* inherent, and those which represent *business rules*.

The *naturally* inherent characteristics include such properties as: a branch office can have *many* salespersons; an employee has one pension record; a supplier can supply *many* parts; a part has only *one* description.

The business rules include such properties as: a particular policyholder will be sent all his bills on the same day regardless of how many policies he has; a given flight number is always the same type of plane; a person may have two addresses, but not three.

The data administrator should distinguish between the *naturally* inherent properties and the business rules. In the case of the latter he needs to determine how viable the assumed rule is. Could it change? Should the data base be set up so that policyholder bills *could* be sent out on different days? Should TYPE-OF-PLANE be identified by FLIGHT-NUMBER or FLIGHT-NUMBER + DATE? Often, the data structure can be set up so as to anticipate changes in the rules.

HIDDEN KEYS

What forces program rewriting is a change in the basic structure of a record. The most common cause of this is that a data item which is an attribute in the record *now* becomes a primary key *later*. It is easy to spot any such data items in the output of a data modeling tool.

The data administrator, systems analysts, and user team should examine each attribute data item in turn and ask: "Could this possibly be used as a primary key in the future?" If data items are found which are potential future primary keys, the decision should be made whether to make them primary keys *now* by giving the modeling tool new input views. If they are made into primary keys now, this will possibly save future redesign with extensive program rewriting.

STABILITY ANALYSIS

The modeling process does not end when the design tool produces an impressive set of output reports and charts. These should then be taken to the users and scrutinized with a set of questions intended to show up any potential instabilities in the model (part 6 of Box 7.2). This step is called *stability analysis.*

It needs to be done thoroughly before the data base is implemented. It is more important with heavy-duty Class II and III data bases than with Class IV, where the software accommodates future change with more flexibility.

The data-base structures will change in the future, but an objective of their design should be to *minimize those types of change that will cause existing application programs to be rewritten.* As we have stressed, it is expensive to rewrite programs—often so expensive that it is avoided or postponed. Achieving the stated objective has a major influence on the *effectiveness* of data processing in all areas.

SUMMARY

Box 7.2 summarizes the steps desirable in creating stable data bases. Some of the items in the box re-

BOX 7.2   Steps in creating stable data bases

The data models are a foundation stone on which so much will be built. The foundation stone needs to be as stable as possible (i.e., it should not change in ways which force application programs to have to be rewritten). The following steps are needed to achieve this:

1. Strategy

- Determine what data bases are to be designed—subject data bases, isolated application data bases, or information system data bases.
- Ensure that the data administrator reports at a high enough level in the enterprise.
- Determine all possible types of end users of a given data base.
- Establish a user team with key individuals who are highly knowledgeable of each type of use of the data base.
- Select a modeling tool and data dictionary which form the bases of a corporate-wide standard.

2. Software Selection

- Select a DBMS which has as many of the properties in Box 7.1 as possible. The DBMS for routine heavy-duty computing will often be different from the DBMS for ad hoc decision support and information retrieval.
- Make it a corporate strategy to prevent proliferation of incompatible DBMSs, understanding that organizations become locked into use of their DBMS.
- Select DBMS report generators, query languages, and application generators which will give the fastest application development and maintenance. This should be one of the most important criteria in DBMS selection.
- Select a data dictionary (today, the data dictionary is usually built into the DBMS itself).
- Select a data modeling tool which together with the dictionary becomes the basis for a corporate-wide standard.

3. Top-Down Planning

- Determine what top-level requirements for information are likely to exist.
- Determine the entities in the enterprise about which data should be stored.
- Create an overview entity chart.
- Cluster the entities into groups, each of which forms the basis for detailed data models (subject data bases, entity supergroups).

(Continued)

Box 7.2 *(Continued)*

4. Input to the Data Modeling Process

- Capture all documents that will be derived from a data base, or will serve as inputs to the data base.
- Determine by discussion with the end users what types of data they want to obtain from the data base, now and in the future.
- Determine from the systems analysis process whether any new record or document requirements are emerging.
- Examine any existing data bases, files, or dictionaries which relate to these data.
- Plan whether existing files or data bases will coexist with the new data base or be converted. If they will coexist, plan the bridge between the old system and the new.
- Employ a data dictionary to document a description of the meaning of each data item.

5. Creating the Data Model

- Employ canonical synthesis, preferably with an automated design tool, or otherwise ensure that the model is in optimal third normal form.
- Inspect each input to see whether it can be simplified.
- Do any of the input data items already exist in the model under a different name or in a slightly different form?
- For each input data item, check that no different item in the model has the same name.
- Employ naming convention standards for selecting data-item names.
- Be sure that concatenated keys are correctly represented in the input to the synthesis process [4, p. 189].
- Be sure that all attributes entered as input are dependent on the *whole* of the key that identifies them [4, p. 192].
- Be sure that the data groups entered as input contain no transitive dependencies [4, p. 137].
- Question the validity of all links that represent business rules, as opposed to the natural inherent properties of the data. Could these rules be changed in the future [4, Chap. 12]?

6. Inspecting the Output of the Data Model

- With the user group, review the data dictionary to ensure that all users agree about the definitions of data items.

Box 7.2 *(Continued)*

- With the user group, review the model to ensure that their data requirements can be derived from it.

- With the user group, brainstorm the possible future uses of the data. For any uses that the model does not serve, create new input to the synthesis process.

- Examine every attribute field in the model to determine whether it could possibly become a primary key in the future [4, p. 205]. (This is a simple step, often not done, which can avoid much grief later.)

- Complete the reverse mapping of any links between keys to identify any possible M:M links (⊏▸━━▸━). The synthesis tool will create an extra concatenated key in the model to take care of any future intersection data [4, p. 209]. This can be changed if no intersection data are possible.

- Examine any links which the synthesis process has deleted, to ensure that they are truly redundant.

- Examine the effect of exploding any concatenated keys, to see whether the resulting single-field data items need to exist separately in the data base.

- If candidate keys exist in the resulting model, check that they are in fact likely to remain candidate keys in the future.

- Check the treatment of any intersecting attributes to ensure that it is the best of the three possible treatments [4, p. 145]. Could the intersecting attribute become a primary key in the future?

- Convert the model to the logical software schema and validate it by checking that every input view can be derived from the software schema.

- Use fast (computerized) redesign after any changes are made, in order to maintain the interest of the users.

7. Physical Considerations

- For each usage path on the model add up the volume of usage, and indicate whether it is batch or fast-response usage. This should be done by the modeling tool.

- For each A ━━▸━ B link determine how many values of B on average are associated with one value of A.

- Use the foregoing data for selecting the optimum representation of the model in the software [4, Chap. 18].

- Does the DBMS permit new attributes to be added to an existing data-item group without causing the programs which use that data-item group to be rewritten? (If not, it should be argued that that is not the right DBMS.)

(Continued)

Box 7.2 *(Continued)*

- Does the DBMS permit secondary-key links to be added to an existing data base without causing the existing programs to be rewritten? (If not, it should be argued that it is not the right DBMS.)

- Does any secondary-key path have a high usage volume? If so, this may suggest that the model be split into separate data bases for machine performance reasons.

quire more detailed explanation, and for this the reader is referred to James Martin's *Managing the Data-Base Environment* [4]. Good data-base management is a complex subject which has often been treated too casually.

The data modeling in an organization needs to be broad in its scope, encompassing the old files and data bases as well as future uses of data. It needs to encompass the many locations where the data will be used.

It should not be regarded as a single task done at one time. It is often too complex for that. Rather, it should be an ongoing process done a small step at a time. The organization's data are steadily cleaned up, removing and documenting the many inconsistencies. A large and complex organization will have multiple different models for different areas. It is easier to do in a small, young organization that is growing up with computers.

The ongoing process of cleaning up, modeling, and documenting the data is an essential part of managing the data-base environment and has a powerful effect on future maintenance costs.

REFERENCES

1. Literature and courses on DATA DESIGNER, a software tool for performing canonical synthesis, Database Design Inc., Ann Arbor, MI.

2. J. Martin and C. Finkelstein, *Information Engineering,* Savant Technical Report 22, Savant Institute, Carnforth, Lancashire, UK, 1981.

3. J. Martin, *An End-User's Guide to Data Base* (Englewood Cliffs, NJ: Prentice-Hall, Inc., 1981).

4. J. Martin, *Managing the Data-Base Environment* (Englewood Cliffs, NJ: Prentice-Hall, Inc., 1982).

8 DOCUMENTATION

THE
DOCUMENTATION
CONTROVERSY Inadequate documentation is a major contributor to the high cost of software maintenance and to the distaste for software maintenance work. For many programs currently used in industry no documentation exists or, perhaps even worse, documentation exists but is incorrect and misleading. Often a maintenance programmer spends days, weeks, or even months trying to debug a program only to find that he was working with an outdated source listing, program flowchart, or design specification.

Documentation is a critical and controversial issue of software maintenance. Documentation, which is expensive and time consuming to produce, soon becomes out of date due to changes to the software. Outdated documentation is not only useless but also may complicate and confuse the already difficult maintenance task. Furthermore, just as for programs, updating documentation may be even more expensive than its original production.

It is not surprising, then, that the intrinsic value of program documentation has frequently been questioned by programmers and managers alike. It has been proposed that the ultimate solution to the documentation problem is to use self-documenting programming languages. Then the program can become its own documentation, completely eliminating the need to develop and maintain documentation separately. When COBOL was designed in 1959, one objective of its English-like syntax was to make COBOL programs self-documenting. PL/1 and other more recent high-level and very high level programming languages offer more powerful control structures to facilitate self-documentation. Structured programming restricts the set of program structures to enhance program readability and thereby make programs self-documenting. Thus far, however, no conventional programming language or programming methodology has succeeded in eliminating the need for documentation. Certain nonprocedural facilities do eliminate the need for most documentation. As with an author writing in English, a programmer may use the syntactic structures provided by a programming language to create either an understandable or an abstruse program.

Documentation can have a profound impact on program understandability. Documentation explaining what a program does, and why, is essential for effectively and efficiently maintaining all but the simplest programs. Documentation is a powerful tool for the maintenance programmer, who must reconstruct the intentions of previous programmers and anticipate the possibilities of future changes.

We have underestimated the need for documentation because we have underestimated the need to change programs. It is interesting to note that the argument used to question the value of documentation is the same argument used to defend it. Because software is frequently changed, documentation is not practical. On the other hand, because software is frequently changed, documentation is essential for performing software maintenance. The purpose of documentation is to make programs more readable by people so that they can be understood, corrected, modified, tested, and used. The general concensus among software professionals is that a well-documented program is easier to work with than an undocumented one.

The controversy over program documentation is really concerned with the type of documentation that is needed rather than the question of whether or not any documentation is needed. Documentation as well as programs must be maintainable, and the key to maintainable documentation is simplicity. Producing voluminous amounts of detailed program documentation requiring a major update effort each time the program is modified can only compound the maintenance burden. Instead, what is needed is succinct, high-quality documentation that is easily accessible and easily updatable. To be maintainable, programs and their associated documentation must be flexible and extensible.

In general, high-level documentation explaining the overall purpose of the program and describing the relationship of the various program components is the most useful. Documentation providing a line-by-line description of the program instructions is extremely time consuming to write, to read, and to update. Such low-level documentation is usually unnecessary and virtually impossible to maintain.

Also, the documentation should fit the program. Small, simple programs require less documentation than large, complex software systems. Programs written, used, and maintained by one individual require less documentation than programs supporting many users and maintained by many different programmers. Programs written in higher-level languages require less documentation than those written in low-level languages.

Good program documentation is a fundamental component in building maintainable software. As Box 8.1 explains, good documentation is documentation that:

BOX 8.1   Program documentation

> Documentation is concerned with the readability of programs. People must be able to read and understand a program to maintain it. The value of documentation has been underestimated because we have underestimated the need to change programs. Although there has been much controversy concerning software documentation, most software experts agree on the following three points:
>
> - Well-documented programs are easier to work with than undocumented programs, but incorrect documentation is far worse than none at all.
> - Good documentation implies conciseness, consistency of style, and is easily updatable.
> - A program should be its own documentation; that is, a well-documented program should take advantage of the self-documenting facilities offered by the language and should have its documentation built into the source code.

- Enhances the readability and usability of programs
- Is easy and inexpensive to produce (and may in part be automatically produced)
- Is easy and inexpensive to maintain

DOCUMENTATION FOR LARGE AND SMALL SOFTWARE SYSTEMS

The need for program documentation increases with system size, complexity, and the number of users. The types of documentation described in this chapter are meant for large, complex software systems such as operating systems, compilers, and on-line transaction processing systems. They are also appropriate for medium-size systems such as inventory control, sales analysis, and payroll. These systems are probably written in third-generation programming languages such as COBOL or PL/1, will be used for many years by many users, and will be modified many times by many different programmers.

In the case of smaller, less complex programs, such extensive documentation is neither necessary nor cost-effective. If a program is written, used, and maintained exclusively by one person, there is little need for such elaborate documentation. However, even in this case, some documentation is helpful, especially if the program will be used over a period of time or if there is a possibility that it may be shared with other users. Unless a program is frequently used, even its original author will tend to forget what he has written and why. At the very least, overview documentation should be included in the source code to explain the basic program functions provided, operating instructions, and user guidelines. Overview documentation is discussed in Chapter 9.

DOCUMENTATION FOR FOURTH-GENERATION LANGUAGES

Overview documentation is also recommended for systems created with fourth-generation languages such as FOCUS, RAMIS, DMS, MAPPER, and NOMAD (Chapter 11). Some nonprocedural languages are largely self-documenting at the detail level. With IBM's DMS, for example, the analyst fills in forms which are largely self-explanatory. The programmer should take advantage of whatever documentation aids are provided by the language. This differs substantially from one fourth-generation language to another.

Programs in fourth-generation languages are often written by one person and this lessens communications problems. The program may be used by many persons and so user documentation is particularly important. It is often quick and easy to make changes. The rule should be made that when changes are made, the user documentation *must* be changed at that time.

It is generally desirable to have on-line user documentation so that users can easily find out at their terminals how to employ the facilities. Figure 8.1 gives an example of on-line user documentation, explaining the data that are on a screen which the user can manipulate or update.

On-line HELP facilities, ability to inquire about each user function, and overview documentation are also needed. Some systems employ simple computer-aided instruction. It is sometimes a principle that the user training courses enable a user to *begin* to use a system and he can extend his abilities with the system himself, on-line.

DOCUMENTATION FOR SOFTWARE PACKAGES

In the case of software packages, good documentation is even more critical than for software used within one organization. (Software packages are discussed in Chapter 15.) The number of users and the life expectancy of the package as well as system size and complexity are important factors in determining the documentation requirements. The longer the package is expected to be marketed, the more likely it will be modified to offer new features and the more need for documentation. However, regardless of the system size, complexity, or life expectancy, customers often expect the same degree of documentation required for the most sophisticated software systems. In this way, the customer can be better

```
ORDER STATUS REPORT

ORDER .PRODUCT.ST.STATUS.INI.PRODUC.PRODUC.SHIP   .PRODUC.SPC.P.S.
NUMBER.NUMBER .CD.DATE  .TAL.PLAN  .ACTUAL.DATE  .TYPE  .COD.R.T.
------.-------.--.------.---.------.------.------.------.---.-.-.

999999 CUSTOMER ORDER NUMBER

       9999999 NUMBER OF PRODUCT ON ORDER

               AA STATUS CODE: OR=ORDERED   SC=SCHEDULED   IP=IN PROGRESS
                               PE=PENDING  OH=ON HOLD    SH=SHIPPED

               899999 DATE WHEN STATUS IS REPORTED (YYMMDD)

               AAA INITIAL OF PERSON REPORTING STATUS

                     899999 PLANNED DATE FOR PRODUCTION (YYMMDD)

                          899999 ACTUAL DATE FOR
                                 PRODUCTION (YYMMDD)

                               899999 SHIPPING DATE (YYMMDD)

                                     999999
                               PRODUCT TYPE NUMBER

                                            AAA
SPECIAL SEARCH CODES USED FOR SEARCHING FOR PRODUCTS GIVEN PRIORITY,
OR SPECIAL CUSTOMER STATUS, OR RESEARCH ITEMS.

                                                  5
                                            PRIORITY RATING
                                                  1
1 INDICATES THAT A SPECIAL TRACKING REPORT EXISTS FOR THIS ORDER.
THIS MAY BE VIEWED BY ENTERING 'SP'
------.-------.--.------.---.------.------.------.------.---.-.-.
 73290 1169083 OR 841221 PTM 850311            8000 BAM 2 1

THE ABOVE LINE IS AN EXAMPLE ITEM WHICH DENOTES AN 8000 SERIES
PRODUCT WHICH HAS BEEN ORDERED BUT NOT YET SCHEDULED.
```

Figure 8.1 Illustration of on-line documentation explaining a report screen to users. This is particularly important if the report fields may be frequently changed.

assured of system maintainability. Also, because he is not allowed to review the internals of a proprietary software package, the customer may use the quality of the system's operation and user documentation as a criterion for selecting a software package and for judging the professionalism of the software vendor.

KINDS OF DOCUMENTATION

Four kinds of documentation are normally created to support application software systems (see Fig. 8.2):

1. User documentation
2. Operations documentation

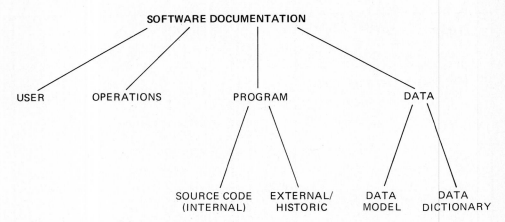

Figure 8.2 Kinds of documentation usually created to support large application systems and programs.

3. Program documentation

4. Data documentation

User documentation provides instructions on how to use the programs. It may consist of a user manual that explains each system function and provides instructions for entering data, interpreting output information, and reacting to error messages. Often better, the user documentation should be on-line, available at his terminal.

Operation documentation is used to direct the execution of programs. It includes run books, run logs, file backup procedures, and so forth.

Program documentation is used by programmers to understand the internal structures of a program and how programs within a software system interact with one another, with the operating system and with other software systems. Program documentation includes source code commentary, external program specification and design documents, system and program flowcharts, cross-sequence maps, and so forth.

DATA DOCUMENTATION   Good documentation is needed for the software data components as well as program components.

A data model and a data dictionary are used to document the data. The data model, preferably a canonical data model, is a graphic representation of the data identifying the inherent structure of the data and their functional dependencies. The data dictionary lists all the data items that are used, their definitions, how and where they are used, and who is responsible for them.

USER DOCUMENTATION

Making a software system more usable from the user's perspective is a very effective way of reducing maintenance costs. A key to improved usability is high-quality user documentation—documentation that is complete, current, accessible, and written in terminology understandable by the user.

Perhaps the best way to develop such documentation is for the user group to write its own. This is appropriate when the software is custom developed for a user group by an internal data-processing department, by an outside consulting group, or by the users themselves, as in the case of fourth-generation languages. In the case of software packages, software vendors are well advised to create user manuals with as much participation as possible from potential users. Because the user presumably knows the application well, he is probably the best qualified to create the user manual. The ultimate utility of a software system in the user's environment is clearly contingent upon user involvement in the software development process. Creating user documentation should be considered the minimal acceptable level of involvement.

When a software system is developed, the user manual should be created as the first step, not the last step, as has been done traditionally. The user manual can form a common basis of system understanding for the user, the developer, and eventually the maintainer.

There are ways to benefit from a "user-written" user manual. First, many misunderstandings concerning system requirements and functions can be avoided since the user defines the requirements. Second, writing the manual serves as a user training exercise to familiarize the user with the system. Finally, the user is in a better position to assume responsibility for deciding on system changes and for updating the user documentation as the system is changed in later life-cycle phases.

Ideally, user documentation should be created when the software is initially developed and then should be updated when changes are made. In the case of on-line systems, the manual should be on-line with the system and should provide a "help" facility to guide even the most inexperienced user. In practice, however, this has not often been the case. For many existing software systems there is little or no user documentation. The current version of the user manual resides only informally in the "heads" of certain key users and is passed by word of mouth among the users. This level of informality can be very dangerous, leading to misunderstandings and frustrations, especially when members of the user group and maintenance group change. In these situations the users' and maintainers' interpretations of what the system does may differ greatly, causing the maintainers to spend much of their time tracking hypothetical errors reported by misinformed users. Encouraging the users to rewrite the user manual to explain correctly how the system works may substantially reduce the maintenance effort.

PROGRAM DOCUMENTATION

Program documentation should describe the program data and procedural components, what the program does, and why the program works as it does.

Good, clear diagrams are an essential part of documentation. Figure 8.3 shows some types of diagrams, relating to structured techniques, which are especially useful.

If the program is structured, the procedural components and their relationships with one another can be graphically represented in a structure chart. If the program is not hierarchically structured, a flowchart can be used to show execution flow from one procedural component to another.

HIPO diagrams and Warnier diagrams are other graphic documentation methods used to show program procedural components. Pseudo-code is an example of a narrative form of documentation used to show the internal structure of a program or a program module. A data-flow diagram graphically portrays the flow of data through a system or program.

The data model and the data dictionary are used to document data. A data model is a graphic representation of data identifying the inherent structure of the data and their functional dependencies. A data dictionary lists all the data items that are used, their definitions, how and where they are used, and who is responsible for each of them.

A logic access map (LAM) shows the sequence of access to a data base. It is drawn on a data model chart showing the logical records used.

A data-base action diagram (DAD) shows the procedure for employing a data base and leads directly to a code skeleton in pseudo-code or the code of a high-level data-base language.

DOCUMENTATION VIEWS

Documentation can give different views of a program. HIPO diagrams and structure charts can give a high-level overview of a program. They explain in general terms what major functions the program performs and what data and procedural components make up the program. On the other hand, pseudo-code and flowcharts can give an instruction-level view of a program. They show where each program variable is initialized, tested, or referenced in the program code.

A high-level and/or a detailed view of a program are important depending on the reader's purpose. If he is searching for a bug, then detailed documentation may guide him to the exact location of the error. If he wants to determine in which of several programs a certain function is performed, high-level documentation may be the most helpful.

Different tools are better suited for a high level of detailed documentation. For example, HIPO diagrams are well suited for high-level documentation that introduces the program to its reader. But at a detailed

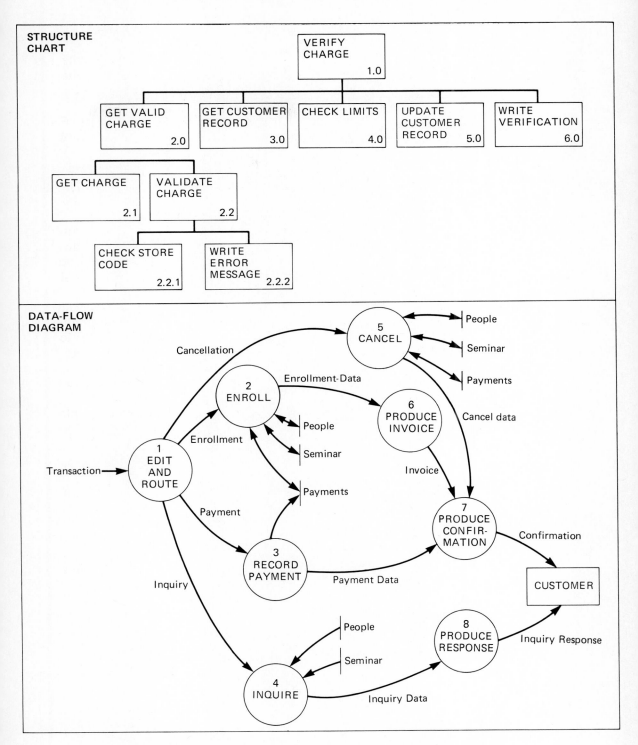

Figure 8.3 Good diagrams form a very important part of external documentation.

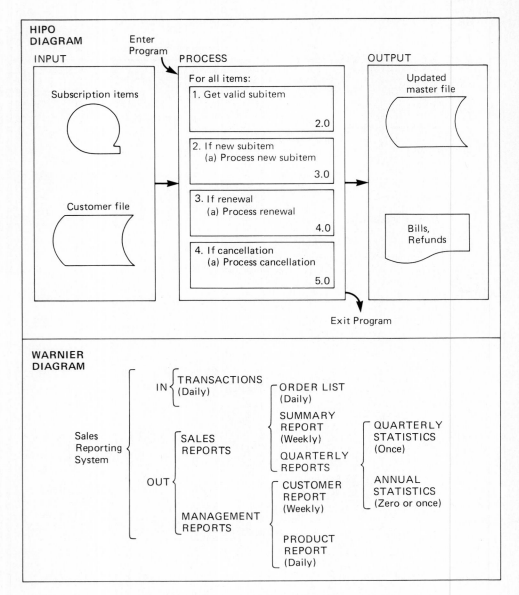

Figure 8.3   (Continued)

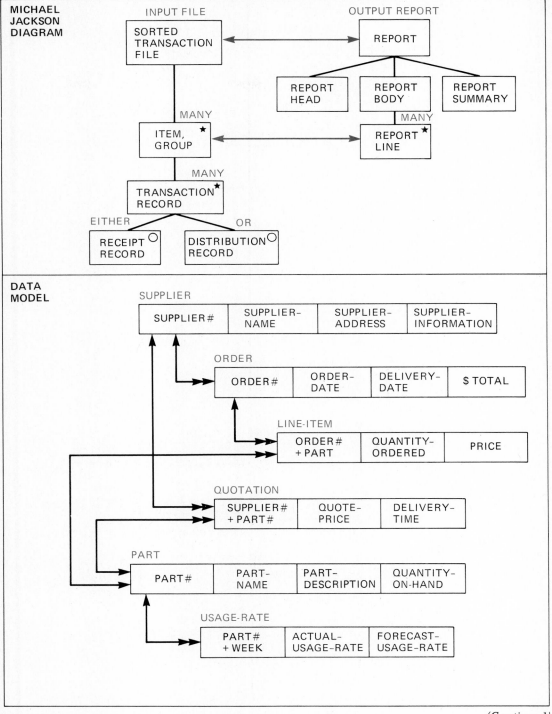

MICHAEL JACKSON DIAGRAM

INPUT FILE

SORTED TRANSACTION FILE

OUTPUT REPORT

REPORT

REPORT HEAD

REPORT BODY

REPORT SUMMARY

MANY

ITEM, GROUP ★

MANY

REPORT LINE ★

MANY

TRANSACTION RECORD ★

EITHER

RECEIPT RECORD ○

OR

DISTRIBUTION RECORD ○

DATA MODEL

SUPPLIER

| SUPPLIER# | SUPPLIER-NAME | SUPPLIER-ADDRESS | SUPPLIER-INFORMATION |

ORDER

| ORDER# | ORDER-DATE | DELIVERY-DATE | $ TOTAL |

LINE-ITEM

| ORDER# + PART | QUANTITY-ORDERED | PRICE |

QUOTATION

| SUPPLIER# + PART# | QUOTE-PRICE | DELIVERY-TIME |

PART

| PART# | PART-NAME | PART-DESCRIPTION | QUANTITY-ON-HAND |

USAGE-RATE

| PART# + WEEK | ACTUAL-USAGE-RATE | FORECAST-USAGE-RATE |

(Continued)

183

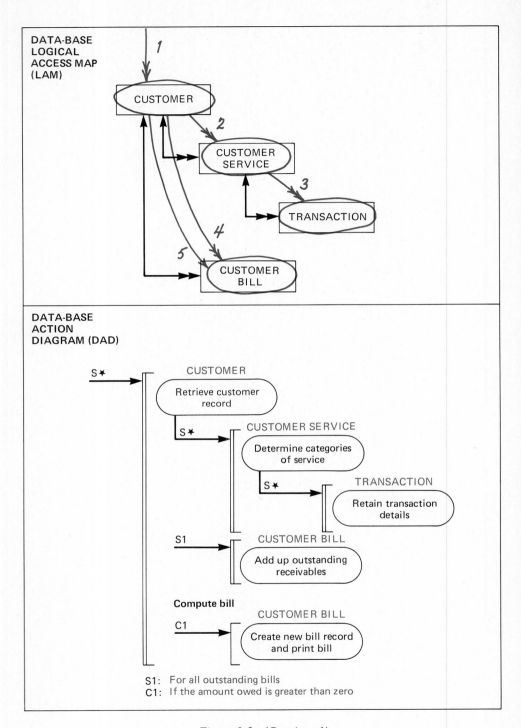

Figure 8.3   (Continued)

```
PSEUDOCODE

            UPDATE-COMPONENT.
              end-of-reserv = 0.
              PERFORM READ-RESERVATION-COMPONENT.
              PFUNTIL end-of-trans = 1 AND end-of-reserv = 1
                IF end-of-reserv = 1 AND end-of-trans = 0
                  PERFORM FINISH-TRANSACTION-COMPONENT
                    ENDIF;
                IF end-of-trans = 1 AND end-of-reserv = 0
                  PERFORM FINISH-RESERVATION-COMPONENT
                ENDIF;
                *Compare flight-number of Reservations-record
                and Transaction-record for an update match.
                IF end-of-trans = 0 OR end-of-reserv = 0
                  IF reservation-flight-number <
                    transaction-flight-number
                    write(New-reservations-record);
                    PERFORM READ-RESERVATION-COMPONENT
                  ELSIF reservation-flight-number >
                    transaction-flight-number
                    print("Reservations record added".
                      Transaction-record);
                    write(New-reservations-record);
                    PERFORM READ-TRANSACTION-COMPONENT
                  ELSIF reservation-flight-number =
                    transaction-flight-number
                    PERFORM UPDATE-RESERVATION-COMPONENT;
                    PERFORM READ-RESERVATION-COMPONENT;
                    PERFORM READ-TRANSACTION-COMPONENT
                  ENDIF
                ENDIF
              ENDPF.
```

Figure 8.3   (Continued)

documentation level, HIPO diagrams can become too cluttered with boxes and arrows to present program details clearly.

EXTERNAL AND INTERNAL DOCUMENTATION

Most documentation tools are used primarily as program development tools. They are used to define the program specifications and to represent the program design. They provide the blueprint for implementing the design into program code. Structure charts and pseudo-code are two good examples. Together they describe the program organizational structure and its internal workings. The programmer translates the structure chart and the pseudo-code instructions into actual programming language instructions during the coding phase.

Documentation tools produce both internal and external program documentation. *Internal documentation* is embedded in the program source code or generated at compilation time. (Internal documentation is discussed in Chapter 9.) Program comments and cross reference listings are examples of internal documentation.

External documentation is separate from the source code. HIPO diagrams and Warnier diagrams are examples of external program documentation.

External program documentation, such as data flow diagrams and pseudo-code, is often discarded once the program is developed. It is considered unnecessary and too expensive to keep it up to date during the remainder of the system life cycle. If a program is well structured and properly documented internally, the program source code can provide all the necessary program documentation.

Maintenance programmers distrust much external documentation because they know that in practice it is seldom updated. Even the external documentation for a newly released system is unlikely to exactly describe the program. The most accurate source of information about a program is the program code and any information generated from the code (e.g., cross-reference listings, automatically generated structure charts, flowcharts). Keeping all the program documentation within or generated from the source code will make it more accessible and more accurate.

Basically, this is a reasonable position, but some important exceptions should be noted. We should distinguish between different types of external documentation:

1. High-level versus detailed
2. Procedural versus data

High-level documentation will change very little, can be easily updated, and is a valuable source of information about a program throughout its life. Overview HIPO diagrams, Warnier diagrams, data flow diagrams, structure charts, and data-base action diagrams are valuable introductions to understanding a complex program.

If the data are properly designed (as discussed in Chapter 7), the data structure will remain stable through the system life. A canonical data model can be largely independent of individual applications of the data and also the software or hardware mechanisms which are employed in representing and using the data. The data model and the data dictionary are valuable tools to aid program understanding. Logical access maps may be associated with the data model.

Other types of external documentation (e.g., program specification documents, pseudo-code, design notes) which give a more detailed, historic description of the program should be kept as reference documents to provide a history of the program.

HISTORIC DOCUMENTATION

Knowing how a software system has evolved during its development and maintenance histories is very useful information to the program maintainer. It is especially helpful in the case of large, complex software systems and for systems that are likely to be maintained by programmers other than the original developers. Because the value of historic software documentation has not been recognized, it is rarely kept. However, it can greatly simplify the maintenance task. For example, understanding the original design intention will guide the maintainer in choosing ways to modify the code that do not jeopardize system integrity. Also, knowing the parts of the system that the developers considered the most difficult may give the maintainer a first clue to where an error might lie.

Three kinds of historic documentation are suggested:

1. System development journal
2. Error history
3. System maintenance journal

SYSTEM DEVELOPMENT JOURNAL

To understand a software system it is necessary to understand how the software was developed as well as what was developed. Recording the system development philosophy, decision-making strategies used, and the reasons for selecting a particular design alternative makes the software more understandable, especially as time goes on and the original developers are no longer available to explain the software. Also, it is useful to record project goals and priorities, experimental techniques and tools used, day-to-day problems, and project successes and failures. Although during the project all this information is probably well known by the developers, it is quickly forgotten after the project is over and the developers move on to other projects and perhaps other organizations.

A system development journal should be created by the developers as part of the development process. When the software is completed and turned over to the maintenance group, the development journal should also be passed on to the maintenance group to help familiarize them with the software.

An excerpt from an actual system development journal is shown in Fig. 8.4. The journal recorded the evolution of the system by answering such questions as:

1. What went wrong in the project (e.g., schedule problems, types of errors)?
2. What was done the right way in the project (e.g., written specifications, a clear definition of system integrity)?

History of Charting Project (4-2-75)

1. System Design

   A. Began June 3, 1974

   B. Comments

      a. Problem with multiple grid groups on chart because logic for grid not consistent with system philosophy and logic not well thought out.

      b. General problem with logic because exceptional cases not well thought out example (row of 0's).

      c. Data control not always strong because:
         i. some data names not meaningful
         ii. not known what units data expressed in example:
            FORMAT-COL-HEIGHT
            CHART-CENTER-FLAG
         iii. not known which modules access which data

      d. Another problem was that we didn't develop a testing philosophy because we didn't know how.

      e. We worked on functions and data intermittently. We defined tables and filled them in later. This way we could postpone decisions. Only time this caused problems is when we couldn't remember what a certain item was used for and who used it.

      f. One big mistake was not understanding arithmetic. We chose COMP instead of COMP-3.

      g. Observation: Data names used during design really stick, so choose meaningful names from the beginning.

      h. Example of Shakey Logic: CHART-AVERAGE changed at least four times!

      i. We did not edit all data put in tables as carefully as we should have.
         example: CD-CHRTPIC-TYPE is valid for which values?

      j. We set up work areas for sections and used prefix to identify each element in a work area.

      k. Many problems were equipment problems.

      l. We had problems with spacing left-hand descriptors and concept of min. bar!

      m. Increase system complexity — with logical ordering concept.

      n. Interesting problems: When to incorporate changes? How to test? What are ramifications to rest of system?
         Observation: Even a simple addition or change can cause problems.

      o. System was delayed because we didn't have test data — profiles were hard to get.

      p. We had problems with special bar — its size, etc.

      q. Many changes made for visual appeal.
         Example: Take out extra half bar on line graph with barred background: put in dash (—) instead of blanks for no data.

   C. Why we did succeed:

      We had conviction in project — our spirit carried us.
      We analyzed process.
      Project was right size.

Figure 8.4 Excerpts from the SMCS development journal.

D. SMCS System Design Approach

   a. Logical modularization of system. Define system from a functional point of view — what task is to be performed? Refine system definition by subdividing program tasks into subtasks. Eventually these subtasks will be refined enough so they can be represented as steps of an algorithm. The steps on the algorithm will be used to build system modules. Each module will be comprised of one or more steps of an algorithm depending on the complexity of the step.

   b. Get a general overview of the system structure; then tackle the hardest part first; consider its interface with the rest of the system and make it as clear and obvious as possible. This is *not* a top-down approach.

   c. Define data requirements in parallel with subtask definition. Use algorithm to define a subtask.

   d. Consistent design approach:

Handle general case

     Design with maintenance in mind:
       i. Other people must maintain so want its process obvious.
       ii. How this piece interfaces with rest of system.

The method for the design of the system was abstraction (i.e., define processing steps in general and then adjust to hand special processing). Abstract away exceptions to the rule and look at common characteristics — then add in special processing.

   System integrity would be preserved by consistently utilizing and applying this approach throughout system design. Emphasis was placed on the development of a general approach which could be used when processing any chart format rather than special processing routines for each chart format. Such an approach could sacrifice efficiency in some cases. However, any loss in execution speed would be compensated by a system which would be easier to maintain. For example, each chart would be plotted in a standard order:

(1) general chart requirements
(2) chart titles
(3) row-by-row
(4) date information at bottom of chart

Figure 8.4 (Continued)

Some organizations have found it more convenient to keep their journal in audio rather than written form.

ERROR HISTORY   A program behavior profile can be constructed using historic documentation. Since a program is likely to behave in the future as it has in the past, a program in which many errors were discovered during its development is likely to continue this trait of error-proneness during its maintenance phase. Furthermore, parts of the program which were more error-prone during the development phases are also likely to be more error-prone during the maintenance phase [1].

   Recording the error history of a program can offer insight into the frequency and type of errors that are likely to occur in the future (see Box 8.2). This will help the maintainer pinpoint troublesome programs and troublesome program modules. Once identified, these programs and modules can be rewritten or replaced to avoid further maintenance problems.

Also, tracing program errors may help identify other maintenance problems. For example, an increase in program errors may indicate that program modifications were made too hastily without sufficient retesting or that the software documentation, technical tools, or programmer expertise were inadequate. An investigation into the cause of the errors may reveal that the errors were "left over" from the software development phase and may suggest ways in which the software development process should be improved. On the other hand, a decrease in program errors may indicate that the software has stabilized and has become relatively error-free or that the system use has decreased. Examples of historic error data are shown in Figs. 8.5, 8.6, and 8.7.

By studying the behavior of software in its operational state we can more realistically evaluate software quality, the validity of our software quality measures, and the effectiveness of our software methodologies.

BOX 8.2   Program test history

The program test history is begun during the development phase and updated each time a new version of the program is produced during the maintenance phase.

- Number of modules tested during development/revision.
- Number of errors discovered during development/revision.
- Average number of errors discovered per module.
- Total number of statements modified to correct errors.
- Average length of time to discover and to correct an error.
- Types of errors discovered and frequency:
    Hardware failure
    Software reaction to hardware failure
    Coding error
    Design error
    Specification error
- List of most error-prone modules.
- List of most complex modules.

```
****** EXPLANATION OF CODES USED ******
|------ SUBSYS IDENTS ------>|<------ CAUSE CODES ------>|<------ OTHER HALT CODING ------>|
  *INQ=DIC INQ      IINQ=INFO INQ        BI=BAD INPUT  PG=PROG ERROR      PROCES = PROCESSING IS INCORRECT
  CINQ=CHG INQ      OTHR=OTHER           CU=CANT DUPL  PR=PROCEDURE       LOOP   = PROGRAM IS LOOPING
  EWO =ENGR WORK ORDER  SORD=SERVICE ORDER   DP=DUPL TR    RE=RECORD ERROR    RECUPD = UPDATE OF RECORD(S) IS INCORRECT
  FACE=INTEFACE     SDUP=SERV URO UPDATE     DS=DESIGN     SS=SYSTEM SOFTW    OUTPUT = OUTPUT MISSING OR INVALID
                                            NT=NO TROB

****** CURRENT MONTHS ACTIVITY ******    *** LAST MONTHS FIGURES ***
* UPDATE THESE FIGURES WHEN CLEARING TR'S =    *** DON'T CHANGE THESE ***
* RECVD CLEARED ON HAND TR'S BEFORE 07/01      * ON HAND OVER 30 DAYS *
    54    38    14                              19    2
```

TR NO.	ISSUED MM/DD/YY	CLEARED MM/DD/YY	HALT/ AEMD IDENT	SUBSYS PGMR IDENT INIT	CAUSE CODE	PROG. TRL.REC	EXPLANATION OF PROBLEM
19701	05/28/81		S80A	OTHR	AIH	PG	0251500	OPEN OF DUMP FILE FAILED DUE TO INSUFFICIENT SPACE
31478	05/29/81	07/13/81	PROCES	CINQ	AIH	DP	TR316C3	USING PICK TO CHNG CNE COS DIST TIE GIVES US TWO
31481	06/01/81	07/15/81	PROCES	IINQ	TLL	PG	0210200	REQUEST W/INV INP SHOULD HALT BUT GIVES OUTPUT FOR WRONG CABLE
31439	06/03/81		H2964	IINQ				HALT OCCURS WHEN PAIR IS DEFECTIVE W/BAD MULTIPLICITY
31491	06/03/81		OUTPUT	SORD				PLEASE PRINT OP MSB ON H019949
31499	06/09/81		OUTPUT	IINQ				CCURS WRONG ON MULTIPLE APPEARANCE
31515	06/10/81		PROCES	SORD				IN C OE SELECTION NOT SELECTING ALL ZERO OE FROM BUCKET
31519	06/11/81		OUTPUT	IINQ				10% PK DUMP NOT PRINTING POS & JK ON HI PAIRS
31520	06/11/81		RECUP	OTHR				W/C.L. SCRUB GIVING HALTS INSTEAD OF FIXING RECORDS
19049	06/12/81		SC03	FACE				DACS BMP PROBLEM
31528	06/16/81		HALT	OTHR				BA3C20041 FROM DAILY REPORTS HAS ZERO KEY FOR CAR RECORDS
31551	06/23/81	07/15/81	OUTPUT	IINQ	TLL	PG	0210200	10% PK DUMP NOT PRINTING REF # ON 100'S
31552	06/23/81		H22319	OTHR				ON CUSTOMER DATA PRINT FOR THEORETICAL PREFX
31553	06/23/81	07/02/81	OUTPUT	OTHR	TLL	NT		CC DUMP MISSING SOME COMPLEMENTS
31554	06/24/81	07/02/81	H03713	OTHR	AIH	PG	0250600	BLOCKING FILE PRINTOUT HALT NO APPARANT RECORD ERROR
31557	06/25/81		RECUP	IINQ				1C UPDATE NOT CHANGING STATUS ON L1 REC W/SCORED AS SESONAL
31562	06/29/81		SOC1	OTHR				** JOB START 211204
31569	06/29/81		RECUP	CINQ				MILO ARDEN SAYS PROGRAMS ALLOWING X-NOX TO BE WO/ISHOULDN'T BE
31570	06/29/81		H29022	IINQ				PAIR NOT IN 5TH RNGE ON "MULTIPLE APPEARANCE"
******	07/01/81	JULY OVER 30 DAY OLD LINE					******
31571	07/01/81	07/06/81	H13020	EWO	AEJ	PG	0213740	DISK EXCEPTION APR WITH 5 DIGIT CABLE NUMBER
31514	07/01/81	07/02/81	H1470Z	EWO	AEJ	PG	0213223	H1470Z TER LOADED WITH MULTIPLE AER CABLES
31575	07/01/81	07/08/81	H13021	EWO	AEJ	PG	0213510	DISK EXCEPTION RUP ON UPDATE ALL
31576	07/01/81	07/01/81	U240	SORD	RCF	RE	CAR	'N' ORDER ARENUS
31577	07/01/81	07/01/81	EWC	EWC	REM	SS		OUT OF RUP IN RUGERS PARK
31578	07/01/81	07/13/81	OUTPUT	CINQ	RCF	PG	0220142	REQUEST 1 TIE CHANGE-BOTH TIES CHANGED
31579	07/01/81		OUTPUT	IINQ				DAILY REPORT PROBLEM ON DELAYED TRANSACTIONS
31580	07/01/81		OUTPUT	CTHR				DAILY REPORT PROBLEM ON DELAYED TRANSACTIONS REF #-NOT MATCH
31581	07/01/81	07/07/81	H15590	EWO	AEJ	PG	0213535	H15590 PRESENT AND FUTURE INR DON'T MATCH
31582	07/01/81	07/01/81	U240	IINQ	RCF	RE	CAR	L1 INFO REQUEST BY SERVICE ADDRESS
31583	07/01/81		H15955	EWO				AX100J101 FROM TPM ON ACTN ORIG
31584	07/01/81	07/10/81	S0C4	SORD	RCF	PG	0201012	3N20586096 3801 CICERO AVIFLR 18
31586	07/02/81		H0C052	IINQ	OHM			MULTIPLE APPEARANCE
31537	07/02/81	07/13/81	OUTPUT	EWC	AEJ	NT		NOT PRINTING 'SAME' CN TO-SIDE WHEN PAIRS-ARE-NOT-CHANGING
31538	07/02/81		OUTPUT	OTHR	AIH	PG	BA30233	SD20-3 L1S RECORD # S/BE 6 DIGITS NOT 9
31589	07/02/81		OUTPUT	EWO				COLOP CODES SCREWED UP ON PC'S
31590	07/02/81		H08653	SDUP				UPDATING 'C' ORDER-ADDING FAM AND SLC
22234	07/03/81	07/06/81	S0C6	FACE	REM	CD	BF600	UPDATING 'C' ORDER ADDING FAM AND SLC
31591	07/03/81		INPUT	IINQ				INVALID INPUT CABLE ON CC DUMP

Figure 8.5 MCC report log.

191

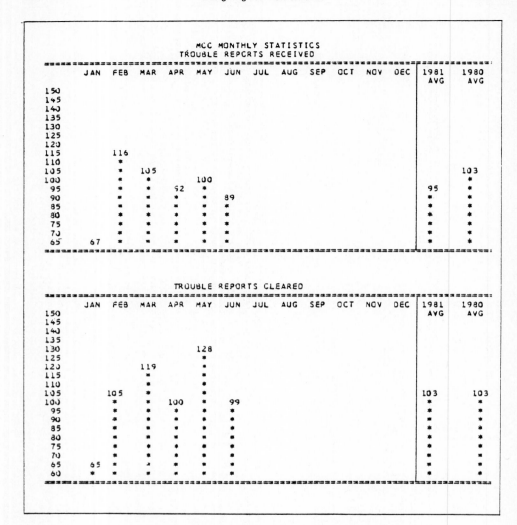

Figure 8.6   MCC monthly statistics.

SYSTEM
MAINTENANCE
JOURNAL

During the software development process, a journal is kept to record how the system was developed. Similarly, during the software maintenance phase, a journal should be kept to record how and why the system is changed. The system maintenance journal contains information such as change philosophy, quality preservation/improvement strategies, problems, trouble spots, and so forth. Understanding the thought process behind the program modifications is the key to understanding what was modified and the probable impact of the modifications. In addition, information on problem reports and their resolutions, change requests and their

```
                        MCC STATUS REPORT
                        ERROR ANALYSIS

******************** SYSTEM STATISTICS ********************************

T.R. ANALYSIS      JAN  FEB  MAR  APR  MAY  JUN  JUL  AUG  SEP  OCT  NOV  DEC 1980
  BY TYPE *                                                               AVG

DESIGN/PROG ERRS  42%  43%  39%  43%  34%  60%                            59%
RECORD ERRORS      9%  10%  13%  10%  13%  11%                             2%
INPUT ERRORS       5%   3%   4%   5%  11%   6%                             4%
SYS SOFTWARE ERR   1%   5%   2%   6%   3%   1%                             -
PROCEDURAL ERRORS  6%  10%  11%   3%   7%   6%                             3%
UNKNOWN            3%   2%   7%   2%   9%   6%                             -
OTHER             15%  20%  19%   0%  17%   7%                             9%
NO TROUBLE FOUND  18%   7%   4%  31%   6%   3%                            21%




************************************************************************

T.R. ANALYSIS      JAN  FEB  MAR  APR  MAY  JUN  JUL  AUG  SEP  OCT  NOV  DEC 1980
  BY SUBSYSTEM *                                                          AVG

SERVICE ORD       32%  23%  33%  22%  16%  23%                            27%
EWO/ROUT ORD      17%  16%  13%   8%  12%  19%                            28%
INQUIRY           20%  11%   8%  12%  30%  35%                            19%
OTHER             31%  50%  47%  58%  41%  22%                            26%

* USES THE CLEARED COUNT FOR CALCULATION
```

Figure 8.7   MCC status report.

disposition, and new version descriptions and new release notices are included in the system maintenance journal.

DOCUMENTATION FOR EXISTING SOFTWARE SYSTEMS

Ideally, documentation is created during the development process and appropriately updated throughout the system life cycle. However, the documentation for many existing software systems currently used in industry is woefully inadequate and virtually nonexistent.

How do the documentation ideas presented in this chapter apply to existing systems? Is it possible or even practical to "go back" and attempt to create good documentation for existing systems? The answer is not a simple "yes" or "no." It depends. It depends on the life expectancy of the system,

BOX 8.3 Guidelines for documenting existing software systems

- Keep the documentation simple.

- Stress high-level documentation. Write up-to-date overview documentation and include it in the source code listing.

- Avoid writing instruction-level comments. If the code is unreadable and must be modified, rewrite it in a more readable manner. User automatic documenting systems when detailed flowcharts are needed to understand the program logic.

- Keep a maintenance journal.

- Record the program error history to identify the most troublesome programs and modules.

- Use automated documentation tools to improve and update existing program documentation (see Chapter 19):

  Cross-reference listers
  Source code reformatters (ADR's MetaCOBOL)
  Automated flowcharters (TRW's FLOWGEN)
  Automated documentors (Amdahl's MAP, General Research Corp's RXVP)
  Structuring engines (Catalyst's COBOL Engine, Caine, Farber & Gordon's FORTRAN Engine)
  Structure checkers (TRW's CODE AUDITOR)
  Programming environments (Bell Labs' UNIX)

its stability, the problems it currently presents to the users, plans to enhance or replace the system, and so forth.

Generally, it is advisable to follow the same strategy suggested for new systems. Keep the documentation simple. Stress high-level documentation. Do not clutter the program code with low-level line-by-line comments. Use automated documentation tools. And most important, do not spend a great deal of time redocumenting a system that should be replaced. Instead, replace it and properly document the new system. Box 8.3 summarizes some general guidelines to follow when documenting existing systems.

REFERENCE

1. H. Mills, "Software Development," *IEEE Trans. on Software Engineering,* Vol. SE-2, No. 4 (December 1976): 265–273.

9 SOURCE CODE STYLE

THE ELEMENTS OF STYLE

Style is normally considered a matter of personal preference and a mark of individuality. But whatever the particulars may be, there are some elements common to any good style. A good style is simple, consistent, and complies with standard conventions. Its rules are not so complicated that the reader becomes bogged down in attempting to understand the form of what is written. Above all, it clarifies, not obscures, what the author is communicating.

The rules of good style apply to programming as well as conventional writing since programs must be read by people. If a program is well written using a good programming style, much of the difficulty of reading programs can disappear.

Programming style and documentation in the source code are discussed in this chapter. They strongly affect the maintainability of programs.

Beyond style, program documentation can provide something extra to enhance readability and more clearly convey the program meaning. High-level program comments explaining what the program does improve program readability. But low-level comments explaining how a program instruction works detract from readability by disrupting the visual scanning of instruction flow and lengthening the text that must be read.

Rather than clutter the program code with a rash of copious comments, a better approach is to employ the following program style and documentation techniques:

1. Selective high-level commentary
2. Meaningful names
3. Indentation
4. Consistent style

5. Structured programming

6. High-level control structures

These techniques lessen the need for program commentary and help make programs self-documenting. In addition, these techniques improve the maintainability of the program documentation. Building the program documentation into the code makes it more readily accessible for review and modification.

SOURCE CODE DOCUMENTATION

Source code documentation addresses three levels of program understanding:

1. Overview

2. Program organization

3. Program instruction

Each successive level provides a more detailed view of the program. All three levels are necessary to maintain a program. If a programmer does not have an overview understanding of the functions performed by the program and generally how these functions have been implemented in the code, he will find it extremely difficult to evaluate effectively the feasibility of expanding or contracting these functions. If a programmer does not understand how the various pieces of a program fit together, he will find it virtually impossible to determine correctly the impact that modifying one piece of the program will have on the other pieces. Or, if a programmer cannot understand each instruction, he will find it exceedingly difficult to isolate the complete cause for a program error and then correctly determine a remedy to rectify it.

OVERVIEW DOCUMENTATION

Overview documentation introduces the program to the reader. Often the need for this first level of program documentation has been overlooked. However, it is essential to all levels of understanding a program. If one must choose among the three levels of source code documentation, overview documentation is the most fundamental and therefore the most essential. Also, it is the easiest to provide and the most stable. Throughout the life of the program, overview documentation is the least likely to require changes. Although the program may be modified frequently to meet changing requirements, the overall function provided and the original design philosophy are likely to remain unchanged. (Of course, this is more likely to happen when the maintenance programmers understand the original design philoso-

BOX 9.1   Overview documentation items

- An overall function summary defining the basic functional components and their relationship to one another.

- An overall data-base summary showing the role of data in the total system, including major files, major data structures, and major clusters.

- A brief explanation of the underlying design philosophy and the programming style used. The portion of a logical data model used, with logical access maps drawn on it.

- Pointers to historic documentation, including design notes, problem reports, version descriptions, new release notices, and error statistics.

- Pointers to more detailed levels of internal program documentation, operating instructions, and user manuals.

phy and are given the maintenance objective to preserve it.) Overview documentation items are listed in Box 9.1.

Overview documentation should be included within the program code in the form of commentary at the beginning of the source listing. It should be brief and general. Also, it should be readable by nontechnical as well as technical readers. An example is shown in Fig. 9.1.

Shneiderman suggests using a narrative form for overview documentation since a prose version will be more easily retained in memory than will a flowchart version [1, pp. 81–85]. Also, a flowchart may be too spread out and less comprehensible to a nontechnical reader.

Documenting the source code should be included as an integral part of the coding process. It should be written by the programmer who writes the code rather than by a separate technical writer. Overview documentation should be written before writing the first line of program code. It should be constructed manually even if an automatic documentation generator is available. Since it is brief and general, it will not be a time-consuming task. But most important, when done manually by the programmer, the programmer has an opportunity to review generally what the program is to do before becoming immersed in the details of coding.

PROGRAM ORGANIZATION DOCUMENTATION

Program organization documentation serves as a program table of contents defining the name, location, and function of each program component. It assumes that the reader possesses a higher level of

```
*
*        VERTICAL-SPACING-DIRECTORY
*
*        THIS ANS COBOL PROGRAM CREATES THE USER CHART FORMAT
*        DIRECTORY BY COMPUTING ALL
*        VALID VERTICAL SPACING COMBINATIONS
*        FOR EACH CHART FORMAT OF THE SMCS
*        SYSTEM.  FOR NON-ROTATED CHARTS
*        (FORMATS 1, 2, 4, 9, 10, 12), VERTICAL
*        REFERS TO THE 8½ INCH DIMENSION
*        ON AN 8½ INCH PAGE.  FOR ROTATED
*        CHARTS (FORMATS 5, 6, 8, 11) VERTICAL
*        REFERS TO THE 11 INCH DIMENSION.
*        THERE ARE FOUR VERSIONS OF SCALING
*        COMBINATIONS:
*        1)   BARS, CHARACTER DATA (FORMATS 1,5,6,8,9,11)
*        2)   BARS, CHARACTER DATA, GRIDS, LINE
*             GRAPHS (FORMAT 2)
*        3)   BARS, CHARACTER DATA, GRIDS (FORMAT 4)
*        4)   BARS, CHARACTER DATA, LINE GRAPHS
*             (FORMATS 10, 12)
*
*        CHART FORMAT DATA IS SUPPLIED BY THE
*        SMCS CHART-PIC-INFO FILE
*
*        ADDITIONAL DOCUMENTATION IS AVAILABLE
*        WITH THE SMCS SYSTEM DOCUMENTATION FILE
*
```

Figure 9.1 Overview documentation for the vertical spacing directory program.

programming expertise than that required for overview documentation and that the program has been constructed as a set of functionally and operationally independent components. It is used by a programmer who is searching for a program error or making a program modification.

Two types of program organization documentation are suggested:

1. Graphic documentation representing the program procedural, data, and control structures
2. Program comments, introducing each program module and data structure

CONTROL STRUCTURE DOCUMENTATION Since the intermodule relationships and control structure may be difficult to discern from reading the code for even a well-structured program, the program organization structure is more clearly defined when graphically represented. A system flowchart or a structure chart in which each program module is represented by a single box is normally

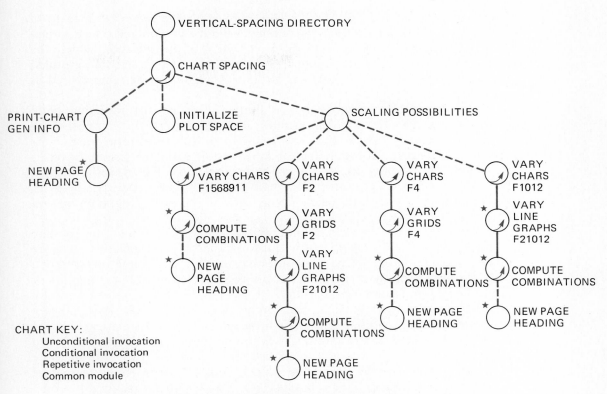

Figure 9.2 Structure chart for the vertical spacing directory program.

used. Attempting to show more detail for any but the smallest programs will make the chart too unwieldy to be useful.

Automatic flowcharting programs (e.g., Amdahl's MAP) can be used to generate the program procedural, data, and control structures. Since they are drawn directly from the source code, the programmer can be certain that the graph correctly represents the code. Also, it is an easy matter to redraw a graph automatically whenever the program is modified. A copy of the graphs can either be kept with the source listing or generated when needed.

An example of a program structure chart is shown in Fig. 9.2. Examples of documentation generated by Amdahl's MAP are included in Chapter 19.

PROGRAM COMMENTS

Shneiderman suggests applying the "chunking" theory to create meaningful program comments [1, pp. 49–53]. He explains that understanding a program is very much like understanding natural language. The syntax of a natural language sentence is used to obtain its semantic meaning. While the syntax is remembered only briefly, the semantic structure is retained for a longer time. This is because syntax items are not remembered one at a time but are grouped together to form a "chunk" of information which the human short-term memory retains. Sentences themselves become grouped together into higher-level semantic structures which can be remembered as one "chunk."

Our short-term memory has a limited capacity for retaining these chunks of information. It can handle about seven chunks at once. Well-known experiments show that the capacity of the short-term memory is about 7 ± 2 chunks. Reorganizing the information into appropriate chunks is important for effective use of our short-term memory. We do this reorganizing *subconsciously* in performing many of life's tasks. We can help by performing it *consciously* when doing certain types of programming and system design tasks.

Similarly, programmers do not understand programs in a line-by-line manner. Instead, they group instructions together to form higher-level, more understandable chunks (e.g., a module that prints a detail line on a report). This is the reason why modularization is such a powerful technique for improving program understandability.

In addition to modularization, program comments can assist the programmer in transforming program instructions into higher-level, more meaningful semantic structures. A comment block should precede each program module in the source code listing. Its purpose is to introduce the module to the reader by describing what the module does. How the module works is *not* described. This is best ascertained by actually reading the code. The comment block should be written by the programmer when the module

BOX 9.2   Module comment block items

- Module purpose—one or two sentences explaining what the module does
- Effective date (last revision)
- Limitations, restrictions, and algorithmic idiosyncrasies
- Accuracy requirements
- Inputs/outputs
- Assumptions
- Error recovery types and procedures
- Information explaining the impact of changes on the other portions of the program—especially in the case of common modules

```
*
*      INITIALIZE-PLOT-SPACE
*
*      THIS MODULE COMPUTES THE VERTICAL AND
*      HORIZONTAL PLOT SPACE AVAILABLE AND
*      THE MINIMUM AND MAXIMUM BAR SIZE FOR
*      A PARTICULAR CHART FORMAT.  VERTICAL
*      PLOT SPACE IS "DOWN" THE CHART FOR NON-
*      ROTATED CHARTS AND "ACROSS" THE CHART
*      FOR ROTATED CHARTS.
*
*      VARIABLES CHANGED IN THIS MODULE
*            SD-PLOT-SPACE-AVAIL
*            SD-MIN-BAR-HEIGHT
*            SD-MAX-BAR-HEIGHT
*            SD-BAR-COUNT
*            SD-CHAR-COUNT
*            SD-GRID-COUNT
*            SD-LINE-GRAPH-COUNT
*            SD-NO-MORE-SPACE
*
*      DATE OF LAST REVISION: 10/20/80
*
```

Figure 9.3 Module comment block for module INITIALIZE-PLOT-SPACE in the vertical spacing directory program.

is coded and appropriately updated each time the module is modified. Information to be included in a module comment block is listed in Box 9.2. Since some program modules will be more difficult to understand than others, the programmer must use some discretion in determining what information will be most helpful. Documenting what is obvious from reading the code may detract from rather than improve on program readability. Minimally, the first two items from the list above should be included.

The comment block should be separated from the module code by one or more blank lines, as shown in Fig. 9.3. An example of a comment block for an internal program table is shown in Fig. 9.4.

INSTRUCTION-LEVEL COMMENTS

Instruction-level comments should rarely be used. Good documentation does not imply that a source comment is required for each program instruction, each control structure, each decision point, or some such arbitrary rule. For example, a programmer does not have to be told that in the following COBOL instruction the line counter is incremented by 1.

ADD + 1 TO LINE-COUNT

```
00056              01    FORMAT-DEPENDENT-WORK.
00057              *     FORMAT-DEPEND-INFO-TABLE
00058              *
00059              *     THE FORMAT-DEPEND-INFO-TABLE CONTAINS VALUES WHICH ARE CONSTANT
00060              *     FOR A PARTICULAR CHART FORMAT.
00061              *
00062              *     FORMAT-MKT-SBGRP-GAP..IS THE FRACTION OF A COL WIDTH BETWEEN
00063              *                           SUBGROUPS WITHIN A PARTICULAR MARKET
00064              *     FORMAT-MIN-BAR IS THE MINIMUM BAR WIDTH FOR A COLUMN OF THE
00065              *        CHART. IT IS MEASURED IN INCHES.
00066              *     FORMAT-CHAR-WIDTH IS THE WIDTH OF A CHARACTER.  IT IS EXPRESSED
00067              *        IN INCHES.
00068              *     FORMAT-CHAR-HEIGHT IS THE HEIGHT OF A CHARACTER EXPRESSED IN
00069              *        INCHES.
00070              *     FORMAT-TOTAL-CHAR-SPACE IS THE TOTAL VERTICAL SPACE IN INCHES
00071              *        REQUIRED FOR A CHARACTER.  IT INCLUDES A FORMAT-CHAR
00072              *        BLANK-SPACE ABOVE THE CHARACTER. THE FORMAT-CHAR-HEIGHT, AND
00073              *        A FORMAT-CHAR-BLANK-SPACE BELOW THE CHARACTER.
00074              *     IF THE CHART IS NON-ROTATED. FORMAT-ORIENTATION = 0  AND IF
00075              *        THE CHART IS ROTATED. FORMAT-ORIENTATION = 90.
00076              *     FORMAT-LEFT-DESC-LEN IS THE SPACE IN INCHES FOR THE
00077              *        DESCRIPTORS WHICH APPEAR DOWN THE LEFT-HAND SIDE OF THE
00078              *        CHART.
00079              *     FORMAT-ORIGIN GIVES THE X AND Y COORDINATES OF THE UPPER LEFT
00080              *        HAND CORNER OF THE CHART WHERE PLOTTING BEGINS.
00081              *     FORMAT-X-SUBGROUP-GAP-PERCENT GIVES THE PERCENT OF A CHART-
00082              *        COL-WIDTH ALLOTTED FOR BLANK SPACE BETWEEN SUBGROUPS.
00083              *     FORMAT-NON-ABUTTED FACTOR IS THE PERCENT OF CHART COLUMN
00084              *        WIDTH BETWEEN BARS.
00085              *     SCALER PROCESSOR WORK
00086              *
00087                    05   FORMAT-DEPEND-INFO-TABLE.
00088                         10   FORMAT-CONSTANTS.
00089              *     FORMAT 01
00090                              15   FILLER                       PIC S9(02)V9(02) COMP
00091                                                                VALUE +1.0.
00092                              15   FILLER                       PIC S9(04)V9(04) COMP
00093                                                                VALUE +0.6.
00094                              15   FILLER                       PIC S9(04)V9(04) COMP
00095                                                                VALUE +0.1.
00096                              15   FILLER                       PIC S9(04)V9(04) COMP
00097                                                                VALUE +0.1.
```

Figure 9.4 Comment block explaining the function of the FORMAL-
DEPENDENT-INFORMATION TABLE in the vertical spacing directory program.

It is obvious from reading the instruction. This sort of documentation is useless and is to be avoided. It may even be detrimental to understandability.
Weinberg explains that the purpose of a comment is "to prepare the mind of
the reader for a proper interpretation of the instruction" [2]. If the instruction is correct, the comment may be helpful. If the instruction is clear as
well as correct, the comment is probably not necessary. But if the instruction
is incorrect, the comment may lead the reader mistakenly to believe that the
instruction is correct and in this way make the error more difficult to detect.

Instruction-level comments should be used only in exceptional circumstances, such as explaining an unusual or complex algorithm or highlight-
ing error-prone program segments and potential ambiguities. Whenever

instruction-level documentation is used, a blank line should be inserted before and after the comment to make it more prominent.

MEANINGFUL NAMES

It is obvious that meaningful names for variables improve program readability. For example, consider the following two COBOL COMPUTE statements:

```
COMPUTE EXPENSES = TRANSPORTATION + MEALS + LODGING
COMPUTE E = E1 + D2 + E3
```

The first COMPUTE statement conveys substantially more information about the program than the second because of the choice of variable names. Proper selection of variable names may be the single most important key to program readability [3].

The results of several programming experiments point out that the more complex a program, the more important meaningful names are to readability [1, pp. 72–74]. Yet many programmers persist in writing programs with meaningless or "cute" variable names (X10, JANE, ENTER-HEAVEN) that give no clue as to what the names logically represent. Why?

There are several possible reasons. The programmer was lazy. The programmer wanted to be cute or witty. The programmer was working against a tight deadline and could not take the time to think of meaningful names. The programmer learned to program using languages such as FORTRAN or BASIC in which the legal length for a variable name was severely limited and therefore not conducive to creating meaningful names. However, the most probable reason is that the programmer did not consider creating meaningful variable names important to building a quality program. Emphasis was placed on building a reliable, efficient program, but little thought was given to building a maintainable program.

This narrow view of program quality has greatly contributed to the development of unmaintainable programs. The value of meaningful variable names in creating understandable, maintainable programs cannot be overemphasized. This applies not only to variable names but also to all programmer-defined names used in a program—program names, paragraph names, procedure names, function names, subroutine names, file names, and so forth. Some general guidelines for choosing meaningful names are listed in Box 9.3.

INDENTATION

The rules for writing in a conventional language include paragraphing, spacing, and indenting guidelines to improve readability. Similar guidelines for writing programs are used to improve program readability. A basic principle of structured programming

BOX 9.3   Guidelines for choosing names

1. Choose names that suggest the logical function performed by a procedure or the purpose of the variable.

> COBOL: EMPLOYEE-NAME
> PL/1:   DEBIT_CHECKING

2. Do not create or use alias names.

3. Make each name unique by avoiding names that are visually similar. Names should differ by at least two characters to provide adequate psychological distances [2].

4. Avoid unnatural spellings for names.

> KATCH for CATCH

5. Take full advantage of what the language allows to create meaningful names.

> COBOL: YEAR-END-DEPRECIATION-ROUTINE

6. Use shorter, abbreviated names for local variables (such as loop indices or subscripts) that are frequently used. Use longer, more descriptive names for global variables that are rarely used [1, pp. 70–72].

7. Use a consistent abbreviation scheme (such as deletion of vowels) to shorten variable names when necessary [3].

> TOTAL →TTL
> DEPARTMENT→DPT

8. Use a common prefix to identify variables that are logically grouped together, such as all the data items contained in a file record or all the local variables belonging to a procedure.

> COBOL:
>
> 01   EMPL-RECORD.
>   05   EMPL-NAME   PIC X (30).
>   05   EMPL-ADDRESS   PIC X (25).

Box 9.3   *(Continued)*

9. Even when allowed, do not use key words of the language to create programmer-defined names.

> IF
> END
> UNTIL
> DO

10. Whenever possible, conform to the data names provided in the data dictionary, or obtain agreement from the data administrator for the names used.

is that standardization of the program form will improve its readability. Structured coding rules typically include the following:

1. Do not code more than one statement per line.

2. If a statement requires multiple lines, indent all continuation lines.

3. Indent the true and false portions of the selection structure to identify its scope more clearly.

4. Use an indentation scheme that accentuates the control structures used to direct statement execution order.

Several experiments have been performed to study the value of such indentation rules [1, pp. 66–90]. The results are quite surprising. It appears that indentation may not be as helpful in improving program readability as assumed. There are two problems:

1. Inappropriate indentation can disrupt program scanning.

2. Incorrect and/or inconsistent indentation can lead to great confusion.

Indentation may cause program statements to be continued on successive lines, making it more difficult to read the program code and to follow the program logic. For example, Shneiderman points out that in deeply nested programs, the code may be severely shifted to the right-hand side of the page [1, pp. 66–90]. Figure 9.5 illustrates how inappropriate indentation can distort program form.

```
IF  RP-CT = 1
    MOVE RP-Y-COOR TO CHART-Y-COOR
ELSE
    COMPUTE RP-SG-STORE = RP-CT - 1
    IF  CD-ROW-CHRTPIC = 59 OR 60 OR
        61 OR 62 OR 69
        SUBTRACT 2 FROM CHART-Y-COOR
        SUBTRACT 1 FROM RP-Y-COOR
    ELSE IF FORMAT-ORIENTATION = 90
            SUBTRACT 4 FROM
            CHART-Y-COOR
        ELSE IF FORMAT-ORIENTATION
            = 0
            IF CHART-FORMAT = 2
                COMPUTE RP-Y-COOR
                = 0
                IF CD-CHRTPIC-TYPE
                = 52
                SUBTRACT
                CHART-COL-WIDTH
                FROM RP-X-COOR
            ELSE IF
                CD-CHRTPIC-TYPE
                    NOT =
                CD-STORE-TYPE
                MOVE
                CD-CHRTPIC-TYPE
                TO
                CD-STORE-TYPE
                PERFORM
                CHANGE-TYPE
                ELSE
                    NEXT
                    SENTENCE
            ELSE
                MOVE 0 TO
                CHART-Y-COOR
        ELSE
            NEXT SENTENCE.
```

Figure 9.5 Indenting deeply nested code can make the code more difficult to read.

One solution is to limit the level of nesting. Usually, three levels is the maximum allowed in a well-structured program. The purpose of this restriction is to preserve readability and understandability. Beyond three levels, it becomes difficult to decipher the program logic.

Indentation can increase the reader's confidence in a program. However, this may be a liability as well as a benefit. It may lull the reader into assuming that the program logic must be correct since the programmer was well organized. Unfortunately, one does not follow the other. Neatness does not necessarily imply correctness.

Consider the following example of an actual COBOL coding error, which required several days to detect:

```
IF GRID-SWITCH = 'Y'
    IF ROW-COUNT = 01
        IF TYPE-CODE = 'A'
            PERFORM TITLE-PRINT
        ELSE
            PERFORM SCALE-PROCESS
    ELSE
        SET LINE-NO TO +1.
```

According to the indentation, it was the programmer's intention to execute the statement

```
SET LINE-NO TO +1
```

when the condition GRID-SWITCH = 'Y' is false. When scanning the code, a reader is likely to assume that the indentation correctly represents the code and interpret it as the programmer intended. However, this is *not* the correct interpretation. The COBOL compiler is oblivious to indentation and instead interprets the code according to the ANS COBOL language rule that for nested IF statements, each ELSE is paired with the first preceding IF that is not already paired with an ELSE. Therefore, the correct indentation is:

```
IF GRID-SWITCH = 'Y'
    IF ROW-COUNT = 01
        IF TYPE-CODE = 'A'
            PERFORM TITLE-PRINT
        ELSE
            PERFORM SCALE-PROCESS
    ELSE
        SET LINE-NO TO +1.
```

The statement

```
SET LINE-NO TO +1
```

is executed when the condition GRID-SWITCH = 'Y' is true and the condition ROW-COUNT = 01 is false. Had no indentation been used, the error might have been easier to detect.

The problems of incorrect indentation and inappropriate indentation can be easily solved by using automatic program formatters (e.g., ADR's

MetaCOBOL, General Research Corporation's RXVP for FORTRAN programs). Or as an alternative to indentation, blank lines can be inserted to highlight the scope of a control structure of functional unit [1, pp. 66–90].

CONSISTENT STYLE, STRUCTURED PROGRAMMING, AND HIGH-LEVEL CONTROL STRUCTURES

Again we can draw an analogy between conventional language and programming language. A consistent programming style is as important to program readability as a consistent writing style is to the readability of an article or a book. When the reader finds that a program is well organized and easy to understand, much of the hestitation to work with the program will disappear.

Because of its emphasis on a consistent, standardized program form, structured programming is a powerful technique for improving program readability. The underlying structured philosophy is quite simple. By using the same form to define a control structure or a module, communication is less susceptible to misunderstanding.

The structured philosophy also advocates the use of the highest possible control structure available in a language. For example, the DO-WHILE structure rather than to GOTO statement is used to implement a loop in a well-structured program. Higher-level control structures decrease program complexity by reducing the number of instructions needed and by imposing a format with a single entry point and single exit point. The latter is the real reason the use of the GOTO statement is restricted in structured programs.

In the 1970s, Dijkstra and others proposed that the GOTO statement be banned as a legal control structure from higher-level programming languages because it is too primitive to be useful as an independent control structure [4]. Its primary use in programs is as a backward branch to create a loop structure. Rather than rebuild a control structure already provided by the language, the programmer should use the highest-level structure available for the sake of program clarity, correctness, and consistency.

Another criticism of the GOTO is that it provides the programmer with an opportunity to obscure program readability. One can easily incorporate afterthoughts into a program by means of forward and backward branches instead of rearranging the program so that the physical occurrence of the code for these modifications reflects their conceptual meaning. In other words, the use of the GOTO statement tends to violate the "principle of locality," which states that the physical placement of program statements should reflect the dynamic flow of the executing program. Such violations lead to "spaghetti" logic. Figure 9.6 shows how spaghetti logic can complicate even a 75-line program. A program that is initially well structured may deteriorate into "spaghetti" code if GOTOs are used to haphazardly insert a "quick fix" into the code.

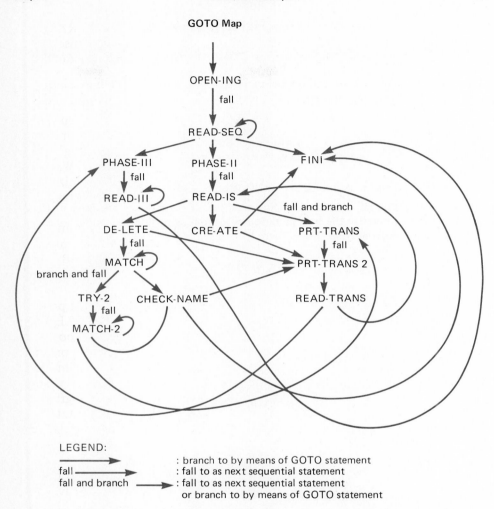

GOTO Map

LEGEND:

──────▶	: branch to by means of GOTO statement
fall ──────▶	: fall to as next sequential statement
fall and branch ──────▶	: fall to as next sequential statement or branch to by means of GOTO statement

Figure 9.6 Because of haphazardly used GOTOs, this 75-line COBOL program has become a mass of "spaghetti" logic.

Finally, use of the GOTO is criticized because it can destroy module independence if the scope of the GOTO is allowed to cross module boundaries (e.g., a branch from one module into the "middle" of another module).

Results from programming experiments conducted to study the use of control structures support Dijkstra's position [1, pp. 66–90]. The more GOTO statements in a program, the more errors the program is likely to have. Higher-level control structures appear to be easier to comprehend, easier to modify, and less error-prone because they have a higher semantic level and avoid machine-related issues. Also, programmers have expressed

BOX 9.4 Program style guidelines

- Use one syntactic form throughout a program [1, pp. 66–90]. For example, in a COBOL program do not use

$$>$$
GREATER THAN
IS GREATER THAN

Choose one format and use it consistently.

- Use parentheses consistently. For example, if parentheses are used in a program to clarify the interpretation of arithmetic or Boolean expressions, always use parentheses. Do not write

$$A < B < C / (D * E * F)$$

and

$$(G * H) / (K * P)$$

in the same COBOL program.
Do not write

$$(X .LT. 0) .OR. Z$$

and

$$A + B .GT. C$$

in the same FORTRAN program.

- Use abbreviations consistently. This rule applies to programmer-defined names, conditions, key words, noise words, and so forth. For example, do not write

IF TYPE-CODE = 2 OR 3 OR 10

and

IF   TYPE-CODE = 2 OR
        TYPE-CODE = 3 OR
        TYPE-CODE = 10

Box 9.4　*(Continued)*

---

in the same COBOL program.
　　Do not write

　　　　　　　　PIC and PICTURE IS

in the same COBOL program.

---

a preference for using higher-level control structures because they improve readability [5].

The structured philosophy is applicable to any programming language—from assembly language to very high-level languages. For example, in FORTRAN the loop structure is implemented with the DO statement, in COBOL with the PERFORM statement, and in PL/1 with the DO statement.

In addition to following the structured programming prescripts for consistency and standardization, a consistent programming style should also be applied when using other programming language structures. Some guidelines are listed in Box 9.4.

REFERENCES

1. B. Shneiderman, *Software Psychology* (Cambridge, MA: Winthrop Publishers, Inc., 1980).

2. G. Weinberg, *The Psychology of Computer Programming* (New York: Van Nostrand Reinhold Company, 1971), pp. 162–164.

3. D. Van Tassel, *Program Style, Design, Efficiency, Debugging, and Testing* (Englewood Cliffs, NJ: Prentice-Hall, Inc., 1978), pp. 1–40.

4. C. McClure, *Reducing COBOL Complexity Through Structured Programming* (New York: Van Nostrand Reinhold Company, 1978), pp. 131–136.

5. C. McClure, *Managing Software Development and Maintenance* (New York: Van Nostrand Reinhold Company, 1978), pp. 13–22.

PART  THE METHODOLOGY REVOLUTION

10 MAKING THE MICE GO AWAY

INTRODUCTION Structured programming and structured design when well executed have a major effect on maintenance costs. For years now, the creators of structured techniques have been trying to make a better mousetrap.

Perhaps our favorite paper on structured techniques is one by G. D. Bergland of the Bell Telephone Laboratories [1]. Bergland describes the program maintenance traumas at McDonald's frozen-food warehouse. (McDonald's in this story is entirely fictional and originally appeared in Michael Jackson seminars.)

The warehouse receives and distributes food items. These items are recorded on punched cards that are sorted by item name. A program must be designed which produces a management report once a week, showing the net change in inventory of each item, as illustrated in Fig. 10.1

Bergland shows four structured approaches to this problem and uses it to illustrate the relative merits of the methods. We will illustrate only the maintenance consequences of the approaches. (Readers interested in structured techniques will find much valuable insight in the paper that we do not try to convey in this chapter.) It might be thought that such a simple application would have no hidden problems, but as we shall see, there are subtle traps for the unwary.

The four approaches are:

1. Hierarchical functional decomposition
2. The data flow design method
3. Data structure design (Jackson methodology)
4. Programming calculus (advocated by Dijkstra)

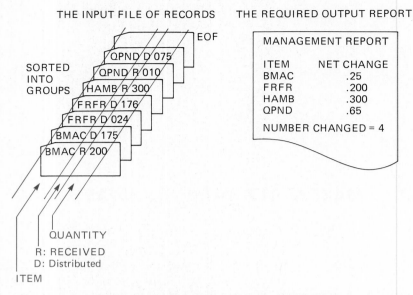

THE INPUT FILE OF RECORDS   THE REQUIRED OUTPUT REPORT

EOF

QPND D 075
QPND R 010
HAMB R 300
FRFR D 176
FRFR D 024
BMAC D 175
BMAC R 200

SORTED
INTO
GROUPS

MANAGEMENT REPORT

ITEM	NET CHANGE
BMAC	.25
FRFR	.200
HAMB	.300
QPND	.65

NUMBER CHANGED = 4

QUANTITY
R: RECEIVED
D: Distributed
ITEM

Figure 10.1   Input and output of the McDonald's warehouse program.

HIERARCHICAL FUNCTIONAL DECOMPOSITION

The hero of the first approach is named Ivan. Let us tell the story in Bergland's own words [1]:

"Ivan is a very 'with it' fellow. He swore off GOTO's years ago. His code is structured like the Eiffel Tower. He can whip out a neatly indented structured program in nothing flat. In doing his design, Ivan was careful to do the five-level, hierarchical, functional decomposition shown in Fig. 10.2

"In this figure, PRODUCE REPORT is shown to be a sequence of PRODUCE HEADING followed by PRODUCE BODY followed by PRODUCE SUMMARY. PRODUCE BODY is shown to be an iteration of PROCESS CARD that is a selection between PROCESS THE FIRST CARD IN GROUP and PROCESS SUBSEQUENT CARD IN GROUP.

"Ivan approached the problem in stages corresponding to the five levels of decomposition shown above:

- First stage (level 1):

```
P:  PRODUCE REPORT;
    STOP;
```

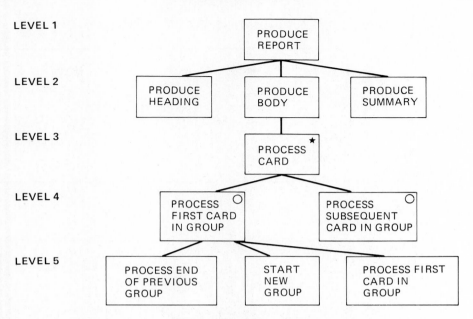

LEVEL 1

LEVEL 2

LEVEL 3

LEVEL 4

LEVEL 5

Figure 10.2 Five-level functional decomposition.

● Second stage (level 2):

```
P:  PRODUCE HEADING;
    PRODUCE BODY;
    PRODUCE SUMMARY;
    STOP;
```

● Third stage (level 3):

```
P:  PRODUCE HEADING;
        READ STF;
        DO WHILE (NOT EOF-STF);
            PROCESS CARD;
            READ STF;
        END;
    PRODUCE SUMMARY;
    STOP;
```

● Fourth stage (level 4), now looking more like a finished product:

```
P:      PRODUCE HEADING;
        READ STF;
        DO WHILE (NOT EOF-STF);
            IF FIRST CARD IN GROUP THEN
                PROCESS FIRST CARD IN GROUP;
                ELSE PROCESS SUBSEQUENT CARD IN GROUP;
            READ STF;
        END;
     PRODUCE SUMMARY;
     STOP;
```

● Final stage (level 5):

```
P:      PRODUCE HEADING;
        READSTF;
        DO WHILE (NOT EOF-STF);
            IF FIRST CARD IN GROUP THEN
                DO:
                    PROCESS END OF PREVIOUS GROUP;
                    PROCESS START OF NEW GROUP;
                    PROCESS CARD;
                END;
            ELSE DO: PROCESS CARD;
                END;
            READ STF;
        END;
     PRODUCE SUMMARY;
     STOP;
```

"Ivan, being very thorough, volume tested his program and turned it over to the users, completely satisfied. Anything beyond this point is called 'maintenance.'

"The program worked well except that some garbage appeared on the first line of the output immediately after the headings. The systems programmers were tinkering with the compiler at the time and Ivan naturally assumed that the garbage would not be there when the compiler was fixed.

"The user was friendly and full of gratitude for the program, so he did not complain about a mere line of garbage characters. It gave the reports a slightly futuristic look appropriate to the computer age. When the reports went to the Board of Directors three months later, they were not so friendly. The problem had to be fixed.

"When the user came down, Ivan was in his cubicle listening to an audio cassette of Dijkstra's Turing lecture. He of course didn't learn anything;

```
P:      PRODUCE HEADING;
        SW1:=0;
             READSTF;
             DO  WHILE (NOT EOF-STF);
                    IF FIRST CARD IN GROUP THEN
                           DO;  IF SW1=1 THEN
                                  DO; PROCESS END OF PREVIOUS GROUP;
                                  END; SW1:=1;
                                        PROCESS START OF NEW GROUP;
                                        PROCESS CARD;
                           END;
                    ELSE DO; PROCESS CARD;
                           END;
                    READ STF;
             END;
        PRODUCE SUMMARY;
        STOP;
```

Figure 10.3   Quick fix 1.

that's the way he had always done his designs. The user showed Ivan a printout.

"After a few MMMs and AAAHHHHs and AAAHHHAAAs, he saw the problem. The first time through the program there was no previous group. Thus the output was just random data. The solution to any first-time-through problem is of course obvious. Add a first-time switch (see Fig. 10.3).

"Six months later our hero was in the McDonald's 'think room' when the user came in and said, 'I put 80 transactions in last week and nothing came out!' Our hero looked at the printout and saw that, indeed, only the heading had come out.

"Ivan knew what the problem was immediately. It must be a hardware problem. After all, his program had been running nearly a year now with only one small complaint.

"Ivan spent most of the night running hardware diagnostics until Steve Saintly (a keypunch operator) wandered by and said, 'With that nation-wide special on Big Macs last week, that's all we handled. Everything else has to wait.'

"A little later, Sally Saintly came by and said, 'Isn't it about time you included those new Zebra Sodas in the Management Report?'

"By this time, Ivan was very discouraged with his diagnostics, so he followed last week's inputs through the code.

"HORRORS! There was only one item group processed last week. Big Macs!

"As Ivan soon discovered, the last item group was never processed. Since only one item group was processed all week (Big Macs), nothing was output. Up until this time only Zebra Sodas had been skipped. Since they were not a big winner, it seems that no one had even cared that they had been left off. In fact everyone assumed they were being left off on purpose. Ivan's solution is shown in Fig. 10.4.

"Meanwhile Sally Saintly asked, 'Why didn't you see that during all the volume testing you did? You tied up the machine for most of a day.'

"The answer again is obvious. In volume testing you put in thousands of inputs but don't look at the output.

"*Passing the Baton.* Six months later Ivan was feeling pretty pleased with himself. He had just turned the program over to a new hire. There would still be some training, but everything should go well. After all, hadn't the program run for nearly a year and one-half with only a couple of small problems? Suddenly the user burst in, 'I thought you fixed this first-line problem and here it is again.'

"Ivan knew immediately what the problem was. The new program librarian whom they had forced him to use had put in an old version of the program that didn't have his first patch in it.

"After many heated comments plus a core dump, Ivan was still baffled. Finally, in desperation, he sat down to look at the input data and found that there wasn't any. Last week a trucker's strike had shut down the warehouse. Nothing came in. Nothing went out. They ran the program anyway. Good grief, who would have thought they would run the program with no inputs!

"The problem, as it turns out, was that the new PROCESS END OF LAST GROUP module needed protection just like the PROCESS END OF

```
P:     PRODUCE HEADING;
       SW1:=0;
           READSTF;
           DO WHILE (NOT EOF-STF);
               IF FIRST CARD IN GROUP THEN
                   DO; IF SW1=1 THEN
                         DO; PROCESS END OF PREVIOUS GROUP;
                       END; SW1:=1;
                           PROCESS START OF NEW GROUP;
                           PROCESS CARD;
                   END;
               ELSE DO; PROCESS CARD;
                   END;
               READ STF;
           END;
                                   PROCESS END OF LAST GROUP;
       PRODUCE SUMMARY;
       STOP;
```

Figure 10.4   Quick fix 2.

```
P:      PRODUCE HEADING;
        SW1:=0;SW2:=0;
            READSTF;
            DO WHILE (NOT EOF-STF);
                IF FIRST CARD IN GROUP THEN
                    DO; IF SW1=1 THEN
                            DO; PROCESS END OF PREVIOUS GROUP;
                        END; SW1:=1;
                                PROCESS START OF NEW GROUP;
                                PROCESS CARD;
                    END;
                ELSE DO; PROCESS CARD;SW2:=1;
                    END;
                READ STF;
            END;IF SW2=1 THEN
                DO; PROCESS END OF LAST GROUP;
                END;
        PRODUCE SUMMARY;
        STOP;
```

Figure 10.5   Quick fix 3.

PREVIOUS GROUP module had before. Since that first-time switch worked so nicely before, it's clearly the solution to apply again (see Fig. 10.5).

"We all know now that Ivan's troubles are all over. Or are they? Two months later Sally Saintly came in and said, 'Where are the Zippo sandwiches?' They were in for two months, but now they've suddenly disappeared from the report.

"After complaining that the new hire was supposed to be maintaining that program now, Ivan looked at the input data and noticed that only one order per item had been issued during the whole run.

"'What happened?' he exclaimed.

"It seems that a new manager, Mary Starr, had started a new policy to try to get things better organized. She had asked each of the stores to place only one order a day instead of placing orders at random. In addition she had said that it would be nice if they could schedule things so that each day the warehouse only had to be concerned with receiving one particular item, and the next day with distributing that item. In addition she wanted the management report program run once a day from now on. The effect on Ivan's program was to drop Zippo sandwiches.

"Instead of moving the set of SW2, the safest thing to do according to the principles of defensive programming is to add an extra set. Since you don't know what you're doing you never touch a previous fix, just add a new one (see Fig. 10.6).

"Now we can all rest assured that Ivan's program works, right?

"The effect of all these changes on the program structure is shown in Fig. 10.7."

```
P:     PRODUCE HEADING;
       SW1:=0; SW2:=0;
           READSTF;
           DO WHILE (NOT EOF-STF);
               IF FIRST CARD IN GROUP THEN
                   DO; IF SW1=1 THEN
                           DO; PROCESS END OF PREVIOUS GROUP;
                       END; SW1:=1;
                               PROCESS START OF NEW GROUP;
                               PROCESS CARD;
                               SW2:=1;
                   END;
               ELSE DO; PROCESS CARD; SW2:=1;
                   END;
               READ STF;
           END; IF SW2=1 THEN
                   DO; PROCESS END OF LAST GROUP;
                   END;
           PRODUCE SUMMARY;
           STOP;
```

Figure 10.6   Quick fix 4.

This story clearly shows the need for better-structured techniques. It is alarming to reflect that Ivan knew more about structured design than many programmers in practice.

THE DATA FLOW DESIGN METHOD

Constantine first proposed the data flow design method [2]. Myers [3] and Yourdon [2] extended it and advocated its use. This type of structuring defines blocks as black boxes which transform an input stream into an output data stream. The data flow graph for the McDonald's problem is shown on the left of Fig. 10.8. This is translated into a hierarchical program structure on the right of Fig. 10.8.

Bergland describes McDonald's second attempt to obtain the inventory reporting programs [1]:

"The heroine who designed the next program was Ivan's sister, Ivy. Ivy is a child of the late 60s. When modular programming came she jumped right on the bandwagon. Her modules had only one extrance and one exit. She passed all her parameters in each call statement. Each of her modules performs only a single logical task, is independent, and can be separately tested. She reads daily from the gospel according to Harlan Mills [4].

"Ivy's program listing is shown in Fig. 10.9.

"Only three of the six modules are shown. The TRANSFORM CARD IMAGES TO CARD GROUP module was lexically included in the GET CARD GROUP module. The other two modules are not necessary for this

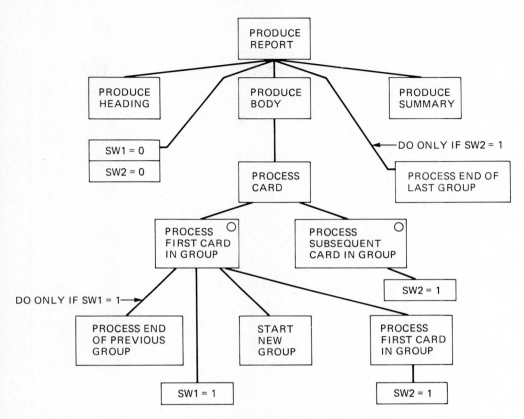

Figure 10.7 Functional decomposition with quick fixes.

particular discussion. Note for starters that the READ CARD module leaves much to be desired.

"*Program Testing.* Ivy has learned to make good use of a program librarian. She wrote the program, gave the coding sheets to the librarian, and went back to her reading. The program librarian faithfully executed his duties and brought back a printout saying, 'CRITEM undefined.'

"It seems that Ivy had forgotten to make sure all her variables had been initialized. Oh well, this should be easy. How about setting CRITEM:=XXXX at the beginning of the GET CARD GROUP module? That would be before CRITEM was used the first time and sort of has a symmetry about it with the way EOG (end of group) is initialized.

"Unfortunately, something just didn't seem right about it. GET CARD GROUP gets executed many times during the program and CRITEM only needs to be initialized once.

"Ivy decided to initialize CRITEM at the beginning instead. Of course,

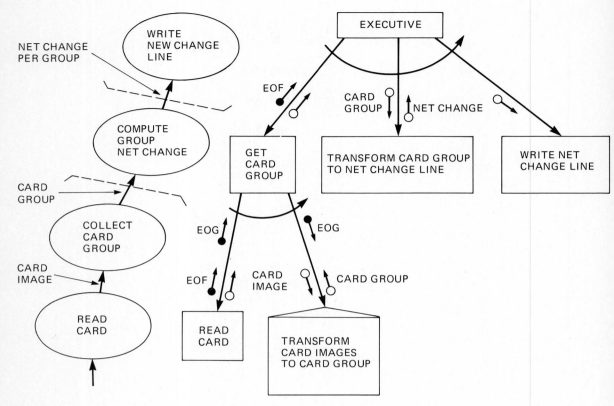

Figure 10.8 Data flow design structure.

```
EXECUTIVE: EOF:=FALSE;
    DO WHILE(EOF=FALSE);
        GET_CARD_GROUP(CG,EOF              );
        TRANSFORM_CG_TO_NC_LINE(CG,NC);
        WRITE_NC_LINE(NC,EOF);
    END;                    STOP;
GET_CARD_GROUP(CG,EOF             ): EOG:=FALSE;1:=0;
    DO WHILE (EOG=FALSE); I:=I+1;
        READ_CARD(C1,EOG,EOF             );CG(I):=CI;
    END;            RETURN;
READ_CARD(CI,EOG,EOF             );
    NEW_CARD:=READ STF;
        IF NEW_CARD_ITEM≠CRITEM THEN
            DO;EOG; = TRUE; CRITEM=NEW_CARD_ITEM;
                        END;
        ELSE      CI:=NEW_CARD;
        IF CI=EOF_STF_THEN EOF:=TRUE; RETURN;
```

Figure 10.9 Data flow design program.

224

that does mean passing it as a parameter up two levels just for being initialized, but that certainly sounds better than a bunch of first-time switches (see Fig. 10.10).

"On the next run, Ivy's efforts were rewarded with some output. Nothing fancy but still some output.

"'What happened to the heading?' exclaimed Ivy. 'That data link must be dropping bits again.'

"'Where did you write out the heading?' asked the program librarian. Enter quick fix 2.

"'Wait, what about that garbage in the front?'

"The problem, of course, is that the program has no way of knowing when it's through with a group until it's already started processing the next group. Thus the first card of a new group serves as a key to tell the rest of the program to send on the previous group. It can't do this, however, without distorting the structure.

"'I think it's time to call out my secret weapon,' said Ivy, 'my UN-READ command.' Enter quick fix 3 (see Fig. 10.11).

"One of the problems in maintenance is that different programmers have different styles. Here we have the same program written by brother and sister (Fig. 10.6 and 10.11) and both think they are doing the best structuring with hierarchical design. If one were to maintain the other's programs there could be still more trouble ahead.

"Ivy's program in Fig. 10.11 worked fine for a few months—not too speedy, but it did work. Then another type of maintenance problem struck:

```
EXECUTIVE: EOF:=FALSE;
     CRITEM:=XXXX;
     DO WHILE(EOF=FALSE);
          GET_CARD_GROUP(CG,EOF,CRITEM          );
          TRANSFORM_CG_TO_NC_LINE(CG,NC);
          WRITE_NC_LINE(NC,EOF);
     END;                     STOP;
GET_CARD_GROUP(CG,EOF,CRITEM          ): EOG:=FALSE;I:=0;
     DO WHILE(EOG=FALSE); I:=I+1;
          READ_CARD(CI,EOG,EOF,CRITEM          );CG(I)=CI;
     END;                     RETURN;
READ_CARD(CI,EOG,EOF,CRITEM          );
     NEW_CARD:=READ STF;
          IF NEW_CARD_ITEM≠CRITEM THEN
               DO;EOG:=TRUE;CRITEM=NEW_CARD_ITEM;
               END;
          ELSE      CI:=NEW_CARD;
          IF CI=EOF_STF THEN EOF:=TRUE; RETURN;
```

Figure 10.10   Quick fix 1.

```
EXECUTIVE: EOF:=FALSE; WRITE HEADING;
      CRITEM:=XXXX;
      DO WHILE(EOF=FALSE);
            GET_CARD_GROUP(CG,EOF,CRITEM       );
            TRANSFORM_CG_TO_NC_LINE(CG,NC);
            WRITE_NC_LINE(NC,EOF);
      END;                    STOP;
GET_CARD_GROUP(CG,EOF,CRITEM       ): EOG:=FALSE;I:=0;
      DO WHILE(EOG=FALSE); I:=I+1;
            READ_CARD(CI,EOG,EOF,CRITEM       );CG(I)=CI;
      END;                    RETURN;
READ_CARD(CI,EOG,EOF,CRITEM       );
      NEW_CARD:=READ STF;
      IF NEW_CARD_ITEM≠CRITEM THEN
            DO;EOG:=TRUE;CRITEM=NEW_CARD_ITEM;
            UNREAD STF; END;
      ELSE       CI:=NEW_CARD;
      IF CI=EOF_STF THEN EOF:=TRUE; RETURN;
```

Figure 10.11   Quick fixes 2 and 3.

"All of a sudden a visit from on high. Big Mac himself came down and said, 'Our people in Provo, Utah, have been trying to bring up your program and it just doesn't work'.

"It turns out that in Provo they never did find it necessary to buy a tape reader. Ivy's UNREAD operation didn't work on cards. This meant that Ivy had to find another way of UNREADing.

"In this data flow design, the equivalent of an UNREAD is messy at best. It corrupts the structure badly, no matter how it's done. Modules end up storing internal states or values, and first-time switches abound.

"In Ivy's case, she chose to read ahead by one, passing state information by SW1 and storing the NEW CARD value within module READ CARD. Other solutions are possible, of course, but it isn't clear that they are a whole lot better (see Fig. 10.12).

"The effect of these changes on the program structure is shown dramatically in Fig. 10.13.

"Ivy has now deviated from a pure tree-structured program. This will make it more difficult for other maintainers to follow. What had been a clean tree structure now has two modules calling the READ CARD module. Some authorities are adamant that deviations from hierarchical program structures should not be allowed. Michael Jackson would say that Ivy has committed *arboricide.*"

```
EXECUTIVE: EOF:=FALSE; WRITE HEADING; SW1:=FALSE;
     CRITEM:=XXXX; READ_CARD(CI,EOG,EOF,CRITEM,SW1);
     DO WHILE(EOF=FALSE);
          GET_CARD_GROUP(CG,EOF,CRITEM,SW1);
          TRANSFORM_CG_TO_NC_LINE(CG,NC);
          WRITE_NC_LINE(NC,EOF);
     END;                    STOP;
GET_CARD_GROUP(CG,EOF,CRITEM,SW1): EOG:=FALSE;I:=0;
     DO WHILE(EOG=FALSE); I:=I+1;
          READ_CARD(CI,EOG,EOF,CRITEM,SW1);CG(I):=CI;
     END;SW1:=TRUE; RETURN;
READ_CARD(CI,EOG,EOF,CRITEM,SW1): IF SW1=FALSE THEN
     NEW_CARD:=READ STF;
          IF NEW_CARD_ITEM≠CRITEM THEN
               DO;EOG:=TRUE;CRITEM=NEW_CARD_ITEM;
               SW1:=TRUE;           END;
          ELSE DO; CI:=NEW_CARD;SW1:=FALSE;END;
          IF CI=EOF_STF THEN EOF:=TRUE; RETURN;
```

Figure 10.12   Quick fix 4.

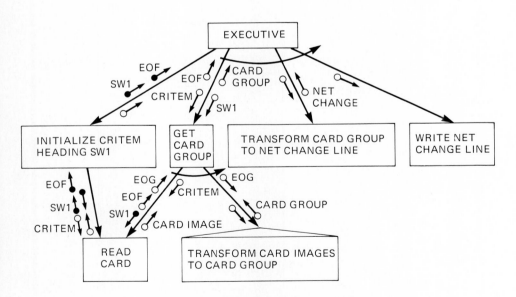

Figure 10.13   Data flow design with fixes.

MICHAEL JACKSON METHODOLOGY   In Michael Jackson's *data structure design* method of programming the program views the world through its data structures [5]. Correct representations of input data and output data lead to precise structures of programs.

Figures 10.14 and 10.15 illustrate this. In Fig. 10.14 are Jackson representations of the data structures which are the input and output of the McDonald's inventory report program. Red lines show one-to-one correspondences between the input and output. REPORT on the right corresponds to SORTED TRANSACTION FILE on the left. In other words, one SORTED TRANSACTION FILE produces one REPORT. Similarly, one ITEM GROUP produces one REPORT LINE.

From these data structures a corresponding program structure is created which encompasses all parts of each data structure. This is shown in Fig. 10.15. Where there are one-to-one correspondences between the input and output, the program block says CONSUME input PRODUCE output. This block in the level below may be broken into more detail, showing computational operations or algorithms which link input and output.

Figure 10.16 shows executable operations allocated to the program

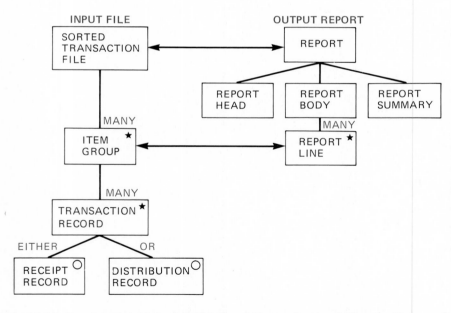

Figure 10.14 Input and output of the McDonald's warehouse problem (a diagram of the data shown in Fig. 10.1) drawn using the Michael Jackson structuring method. The red lines show one-to-one correspondence between input and output.

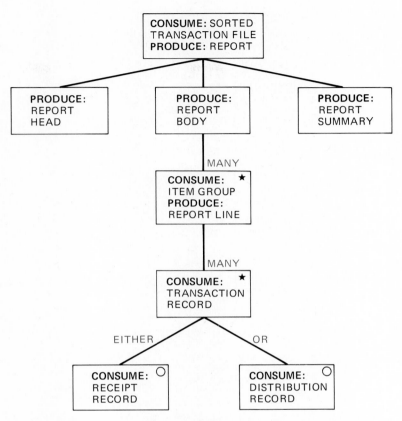

Figure 10.15 Program structure produced from the data structures shown in Fig. 10.15 (Michael Jackson methodology).

structure of Fig. 10.15. Jackson methodology provides rules for checking both this allocation and the program structure.

Figure 10.17 shows the McDonald's program converted to structured text.

Figure 10.18 shows the structure text converted into a program.

Jackson methodology helps to avoid the problems mentioned in the earlier versions of the program. Major users of the methodology claim that, at least for straightforward data processing, it leads to code with fewer problems than the other forms of structuring in common use. When conscientiously adhered to and documented it can make maintenance easier *if* the maintainers are also trained in the methodology. In the United States there are, however, far fewer programmers trained in this technique than in other structured techniques.

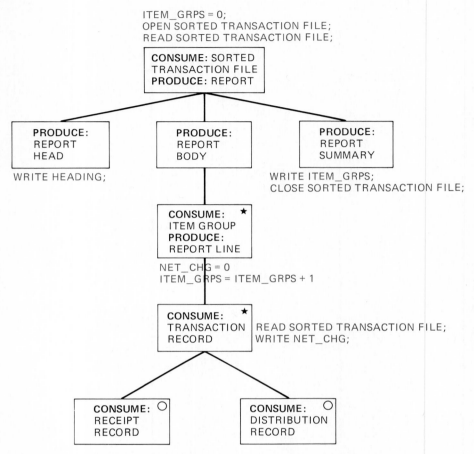

Figure 10.16 Executable operations allocated to the program structure of Fig. 10.15.

PROGRAMMING CALCULUS

Bergland's last version of the McDonald's program is mathematically structured. It uses programming calculus as advocated by Dijkstra [6, 7]. Bergland does not describe how any of the characters at McDonald's used it (presumably because none of them could understand it).

The program is elegant, but few maintainers could preserve the elegance when changes are needed. We will not indulge in a lengthy explanation of the mathematics here, but the following final version of the program gives the flavor of skills needed:

```
P seq
    item_grps:=0;
    open stf; read stf;
    write heading;
    P-BODY itr until (eof-stf)
        C-ITEM-GRP-P-REPT-LINE seq
            net_chg:=0;
            item_grps:=item_grps+1;
            critem:=next item;
            PRLBDY itr while (next item=critem);
                C-TRANS-REC seq
                    CTRBDY sel (code=R)
                        net_chg:=net_chg+qty;
                    CTRBDY alt (code=D)
                        net_chg:=net_chg-qty;
                    CTRBDY end
                    read stf;
                C-TRANS-REC end
            PRLBDY end
            write net_chg;
        C-ITEM-GRP-P-REPT-LINE end
    P-BODY end
    write item_grps; close stf;
P end
```

Figure 10.17　Structure text derived from the structure in Fig. 10.16.

$$\hat{m},i,\hat{c}:=1,0,0;$$
$$\{P\}$$
$$\textbf{do } \hat{m} \neq m \rightarrow$$
$$\quad \textbf{if } f(\hat{m})=f(\hat{m}+1) \rightarrow \hat{c}:=\hat{c}+q(\hat{m})$$
$$\quad \textbf{|} f(\hat{m})\neq f(\hat{m}+1) \rightarrow i:=i+1;c(i):=\hat{c}+q(\hat{m});\hat{c}:=0$$
$$\quad \textbf{fi};$$
$$\quad \hat{m}:=\hat{m}+1 \; \{P\} \; \bullet$$
$$\textbf{od}$$
$$\{R\}$$

The desired result R and invariant P are expressed separately.

Dijkstra's programming calculus is an important development in the theory of programming. However, it requires considerable mathematical maturity for even the most simple program. It is not used for large, complex programs.

MAKING THE MICE GO AWAY

Of the four approaches, it appears that in today's commercial practice Jackson's methodology leads to the most error-free code and to the most maintainable code if the documentation contains thorough diagrams and structure text, and also if the maintainers are experienced in the technique.

```
PB:             item_grps:=0;
                open stf;
                read stf;
                write heading;
PBB:            do while (not eof-stf);
                    net_chg:=0;
                    item_grps:=item_grps+1;
                    critem:=next item;
PRLBB:          do while (next item=critem);
CTRBB:              if (code=R) then
                        net_chg:=net_chg+qty;
                    else if (code=D) then
CTRBE:                  net_chg:=net_chg-qty;
                    read stf;
PRLBE:          end;
                write net_chg;
PBE:            end;
                write summary;
PE:             close stf;
```

Figure 10.18   Final data structure design program.

But now we want to explain why we gave this chapter such a strange title. The search for better structuring techniques, immensely important in the computer industry, is like the search for a better mousetrap. Suppose that we could find a different type of solution that would make the mice go away—avoid the need for programming in a language such as COBOL or PL/1 with the attendant problems we have described.

New ways to create programs are now coming into existence. Much conventional programming for commercial DP can be avoided with new types of facilities—report generators, query languages, application generators, and nonprocedural languages which permit the description of a result required rather than a step-by-step program for obtaining the result.

These new facilities avoid most of the problems described in this chapter, and give results which are much easier to change. In many cases the new facilities are so simple to use that end users employ them, generating and modifying their own files and reports.

How could the McDonald's problem have been solved with these facilities?

NOMAD   NOMAD2, a language marketed by National CSS,
                                   employs a relational data-base management system

and a variety of commands for manipulating data in the data base [8]. In our example the warehouse deck of cards is not a data base. It is an external file called WAREHOUSE. We tell this to NOMAD by saying

```
MASTER WAREHOUSE EXTERNALFILE
```

We can then use report generator commands which are both easy to use and powerful. The user typically adjusts the format of his reports interactively until he likes the result, and then catalogs the procedure. We do not have to bother about which is the first card or end of file. The software takes care of such considerations.

The cards in Fig. 10.1 contain three fields. The programmer defines these as follows:

```
MASTER WAREHOUSE EXTERNALFILE

    ITEM PRODUCT A4
    ITEM STATUS A1
    ITEM QUANTITY 999
```

He may go to define two more fields for the quantities received and distributed, thus:

```
DEFINE RECEIVED AS 99,999 = (IF CODE = 'R'
    THEN QUANTITY ELSE 0)
DEFINE DISTRIBUTED AS 99,999 = (IF CODE = 'D'
    THEN QUANTITY ELSE 0)
```

What we have done so far is rather like the Data Division of COBOL except that with NOMAD we only have to do it once, as with a data-base dictionary; with COBOL it has to be rewritten in each program. Furthermore, the COBOL Data Division cannot include dynamic statements such as IF CODE = 'R' THEN . . .

The programmer (or end user) may now write statements which do calculations, sort and merge the data, generate reports, plot charts, and so on. For the report needed here he may write:

```
DATABASE WAREHOUSE
LIST UNIQUE (PRODUCT) SET &PROD
    BY PRODUCT SUM (RECEIVED) SET &REC
            SUM (DISTRIBUTED) SET &DIST
            (&REC-&DIST) HEADING 'NET-CHANGE'
TITLE 'MCDONALD'S WAREHOUSE REPORT'
FOOTING 'NUMBER CHANGED = ' &PROD
```

This is the complete program (whereas the earlier ones in this chapter were not complete). &xxx refers to temporary variables kept for the duration of this run.

The factors that caused problems earlier in this chapter have simply gone away—end-of-last-group problems, garbage headings, groups with no entries, clumsy switches, "unreading," first and last card problems. The software deals with such problems automatically. The resulting report can be adjusted in minutes to change its format, produce statistics, alter the heading, and so on. Most maintenance is simple and speedy.

RAMIS   A diversity of other languages are similarly powerful. RAMIS II, from Mathematica Products Group [9], would solve the problem as follows. After the three fields on each card are declared, three extra fields are defined, thus:

```
DEFINE FILE WAREHOUSE:
RECEIVED/I9 = IF CODE IS 'R' THEN QUANTITY ELSE 0;
DISTRIBUTED/I9 = IF CODE IS 'D' THEN QUANTITY ELSE 0;
NET_CHANGE/I9 = RECEIVED - DISTRIBUTED:
END;
```

A variety of reports can then be created with code such as the following:

```
TABLE
'MCDONDALD'S WAREHOUSE REPORT'
FILE WAREHOUSE
SUM RECEIVED AND DISTRIBUTED AND NET_CHANGE
AS 'INCREASE, (DECREASE)' EDIT PARENS
BY PRODUCT
END
```

Again this solves the whole problem. The body of the report consists of four columns: PRODUCT, RECEIVED, DISTRIBUTED, and NET CHANGE. The first three columns take the relevant fieldname as their default titles. The fourth column is given a two-line title:

```
INCREASE
(DECREASE)
```

and is edited so that negative values are enclosed in parentheses.

The report is sequenced by PRODUCT (independent of the order of the file) and SUMmed to produce one line per PRODUCT. The report is followed by a message indicating the number of cards read and report lines produced. As with NOMAD, such operations as numbering the pages of the reports, and repeating the title at the head of each page, are done automatically.

EASE OF MAINTENANCE

In DP installations everywhere today one finds programmers writing COBOL or PL/1 programs that need careful structuring, when a higher-level language would give direct results simply. Not only does the very high level language permit results to be obtained in a tenth of the time, but the results are usually free from subtle errors and can be easily modified. Debugging maintenance largely disappears and enhancement maintenance becomes easy, fast, and inexpensive. The problems discussed in the body of the chapter mostly go away.

The new techniques are not appropriate for all applications, but they *are* appropriate for the majority of commercial data processing. The new languages have a rich set of functions which can be used, and usually allow exits into COBOL or lower-level code where routines are needed that require such code.

UNLEARNING THE OLD TECHNIQUES

Languages such as NOMAD and RAMIS are often employed by *end users*. Where this happens the rule should be applied that users do their own enhancement maintenance. In practice, where this approach has spread it has resulted in users adapting computing to their own needs much better than is common with classical DP.

A curious phenomenon can be observed with this form of application development. Experienced programmers using the new languages often write worse code than end users who have learned to employ computers for the first time. The reason is that experienced programmers still tend to think in COBOL-like terms, or apply the reasoning of the body of this chapter. NOMAD professionals sometimes refer to NOMAD programs written by old COBOL programmers as "NOBOL" programs!

We gave the McDonald's warehouse program to a senior systems consultant who is now a representative for a language similar to NOMAD and RAMIS. The result he produced is the following:

```
DO PRINT_HEADINGS
GET TRANSACTION
WHILE TRANSACTION <> "END"
.LAST_ITEM= THIS_ITEM
.WHILE LAST_ITEM= THIS_ITEM AND TRANSACTION <> "END"
..DO ACCUMULATE
..GET TRANSACTION
.END
.DO SUMMARY_LINE
END
DO TOTAL_LINE
STOP
```

This is well structured in conventional terms, but it completely fails to use the power of the language. It is complex in structure compared with the NOMAD and RAMIS examples above (and is far from a complete program). This style is much more likely to have bugs and maintenance problems than when the nonprocedural power of the language is used to avoid DO or WHILE or other loop or branch constructs.

Our message, then, is not only "use nonprocedural languages" but also "use them nonprocedurally." This, for conventional programmers, needs new thinking and *unlearning* of old skills they are proud of.

An advertisement used by the vendor of one of the new languages shows busy end users obtaining results from terminals, and in the foreground an elderly monk at a gothic desk is decorating a parchment scroll with illuminated letters showing COBOL-like code.

REFERENCES

1. G. D. Bergland, "A Guided Tour of Program Design Methodologies," *IEEE Computing,* October 1981, pp. 13–37.

2. E. D. Yourdon and L. L. Constantine, *Structured Design* (New York: Yourdon Press, 1975).

3. G. J. Myers, *Reliable Software Through Composite Design,* (New York: Petrocelli/Charter, 1975).

4. R. C. Linger, H. D. Mills, and B. I. Witt, *Structured Programming Theory and Practice* (Reading, MA: Addison-Wesley Publishing Co., Inc., 1979).

5. M. A. Jackson, *Principles of Program Design* (New York: Academic Press, Inc., 1975).

6. E. W. Dijkstra, *A Discipline of Programming* (Englewood Cliffs, NJ: Prentice-Hall, Inc., 1976).

7. E. W. Dijkstra and D. Gries, "Introduction to Programming Methodologies," Ninth Institute in Computer Science, University of California, Santa Cruz, August 1979.

8. *NOMAD 2 Reference Manual* and other literature on NOMAD are available from National CSS, Wilton, CT 06897.

9. *RAMIS II Reference Manual* and other literature on RAMIS are available from Mathematica Products Group, Princeton Station Office Park, P.O. Box 2392, Princeton, NJ 08540.

11   USE OF FOURTH-GENERATION LANGUAGES

INTRODUCTION   In the early days of the U.S. car industry, production volumes were growing fast and a well-known sociologist was asked to predict the total number of automobiles that would ever be manufactured. After a great deal of study the sociologist reported that no more than 2 million would be manufactured in the life cycle of the car. If the car lasted 10 years on average, the maximum annual production would never exceed 200,000. This conclusion was based on the much-researched figure that no more than 2 million people would be willing to serve as chauffeurs.

Today we might conclude that no more than 2 million people in the United States would be likely to become professional programmers—six times as many programmers as there are today. Computers will increase in speed by a factor of 10 in less than a decade and require, say, six times as much programming. At that time, the sociologist might calculate there could be no more computers than there are today because of a lack of programmers.

Henry Ford created not only a mass-production line, but also simplified the controls of his Model T so that most people could drive it. The computer industry will have Model-T-like computers mass-produced with microelectronics. They will only sell in the vast quantities possible if they can be put to work without professional programmers. This is now beginning to happen. Application development without programmers is perhaps the most important revolution in computing since the invention of the transistor.

FOURTH-GENERATION LANGUAGES   The alternative to professional programmers is systems being developed by end users or by analysts working directly with the users. It is made practical by a new breed of languages, called *fourth-generation languages.*

A characteristic of such languages is that *an analyst can obtain results faster than he could write specifications for a programmer.* The analyst then works hand in hand with the user, creating what the user asks for and refining it in a step-by-step fashion to adapt it better to the user's needs.

Some fourth-generation languages are sufficiently user friendly that end users can obtain the results they need by themselves, especially if data systems with appropriate data are made available to them.

The first generation of computer languages was *machine language,* which came into use in the 1940s and 1950s. It used no compilers, assemblers, or interpreters.

The second generation comprised various forms of *assembler language,* which came into use in the late 1950s. The early assembler languages would optimize the position of program instructions on a drum which stored the programs. Later, attempts were made to create machine-independent assembler languages.

The third generation, called *high-level* languages, came into use in the 1960s. Some of these, such as ALGOL and FORTRAN, were for scientific work; some, such as COBOL, were for commercial work. COBOL became by far the most commonly used computer language. Some languages, such as PL/1 and later Ada, encompassed both scientific and commercial computing. Manufacturer-independent standards were created for these languages, but portability was still sometimes a problem.

Fourth-generaration languages were created for two principal reasons: first, so that nonprogrammers could obtain results from computers, and second, to greatly speed up the programming process. A proliferation of such languages, differing widely in their syntax and capability, has emerged. There are, as yet, no standards. New language ideas are emerging too rapidly. Most fourth-generation languages link into a data-base system. Some allow users to create their own personal data base. Some create and employ relational data bases because these provide more powerful and flexible user commands than do traditional data bases. Some fourth-generation languages are very user friendly and users become competent at obtaining useful results after a two-day training course.

With most fourth-generation languages a user does not have to specify how to do everything. Instead, the compiler or interpreter makes intelligent assumptions about what it thinks the user needs. For example, it may automatically select a useful format for a report, put page numbers on it, select chart types for graphics display, put labels on the axes or on column headings, and ask the user in a friendly, understandable fashion when it needs more information. Where a language makes intelligent default assumptions, these assumptions are likely to become steadily more intelligent as the language evolves and improves. An assumption behind such languages is that a relatively large amount of computer power can be used for compiling or interpreting.

There were a few fourth-generation languages in isolated use in the 1970s. At the start of the 1980s such languages began to proliferate both in number and usage, and it became clear that they represented a major trend of vital DP importance.

PROCEDURAL AND NONPROCEDURAL CODE

Some of these languages are referred to as *nonprocedural languages*. "Procedural" and "nonprocedural" is a useful and much used language distinction. A procedural language specifies *how* something is accomplished. A nonprocedural language specifies *what* is accomplished but not in detail *how*. Thus languages such as COBOL and PL/1 are procedural. Their programmers give precisely detailed instructions for how each action is accomplished. An application generator whose users fill in forms to tell it what to do is nonprocedural. The user merely says *what* is to be done and is not concerned with the detailed procedure for *how* it is done. Most professionals say that using such a generator is *not* programming.

Most query languages, report generators, graphics packages, and application generators are nonprocedural. However some high-level *programming* languages are now acquiring nonprocedural capabilities. NOMAD, for example, is a high-level language with which some end users obtain fast results from a computer. Most professionals would call it a programming language because it has IF statements and DO loops. However results can be obtained with brief nonprocedural statements such as

LIST BY CUSTOMER AVERAGE (INVOICE TOTAL).

This is a complete "program." It leaves the software to decide how the list should be formatted, when to skip pages, number pages, how to sort into CUSTOMER sequence, and how to compute an average.

We avoid the issue of what is "programming" and consider instead *programmers*. The term "programmer" in this book refers to a person who is a full-time creator of code. This is usually, but not always, procedural code. Our "programmer" is not an accountant, scientist, or systems analyst who programs occasionally to assist in doing his main job. Some enterprises today encourage the creation of application by end users or systems analysts rather than by full-time coders. Fourth-generation languages, then, can be either procedural or nonprocedural or both.

Nonprocedural languages are intelligent in the sense that they make intelligent assumptions about how to create the required results. Over the years ahead we will see them becoming *more* intelligent. This represents a higher level of automation of the application creation process. It can be designed so that maintenance changes are much easier to make.

EFFECTS ON   The move to fourth-generation languages probably
MAINTENANCE   has a greater effect on maintenance than any
                       other action DP can take, especially if it is linked
to tightly managed data administration. It has several types of effects, as follows:

- The simple hidden errors illustrated in Chapter 10 are avoided to a large extent. A good fourth-generation language and compiler should not have problems with determining which is the first or last record. Loops and program structures are often made easier to design correctly. The quality of generated code is usually good.

- Programs cannot only be created much faster, they can also be *changed* much faster.

- The traditional cycle of formal specification, design, and programming disappears for some applications. Many maintenance changes no longer have to be fed through this lengthy cycle. They can be performed quickly, when required. Some installations have reported that 80% of maintenance changes are made in one hour with application generators or other fourth-generation aids, instead of months as previously.

- With good fourth-generation languages it is much easier to understand another person's application—the first step toward modifying it.

- Many fourth-generation languages disallow clumsy or ill-structured program constructs which cause trouble later.

- Many fourth-generation languages are linked to data management systems with built-in dictionaries. The programmer cannot misrepresent the data or fail to declare variables.

- Many fourth-generation facilities are self-documenting. Poor documentation is less likely to be a cause of maintenance difficulties.

- End users can sometimes make their own enhancements, especially to the reports and displays that are generated. This lessens DP's work on enhancement maintenance.

- Sometimes end users generate and maintain entire applications.

There may also be some negative effects of a move to fourth-generation languages:

- Users sometimes become euphoric about creating their own applications and do so without controls, structuring, auditability, or data administration.

- A few languages are difficult to maintain. (APL, although not strictly a fourth-generation language, permits users to write code that can be nearly impossible for other persons to comprehend. In some financial organizations, when investment analysts leave, their APL programs are abandoned.)

- Some persons try to use application generators for applications which eventually become too complex for the language in question.

- Many new languages have the characteristic that they cannot create all types of applications. They are not general-purpose. That is a price we may have to pay for the great productivity improvements which fourth-generation languages bring. In this case we have to *select the language to fit the application.* This is repugnant to some programmers and purists. But it is a vitally important fact that languages of limited scope are enabling users to obtain the results they need *fast,* whereas the traditional programming process in COBOL or PL/1 did not.

If, however, a language or generator is used for an application that is beyond its scope, this will cause problems. Sometimes an application generator has been abandoned after much work because it was not appropriate for the application or the future maintenance changes to the application.

CHARACTERISTICS OF FOURTH-GENERATION LANGUAGES

Now that we have the term *fourth-generation language,* it is likely that every new language will be called "fourth generation" by its advertising copywriter. Some new languages, however, have more the characteristics of third-generation languages. For language to be worth being called "fourth generation," it should have the following characteristics:

1. It is user friendly.
2. A nonprofessional programmer can obtain results with it.
3. It employs a data management system directly.
4. Procedural code requires an order of magnitude fewer instructions than COBOL.
5. Nonprocedural code is used where possible.
6. It makes intelligent default assumptions about what the user wants, where possible.
7. It is designed for on-line operation.
8. It enforces or encourages structured code.
9. It is easy to understand another person's code.
10. Non-DP users can learn a subset of the language in a two-day training course.
11. It is designed for easy debugging.
12. Results can be obtained in an order of magnitude less time than with COBOL or PL/1.
13. It automates documentation where possible.
14. It is designed for ease of maintenance.

CHANGES IN REPORTS Most enhancement maintenance requested by users relates to *output* rather than *input*. The users want different reports, better screen output, a different cut through the data, and so on.

If the users learn to employ a good report generator and calculation facility they can extract much of the information they require from a data system and adjust it to their needs. This method of operation removes a good portion of the need for enhancement maintenance. If the input to the data system is from data-entry software which permits modifications in procedures to be made easily, programming maintenance is further avoided.

SEVEN TYPES OF SOFTWARE Software being used for application development without professional programmers falls into seven categories:

1. Simple-Query Facilities

These have existed since the earliest disk storage devices. They enable stored records to be printed or displayed in a suitable format.

2. Complex-Query Languages

These are data-base user languages which permit the formulation of queries which may relate to multiple records. The queries sometimes invoke complex data-base searching or the joining of multiple records: for example, "LIST ALL U.S. SHIPS WITHIN 500 MILES OF THE STRAITS OF HORMUZ CARRYING CREWMEMBERS WITH EXPERIENCE IN DESERT COMBAT." Because of the searching and joining, only certain data-base systems are appropriate for on-line use of such languages.

Many data-base user languages now exist. They differ greatly in their syntax and structure. Some are marketed by the vendors of their host data-base management systems; others are marketed by independent software houses.

Many query languages permit the users to enter and update data as well as query it. With some, users can create their own files.

3. Report Generators

These are facilities for extracting data from a file or data base and formatting it into reports. Good report generators allow substantial arithmetic or logic to be performed on the data before they are displayed or printed.

Some report generators are independent of data-base or query facilities. Others are an extension of data-base query languages. Ideally, an end user should be able to start by learning to make simple data-base queries and should steadily extend her or his skill to data manipulation and report formatting. The report generator should be an extension of the query language; many are not.

4. Graphics Languages

Graphics terminals are dropping in cost and give a particularly attractive way for certain types of end users to display and manipulate data. Software for interactive graphics is steadily improving. It can enable users to ask for data and specify how they want it charted. They can search files or data bases and chart information according to different criteria. Like report generators, some graphics packages allow considerable arithmetical and logical manipulation of the data.

5. Application Generators

These contain modules which permit an entire application to be generated. The input can be specified, and validation rules applied which specify what action is required, what logic, arithmetic is to be performed, and what output is created. Most application generators operate with data bases. They can greatly speed up application development.

Some applications can be generated only partially. They require certain operations which the application generator cannot create. It is still useful to employ the generator provided that it has an *escape* mechanism which permits the inclusion of routines written in a program language.

Some application generators are designed to create heavy-duty applications in which efficient coding and data accesses are needed because of the high transaction volumes.

6. Very High Level Programming Languages

Some programming languages are designed for end users. Some are designed so that they use a much smaller number of instructions than a language such as COBOL, FORTRAN, or PL/1 and permit much faster application development.

Languages employed by sophisticated end users include BASIC and APL. More powerful (in that it uses fewer instructions) is NOMAD, which is designed to operate with a relational data base.

With high-level languages such as NOMAD, the user can say LIST, TITLE, INSERT, AVERAGE, SORT, SUM, and so on. He need not describe in code the format of a report. The interpreter selects a reasonable format and the user can adjust it if he wishes.

Cost studies have indicated that the cost per line of code is typically $10 in the United States (although it varies from $5 to over $300 [1], and this cost is largely independent of the language. A COBOL program often has 20 to 40 times as many lines of code as the same application written in a very high level language.

7. Parameterized Application Packages

Packages can be purchased for running certain applications. These pre-programmed packages are increasing in number, diversity, and quality. They often require a considerable amount of tailoring to fit the organization that installs them and are designed with parameters that can be chosen to modify their operation. The parameterization is the key to success in many cases. As the marketplace for packages grows, they tend to be built with a richer set of parameters so that they have wider applicability.

Some application packages are marketed directly to end users so that they can avoid involvement with their DP department. Some are designed to operate on end-user minicomputers.

SUITABLE FOR END USERS? There are many types of software in the categories described above. Most vendors of such software claim that it is "designed for end users." In many cases this claim is questionable because the software requires more skill and training than most users will acquire. In many cases the software should be used by systems analysts who work with the end users.

Some of the software noted above is excellent for end users. Some of the best data-base query and update facilities can be employed by users who have never touched a terminal before: for example, VIEWDATA sets [2], IBM's QUERY-BY-EXAMPLE, and INTELLECT.

We might classify something as "suitable for end users" if typical end users can learn how to use it and obtain valuable results in a two-day training course and then not forget how to use it if they leave it for several weeks. (They *would* forget codes and mnemonics.) End users could not adapt fully to IBM's application generators DMS or ADF, for example, in a two-day course. With these criteria we can categorize the software *for application development without conventional programming* by means of the matrix shown in Fig. 11.1.

The reader might like to fill in Fig. 11.1 with software with which he or she is familiar. There is scope for argument about which compartment in Fig. 11.1 certain facilities fit into. Many fit into more than one. For example, a good data-base language might be *both* a complex query language and a report generator. A language might be categorized as suitable for end users *and* suitable for DP professionals, because the users can learn (in two days) to use *some* of its facilities, but not all. This is the case with the programming language APL, for example. A child can learn to use a small subset

	Suitable for End Users	Suitable for DP Professionals
Simple-Query Facilities		
Complex-Query Languages		
Report Generators		
Graphics Languages		
Application Generators		
Very High-Level Programming Languages		
Parameterized Application Packages		

Figure 11.1 Categorization of facilities for application creation without conventional programming.

of APL in two days, but it takes a skilled professional months to master all of APL's capabilities.

A desirable property of a language is that it should be *easy to start to use it,* but that the user can continue to learn more about it and improve his skills for a long time. Languages with this property should be taught in subsets. If a language has a beginners' subset which can be well learnt in *one* day, many users will cross the threshold from being mystified outsiders to being initiate members of the club.

We sometimes use the term *end user* as though it referred to one breed of creature. In reality, computer end users vary across the entire spectrum of humanity both in skills and in motivation. Some budget plannners and production schedulers work wonders with the new languages. But most users are frightened of terminals and do not yet dream that they could instruct computers to go to work for them. A sensitive seduction process is needed to encourage them to join the club—and many are too set in their ways to be seduced.

In the long run it is certain that much computing will be user driven. In the early days of the motor car, technology improved and a chauffeur became unnecessary. Technology will increasingly improve the user interface to computers so that for many applications users will not need a computer-chauffeur.

INTEGRATED LANGUAGES

Although some languages fall into *one* of the seven categories in Fig. 11.1, it is desirable to have languages that are in multiple categories. Some report generators, for example, are entirely separate from query languages, and some data-base query languages do not have a report generation capability. It would be preferable for a user to learn a query language with which he could steadily extend his skills and become able to create reports with useful formats. He should also be able to create business graphics. Similarly, the language should be extendable so that it is a full application generator.

ESCAPE FEATURE Application generators are not capable of generating all applications. Sometimes they lack the capability to generate particular logic or algorithms which are needed. Too often a generator is rejected for this reason. An important feature of a generator is the capability to associate with it modules of logic written in programming languages. This is sometimes called an *escape* feature. Where possible, it is desirable that the user of the generator be able to use the language to which the escape is made.

In some cases a programmer is required to handle the escape language, but if the programmer is part of the DP department doing conventional coding, the problems with programming backlog will affect the use of the generator.

Ideally, then, the products in Fig. 11.1 should be integrated as much as possible. The query language should support the creation of reports and graphics and be the basis of an application generator. A high-level programming language should be available both for use in its own right and for escape from the application generator. Most products in existence today do not yet have this degree of integration. Computer manufacturers and software houses have often created separate languages for data-base query, report generation, graphics, application generation, and high-level programming.

Several query languages and report generators today are suitable for end users, but many application generators at the time of writing are not. Application generators can be designed for end users and some good ones exist. There is *much* software of these types on the market.

ON-LINE OR A further categorization of the software in Fig.
OFF-LINE? 11.1 can indicate whether it is on-line or off-line. Some query languages, report generators, and application generators operate interactively at a terminal; some operate off-line with the users or systems analysts filling in forms or coding sheets.

The use of forms gives the user time to think about what he needs. In some cases he may fill in the forms at home or away from his office.

Nevertheless, on-line operation can be much more satisfactory if it is well designed psychologically. It can lead the user to do what is required a step at a time. It can check the user's input as he creates it. It can make tutorial explanations available on-line and can assist if the user presses a HELP key. On-line operation can generally be made much more versatile than off-line operation. When the product types in Fig. 11.1 are integrated, on-line operation can make a wide range of features available to the user.

EFFICIENCY

An argument often voiced *against* application generators and the other facilities of Fig. 11.1 is that they generate inefficient code and use an excessive amount of computer time. It is important to realize that this is true with some but not with others. It is an important characteristic to examine when selecting such software, but not a blanket argument against its use. *Surprisingly, perhaps, some application generators create object code which is better than the same applications programmed in COBOL or PL/1.* The reason for this is that statements in the generator language result in the use of blocks of code which have been written in assembler language and tightly optimized. These assembler blocks are better optimized than the object code which is compiled from COBOL or PL/1. On the other hand, the worst of both worlds is a generator that generates COBOL (or PL/1) source code, which is then compiled.

Some generators also use less compile time than COBOL or PL/1. IBM's DMS (Development Management System) commonly takes a sixth of the compile time of the same functions written in COBOL. The reason for this is that it generates major blocks of code *which are precompiled.*

Some generators work interpretively; some work with compiled code. As elsewhere, *compilation* can give better machine performance than interpretive operation. Compilation is desirable for repetitive operations.

There may be an increase in hardware costs due to the languages being interpreted rather than compiled. In many cases, however, the cost of running a program is small compared with the cost of creating it.

A study by Kendall [3] found that many programs used more machine cycles *during development* than they used in their entire lives in execution. This is often the case with very large or complex programs because these are not run as frequently as the programs that process routine operations or paperwork, which can usually be *generated.*

In a typical installation 50% of the applications consume 2% of the machine time. Only 2% of the applications consume 50% of the machine time [4]. The latter 2% might be coded with high machine efficiency.

Again, typically, 90% of the applications cost more to develop and compile with conventional programs than to run for their entire lifetime [4]. In addition, the difference in lifetime maintenance costs between COBOL and fourth-generation languages is usually even greater. Money saving for these programs needs to concentrate on the development cost rather than on the running cost.

Applications created for high-volume operation need to be efficient. Some application generators are designed to give efficiency with heavy-duty systems; others are designed for ad hoc operation for one-off reports or low-volume activity.

In some cases an expert is needed to extract good performance from the software. The expert may make an application run twice as fast by using a different data-base design. He may save more time by sorting the input or changing the operation sequence. In some cases experts on the software improve its performance by a much larger factor.

When choosing the software it is necessary to decide whether machine efficiency is a selection criterion. If its use is for a few transactions a day, machine efficiency does not matter at all. However, it is also important to use generators for heavy-duty applications as well as for low-volume ones.

PLUNGING COMPUTER COSTS   Today, computers are dropping in cost. Mass-production techniques are in sight which could turn out computers like they turn out newsprint. We will eventually have an IBM/370-like computer on a single chip. No white-collar worker should be without one.

In the next 10 years computers will increase in speed by a factor of at least 10, perhaps much more. As they plunge in cost, many will be sold. It is estimated that the number of computers used for scientific and commercial applications will continue to grow at 25% per year at least. It is growing faster than that now.

If we assume no increase in programming productivity, the figures indicate that in 10 years the industry will need 93.1 times as many programmers as now. There are approximately 300,000 programmers in the United States today. That suggests about 28 million programmers in 10 years' time. Before long, the entire American work force would be needed to program its computers. Ridiculous!

Another way of looking at the same figures is that the number of applications in today's data processing centers is growing at 45% per year. This figure comes from an IBM survey. The growth seems likely to continue. Many potential applications which users need are never mentioned by the users today because the *documented* application backlog is so great. Ten years' growth of 45% per year multiplies the number of applications by 41.1. At the same time the number of data-processing centers will grow, perhaps by a factor of 10 in the next 10 years because of the rapidly dropping cost of computers.

Any set of estimates of computing power 10 years hence indicates that the *productivity of application development needs to increase by two orders of magnitude* during the next 10 years.

The productivity of writing programs in languages such as COBOL, FORTRAN, or PL/1 is indeed improving, but only slowly. In installations where it has been used well, structured programming has improved programmer productivity. Typical installations quote a 10% or so improvement. It is rare to find a case where structured techniques have in reality increased programmer productivity by more than 25% [5]. Some installations state that there is no measurable improvement. It appears that structured programming might reduce the figure of 28 million programmers to about 20 million or so if we are optimistic about it!

Worse, the program coding is only part of the task. In a typical installation, writing and testing new program code takes only 14% of the human DP resources. The rest is spent on system analysis, writing program specifications, documenting the programs, and maintenance. (This figure is also from an IBM survey.)

Clearly, if the computer industry is to find markets for the acres of silicon chips that it will produce, fundamentally new methods of application development are needed. Indeed, if this is not done, it is doubtful whether some of the large computer vendors will survive the plunge in costs of their hardware. The challenge for programmers today is to automate their own job where possible, but many do not welcome this prospect! The profession that has done the most to change other people's jobs is reluctant to have its own job changed.

**PEOPLE COSTS
VERSUS
COMPUTER COSTS**

Figure 11.2 shows how the costs of computer time and people time are changing. In 1979 the curves of Fig. 11.2 crossed, making computer time (of the power shown) cheaper than people time. The vertical scale of Fig. 11.2 is logarithmic, so the rate of change is great. Before long the cost of a person for an hour will be 10 times greater than the cost of a computer for an hour.

The number of computers being delivered is increasing very rapidly. This is not reflected in the curves of Fig. 11.2. By the time the curves in Fig. 11.2 crossed, the United States was delivering more computers per year than it was producing science and engineering graduates per year.

Figure 11.2 represents an inexorable trend that will continue. Sooner or later the techniques of commercial DP programming and analysis *must* change. For most corporations today the question is not *whether* the methods will change but how soon the corporations will adapt new methods which are working elsewhere.

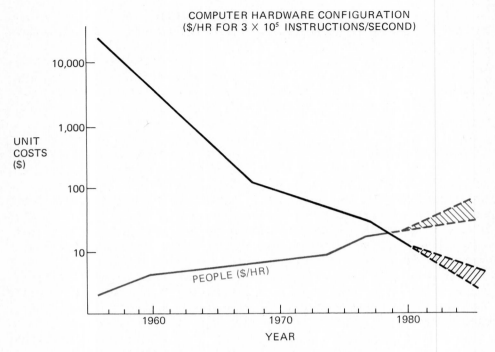

COMPUTER HARDWARE CONFIGURATION
($/HR FOR 3 × 10⁵ INSTRUCTIONS/SECOND)

Figure 11.2 Comparison of the cost of computers with the cost of people in the United States. In 1979, computer time (at 3×10^5 instructions per second) became cheaper than people time. (Note that the vertical scale is logarithmic.)

APPLICATION BACKLOG

We have stressed that the demand for new applications is rising faster than DP can supply them. The inbalance between demand and supply is steadily becoming worse. Because of this, the backlog of applications which are needed is growing. Most corporations now have a backlog of three or four years. One New York bank informed us that its backlog was seven years. This situation is likely to become worse as machines drop in cost, unless better methods of creating applications are found. In one typical corporation there is a backlog of 70 applications. In the previous 12 months only 19 applications were created. The acknowledged demand for new applications is growing faster than applications are being created.

Even though today's application backlogs are so long, they reveal only part of the story. When the documented backlog is several years (as it is in most installations), the end users do not even consider making requests for many of the applications they need. There is thus an *invisible backlog*.

A study at the Sloan School [6] showed that the invisible backlog is much larger than the official backlog—168% of it. The Sloan survey indicated that the declared backlog is 68% of the installed base of applications in typical U.S. corporations. The invisible backlog is 112% of the installed base.

Together the declared and undeclared application backlog are 179% of the installed base of applications. This is an awesome figure, indicating how much harm is being done by the slowness of today's application development and maintenance process.

TWO SOLUTIONS　　　Fourth-generation languages provide two types of solutions to the problem of slow application development. First, they can greatly speed up the development of applications by DP. Second, the user-friendly languages permit end users to generate their own reports and create their own applications. Often the best approach is to have DP analysts working directly with end users to create applications with them, using nonprocedural languages where possible so that results may be obtained very quickly and repetitively modified.

Both development by users and development by DP with fourth-generation languages proceeds faster when the data are already designed. Wherever possible the use of fourth-generation languages should link into data models. This avoids proliferation of incompatible data and lessens the likelihood of later redesign, because the data are designed for stability and transferability.

HUGE GAINS IN　　　The most important thing to understand about the
PRODUCTIVITY　　　use of fourth-generation languages is that *huge*
　　　　　　　　　　gains in application development and maintenance productivity are being achieved with them in practice. The best results are far too spectacular to be ignored.

Figure 11.3 gives numbers of programs installed per person-month at Playtex, Inc. [7] using COBOL versus using ADF (IBM's Application Development Facility, which employs an IMS data base). For the types of applications shown there is an 80.7 times improvement in the productivity of application creation. For some applications in Playtex, ADF was not used, but these were in the minority. It is normal to find an improvement in productivity by a factor of 10 when moving from COBOL or PL/1 to fourth-generation languages; it is not uncommon to find an improvement by a factor of 20 [8].

The second most important thing to understand is that these products and these gains in productivity make desirable an approach to application creation which is quite different from the traditional methods. Chapter 12 describes this.

Whereas some organizations have achieved huge productivity gains such

Programs installed per person-month		
PROGRAM TYPE	USING COBOL	USING ADF
Inventory locator	.3675	20.44
Order billing	.1365	35.11
Order processing	.3220	11.11
AVERAGE	.2753	22.22
Average improvement		80.71

Figure 11.3 Application development productivity figures from Playtex, Inc. [7].

as those in Fig. 11.3, others have not. Some have attempted to use ADF (the application generator which achieved the results shown in Fig. 11.3) and have abandoned it. There are several reasons for this huge difference in experience. First, substantial training is needed to use some application generators. Sometimes the commitment to training is not made. Second, the application generators and other aids are not suitable for every application. They need to be used where appropriate. Sometimes the application, its dialogue, or its screen formats need to be adapted to fit what can be generated. The range of applications for which they are valuable can be greatly extended by using them in conjunction with conventional code where necessary. Third, to achieve high productivity, changes in DP management and methodology are needed. It is sometimes the group with little experience of conventional DP procedures that achieves the best results. Fourth, the analysis and design of information resources in an enterprise has not been done. Some management information applications require a substantial base of data to be available in data systems. Once the raw data are available, reports or applications using the data can be created quickly.

TECHNIQUES ANALYST

At the time of writing, the software to automate application generation has many shortcomings. It is rapidly improving, but today the software method needs to be selected to fit the application. No single type of software is appropriate for all applications.

The selection process is a key to success. Higher productivity can often be achieved by using more than one type of software for one application area: for example, an application generator for DP professionals, certain routines written with conventional programming, and a data-base query language and report generator for end users.

It is desirable to have an analyst who is familiar with the capabilities of these diverse languages and software packages and who will decide what language should be used for each application. He may also be responsible for deciding what training is needed. The number of different languages needs to be kept as small as it can be and still maximize productivity. This analyst might be called a *techniques analyst.*

The techniques analyst should be familiar with figures quoted in the industry for typical productivity with different methods. In some organizations he will meet much opposition from DP people who are resistant to changing their methods, standards, and hallowed procedures manuals. However, the figures for productivity improvements are too big to ignore [8].

The techniques analyst should be familiar with maintainability requirements and maintenance costs. He should recommend the use of languages and tools that minimize long-range maintenance costs. Often the primary justification for the move to fourth-generation techniques is the cost of maintenance.

REDEVELOPING OLD APPLICATIONS

If new applications are developed with fourth-generation techniques, a large DP installation may become split between practitioners of the new approach and maintainers of the mass of old applications in old languages. The morale of the latter group may become low.

As the new techniques spread, a calculation needs to be made about whether the old applications *should* be maintained. Often, the estimated cost of maintaining them for five years is greater than the cost of rebuilding them with the techniques of new languages, clean structuring, data administration, stable data models, and report generators. It is often cheaper and better to scrap those old applications with high maintenance costs and recreate them. A phased plan for doing this should be created.

REFERENCES

1. J. H. Lehman, "How Software Projects Are Really Managed," *Datamation,* January 1979.

2. J. Martin, *Viewdata and the Information Society* (Englewood Cliffs, NJ: Prentice-Hall, Inc., 1982).

3. R. C. Kendall, "Management Perspectives on Programs, Programming and Productivity," Proceedings of Guide 45, Atlanta, GA, November 1977.

4. W. R. Bradshaw, "Application Development Productivity Within IBM Information Systems," Guide and Share Application Development Symposium, Monterey, SHARE, Inc., New York, 1979.

5. T. Capers Jones (IBM), "The Limits to Programming Productivity," Guide and Share Application Development Symposium, Monterey, SHARE, INC., New York, 1979.

6. R. B. Rosenberger, "The Information Center," SHARE Proceedings No. 56, Session M372, March 1981.

7. IBM brochure, "IMS/VS Users Talk About Productivity and Control," G520-3511-0 IBM Corp, White Plains, NY 10604, 1980.

8. J. Martin, *Application Development Without Programmers* (Englewood Cliffs, NJ: Prentice-Hall, Inc., 1982), Box 3.1.

12 USER-DRIVEN COMPUTING

INTRODUCTION   The largest single cause of maintenance is users changing their requirements. It is unreasonable to expect them *not* to change their requirements, because their business is changing and they *ought* to invent better procedures as they better understand the possibilities for automation. What is needed is not a management technique that tries to suppress change, but rather computing techniques that make change easy and quick to accomplish.

The term "paperless office" is sometimes used to describe a modern DP environment. It implies that data will be entered directly into terminals at or close to their source, stored and manipulated in electronic systems, and information made available for analysis at terminals. Form-filling, paperwork flow, and batch printouts will largely disappear.

This environment depends on several technological developments:

1. Terminals coming into widespread use. When manufactured in large enough quantities, a visual display terminal, which has almost no moving parts, can be as cheap as an electric typewriter which has many intricate moving mechanisms.

2. Data storage software permitting information retrieval systems and data-base systems, some of which are more flexible than those of the 1970s.

3. Data networks making the computer and data systems easily accessible.

4. User-friendly computer languages that enable diverse users to extract the information they need flexibly from the data systems.

5. Software that radically changes the process of creating simple DP applications so that the time delays, problems, and expensive maintenance of conventional programming can be avoided. A more flexible, user-driven evolution of paperless administrative procedures and decision support can then evolve at a rapid rate.

All of these developments in technology exist today but in some organizations are not yet put to good use.

To employ these technologies requires fundamental changes in systems analysis and design procedures. Together with these changes, new patterns of DP management are required. This book is concerned with the new forms of analysis, design, and management.

THE PROBLEM OF SLOW APPLICATION DEVELOPMENT

Once they start to use terminals and begin to understand data processing, white-collar workers perceive all manner of ways in which they could put computers to work. They know what information they would like to have on their terminals. They begin to realize how computers could save them time, improve administrative procedures, enable them to make better decisions, or do a better job. An enormous number of good ideas about how to use information systems have bubbled up from the shop floor, the distribution area, and other areas of an organization when this has been encouraged [1, Chap. 11].

The problem is that until recently most of these ideas could not be implemented because the processes of systems analysis, programming, and maintenance were too slow. Most application programs are individually designed and hand coded with very slow methods.

Application programming is one of the most labor-intensive jobs known. We are now beginning to perceive how to automate much of it. To do so, we need better software, which is becoming available. A vital characteristic of such software ought to be that users or systems analysts can make changes to applications in a flexible fashion, without employing programmers. Only then will computing escape the straitjacket of today's application maintenance. The challenge of data processing today is how to introduce a high level of automation without introducing rigidity of procedures.

PROBLEMS WITH CONVENTIONAL APPLICATION DEVELOPMENT

DP productivity alone would be a powerful reason for moving from conventional systems analysis and programming to more automated forms of application creation. There is, however, another reason that is sometimes more powerful: in many situations the conventional development process *does not work*.

Time and time again one finds stories of a system being cut over after years of development effort and the end users saying it is not what they want, or trying it for a while and then giving up. Frequently, after using a system laboriously created for a few weeks, the users say they want something different.

A common reaction to this unfortunate situation is to say that the requirements were not specified thoroughly enough. So more elaborate procedures have been devised for requirements specification, sometimes resulting in voluminous documentation. But even with such specifications the results have been unsatisfactory.

The fact is that many of the most important potential users of DP do not know what they want until they *experience* using the system. When they first experience it, many changes are needed to make them comfortable with it and to meet their *basic* requirements. Once comfortable with it, their imaginations go to work and they think of all manner of different functions and variations on the theme that would be useful to them. And they want these changes *immediately*.

MORE RIGOROUS SPECIFICATIONS

Many DP organizations have realized that their application creation process is not working to the satisfaction of the users, and have taken steps to correct this. Unfortunately, the steps they take often make the situation worse.

Steps are often taken to enforce more formal procedures. Application creation, it is said, must be converted from a sloppy ad hoc operation to one that follows rules and has thorough management control.

The U.S. Department of Defense recognized that it had software problems and *mandated* certain actions in response to them, in DOD Directive 5000.29. A major concern in creating this directive was that the programs created did not meet the user's requirements. The directive specified more formal requirements documentation prior to the design, coding, and testing. A Computer Resource Life-Cycle Management Plan was specified, as shown in Fig. 12.1, and depicted certain milestones that are to be attained and documented. The milestones are to be used to "ensure the proper sequence of analysis, design, implementation, integration, test, deployment, and maintenance" [2]. Figure 12.2 shows another such development life cycle, this one from a large aerospace corporation.

This approach formalizes the conventional wisdom of programming development and can work well *if and only if* the end user's requirements can be specified in fine detail before design and coding begins. With some systems they can and with others they cannot. The requirements for missile control *can* be specified completely beforehand. The requirements for management information systems *cannot* be specified beforehand and almost every attempt to do so has failed. The requirements change as soon as an executive starts to use his terminal.

This point is vitally important for maintenance. If we try to use rigid specification, development, and maintenance techniques for systems requiring constant dynamic change, we are doomed to failure.

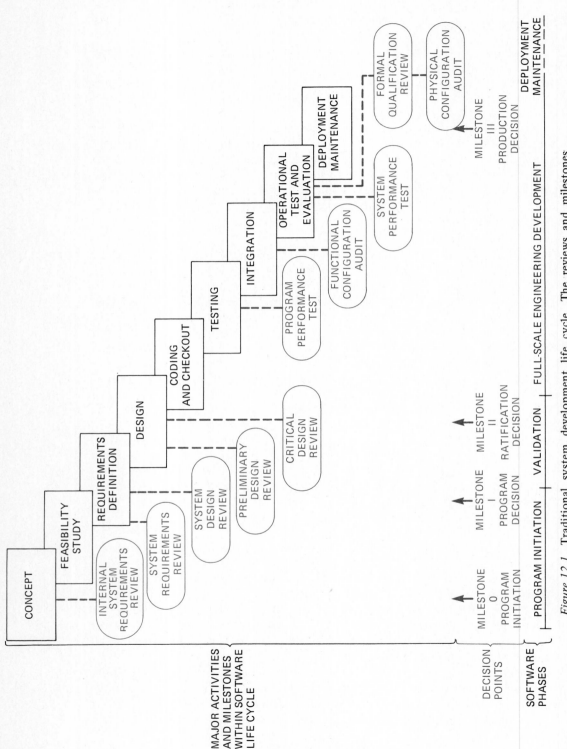

Figure 12.1 Traditional system development life cycle. The reviews and milestones shown here are those required in the U.S. Department of Defense. (Redrawn from Ref. 2.)

SYSTEM DEVELOPMENT LIFE CYCLE

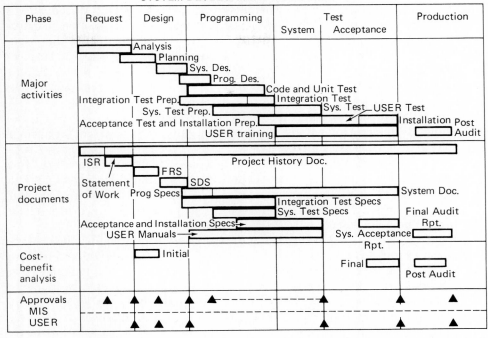

Figure 12.2 Pratt & Whitney life cycle.

FAILURES

In one large insurance company a system was developed for claim processing that would put terminals in all the branch offices. It took about three years to develop at a cost of about $4 million. To ensure that the end users were well understood, an end-user manager was moved into a high position in the development process. When the first terminals were cut over, to everybody's horror the users gave up using them after a short period. They perceived the system as unsatisfactory compared with their previous method. The system was eventually abandoned.

A Department of Defense study was conducted in 1977 of 10 major automated systems. It concluded that all 10 systems had *unstable and changing* requirements.

IBM designed a system to automate two Japanese newspapers—Asaki and Nikei. What do editors of a newspapers really want at their terminals? They did not know. When the system was first installed it was not useful to the editors, and IBM lost about $2 million on the software development effort [3]. Undaunted, newspaper automation continued. Years later, after a great effort, a requirements document of *2400 pages* was produced. It was created to automate several U.S. newspapers. It was so thorough that management thought *nothing* could go wrong. But, unfortunately, when the document was used to settle questions, the developers and their customers interpreted it differently! Both worked in good faith, but the difficulty of specifying the processes in sufficient detail for programming was too great [3].

The difficult of writing adequate requirements specifications has resulted in some spectacular court cases. In the early 1970s two major airlines sued their computer suppliers who were to provide the application programs, after $40 million had been spent, because the application programs were perceived to be unworkable. At the time of writing, a European bank is in court for a $70 million claim over application software. The U.S. Air Force spent more than $300 million in a futile attempt to automate an Advanced Logistics System (ALS) [3].

Used correctly, the computer represents an extension of man's mind, freeing him from his limitations by being able to process the masses of data that inundate him. The computer can act as a multiplier of man's creative and reasoning abilities—for human beings can learn from experience in a way that perhaps the computer will never be able to emulate.

But used incorrectly, the computer opens up a potential for disaster on a scale never before imagined. Computers carry out unerringly the instructions we give them. And it is human to err. If our instructions are faulty, those faulty instructions will be carried out at a speed and in a way never before experienced.

The computer application systems we use today consume enormous amounts of time and money in their construction. But once built, the complexity of (most) application development techniques defies both correction of errors and enhancement maintenance.

For every big failure that hits the headlines there are a thousand small ones where ordinary end users abandon their terminal or complain that it does not do what they want. This can become a disaster when it results in the inability of organizations to respond to changing economic or competitive environments. The computer systems developed to enable organizations to be more responsive were based upon automation of the procedures presently in use by the organization. The error made was the assumption that those procedures would not change: that they would be appropriate not only for the needs of today, but also for the needs of the organization into the future.

Once developed, conventional computer programs are difficult to change to respond to a different external environment. We are locked in a thickening morass of worsening maintenance complexity.

SOLUTION   What is the solution?

It is essential to distinguish between systems that need dynamic user-driven modification of requirements after the system is initially implemented and systems that need complete, formal, requirements analysis and specification before implementation. Many commercial and administrative data processing and systems oriented to human needs fall into the former category. We will refer to these two types of systems by the terms *user-driven computing* and *prespecified computing.*

User-driven computing needs fourth-generation languages and where possible *nonprocedural* techniques. User-friendly languages and data management systems are needed so that users or systems analysts can dynamically and easily modify what they obtain from computers. Nonprocedural languages may be used for creating prototypes; or they may be used for creating the final result.

Much modern data processing should employ stable data systems in conjunction with *user-driven* computing to create applications. User-driven computing needs a change in the role of the systems analyst. It often results in fast step-by-step incremental modification of terminal screens and applications.

Although these methods work well for most ordinary data processing, they are not appropriate for highly complex, technical systems such as those for refinery operation, satellite image processing, air traffic control, or moon launches. With these, a formal requirements specification and the development life cycle of Fig. 12.1 or 12.2 with tight controls are needed— *prespecified computing.*

Box 12.1 shows characteristics of *user-driven* and *prespecified* computing.

Most computing which ought to be *user-driven* is being developed today as *prespecified* computing. A drastic change in the management of application development is needed, together with the introduction of the new software and techniques. It is not clear how much computing ought to be user-driven rather than prespecified. When the power and efficiency of application generators increases substantially, and information analysis and data modeling has been done, it is likely that user-driven methods will be employable for most (but not all) commercial data processing, rather than the long development cycle of traditional DP. The data should be analyzed, modeled, and documented. After that, there is scope for much argument about what ought to be prespecified.

It is not *only* user-driven computing that should employ the new software. The productivity of developing prespecified computing of certain types is greatly improved by the use of application generators such as IBM's DMS or ADF, or the use of higher-level languages such as NOMAD, MANTIS, NATURAL, or IDEAL.

BOX 12.1   **The distinction between prespecified computing and user-driven computing. Much of what has been** *prespecified* **ought to be** *user-driven* **with today's software.**

Prespecified Computing

● Formal requirements specifications are created.

● A development cycle such as that in Fig. 12.1 or 12.2 is employed.

● Programs are formally documented.

● The application development time is many months or years.

● Maintenance is formal, slow, and expensive.

Examples: Compiler writing, airline reservations, air traffic control, missile guidance, software development.

User-Driven Computing

● Users do not know in detail what they want until they use a version of it and then they modify it quickly and often, frequently. Consequently, formal requirement specification linked to slow application programming is doomed to failure.

● Applications are created with a generator or other software, more quickly than the time it takes to write specifications.

● The system is self-documenting, or interactive documentation is created when the application is created.

● Users create their own applications or work with an analyst who does this in cooperation with them. A separate programming department is not used.

● The application development time is days or at most weeks.

● Maintenance is continuous. Incremental changes are made constantly to the applications by the users or the analyst who assists them.

● The process may employ data models and data systems which are centrally created with the information engineering processes.

● Control is imposed via the data models, dictionary, and authorization procedures.

Examples: Administrative procedures, shop floor control, information systems, decision support, paperwork avoidance.

Prespecified computing needs new methods because the old methods are too slow. *User-driven computing* needs new methods because the old methods *do not work.*

PROBLEMS WITH PROCESS SPECIFICATION   Specification documents, whether done with structured analysis or traditional analysis, are extremely important in the *traditional* DP life cycle. They guide the programmers and are supposed to answer the numerous questions that will arise about the system. In practice we ask too much of them. There is really little hope that they can provide perfect communication between the programmers and the end users.

The specification document usually has the following unfortunate characteristics: It is so long that key managers do not read it all. They read the summary. It is incredibly boring, and this causes it to be only scanned by many people who should read it fully. It contains technical terms, systems analysis charts, and various forms of professional shorthand which the end users do not fully understand. It contains words that have very precise meanings in the user areas but that the programmers do not understand, and most systems analysts do not appreciate their nuances.

The end users fail to comprehend things that are *obvious* to the computer staff, and vice versa. A programmer cannot be expected to know that *benefit-effective-date* is different from *benefit-posted-date,* although that is obvious to the end user. A DP professional may not realize that an oil well has many different definitions or that the oil it accesses spreads underground to areas with different ownership. A user may have signed off on a document referring to *rating basis* without understanding that the systems analyst meant something entirely different by that. The DP professional might read phrases like the following over and over again without knowing what they mean: "indicates the date on which a given qualification was verified in the context of the structure within which it existed." (A real example! Its meaning is obvious to the end users in question.) There are endless such examples.

Much of the vital specification document is misinterpreted on both sides. Often its readers *think* they understand it but in fact do not.

Sometimes much trivia and/or "motherhood" are added to the document. Both sides understand this. It increases the comfort level but has zero value.

Specification documents are bad enough with batch processing; with interactive systems they tend to be worse because they cannot capture the dynamic quality of the user interaction. How many users will know what to do when confronted with a new screen? What happens when the user keys in something stupid? What is the effect of response time? Will the user prompting be effective? Is the dialogue too long-winded? Most users cannot obtain a feeling for what using a dialogue will be like when they read its specification.

USER SIGN-OFF

The users are coerced to sign-off on the specification document. They know that until they do that the detailed design and programming will not begin. DP hopes that the need to sign off will encourage the users to check the document very carefully and find any errors before programming starts.

SPECIFICATION FREEZE

It is important in the traditional development cycle to *freeze* the specifications when programming begins. Usually, the sign-off represents this freeze. The sign-off is invariably a moment of apprehension on both sides. The users are not sure whether it is really what they want. They often feel that their views on the system are changing as they learn and think more about it. Halfway up a learning curve the specifications are *frozen*.

DP is apprehensive because they are not sure that they understand all the user's needs. They are about to put much effort into the implementation and any imperfections in the specifications will prove expensive.

BUGS

Not surprisingly, the specification document contains errors. In most installations there are more bugs in specifications than in program coding. In one typical case a large corporation found that 64% of its bugs were in requirements analysis and design—in spite of a formal sign-off by the user departments. Even worse, *45% of these bugs were discovered after the acceptance tests for the finished applications were completed.*

This corporation had a formal development life cycle not unlike Fig. 12.1, and was following its installation standards meticulously. It was using a formal method of structured analysis in creating the specifications.

If there is not a formal structured method of system specification, the situation is usually worse. Figure 12.3 shows the distribution of bugs in a large bank before it moved to structured analysis. Fifty-six percent were in the requirements document; 27% were in design, and most of these were related to misinterpretation of the requirements document.

The bugs in the requirements specification are much more time consuming and expensive to correct than those in coding. Figure 12.3 illustrates this. Ninety-five percent of the cost of correcting bugs in this bank was for the bugs in requirements and design. The ratios in Fig. 12.3 are typical of many installations.

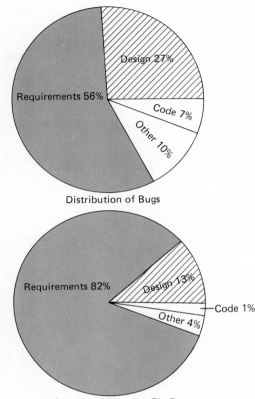

Distribution of Bugs

Figure 12.3 In a typical installation with a traditional development methodology, more bugs occur in requirements specification and design than in coding. The bugs in requirements specification are much the most expensive to correct. (Charts from Ref. 4.)

Distribution of Effort to Fix Bugs

THE UNCERTAINTY PRINCIPLE

The uncertainty principle in physics says that the act of observing subatomic events *changes* those events. There is an uncertainty principle with data processing. The act of providing what an end user says he needs *changes* his perception of those needs.

The mere act of implementing a user-driven system changes the requirements for that system. The solution to a problem changes the problem.

As the system becomes live it will affect the rest of the department in a variety of unforeseen ways. It suddenly becomes possible to move work from one person's screen to another. Salesmen can suddenly provide a service that was previously so difficult that they ignored it, and demands for that service boom. A manager suddenly sees information that was previously hidden from him, so he makes changes in the department. Some users do not like the system and insist on using their previous methods. Others want new types of reports or want the computer to do calculations not in the system requirements.

The system has many unforeseen psychological effects. It may make some employees feel unwanted and resentful. Some become prima donnas with the new terminals. It changes the organizational interaction and power patterns.

END-USER LEARNING CURVE

End users have a long learning curve to climb in assessing how they should use today's data processing. They cannot climb far on this curve as long as it remains at the talking stage. It is only when they have a terminal and use it on their own work that they begin to understand the reality of the computer's challenge and limitations. Their imagination slowly begins to realize what they *could* do with that screen. After implementation the users have a common basis for discussion of the system. They argue at lunch about what it does well and badly, what it ought to do better, and how it could benefit them in different ways from what it is doing now. They would like to modify its behavior *quickly*.

In many cases the functions of a user-driven system when first installed are less than a tenth of those they feel they need a few months after installation. These new functions are more valuable because they are based on experience. But the rigid development cycle prevents them from making the changes they want.

The system makes it possible to have more finely structured inventory reorder points. The reordering rules can now be changed easily to better adapt to seasonal peaks. It becomes possible to deal with problems on the shop floor that were quietly ignored before, but to do so needs additions to the data base, or different patterns of data entry.

It is often the case that the end user does not know what he wants until he gets it. When he gets it he wants something different.

In spite of this, the basic data in the organization—the entities and attributes—remain the same. Therefore, what is needed is a different approach to application development, which has proved highly successful in some installations. Its characteristics are summarized in Box 12.2.

A NEW APPROACH

The new approach in its most powerful form is illustrated in Fig. 12.4. The data that are needed to run the organization are determined with the bottom two blocks; these data are designed into stable data models, and implemented in data systems. The end users or systems analysts working with them can generate the information they want from the data systems using nonprocedural or other *fourth-generation languages*.

Users can also enter data, build their own electronic filing cabinets,

BOX 12.2   A new type of application development

For most, but not all, commercial data processing, a form of application development is needed which differs from conventional DP. It should be designed to speed up development and minimize maintenance time. At its best it produces very impressive results compared with the traditional DP development cycle.

Its characteristics are as follows:

- It uses application generators, report generators, nonprocedural languages, and other fourth-generation languages where possible (Chapter 11).

- Using this software, application creation is *fast*.

- Using this software, applications can be modified *quickly*.

- The applications use data systems built with data models which constitute a soundly planned foundation stone designed to be as stable as possible (Chapter 5).

- Users and management participate extensively in creating the data models [5] .

- Information resource planning is treated as a senior management function and employs proven methodologies [6] .

- Where possible, end users or systems analysts working directly with end users create their own applications at a terminal, using data systems [1] .

- Where possible, end users or systems analysts working directly with end users maintain their own applications interactively.

- Data-base action diagrams [7] are used where necessary to chart procedures.

- Class IV data systems, which are more flexible than traditional data-base systems (Chapter 5), are used where transaction rates are not too high.

- Where conventional programs are written, this is not done without prototyping (Chapter 13). Prototypes largely replace the use of lengthy written requirements documents. Where possible, the prototype is converted directly into the application.

- The creation of information systems is incremental and interactive, as opposed to the single great-leap-forward associated with requirements documentation and a specification freeze.

(*Continued*)

Box 12.2 *(Continued)*

- Management controls are employed, linked to the data models, to prevent the spread of incompatible data.
- Information center management is used extensively but tightly linked to the data administration process.
- Many systems analysts assume the role of consultants, encouraging and helping users to employ the new tools and information sources, and creating applications for them.

search or reorganize their own data, explore "what-if?" questions with their data, and generate reports and graphics.

Sometimes end users create their own procedures and sometimes systems analysts work with them. This is the procedure formation block of Fig. 12.4. Techniques can be used which greatly simplify the design of procedures, given that data models exist and that fourth-generation languages are used. The procedures can be rapidly implemented and easily changed with fourth-generation languages.

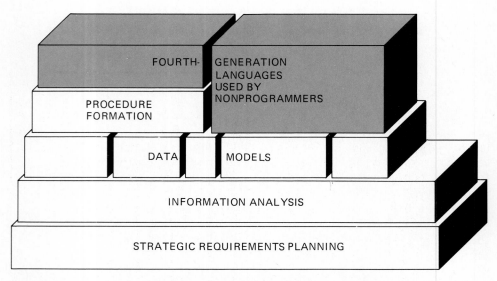

Figure 12.4 Information system development in its most powerful form.

CHANGE IN DEMAND   The types of applications that are needed by users are changing. Many corporations have already built their routine DP applications, such as payroll, invoicing, and bill-of-materials breakdown. Their primary needs now relate to providing better information to the various management processes.

The Sloan School study breaks down the applications requested by user management into four types [8]:

- *Monitor:* routine systems that monitor daily transactions and produce standard reports on a fixed schedule
- *Exception:* systems that produce predefined reports about predefined exception conditions
- *Inquiry:* systems that provide flexible inquiry capability, enabling users to design and change their own reports when they wish
- *Analysis:* systems that provide powerful means of analyzing the data in data bases in order to support decision making (e.g., optimization, modeling, "what-if?" questions, simulation, and statistics)

The study indicated that the ratios of these applications was approximately the same in the invisible backlog as it was in the declared backlog, but substantially different from the installed mix of applications. User management are asking for *six* times as many *analysis* systems, *three* times as many *query* systems, and *twice* as many *exception* systems as are currently installed. Professor Alloway, who conducted the study, projects the future demand as:

- 12 times as many *analysis* systems as currently installed
- 4 times as many *query* systems
- 1.5 times as many *exception* systems
- $\frac{1}{4}$ of the number of *monitor* systems

The analysis and query categories are *demand* systems which cannot generally be prespecified. They need to satisfy the need for information *when it arises,* and when the users see the information they are likely to change their requirements. These growing system categories are much worse for maintenance if programming is done in the traditional way. It is therefore vital to bypass the traditional systems analysis stages of writing specification documents. Such applications need to be created quickly and flexibly with very high level languages by the end users or technical assistants who help them. The raw data need to be accessible and well designed. The languages should be chosen so as to facilitate easy and ongoing modification of the application, preferably by the end users.

Finding or analyzing the requisite information is usually an iterative process. It is common to hear an executive say, "I don't know what I want, but I'll recognize it when I see it" [8]. The data in different records may be associated in different ways, often on a trial-and-error basis. The decision maker says: "Let's try a different cut at the data." The decision makers often want the data immediately—including the ones who say, "I don't know what I want but. . . ."

When managers are provided with preplanned listings of data, it is a common sight to see them scanning the data and using a pocket calculator, trying, often with inadequate success, to make estimates create information not provided. Such users should be able to browse in large data systems, extract the information they need, put it into palatable forms, do calculations on it, plot the results, and create charts and reports. Languages with which end users can perform these activities are now excellent.

THE FALLACY OF PROGRESSIVE SUMMARIZATION

Data processing often tries to serve the needs of managers with summaries of data. The higher the level of management, the greater the degree of aggregation or summary. In fact, top-level managers often have questions more subtle or complex than those which can be answered by the preplanned summaries. It is because managers' needs are different that they are seen inadequately manipulating with pocket calculators the data they are given.

What they really need is the ability to have questions relating to the data answered *when they arise.* They need to be able to access, or have assistants who can access, all the relevant data, summarize and do calculations with the data, ask "what if?" questions, and so on.

Top-level managers certainly need summaries. They need an essence distilling from the unwieldy mass of data, but that essence is likely to be different as different problems and needs arise, and sometimes these needs require a detailed examination of portions of the data.

DIFFERENT PATTERNS

These different patterns of user needs require a different approach to the DP development. The attempt to meet such needs with structured analysis and structured COBOL seems doomed to failure. Instead, corporations need appropriate data systems establishment—Class III or, more often, Class IV. The raw data in an enterprise can be identified independently of how they are used, as described in this book, and normalized records can be made available for analysis in unanticipated ways with the powerful new languages. The user query and analysis process will often be ad hoc and trial and error.

Box 12.3 lists typical characteristics of decision support systems. This very important use of computers requires fourth-generation languages (even

BOX 12.3   Characteristics of decision support systems

Immediacy:

The information is often needed quickly to support an urgent management decision. There is no time for the traditional systems analysis specification cycle.

Often Unanticipatable:

Although some decision needs can be anticipated, many arise which are unforeseen crisis decisions: "What is the effect of a sudden vendor strike?" "How will the price increase affect the cash flow?"

Existing Data Types:

Although the decision need may be unanticipatable, the data types have usually existed long before and can be stored in data systems for future extraction and analysis.

Unstructured Processes:

Whereas processes for routine operations can be highly structured, processes for decision support often cannot be. One question often leads the decision maker to another in an iterative fashion.

Structured Data:

The data have properties independent of how they are used, which enable them to be structured into third-normal-form records.

Flexible Data Use:

The decision maker sometimes says: "I don't know what I want, but I'll recognize it when I see it." He is often investigating complex situations with multiple interrelated factors. A flexible data system is needed so that different data from different normalized records can be freely associated (as in a relational data base).

Short Life:

Many applications are once-only, or have a short life. Some applications may be found useful enough to be cataloged for repetitive use.

(*Continued*)

Box 12.3 *(Continued)*

Speed:

Speed may be more important than completeness. Approximate results before a decision is made are more valuable than exact results after it has been made.

Personal:

Decision makers often have personal styles and needs. A program created for one person is often not usable by a different decision maker.

Non-DP-Trained Users:

The users are usually not trained in DP. They often do not use a keyboard for any other purpose.

Busy Users:

The users are often busy handling a wide diversity of situations in a day. They are usually too short of time to learn complex languages and would rapidly forget mnemonics. Highly user-friendly dialogue structures are needed.

Noncurrent Data:

Most decision support does not need data which are current up to the second. Usually, an extraction of yesterday's or last week's data will suffice. Many decisions need historical or time-series data so that trends and changing data relationships can be examined. Managers often learn from the past and relate it to the current situation.

Calculations:

Decision makers need an easy means of expressing calculations which they can apply to the data. Often they modify the calculations in an iterative fashion.

"What-If?" Questions:

Many decisions are better made if multiple "what-if?" questions are posed. This can often be done simply by changing certain data values and calculating the effects. Users may create their own

Box 12.3 *(Continued)*

versions of the data with "what if?" modifications made to the data.

Graphics:

Graphics displays provide a useful way of understanding data and exploring the potential effects of decisions.

Off-Line Study:

Some managers need to print reports of data or analyses for off-line study, for example, at home.

Easy Access:

The system must be easy to access and constantly available. Any obstacle or inhibitor tends to frustrate and put off the potential user.

Response Time:

Fairly fast on-line response time is needed, so that data can be searched and alternative analysis developed, modified, and compared.

Justification:

Tangible numeric justification for decision support systems is often missing. Cost-benefit studies are often not done. However, the value of better informed decisions is often high and management's complaints usually relate to the insufficiency of systems rather than to their cost.

All Levels of Management:

Decision support systems are needed at all levels of management:

- *Operations management* for tracking and analyzing operational alternatives.
- *Tactical management* for developing alternative plans, comparing actual to planned performance, and evaluating sudden opportunities or crises.
- *Strategic management* for evaluating strategies in a simulated rather than a real environment.

more than other categories of systems) and needs the type of DP management described in the following chapter.

DISCIPLINE

User-driven computing, we believe, is *essential* for certain types of systems. Without it, the maintenance cost and inflexibility will be extremely damaging. User-driven computing implies application creation without programmers; it certainly does not imply application creation without controls. Applications may be built by end users; more often, applications are built by analysts working with users. Users may learn to create their own reports or graphics displays even though they do not build the system.

The whole idea of user-drive computing encounters great emotional resistance in many installations. There are several reasons for this. First, to many DP people the whole idea of application creation without programmers still seems strange and alien to the God-given order. Second, programmers, not surprisingly, resist the idea and concoct scornful arguments against it. Higher DP executives can be alarmed by it also and sometimes envision their empires dwindling if end-user departments learn to create their own applications.

A major reason for resistance is that DP organizations have struggled to achieve discipline in the DP development process. This process used to be an unruly free-for-all until standards and guidelines were established relatively recently. The standards and methods have assumed the force of law, have been taught to all DP staff in an organization, and are regarded as a vital necessity in the crusade against unstructured methods, unmaintainable code, nonportable programs, and lack of scientific discipline. The installation standards, religiously adhered to, have frozen the methodologies of large installations at a time when the technology is plunging into new forms.

Discipline is certainly needed. This can come from the formal data modeling and information engineering techniques. Information engineering establishes a framework, as discussed in Chapter 14. Within that framework end users should be free to employ the data made available to them.

One typical corporation with many computer installations in many countries spent much effort in the 1970s perfecting a project management system. This incorporates installation standards, guidelines, and some software for project control. It is referred to as the installation "Bible." No DP manager will admit that he does not use it; to do so would be detrimental to his career.

If the Bible is followed literally, it prevents DP managers and analysts from achieving high productivity. It insists on having elaborate formal specifications for all applications. These are typically an inch or more thick. It is not possible to do prototyping and remain within the project management system. Interactive use of report generators and application generators results in applications being created and adjusted to fit the users' needs much better than what is usually specified in the formal specifications. Furthermore, the Bible would prevent end users from doing their own application creation.

Some organizations have standards specifying that only certain languages may be used. They exclude all new languages. The U.S. Department of Defense took action to reduce the proliferation of languages and increase the transfer of software among new systems. DOD Instruction 5000.31 listed seven languages which it called HOLs (high-order languages) and restricted application development to these [9]. Whichever language is selected, 100% of the programming must be done in it except possibly for optimized subroutines written in assembler or machine language. All seven of the HOLs are procedural and should be regarded as *low*-level languages compared with NOMAD, FOCUS, MAPPER, MANTIS, or other fourth-generation languages. The DOD Instruction thus prohibits high-productivity techniques.

Other government departments are still issuing application development directives which lock their vast organizations into conventional procedural techniques. Often such directives have been developed with high-powered academic participation and much exhortation about making programming more professional. A paper about the Department of Defense programming directives states: "The theme pervading all of these steps is to elevate software policy, practices, procedure, and technology from an artistic enterprise to a true engineering discipline" [10]. These directives prevent the use of the new methods with which more flexible organizations have speeded up their application creation by a factor of 10 or more.

The installation standards, then, so laboriously created in many organizations, are full of trip wires which prevent the productivity increases which new methods and end users are demanding. It is not easy to reverse the standards, because so many people have been trained and drilled in their use.

A WALL BETWEEN USER AND PROGRAMMER

The traditional techniques for application development tend to build a wall between the application *user* and the application *creator*. The programmer is kept away from the end user.

First there is the formal development life cycle, of which Figs. 12.1 and 12.2 are typical. Written requirement specifications are created. This takes much time but is rarely adequate.

The specifications must be *frozen* at the start of the design and coding phase. Often they are frozen when the ideas about what the system ought to do are still fluid. The user often does not know what he wants until he sees it on a terminal and uses it. This is becoming increasingly so as we move to more complex applications. We have now done the simple, easily standardized applications—payroll, invoicing, and the like—and are faced with more subtle and valuable applications, such as decision support systems, operations control, and financial planning. With these applications a rapid rate of adjustment is needed as the end users begin to change their methods of working. With many such applications, *prototypes* should be created quickly to see if the users like them. The prototypes should be rapidly changeable.

In this environment it is vital that the application creator work hand in hand with the application users. The systems analyst who learns to understand the user's needs should himself create the application and work with the user to adjust it interactively. For most applications this can be done with the new software for generating applications, graphics, reports and database queries. In a few cases, the systems analyst will need to call on the services of a programmer to create complex algorithms, but not (with good software) to create the end-user interface.

Programming in a language such as COBOL or PL/1 takes a long time. The programmer must document his code. In typical installations that are well controlled through a development standards manual, there are about 10 pages of program documentation to each 1000 lines of code. In some installations documentation never gets done.

Often a production line is established for the use of programmers. Jobs for coding wait in a queue until a programmer is free. This maximizes the use of programmers—the scarcest resource—but adds further to the overall elapsed time.

The user sees a multiyear delay before work starts on the application he needs. When work is under way, the time between specifying requirements and obtaining results is so long that during this time the requirements have changed. Many end users, now beginning to understand what computers could do for them, do not formally notify DP of their need because of overload on DP and the multiyear backlog.

The DP creation process is further slowed down by errors which have to be corrected. As indicated in Fig. 12.3, most errors are in requirements analysis or interpretation and design.

Errors in analysis become less of a problem when the analysts can create the applications themselves, quickly, and show them to the end users. Relatively fast end-user feedback enables the analysts to make adjustments while they are still familiar with what they created. This fast cycle of application creation and feedback, using the new application generation software, makes prototyping and adjustment a natural procedure.

Program bugs are reduced by the move to higher-level application creation facilities. Errors are also reduced by removing, where possible, the traditional interaction between systems analyst and programmer. Too often the analysts' program specifications are misinterpreted. When the analyst *creates* the application directly, this cause of errors is removed.

To build this wall between application user and application creator is the worst thing we could do. It is becoming more serious as we evolve to more user-driven applications. New methods of application creation are vital to the future of the computer industry. This future lies with vendors who make possible application creation without the wall.

USER-DRIVEN
PRODUCTION
SYSTEMS

It is sometimes thought that end-user languages are appropriate only for information systems or decision support. They are sometimes referred to generically as *query languages* by people who do not realize that their capabilities are much broader. The good ones can tackle data entry and control, data-base specification and building, arithmetic and logic operations, and complete application generation. Because of this capability they are employed by end users in some corporations to create *production systems* as well as information and decision-support systems. Some of the production systems created by end users are spectacular by any measure.

In some organizations the capability for end users to eliminate their own paperwork has spread pervasively. Data are entered at their source into data-base systems. Electronic files are generated by the end users and data in them are made accessible to other users who need those data. Paper flow is eliminated because many different users can access the data, often viewing it in different ways.

Users are trained to employ the end-user language, encouraged to increase their fluency with it, and motivated to think up ways in which they can improve administrative efficiency. In some corporations end-user-created terminal procedures have enabled a major increase in work load to be absorbed without any increase in administrative staff.

After two or three years of end users creating new terminal uses in an organization, the overall pattern of administrative procedures and information usage is completely changed. It is through this process that the paperless administrative environment becomes as different in shape from the earlier paper-oriented one as today's horseless carriage is from horse-drawn carriages.

User-driven computing is a powerful and exciting trend. *Motivation* of white-collar workers is a complex subject. Why do some work so hard while others do not? Psychologists have found that when workers can design their own work they are usually much more highly motivated. Nonprocedural user-friendly terminal languages are enabling them to do that, where such methods have taken hold.

However, user-driven computing can be a formula for chaos if it is not linked to well-planned data systems. The data administration function is vital in the support of user-driven computing.

SOLVING THE WRONG PROBLEM

Much of today's research into the development process is oriented toward improving the existing methods. Improve programming with the move to structured programming. Improve systems analysis with the move to structured analysis. Formalize the life cycle of Fig. 12.1 and provide tools for documentation and review. Add yet more instruction types and reserved words to COBOL. Adapt languages and compilers for better structured programming. And so on.

In a sense these activites (although highly valuable because such conventional programming will remain) are solving the wrong problem. The important problem is how to migrate from conventional programming and the life cycle of Fig. 12.1 to development methodologies which are fast, flexible, interactive, and employable by end users; methodologies in which interactive prototyping replaces formal, voluminous specifications which must be frozen; methodologies with which end users can create and continuously modify their own applications; and methodologies in which data are analyzed, structured, and made available independently.

If a hammer is not achieving much success in fixing screws, the solution is not to obtain a better hammer. The problem is that the wrong methodology is being used. More appropriate tools are now available for DP development. In some cases DP managers still want to use the old development life cycle even with the new tools. This is rather like the old hammer enthusiasts driving in screws by hitting them hard with the handle of the screwdriver.

Daniel McCracken tells a parable about a man with an old car who wanted to go from New York to California in a day. He souped up the engine, changed the transmission, and modified the car any way he could to make it faster. He fitted it with superb police radar detectors, but the attempt to make it sufficiently fast was doomed before it began. When told that he could use a different technology to get to California—take a jet—he said: "Oh those things! They'll never fly!" Many programmers have the same attitude to application generators.

VARIETIES OF END USERS

Society has endless varieties of people, with enormously differing interests and skills. The same is true of computer end users. It is desirable that they should have available a wide variety of techniques for using the computing power which is now spreading to the users. A type of dialogue structure that is good for one user is not necessarily good for another. Some end users will learn to program; most will not. Some end users will learn mnemonics; most will not. Some end users will be happy with simple menu selection dialogues; others will find these slow and restricting.

We sometimes make the mistake of talking about "end users" as though they were all the same. In fact, they are as diverse as all of Shakespeare.

Whereas the new software gives one class of users terminal dialogues of extreme simplicity, other software offers the capability to use sophisticated languages. To all these different groups, usability should be the prime consideration. Value to users is of more concern than machine performance.

The *role* of the end user is being changed by a variety of technologies: microelectronics, desktop computers, minicomputers, distributed processing, better terminal dialogue facilities. As a result, the numbers of end users are growing fast.

Today, because of the backlog with low-level application development techniques, many DP managers perceive the pressure from end users for applications as being excessive. *In reality, however, most end users have barely begun to realize the potential of computing for improving how they do their job.*

SPECTACULAR END-USER SYSTEMS

There are a variety of case histories of end users having created comprehensive systems with multiple applications, which are by any standards spectacular [1]. The moral of such case histories is that *we have grossly underestimated end users.*

Some end users are amazingly bright people. They need the right tools and encouragement. Many end users want to create their own facilities but have not been given the tools to do it. The majority have not yet glimpsed the possibilities. In showing a user-created system to one typical end user the comment was made: "If I had something like that I could save 40 to 60 hours a month." This realization needs to spread among white-collar workers everywhere (and some blue-collar ones).

When writing this book we talked to software and system architects in the computer and software industry. All of them understood the need for improving the productivity of application creation, but almost all of them thought that this must come via DP experts. Highly influential software architects talked about the end users as though they were idiots and told one story after another to reinforce this view. There are certainly top executives who will never cross the cultural threshold into using their own terminal. There are certainly bigoted users who describe computer staff as "little tin Hitlers." But there is also a vast world of intelligent users with problems to solve if only they had the right encouragement and tools.

Box 12.4 lists reasons why end users should use computers directly. Much computing *ought* to be end-user driven. To create end-user driven computing the following facilities are needed:

- An interactive system with screen terminals.
- Application generation software that is data based and report oriented, preferably with graphics capability.

BOX 12.4   Reasons why end users should "do their own thing" with computers

- Only the end users truly understand the subtleties of their own applications (especially if they are complex).
- The end users should be made *responsible* for how they employ computers.
- End users can obtain the applications they want earlier, thereby relieving the extreme frustration with DP that some end users feel.
- Spontaneous demands for information may be satisfied quickly.
- End users should be encouraged to use their imagination about what computers can do for them.
- The total number of people working on application development can be much larger.
- The understanding of what is needed comes slowly with experience in using the system. A facility is needed with which users can make many rapid modifications to their system.
- Complex administrative procedures tend to evolve a step at a time, each step being a reaction to current problems and pressures. Computerized procedures should evolve in the same way.
- End users are much brighter than many DP professionals admit; the best of them can be highly inventive in their use of computers.
- The traditional development life cycle (Figs. 12.1 and 12.2) does not work for user-driven systems.

- Software that is elegantly human-factored and easy to use.
- Linkage to appropriate on-line data systems.
- Data in the data systems which have been planned with substantial user involvement with the techniques of information engineering.
- A complete absence of DP jargon. There is no need for difficult words or acronyms.
- Software that end users can learn to use well in two days.
- Good instruction, encouragement, and sympathy.
- Self-teaching software in which the HELP function is skillfully written. Computer-aided teaching at the terminal should guide and test the user and encourage him to experiment.
- A management approach which seeks out the early adapters and motivates them to encourage their less adventurous colleagues.

- Tools built into the software for managing and controlling its use.

- Encouragement and cooperation from DP, not competition with and isolation from DP.

- Good security and authorization controls.

- DP information center management, described next, linking the user-driven activities to the other corporate computing, data-base, and network resources.

- General management that motivates end users to invent and acquire the facilities they need.

THE INFORMATION CENTER CONCEPT

The installation Bible is not going to be abandoned overnight, nor should it. What is happening instead is that *alternative* means of creating applications are coming into existence which now coexist with the traditional methods.

In some cases end users have created the alternative method, without DP approval. User departments acquire their own minicomputer or use software that permits fast application creation. Sometimes they use time-sharing services with languages such as NOMAD or a partition of a mainframe with languages such as MAPPER. DP executives in some organizations have tried to stop this uncontrolled spread of minicomputers and languages. In other cases they have allowed it to happen, only too glad to get some of the end users off their back. The *uncontrolled* spread of minicomputers, however, can store up trouble for the future because multiple versions of incompatible data, and multiple machines which cannot be linked into networks, come into existence.

A valuable approach is the *information center* concept. The information center is a group within the DP organization designed to serve the end users directly and speedily. The group is aware of which data bases exist and sometimes sets up other data bases. It makes this information available to end users, employing the types of languages described in this book. Information center consultants work with the end users and create, where possible, the applications they want. The consultants help to create the decision support systems, personal computing facilities, information retrieval systems, and organizational support systems. A major reason for establishing this mode of operation has been the extreme dissatisfaction expressed by end users about the way DP has been responding to their information needs.

The consultants encourage the users to employ the information facilities which already exist. They sit at terminals with the users to create the cataloged query procedures, report generation routines, or graphics generation routines. They train the users to employ these facilities.

Where more complex applications are needed, the information center consultants decide how they can be created, selecting, where possible, an application generator or language which avoids the formal programming development cycle of Figs. 12.1 and 12.2.

Prototyping allows new frontiers to be explored. Sometimes a system is created which users will never employ. This can be done quickly with the application generators and not too much time is wasted. The lessons learned enable better design next time.

The end users need much training and handholding in adapting to new systems. The information center consultant can work closely with users, showing them how to employ the facilities. In some cases substantial use is made of computer-based training. IBM's IIS (Interactive Instruction System) is used extensively in some installations for training end users. It is sometimes used for prototyping. It is used to simulate an end-user terminal dialogue before detailed programs are generated.

CONTROL OF USER-DRIVEN COMPUTING

To make user-driven computing fully effective, a management style is needed which both encourages and controls it. Techniques need to be employed which are fully cognizant of the maintenance problem. The following chapters describe such techniques. Chapter 13 discusses prototyping. Chapter 14 discusses a disciplined approach to data-centered application creation—information engineering—and the linkage of this discipline to information center management.

REFERENCES

1. Examples are described in J. Martin, *Application Development Without Programmers* (Englewood Cliffs, NJ: Prentice-Hall, Inc., 1982).

2. U.S. Department of Defense Directive 5000.29, *Management of Computer Resources in Major Defense Systems.*

3. J. Fox, *Managing Software* (Englewood Cliffs, NJ: Prentice-Hall, Inc., 1981).

4. T. de Marco, *Structured Analysis and System Specification* (New York: Yourdon, Inc., 1978).

5. J. Martin, *Managing the Data-base Environment* (Englewood Cliffs, NJ: Prentice-Hall, Inc., 1983).

6. J. Martin and C. Finkelstein, *Information Engineering,* Savant Technical Report 22, Savant Institute, Carnforth, Lancashire, UK, 1981.

7. J. Martin, *Fourth-Generation Languages,* Savant Technical Report 25, Savant Institute, Carnforth, Lancashire, UK, 1982.

8. R. B. Rosenberger, "The Information Center," SHARE Proceedings No. 56, Session M372, March 1981.

9. J. H. Lehman, "How Software Projects Are Really Managed," *Datamation,* January 1979.

10. U.S. Department of Defense Instruction 5000.31, *Interim List of D.D. Approved High-Order Programming Languages.*

13 PROTOTYPING

The concept of prototyping is particularly important to maintenance.

With most complex engineering a prototype is created before the final product is *built*. This is done to test the principles, ensure that the system works, and obtain design feedback which enables the design to be adjusted before the big money is spent. A chemical plant is built in a laboratory form before the plant is finally designed. The hull shape of a boat is tested. A new airplane is simulated in a variety of ways before it is built.

Complex data processing systems need prototyping more than most engineering systems because there is much to learn from a pilot operation and many changes are likely to be made. Prototypes help to solve the problems of systems not working in the way the end users really need, and this greatly reduces the modifications that are eventually requested.

In a sense the system created by the traditional DP life cycle (Figs. 12.1 and 12.2) is a prototype. It is not *meant* to be a prototype and is not regarded as such, but it has all the imperfections of a prototype. These imperfections are expensive to correct, so they often remain in the system, leading eventually to costly maintenance.

The reason DP prototypes were not generally used until the 1980s was that the cost of programming a prototype was about as high as the cost of programming the live working system. Fourth-generation languages enable prototypes to be created relatively cheaply.

A systems analyst working with an end user can create and demonstrate dialogues for data-base queries, report generation, and manipulation of screen information. The analyst discusses an end user's needs with him and then creates a specimen dialogue on a terminal. This might take him an hour or a week, depending on the complexity and the language that is being used. Initially, he ignores questions of transaction loads and machine performance.

The end user is shown the dialogue and quickly trained to use it. Usually, he has some suggestions for changes he would like and the analyst makes these. The user may add subtotals or extra columns. He may want to perform certain calculations. The analyst may show him the different types of charts that could be created—scatter plots, bar charts, charts with regression lines, linear versus log scales, and so on. The user remembers a different type of customer, or some union rule that was forgotten, or other factors that only the user would be likely to know.

Often major misunderstandings surface, and/or ambiguities and inconsistencies are uncovered. Different users have different interpretations of the same data. Omissions are found. The users think of other features they would like added. The users may find parts of the system difficult to use, or confusing, so that screen clarification or on-line *help* facilities can be improved.

When users operate a system for a few weeks it *always* changes their perception about what they really want. Prototyping allows this to occur early in the development cycle, not after implementation, when change is expensive.

As the analyst and user continue their discussion of what is needed, the running prototype is now a focus of the debate which helps to ensure that they are both talking about the same thing. The screens are printed and the end user takes them home to think about them. The analyst works further, improving the screen interaction, adding new features, and improving the displays.

Finally, the user is satisfied, excited, and says: "When can I get it?" In some cases he can have it very quickly. The data base exists and the prototype can become the final application. In other cases he cannot have it yet because design work is needed to achieve machine efficiency, security, auditability, telecommunications networking, or to create the data base.

In the latter case the prototype becomes, in effect, the requirements document for application programming.

PROTOTYPING SOFTWARE

The software used for prototyping is often the same that we described in Chapter 11—application generators, report generators, data management systems, screen design aids, and so on. Its most important characteristic is that it should permit prototyping to be performed *quickly*. Prototyping requires a *quick and inexpensive* means of testing a trial balloon.

The second most important characteristic is that users, or analysts working with them, should be able to make adjustments quickly and easily.

These two characteristics are also at the top of the requirements list for fourth-generation languages designed to minimize the personnel needed for application creation and maintenance. Is there any difference in the requirements for a prototyping language and a development language?

Yes. The development language may be designed to give good machine performance, whereas this is not a concern in the prototyping language. The development language may give one fixed type of screen format; the prototyper may want more flexibility in designing and experimenting with different screen layouts. The development language may employ a traditional data-base management system; the prototyping language may employ an easy-to-implement data management system (Class IV in Box 5.2).

In spite of these differences there is a good reason to make the prototyping language the same as the development language. This reason is that the prototype may evolve into the final system. This has several advantages. First, it saves much development time. Second, it gives continuity between the prototype and the final system as the users become familiar with the final system. Third, it makes it possible to modify the final system in the same way as modifying the prototype.

Box 13.1 lists characteristics to look for in the selection of a prototyping language.

WHY CONVERT?

If the prototype can become the final system, why convert it to a system developed with a traditional language?

There are powerful reasons *not* to convert it to COBOL or other third-generation languages. As soon as it is rewritten in COBOL it is expensive to maintain, whereas if it remains in the prototyping language, modifications are easy to make.

The most common argument *for* conversion is machine performance.

As we discussed in Chapter 11, machine performance is a major concern only for heavy-duty applications. Fifty percent of the applications in a typical DP installation consume a total of 2% of the machine cycles. Their machine costs are *much* less than their maintenance costs in COBOL. Furthermore, some application generators which are appropriate for prototyping are designed to give good machine performance—sometimes better than COBOL applications, where their building blocks are tightly coded in machine language.

DP staff feeling the urge to convert prototypes to COBOL should calculate the costs of conversion plus, say, five years' maintenance, and compare these costs with the machine savings and costs of maintenance in the prototyping languages. There is another more subtle cost of having the application in third-generation languages—they inhibit change; and the inability to change the system may result in lost business opportunities or inefficiencies.

BOX 13.1 Characteristics to look for in the selection of a prototyping language

- How rich are its functions?
  - Simple query
  - Complex query
  - Report generator
  - Graphics generator
  - Application generator
  - High-level programming
- Are there intelligent default assumptions if details are unspecified?
- Is it easy to design and change screen formats?
- Can it also be used as a development language?
- Can it generate
  - compares?
  - logic operations
  - Boolean algebra?
  - conditional clauses?
  - loops?
  - subroutines?
- Is it on-line or off-line?
- Is it suitable for end users, systems analysts, or programmers?
- Is the language syntax good for maintenance? (With some it is easy to understand another person's code; with others it is difficult.)
- Does it use a standard DBMS, its own simple DBMS, or files?
- Is it DBMS-independent?
- Is file design provided for automatically?
- What support facilities does it have?
  - DBMS
  - Concurrency controls
  - Security
  - Logging and audit tools
  - Recovery and restart
  - Dynamic data-base modification
  - Data dictionary
  - Procedure library
  - Terminal driver
- Is multithread operation supported?
- Dialogue ease of use: Is it easy to learn? Is it easy to remember?
- Does it force the operator to remember mnemonics, formats, or fixed sequences?
- Is it self-teaching, with computer-aided instruction or effective responses to HELP requests on all its functions?

Box 13.1 *(Continued)*

- Is it easy to install? Can it be installed without systems programmers, or does it require complex systems programming?

- Is it operating system-independent?

- Is it terminal-independent?

- Does it have its own terminal driver?

- How good is the quality, appearance, and richness of the reports, displays, or graphics?

- Can it store cataloged procedures? Can these be parameterized?

- Does it use color?

- Can it operate at different levels of verboseness in its dialogue?

- Does it have simple obvious-to-use sign-on procedures?

- Does it have good, clear documentation?

- Is it easy to debug? Does it have good testing tools?

- Does it give clear self-explanatory error messages?

- Can new data be added dynamically (while other users are employing its data base)?

- Can the data-base structure be changed dynamically (while other users are employing its data base)?

- Can new secondary indices (or other search mechanisms) be added for any field? At any time?

- Can data be automatically extracted from an existing data base or file system and rebuilt for this system?

- Can data be moved from this system to a separate file or data-base system?

- Does the organization selling it give good service and support?

- Does it employ a dictionary?
    Active or passive dictionary?
    Is it linked to a major DBMS dictionary?
    Can it use aliases?
    Does it store or generate column heading or report and chart labels?

- Can it generate good security and privacy locks?

- Can it generate good auditing features?
    Automatic audit trails
    Accuracy controls
    Logs of usage

- Can it be used for accurate data-entry operations?

- Does it have good protection from system crashes?

Other important reasons for rebuilding the prototype are to achieve better security, integrity controls, protection from crashes, reliability, and auditability. The ability to have larger data bases, more terminals, a better network, or higher transaction volumes may be other reasons.

When the DP group initially selects the prototyping technique, they should have in mind the desirability of making the prototype into the final system.

THREE TYPES OF APPLICATION DEVELOPMENT

We thus have three types of application development:

1. Traditional development with a life cycle like that in Figs. 12.1 and 12.2. This has the problems which we have discussed.

2. Use of an application generator as a prototyping tool. The end user interacts with the prototype and the systems analyst modifies it until it is a suitable model for application programming. The prototyping tool alleviates as much of the need for separate requirements documentation as possible. Modules of code may be created by the prototyping tool to alleviate the need for programming *all* of the application.

3. Use of an application generator (or other software in Fig. 11.1) to develop the entire application. The prototype becomes the application. No separate use is made of professional programmers. An end user and DP analyst may work together to create the applications.

The third of these development approaches can be used for most but not all commercial data processing. For many data-processing applications there need be little concern with machine efficiency because they do not run frequently. Only a small proportion are high-volume applications.

For heavy-duty applications, high machine efficiency is needed. This can be achieved in one of three ways:

1. First, we have stressed that some fourth-generation languages are designed to achieve high machine efficiency. A specialist who knows all the tricks with an application generator can sometimes achieve much more efficient results than the average analyst. The analyst may create a heavy-duty application in DMS or ADF and then hand it over to a DMS or ADF "acrobat" for optimization.

2. There may be certain routines which are time-eaters. These can be isolated and programmed in a more efficient language if the generator has suitable EXITS.

3. The entire application may be reprogrammed for efficiency. The generator version is used to guide the programming team instead of written requirements documentation. Sometimes the generator creates only part of what is needed, so a hybrid of generator input/output and written specifications is needed.

Box 13.2 lists typical characteristics of these three approaches to application development. In many large corporations all three types of develop-

BOX 13.2 Three types of application development

	Conventional Application Development (As in Figs. 12.1 and 12.2)	Information Engineering and Fourth-Generation Languages	
		Use of a Prototyping Aid Followed by Programming	Application Development Without Professional Programmers
Requirements Analysis	A time-consuming, formal operation, often delayed by long application backlog.	The user's imagination is stimulated. He may work at a a screen with an analyst to develop requirements.	The user's imagination is stimulated. He may develop his own requirements, or work with an analyst.
System Specification Document	Lengthy document. Boring. Often inadequate.	Produced by proto-typing aid. Precise and tested.	Disappears.
User Sign-off	User is often not sure on what he is signing off. He cannot perceive all the subtleties.	User sees the results and may modify them many times before signing off.	No formal sign-off. Adjustment and modification is an ongoing process.
Data	Often designed separately for each application.	Planned with information analysis and data modeling.	Planned with infor-mation analysis and data modeling. Made available in data systems.
Coding and Testing	Slow. Expensive. Often delayed because of backlog.	The prototype is converted to more efficient code. Relatively quick and error-free.	Quick. Inexpensive. Disappears to a large extent.
Documentation	Tedious. Time consuming.	May be partly automated. Interactive training and HELP responses may be created on-line.	Largely automatic. Interactive training and HELP responses are created on-line.
Maintenance	Slow. Expensive. Often late.	Less slow. Less expensive. Less late. Fewer modification are needed to the final system.	A continuing process, with user and analyst making adjustments.

ment are likely to coexist. A good DP executive will organize his operation so that they *can* coexist. In some corporations the DP department uses only the traditional development life cycle, and the end users have bypassed the DP department, using the new languages to create their own applications more quickly and satisfactorily.

The mature DP executive should *welcome* end users creating their own applications and not fight it. He should regard it as his job to provide them with the software tools, networks, and consultant systems analysts that they need. But particularly important, he should link their activities to the data modeling and data systems created by information engineering.

PARTIAL SYSTEM PROTOTYPING   Some prototyping efforts create a pilot version of a complete application. Some tackle only one facet of an application. Partial system prototyping has proven particularly valuable on some systems. Often DP managers have not considered this approach because they assume that a complete system prototype is needed. Partial system prototyping can be easier and there may be less excuse for not using it. Partial prototypes are of a variety of different forms:

• *Dialogue prototype.* The prototype simulates the intended terminal interaction. This is probably the most common form of partial prototyping. It allows the end users to see what they will be receiving, play with it, suggest omissions, improve the ease of comprehension, generally react to the dialogue, and finally sign off on its development. Various software products can be used as dialogue simulators.

The design of the terminal dialogue greatly affects the usability and users' perception of the system. Many systems have been partial failures because of poor terminal dialogues. Amazingly, many systems analysts and programmers are not trained in what constitutes a psychologically effective dialogue. They often create dialogues which are muddled, not clean, and which confuse some of the users. It helps to build a prototype dialogue which can be tested, criticized, and improved before final implementation.

• *Data entry.* One group of users may perform data entry. The data-entry subsystem may be prototyped and adjusted independently and may be linked to an existing system. Data-entry prototyping may be done to check the speed and accuracy of the data entry. Validity and integrity checks may be tested.

Some systems have been split into a *front end* and *back office.* The front end is interactive. The back office consists of multiple batch updating runs. The front end may be prototyped independently using software such as MAPPER, FOCUS, RAMIS, or NOMAD. The back office may remain in the form of COBOL programs.

• *Reporting system.* The reports provided to users may be tried out on them before full system implementation. They may be either batch or on-line. Often many adjustments are made in the reporting subsystem. Report generators may be used, such as RPG, NOMAD, or ADRS.

- *Data system.* A prototype data base may be implemented with a small number of records. Users and analysts interact with it, generating reports or displaying information which might be useful to them. This interaction often results in requests for different types of data, new fields, or different ways of organizing the data.

With some prototyping tools, users or analysts have the ability to build their own files, manipulate them, and display information from them. Such tools are used to explore how the users will employ information, and what should be in the data base.

- *Calculations and logic.* Sometimes the logic of an application, or the calculations, are complex. Actuaries, engineers, investment analysts, or other such users may use a language such as APL to build examples of the computations they need. These may then be incorporated into larger systems, perhaps linked to other applications, to data bases, or to many terminals. The users may employ their APL prototypes to check the accuracy of the results.

- *Application package.* An application package may be tried out with a small group of users to determine whether it is satisfactory. The need for various modifications may become clear. These are tried out before the package is linked to other applications or put into volume use.

- *Concept.* Sometimes the concept of an application is in question. It needs testing and refining before too much money is spent on building the system. The test may be done with a quick-to-implement data management system. Standard data-entry screens and standard report formats may be used so that the concepts may be tested and refined without too much work. Later, application-specific reports or screens may be built.

DIFFERENT HARDWARE

Sometimes prototyping is done on different hardware from that of the final system. This may be because the final hardware is not yet available. It may be because it is much easier to experiment on a small minicomputer than on the final complex system. Prototyping aids need to be selected which are easily adaptable to the final hardware.

REAL DATA

With some prototyping the analyst creates small files of made-up data to illustrate what the system will do. In other cases made-up data are not good enough. The users need to update real data or explore complex data bases in order to experience what the proposed system will do for them.

If real data are required, the users may be given prototypes connected to a *live* data system or may be given data that have been *extracted* from a live data system. The latter is generally safer and more flexible.

If the users do not update the data they may be given report generators or other facilities which *use* data in a live data base but which cannot *modify* the data. Often, however, the users want to manipulate or update the data. They should then be given extracted data to do this with and locked out of the live data.

In some prototyping efforts the users ask for information of various types. The analyst must find out where such data exist, capture them, and reconstruct them in the data management system of the prototyping tool. Sometimes they exist on batch files, sometimes in corporate data bases; sometimes they can be obtained from external sources.

When real data are used the prototype sometimes grows into a system that the users do not want to give up; it becomes a real working system.

THROWAWAY PILOTS

When prototyping becomes very easy, the development organization or end-user groups themselves may create pilot systems and try them out to see whether other end users like them. In some organizations a third or so of the pilots created fall into disuse, whereas some are perceived as being very valuable.

By use of throwaway pilots, system designers can discover the requirements and refinements that end users will actually employ. It is a trial-and-error process: build a pilot, observe it in use, evaluate, revise it where necessary, or replace it with a different version; do not worry if some of the pilots are abandoned.

THE DEVELOPMENT PROCESS WITH PROTOTYPING

Prototyping, illustrated in Fig. 13.1, creates a different cycle of DP development from the traditional one. Because prototypes vary widely in their character and use, there are widely different versions of this life cycle.

The first step in Fig. 13.1 is the broad determination of what the end users need. Often the users make a request. An analyst studies it, determines what data it requires, and determines how it might be prototyped. For small systems this can be informal, without any written specifications. For large systems it might involve detailed written descriptions of what data are needed, data flow diagrams, or event diagrams showing how a data base will be used.

In the second step a working prototype is created. It is important that this be done *quickly*. The prototype may use the standard default options of

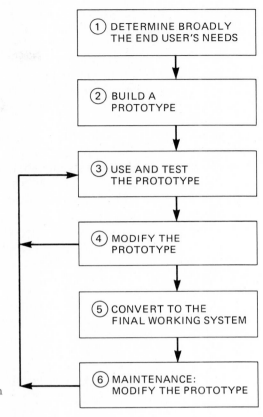

Figure 13.1 Development life cycle with prototyping.

a nonprocedural facility or data management system in order to demonstrate something to the users quickly. It may initially demonstrate only the major functions and not yet include peripheral details, auditors' requirements, and so on.

The third step may progress from an initial demonstration to a small group of users, to a more thorough and refined test with multiple users. Some changes requested by users can be made at the screen when they request them. Other requests are noted for later modifications. With some prototyping tools, end users with terminals in multiple locations may employ the prototype, and may record their requests or comments at the terminal.

Sometimes the initial prototypes may be inappropriate, so that they are scrapped and different ones created. When the prototype reaches an acceptable state, multiple users may be trained to use it and to experiment with it.

To demonstrate the prototype's usefulness to management, managers may be asked to bring demonstration questions which they would like the system to be able to answer. The analysts who created the prototype will either demonstrate this ability or expand the system if possible to meet the requirements.

If in step 5 a conversion to different software takes place, the original version should be kept. The original version may be needed for future enhancement maintenance, feeding back to step 3, as shown in Fig. 13.1

RESISTANCE

Prototyping seems so vital to the development process, and has in practice saved so much money in maintenance, that it is amazing that so many systems are still developed without prototypes. The reason seems to be reluctance on the part of DP managers to change their methods, and lack of education about the tools now available.

14 INFORMATION ENGINEERING

INTRODUCTION The term *software engineering* refers to the set of disciplines used for specifying, designing, and programming computer software. Software engineering techniques became formalized in the 1970s. They encompass software development methodologies such as structured programming, structured design, and structured analysis, and tools to support these [1]. They are vital in the creation of complex software with complex logic.

In much commercial data processing the need to program complex software can be avoided, especially when fourth-generation languages are used. Much commercial data processing is concerned with capturing data, updating files, creating routine documents, generating reports, and providing the information needed to support decision making. The design of the logic can be made relatively simple by appropriate data-base techniques, but it is complex to create the right data bases and tools for their effective use. Different techniques are needed from those of software engineering. The techniques of the 1970s were rarely good enough, and many information systems were inadequate for the needs of corporate management.

The term *information engineering* refers to the set of interrelated disciplines which are needed to build a computerized enterprise based on today's data systems. Today, some corporations have excellent information systems. Information engineering formalizes the techniques by which they were created. It uses different types of diagrams and methods from software engineering.

The primary focus of information engineering is on the data that are stored and maintained by computers and the information that is distilled from these data. The primary focus of software engineering is the logic that is used in computerized processes. Information engineering seeks to minimize the programming of complex logic and the creation of entangled program interactions. In doing so it minimizes the maintenance difficulties associated with complex custom-built programs.

To minimize maintenance costs in commercial data processing we believe that an organization should minimize the need for the *software engineering* it performs and maximize *information engineering.*

The basic premise of information engineering is that data lie at the heart of modern data processing. This is illustrated in Fig. 14.1. The data are stored and updated with the aid of various types of data systems software. The processes on the left in Fig. 14.1 *create* and *modify* the data. The data must be captured and entered with appropriate accuracy controls. The data will be updated periodically. The processes on the right in Fig. 14.1 *use* the data. Routine documents such as invoices, receipts, freightbills, and work tickets are printed. Executives or professionals sometimes search for information. They create summaries or analyses of the data, and produce charts and reports. They ask "what if?" questions and use the data for helping them make decisions. Auditors check the data and attempt to ensure that they are not misused.

The data in Fig. 14.1 may be in multiple data systems. They may be stored in different ways. They may be distributed. They are often updated and used by means of transmission links and terminals.

A set of *actions* occur that relate to the data. A simple action applies to one record. This action may create, read, update, or delete the record. A

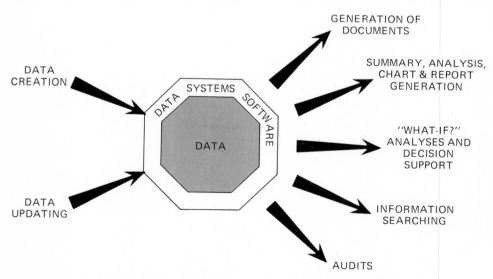

Figure 14.1 Most modern data processing is composed of actions that create and modify data, with appropriate accuracy controls, and processes that use, analyze, summarize, and manipulate data, or print documents from the data.

compound action applies to an entire logical file or relation. We define database actions in more detail elsewhere [2].

The actions are controlled by various *conditions.* Some actions *trigger* other actions. An on-line *procedure* consists of a sequence of actions with associated logic, controlled by certain conditions. We use a diagramming technique to represent these procedures and convert them to highly structured, easily maintainable program code.

DATA ARE STABLE; PROCEDURES ARE NOT　　A basic premise of information engineering is that the *types* of data used in an enterprise do not change very much. An *entity* is something about which we store data—for example, customers, parts, employees, machine tools. The entity *types* do not change from year to year except for the occasional (rare) addition of new entity types. The types of *attributes* that we store about these entities also rarely change. The *values* of data change constantly, like the data in a flight information board at an airport, but the *structure* of the data does not change much if it was well designed to begin with.

As discussed in Chapter 5, if we have a given collection of data items, we can identify which data items are functionally dependent on which other data items; given this knowledge there is one and only one minimal nonredundant structure (canonical model) of the data. Thus we can make a firm, unchanging statement about the structuring of data. However, the processes that employ the data are likely to change frequently. The methods and procedures and the information needs of executives change fundamentally. The computer programs, processes, networks, and hardware change, but the basic types of data remain the same. The data thus form a relatively stable foundation on which computer processes are built. These processes will change constantly and it is desirable to make this change as quick and easy as possible.

Data are usable only when correctly identified and structured so that they have the necessary flexibility. This is not a simple task. Many early attempts to build corporate information systems failed. Now, success often follows where appropriate methodologies are used.

Because the basic types are stable while procedures tend to change, *data-oriented* forms of structured techniques succeed if correctly applied where *procedure-oriented* techniques have failed. Many of the procedure-oriented techniques have resulted in systems which are slow to implement and difficult to change so that maintenance has become a burden. Information engineering seeks to fulfill *rapidly* management's changing needs for information. We can obtain and change results quickly once the necessary data infrastructure is established.

Stress is placed on the information resources that are needed to manage an enterprise effectively. Information is becoming regarded as one of the basic resources of business, together with capital, personnel, and production. Much has been said about the *value* of *information resource management,* but too often effective techniques have been missing.

NONPROCEDURAL LANGUAGES PLUS TIGHT DATA CONTROL   We have stressed the use of nonprocedural languages and Class IV data systems. The flexibility and user friendliness of these facilities enables organizations to overcome the rigidity of conventional data processing. The danger of such facilities is that they make it possible for end users or analysts everywhere to invent their own data and create their own procedures. When this happens chaos can spread rapidly. It becomes impossible to extract the overviews of data from multiple areas which are needed for management control. One form of maintenance has been avoided but another has been created because the incompatible systems have to be converted or linked together.

The best option occurs when not only are user-friendly facilities for system creation employed to the full, but are linked to data models which represent the data in the enterprise in the most stable fashion. The information needed for efficient functioning of the enterprise is made available on Class III and Class IV data-base systems with which nonprocedural languages are employed. It is this combination which information engineering seeks to establish—flexible user-friendly facilities linked to firm management and design of data resources. As Fig. 14.2 illustrates, this is a powerful combination.

AN INTEGRATED SET OF METHODOLOGIES   Information engineering provides an integrated set of methodologies, as shown in Fig. 14.3. In this diagram each block is dependent on the one beneath it. However, as we shall see, the blocks can be as-

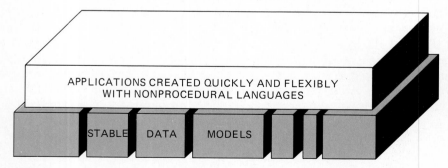

APPLICATIONS CREATED QUICKLY AND FLEXIBLY WITH NONPROCEDURAL LANGUAGES

STABLE DATA MODELS

Figure 14.2 The highest productivity development and most maintainable systems result from the use of nonprocedural languages applied to data in stable data models.

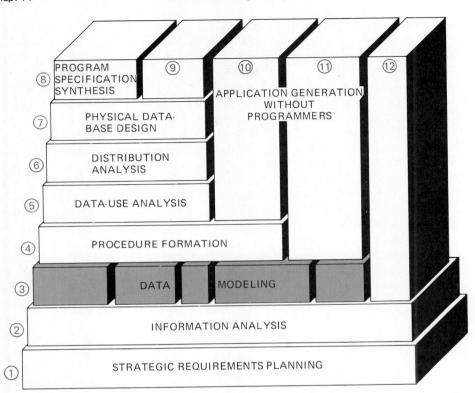

Figure 14.3 Basic building blocks of information engineering. Each block depends on the one beneath it. In some enterprises the bottom one or two blocks are missing.

sembled in different ways. We have drawn the methodologies as building blocks so that we can build somewhat different edifices with them.

(1) The stone on which all the others rest in Fig. 14.3 is *strategic requirements planning*. This attempts to determine the objectives of the enterprise and what information is needed for enabling it to accomplish its objectives. The edifice of Fig. 14.3 can be built without strategic requirements planning, but to do so is like erecting a building on soft ground without good foundations.

(2) The next stage is *information analysis*. This is a top-down analysis of the types of data that must be kept and how they relate to one another. Information analysis is sometimes done across an entire enterprise; sometimes it is done for one division, subsidiary, factory, or portion of an enterprise.

(3) The third stage is *data modeling*. Information analysis surveys the types of data needed. It creates an information model which is a broad overview but which does not contain all the details needed for data-base implementa-

tion. Data modeling creates the detailed logical data-base design and attempts to make it as stable as possible before it is implemented. Stage 3 is an extension of stage 2 which carries it into more detail and applies various checks for stability.

One of the important realizations that led to information engineering is that data exist in an organization and can be described *independently of how the data are used.* Furthermore, the data need to be structured. We must not group any old collection of data items into a record. The data have certain inherent properties which lead to correct structuring. These properties are, again, *independent of how the data are used.* If we structure data in a way which violates their inherent properties, it is likely that we will have to restructure them in the future, and that restructuring will be expensive because programs using the earlier structure will have to be rewritten. If we structure data in accordance with their inherent properties, the structure will be stable. Data synthesis, described in Chapter 6, is a formal technique for analyzing the data in an organization and building them into stable data-base structures called *data models.*

Data modeling is often done without *information analysis.* Information analysis cannot be achieved without senior management support, and that is often lacking. However, to build a fully computerized corporation it is vital to harness the perspectives of top management and put the bottom two blocks of Fig. 14.3 in place.

④ The fourth block of Fig. 14.3 is *procedure formation.* Procedure formation identifies *actions* that change or use the data base. It indicates what *actions* trigger or follow from other *actions.* The *actions* are related to various conditions. When different conditions exist, different *actions* occur. Procedure formation uses a simple diagramming technique to represent the *actions* and group them into procedure charts.

The procedure charts can be simply converted into specifications written in structured English. Structured English is a concise semiformal language which tells programmers what to code. It mirrors the structure of that code and results in fast, relatively error-free coding. It replaces conventional program specifications, but can be read and inspected by end users with brief training. This is the step labeled *program specification synthesis,* level 8, in Fig. 14.3.

The logic defined by procedure formation can be extended by clerks (with no computer experience) directly into formal structured English program specifications, for translation by coders or programmers into appropriate source program statements. Or it can be applied by programmers for direct specification of source program logic from the output of procedure formation. The result is the synthesis of program logic which automatically exhibits high functional cohesiveness (the end objective of structured design). This program logic can be implemented using "traditional" languages such as COBOL, PL/1, or Pascal, or may instead be implemented using end-user languages such as NOMAD or FOCUS or very high level programming languages such as MANTIS. It may be possible to automate the generation of programs from the procedure charts.

(5) *Data use analysis* provides a formal way of collecting and diagramming the usage information ready for *physical data-base design,* which is shown as stage 7 in Fig. 14.3. Data modeling results in the logical design of a data base. A variety of decisions have to be made before that design is implemented physically. The decisions depend on how the data are likely to be used. What are the usage paths through the data base, and what are their volumes of use and response time needs? This information is gathered in the stage labeled *data use analysis* in Fig. 14.3.

(6) Data models may or may not be split for implementation in separate data bases. This may be done for performance reasons. There are many other possible reasons for distributing data or processing power. Stage 6 of Fig. 14.3 is *distribution analysis.*

(7) Stage 7 relates to the conversion of the data models and procedures into physical data-base design.

(8) Stage 8 synthesizes the different procedures to integrate their *actions* where possible, further document the data changes, and produce functionally cohesive program code.

(9) One of the most important new directions of data processing is the development of powerful end-user languages which enable results to be obtained without the use of professional programmers. As described in Chapter 11, such languages may be employed by end users or, more commonly, by systems analysts directly aiding the end users.

Figure 14.3 illustrates four types of application generation without programmers, labeled 9, 10, 11, and 12.

Type 9 uses an existing data base. The user employs a query language, report generator, or application generator which works in conjunction with the data base.

(10) Sometimes the users (or systems analysts they work with) create production systems in which multiple *actions* happen and are interrelated. They should diagram these actions with the data-base action diagrams used in the procedure formation stage of information engineering. The diagrams will assist in creating appropriate results and integrity checks with the end-user languages (10 in Fig. 14.3).

Sometimes the language in question does not link to a separate data-base management system or to an existing data base. Instead, it employs its own data-base facility which permits users to create their own logical files and manipulate or merge other logical files. Such software is sometimes used for personal computing. It is desirable to distinguish between two types of use—that in which the *data* used are purely personal and not employed by or relevant to any other person elsewhere in the organization, and that in which data are shared or needed elsewhere. In the latter case the data need to be linked into the information engineering processes; the user should not be left free to create his or her own data structures because these will usually be incompatible with the same data elsewhere.

⑪ ⑫   The users may be constrained to use data that conform to the data models developed by the information engineering process (11 in Fig. 14.3). They may use data planned at a lower level of detail in the information analysis process (12 in Fig. 14.3).

The blocks of Fig. 14.3 are described and illustrated in detail in the book *Information Engineering,* by Martin and Finkelstein [3].

CONVENTIONAL PROGRAMMING

Although the use of the new languages which give faster results, and application development without professional programmers, are both desirable and practical, in many installations conventional programming will still be used. Figure 14.4 shows conventional programming used with information engineering.

THE ESSENTIAL NEED FOR USER PARTICIPATION

A basic premise of information engineering is that the users of the information must be thoroughly involved. For the first two decades of data processing, systems analysts assumed that they could fully understand the users' data and what the users' information needs were. They were wrong, often catastrophically so. Many early management information systems were failures.

Data are full of subtleties and unexpected complexitites that are difficult for analysts to discover. Help is needed from the users of the data, who do understand. In one large bank a data base was built which contained an important field called *float.* The data administrator thought it was obvious what a banker meant by float. However, the data base had to serve both sides of the Atlantic and it was discovered (too late) that a British banker defined float differently from his American counterpart. The systems analysts or data administrator could not have been expected to know that, but the bankers said: "Of course they're different; any fool knows that." Data are full of such mismatched definitions and relationships, which can play havoc with data-base systems. To flush them out we need simple techniques for involving the end users—for harnessing the knowledge of the persons who work with the data.

Even more difficult for the analyst is to understand what types of information a user really needs for making decisions. The higher we go in the management tree the harder it becomes to understand the diversity and complexity of the decision-making processes. Analysts have often guessed

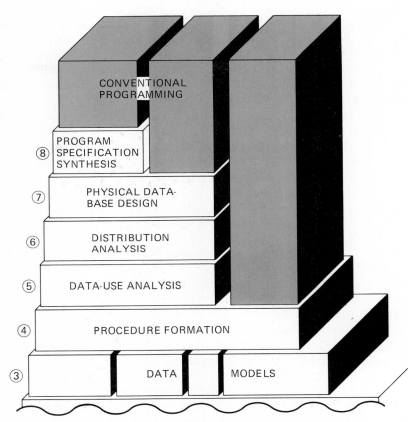

Figure 14.4 Conventional programming used with information engineering. (In general, languages that avoid the need for professional programmers should be used where practical.)

what information they think a manager needs or ought to need. Unfortunately, most analysts do not understand the minds of the business managers or the subtleties of their decision-making processes. In many cases senior managers have never been able to analyze their own decision-making processes and information needs.

The solution to these problems lies in thorough analysis of data used in running an enterprise and the establishment of these data in systems that permit new uses or new forms of decision-making employing the data. Once the data are established in appropriate forms of electronic filing, the users must be able to find the data they need quickly and flexibly, and analyze, summarize, and process those data using a terminal. They should employ their own user-friendly language, or work with a specialist who can obtain results for them very quickly—bypassing the lengthy, slow methods of traditional systems analysis and programming in languages such as COBOL or PL/1.

The software to make this possible now exists, and is relatively new. To employ it effectively new forms of DP analysis and management are needed. The new techniques need to be integrated into one overall discipline—*information engineering.*

Information engineering needs to provide a set of linked methodologies which break down the communication barriers between end users, operational management, senior management, and data processing staff. Traditionally, systems analysts and programmers have designed their own data. Programmers have embedded their own data into their programs.

Most of the books and courses on structured analysis still encourage the analyst to design his own data. Most analysts create data which are tailored to the specific application on which they are working. Those data are needed for many functions elsewhere in the corporation, but those functions are not within the current purview of the analyst. The analyst's work is of necessity narrowly focused.

The result is that analysts in different parts of the enterprise create their own designs for what are really the same data. What should be the same data item is given different names in different places and represented with different bit structures. What should be the same logical records are built containing different collections of data items. Incompatible data structures are used where they ought to be compatible.

As time goes by, the collection of incompatible data becomes greater and greater. A worse and worse mess is made of the data. A Tower of Babel grows in data, and eventually expensive conversions are necessary.

Information engineering takes a fundamentally different approach. Most of the data that are needed to run a corporation already exist. A typical corporation has several hundred *entities* (if the redundant ones are not counted separately). Information engineering identifies these and identifies whether any new data are needed in order to better meet the objectives of the enterprise and its departments. Data have properties of their own, inherent properties which are independent of how they are used. Certain data items are related to other data items, independently of usage. Information engineering identifies these properties and creates models of the data. It uses techniques for making these logical data structures as *stable* as possible. The mechanics of this are computerized. Computerized documentation of data and drawings of data structures then become available for all analysts to use.

If an analyst or programmer starts when the data structures have already been defined, much of his work is already done. The data-oriented approach changes the analysis and design. Much of the design process should now ask: "What single *actions* change or use these data? And how are the actions related?" Each takes a single action employing the data.

This approach leads us to a different diagramming technique—data-base action diagrams. Data-base action diagrams are fundamentally different from the data flow diagrams of structured analysis. Often in an on-line data-base environment, *no data flow.* Instead, a succession of discrete actions occur, each action using one logical data record. We convert the data-base action diagrams directly into structured English program specifications, or sometimes directly into the code of fourth-generation languages.

INCREASED USER INVOLVEMENT
A good part of maintenance arises from inadequate involvement of end users in the design of systems.

Methodologies are needed that harness the knowledge of DP users, ranging from top management to low-level staff. The methodologies must be designed to encourage this involvement and make it easy for users to participate.

The preceding chapter discussed prototyping. Other forms of user involvement are as follows (Fig. 14.5):

1. Strategic Requirements Planning

Strategic requirements planning can be done only with strong top management participation. Such planning must establish with senior management the strategic direction and objectives of the organization for the future. It is desirable to establish the factors critical for success and how they can be measured, achieved, and translated into objectives and motivational schemes for employees. Figure 14.6 illustrates the desirable stages of corporate planning as it relates to information systems.

Critical success factor analysis is a technique originated by Rockhart [4] for determining those factors most important in making an enterprise succeed fully, and translating them into controls and measurements. The identification of critical success factors and the strategic requirements planning lead to objectives being set for business units, departments, or individuals. Measurements need to be devised relating to these objectives so that overall control can be achieved.

2. Information Analysis

Information analysis involves management and business analysts in creating a top-down overview of the data required for running the enterprise. It enables senior users to translate their knowledge of the organization into overview representations of the data needed.

3. Data Modeling

Information analysis gives an overview of the data used in an enterprise; data modeling fills in the details. This process, shown as stage 3 in Figs. 14.3

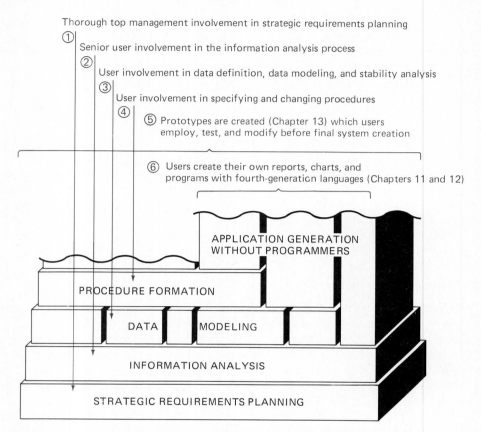

Figure 14.5 A good part of maintenance expense arises from inadequate involvement of end users in the design of systems. The information engineering processes should be designed for end-user involvement in multiple ways as shown here.

and 14.5, also needs end-user help. In some cases the users may be at a lower level than those who helped in information analysis. They are people who understand their own data better than an unaided systems analyst is likely to. Teams of users from given areas are asked to participate in checking the detailed data models for their area. A set of steps is taken with the users to make the data models as stable as possible (Box 7.2).

4. Procedure Formation

Procedure formation provides a method for use with user management and business analysts which enables new procedures (based on data modeling) to be designed. Procedure formation identifies business opportunities that

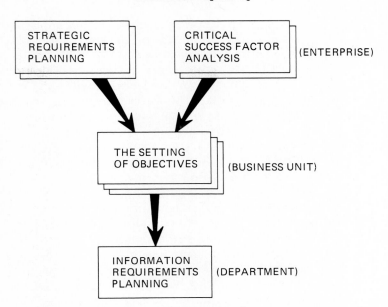

Figure 14.6 Top-level strategic planning leads to the setting of objectives and the determination of information requirements for measuring and controlling the accomplishment of objectives.

result from use of integrated data models. It builds those procedures from an examination of *actions* used to change data in the data model. It identifies the controls that must be observed. In also allows the data model to be quality tested as to its ability to support management decisions.

5. Application Development Without Programmers

User-friendly software for application creation leads to fundamentally changed methods of application development in which the user plays a much greater role. Where programmers are not employed, the end user either creates his own applications or works closely with an analyst who creates them. The analyst no longer writes specifications for programs (structured or otherwise) which are bewildering to the end user. Instead, he creates results which the user can see and play with at a terminal. The user frequently modifies the results or works with the analyst to modify them. A pattern of application creation then emerges that is user driven and that can proceed by means of multiple small incremental changes. This step-by-step evolution enables the results to be tailored to the user's changing needs and perceptions. The slow and expensive hassle of conventional program maintenance gives way to a much more flexible environment in which changes can be made easily and quickly.

TWO IMAGES

The reader should create in his mind two vividly contrasting images of the use of computers in an enterprise. In the *first image* all application creation is done by a hard-pressed DP group using COBOL, with formal systems analysis and requirements specification. Structured analysis and structured programming are used—in fact, the best of the structured software techniques. However, there is an application backlog of years, and an invisible backlog which is even greater. The users seem to be remarkably unsatisfied with the results when they get them, but have difficulty getting changes made. There are many needs to modify old applications, but DP is bogged down in maintenance and reluctant to agree to modifications. Top management perceives DP as a problem. End users are trying to bypass DP by obtaining their own mini-computers, but this has not been very satisfactory either.

The *second image* is one in which DP has done information analysis and data modeling throughout the enterprise and has made the data available on data-base systems. Users have terminals with which they can access these data. Some use a simple query language designed to be as user friendly as possible. Others use a language with which they can manipulate the data, extract their own files, perform data entry, and ask "what-if?" questions. The shop floor supervisors, expeditors, and the purchasing, marketing, and personnel departments all create computerized reporting and control procedures with a data-base-oriented application generator. This increases the productivity and efficiency of these departments, decreases the capital tied up in inventory, work-in-progress, and machine tools, and improves customer service. The financial staff, budget controllers, planners, and engineers create and modify the programs they need in NOMAD, FOCUS, and so on. DP operates an information center designed to give users the maximum help in finding the information they need, processing it or reformatting it to their requirements, and generating procedures and reports. Many DP representatives have become consultants, helpers, and instructors to the end users. Systems analysts work interactively with the end users to create their applications. Almost all data are on-line. Almost all users who need computing have access to terminals. The systems analysts almost never write specifications. They create prototypes of applications interactively, charting complex procedures with data-base action diagrams which they can convert directly into code with fourth-generation languages. The languages and techniques used are selected for ease of change, user-friendliness, and speed of application creation. DP creates the data bases, networks, and infrastructure necessary to support this activity. End users of many types throughout the corporation are inventing how they use computers to improve their own productivity and are constantly adjusting their own applications.

The *second image* is what computing *ought* to be like. It needs support facilities created by DP. It needs substantial coordination, which is what information engineering is all about.

Today's software makes it practical for many end users to do their own application generation. Whether they do it themselves or with help from a DP specialist, it needs to be done within a managed framework. This chapter is concerned with that management.

THE NEED FOR MANAGEMENT

The reasons why we need to manage user-driven computing are as follows:

- To ensure that data entered and updated by the users are employed to their full potential rather than being in isolated personal electronic filing cabinets
- To assist users so that they develop applications as efficiently as possible
- To encourage the rapid spread of user-driven computing
- The ensure that adequate accuracy controls on data are used
- The avoid unnecessary redundancy in application creation
- To avoid integrity problems caused by multiple updating of data
- To ensure that the systems built are auditable and secure, where necessary
- To link end-user activities into the various stages of information engineering

The information center concept mentioned in Chapter 12 is intended to provide management of, and support for, user-driven computing.

The overriding objective of information center management is to speed up greatly the creation of applications that end users require. The queue for conventional development, with its long application backlog, is *bypassed*.

One DP department was required to calculate the return on investment of all DP-developed applications. The average was 37%, with an average payback period of 30 months. This same DP department created an information center. This gave 100% return on investment [1]. A vice-president of the company described the information center as "our single most important productivity tool."

In most cases data bases are used—sometimes Class III, more often Class IV. Most information centers support the concept of end users developing their own applications. Some additionally use systems analysts to develop applications working in conjunction with end users, but without employing programmers, writing program specifications, or indulging in the time-consuming systems analysis techniques of flowcharting, data flow diagramming, or structured analysis.

The information center concept should support a natural division of labor between the end users and DP staff. Each group provides what it is best equipped for. The end users know what information, reports, and decision support they need in order to do their jobs well, and usually they need results quickly. The DP support group knows how these results can be obtained. The two groups work together in close partnership, balancing their resources for maximum productivity. To achieve this result the end users must be trained, encouraged, and motivated, and their competence developed to a point where they can generate and manipulate the reports that they need, perform calculations, answer "what if?" questions, perform simulations, and so on. In some cases end users have created major operations systems.

EXECUTIVE'S WORKBENCH

The terminal installed for an end user by the information center provides a variety of services. It has been described with the terms *executive workbench, professional workbench,* or *administrative workbench.*

Like a carpenter's workbench, the *administrative workbench* provides a set of well-organized tools. These assist the professional, manager, or the staff to manipulate data or carry out activities such as those shown in Fig. 14.7. Display terminals are used, sometimes with color and sometimes with graphics capability.

Information centers differ greatly in the amount of data they make available to users. Some extract data from production systems and make these available for user manipulation and decision-support activities. Some merely support the user's own data input for his own applications. Others operate major general-purpose information retrieval systems to which new data can be added whenever requested.

Office automation (office-of-the-future) facilities are spreading rapidly in some organizations, providing mailbox facilities, automated in-basket processing, and other services. These ought to be linked with the information center service. The office-of-the-future and information center concepts are becoming closely integrated in some organizations. Most office-of-the-future services should be regarded as additional tools for the administrative or professional workbench.

Figure 14.7 illustrates the administrative workbench concept. A particularly important facility in an executive workbench is the capability for the executive to create and adjust his own control mechanisms.

VIRTUAL FILING CABINET

In some cases the data accessible by users are perceived as being in an electronic filing cabinet to which the users have personal access. Users have several types of reports in their *virtual filing cabinet.* They can specify the type of data they want to see, what calculations should be done on them, and how they should be sorted and presented. They may ask to see data only when they exceed certain parameters. They can determine when "exceptions" should be brought to their notice.

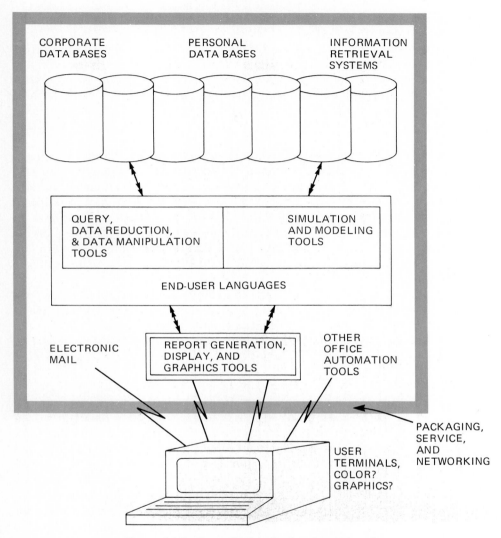

Figure 14.7 Executive/professional workbench.

In some cases the data in the users' virtual filing cabinets will be derived from the master data bases (or files) which are used for the main production processes. In some cases the users will create their own personal files. Often the users will enter and maintain data that are important to their particular areas. These data, with appropriate security, audit, and accuracy checks, are moved across to the central master data bases.

The users can transmit data from their virtual filing cabinets to other users. They can generate reports that highlight important information and have these printed if necessary.

The concept of users' virtual filing cabinets combined with computing and report generation capability is powerful. In IBM's Yorktown Heights research laboratory this approach led to an *increase of 1300% in computer utilization* by managers and professionals, *with no system development department* since all projects were handled by the users. A small, highly skilled support group helped the users and spread the usage of packaged tools.

In a much more spectacular example end users on the Santa Fe railroad created their own *operations* system to avoid paperwork and speed up railroad operations. This system grew until it processed more than $2\frac{1}{2}$ million transactions a day from more than 2000 terminals throughout the railroad. It had a major effect on the profitability of the railroad, allowing it to double the freight it carried without an increase in administrative staff. It permitted many changes in railroad operations and experiments in train and container usage, because the users could adapt the computer system quickly to reflect the changes.

Many DP executives and analysts are skeptical about this Santa Fe system until they see it in operation and investigate how it was created. It is a truly impressive computer system and it is easy to do enhancement maintenance with it. Its development methods are now being emulated elsewhere.

INFORMATION CENTER SUPPORT

In many organizations DP executives have tried to stop end users from developing their own applications. In other organizations they have allowed it to happen, only too glad to get some of the end users off their backs. End-user development is a force that should be harnessed, encouraged, and supported to the full, but if it happens in an *uncontrolled* fashion it can store up trouble for the future because multiple versions of incompatible data come into existence, and multiple machines cannot be interlinked.

The information center concept encourages and supports end-user development of their own applications. The information center is a group within the DP organization designed to serve the end users directly and speedily. The group is aware of what data bases exist and sometimes sets up other data bases. It makes this information available for end users to access and manipulate. Information center consultants work with the end users. The consultants help users to create decision support systems, personal computing facilities, information retrieval systems, and organizational support systems. A major reason for establishing this mode of operation has been the extreme dissatisfaction expressed by end users about the way DP has been responding to their information needs.

The consultants encourage the users to employ the information facilities that already exist. They sit at terminals with the users to create the cataloged query procedures, report generation routines, or graphics generation routines. They train the users to employ these facilities.

Where more complex applications are needed, the information center consultants decide how they can be created, selecting, where possible, an application generator, language, or package which avoids the formal, slow, programming development cycle.

CONNECTION TO DATA ADMINISTRATION

Some information centers have been developed without any link to the data administration process. This is clearly disadvantageous. It is better to *regard the provision of an information center as an integral part of information engineering.*

The information center needs access, potentially, to any of the information in an organization. It needs to comprehend fully the information resources and data models, and have access to the data dictionaries.

A well-run information center is in close contact with the information needs of users and management. Its knowledge of their requirements should be fed into the information analysis process.

If an information center is not in operation, the interviewing and involvement of senior management can seem to them like a one-way process. They make lots of statements about information needs and for a long time see no improvement in the information provided by DP. An information center can make this a two-way street. It can capture the types of data which managers need and make them available in Class IV data bases with good end-user languages. Providing such information to management as quickly as possible helps to clarify what their real needs are. The models of data become more useful and realistic.

Perhaps the biggest danger of information center operation, or of the spread of minicomputers and software for user-driven computing, is that multiple uncoordinated data structures will be used. These lead to maintenance and conversion costs later, or to an inability to interlink systems in important ways. The answer to this is well-controlled data administration. The data in the end users' files or Class IV data bases must be compatible, where necessary, with the data in the production data bases.

Data are often extracted from production system data bases and moved to separate information center data bases, as shown in Fig. 5.6. Sometimes they are moved back in the opposite direction, with suitable accuracy controls. These operations require common data administration and, ideally, the same data dictionary.

DATA COORDINATOR

If end users are given the capability to create their own files, using systems such as Univac's MAPPER, for example, data-item formats and definitions should be derived from a common dictionary. Sometimes in such installations a *data coordinator* is used. This person, sometimes a specially trained end user, ensures consistency among the users' data. This data coordinator ought to report (at least for data administration purposes) to the official data administrator.

The data coordinator may have functions such as the following:

- Be aware of what data models exist and ensure that users' data are made consistent with such models.
- Make the dictionary definitions of data available to the users.
- Where the users' data are not yet represented in data models, coordinate with the data administrator to see if the data being created can be input to the modeling process.
- Generally, liaise with the data administrator about the users' data.
- Guide and encourage the users in employing data.
- Train the users.
- Move infrequently used reports or data off-line (if this is not done automatically).
- Remove infrequently used "user views" of data.
- Establish techniques for informing users what data exist.
- Contribute to a newsletter about the information center and its services.

CONFLICT IN SPEED OF RESULTS   There may be a conflict between the information engineering process and the information center operation. The purpose of the information center is to obtain results for end users as quickly as possible. Information analysis and data modeling, on the other hand, take a long time and might delay the delivery of quick results.

The answer to this conflict is to get the data modeling done as soon as possible. Once the data models are completed and implemented, results may be obtained very quickly. Until that has been done a compromise is often necessary. Data for a given application may be captured, normalized by the information center analysts, and converted to the form needed by the user languages. Such data may have to be retrofitted later to the detailed models as they emerge. But the modeling process should not hold up getting valuable results to the users quickly. Data models should be created first for those areas that need quick results. This should be done quickly using a computerized modeling tool.

The sooner the data models are in place, the sooner the enterprise can benefit fully from the information center methods, without incurring high maintenance costs due to uncoordinated data. To move rapidly into user-driven computing without information engineering is to risk a rapid spread of incompatible data as different users devise their own data. The mess in data will rapidly become worse.

**INFORMATION
CENTER
ORGANIZATION**

Figure 14.8 shows a type of information center organization that works well in some corporations. Data-processing development is split into two parts, conventional development and the information center. Both link to the data administration function, which has a vital role in standardizing the data that must pass between the two areas, and in linking both areas into the information engineering processes.

The information center reports to the overall DP executive. Its staff consists of general consultants who work with the end users and specialists who are expert on end-user products. These staff train and assist the end users, create applications for them, and where practicable encourage them to solve their own problems with the end-user languages.

An organization in the grip of traditional DP standards and methods can make a small beginning by initially having only a few staff using the information center methods. The objective should be that as the information center methods are demonstrated to work well, they should take over a rapidly increasing proportion of the DP development.

The information center must relate closely to the data administration function, which is a vital part of conventional DP development (if it is well

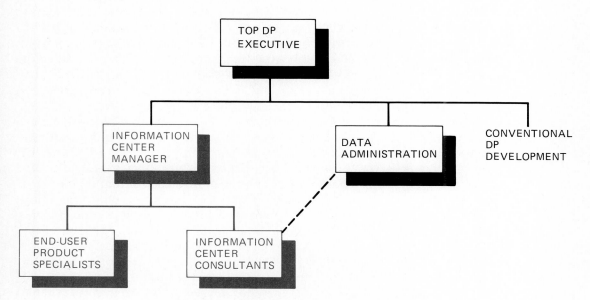

Figure 14.8   Information center organization.

managed). The information center consultants will use the data bases, request additional data bases, and participate in all stages of the information engineering processes. The information center may design and operate its own data bases for decision support and information-retrieval systems. The data in these will often be derived from conventional DP production-oriented data bases, and conform to the information engineering data models and data dictionary.

Sometimes as end-user application can be created partially but not completely with the application generators or nonprocedural languages. An important feature of these facilities is an *escape* mechanism or the ability to call subroutines of conventional programming. For this purpose the information center may be able to call upon programmers from the conventional DP group. If, however, this can be done only with a long delay because of the conventional application backlog, the information center may acquire some programming skill of its own.

DIFFERENCES IN SCOPE

Information centers in existence differ greatly in their scope. Some are a small operation within a DP department, sometimes without a full-time manager. Some support *only* development by end users. Some computer vendors' proposals for information centers state that a basic principle is that *only* end users should do the development—the information center should merely give them the tools, systems, and training. However, many of the most valuable information centers employ systems analysts or information center "consultants" who *do* create applications working hand in hand with the users, but do not write program specifications for separate programmers to code. These analysts employ nonprocedural application generators or report generators which can obtain results *fast* without conventional programming. They can complete the application faster than writing programming specifications, so the traditional development cycle disappears.

Some information centers do no work on routine production systems, but only on ad hoc systems—information systems and decision support systems. Others are organized so that *all* application development without programmers goes via the information center (which may be called a different name). Some of the nonprocedural languages which a nonprogramming systems analyst can employ are appropriate for creating certain production systems as well as information systems, and produce suitably efficient machine code. IBM's DMS (Development Management System), for example, is used by nonprogramming analysts to create production systems.

Figure 14.9 splits application development into six categories. Some information centers do category 1 only. Some do categories 1 and 2. Some do categories 1 and 4, and some 1, 2, 4, and 5. In the authors' view it is desirable to support all forms of application development without programmers.

	DEVELOPMENT BY END USERS ALONE	DEVELOPMENT BY SYSTEMS ANALYSTS WORKING WITH END USERS	DEVELOPMENT BY ANALYSTS AND PROGRAMMERS
INFORMATION RETRIEVAL AND DECISION SUPPORT SYSTEMS	1	2	3
ROUTINE PROCESSING SYSTEMS	4	5	6

Figure 14.9 Some information centers support development by end users only—category 1. Some support categories 1 and 2. Some support all application development without programmers—categories 1, 2, 4, and 5.

Sometimes information centers have been set up with the blunt insistence that the staff do *no* application development. Often in such cases the DP department itself has used the information center for its own development because this is quicker than conventional techniques. This leads to another type of organization in which the information center provides support staff assisting both the DP department and the end users. It is generally better that the information center be separate from conventional DP so that it can fully develop the counterculture of application development by new methods.

The information center *should* develop applications itself so that it becomes totally familiar with the problems, and thus can better support the user development, and also because the best form of development is often users and information center staff working jointly on creating applications. It should, where possible, insist that users *document* their own applications and learn how to modify (maintain) them. The information center should avoid the trap of having a large number of programs to maintain (e.g., APL).

FUNCTIONS OF IC STAFF　　　Selection of the techniques or software is one of many services that should be provided by the information center staff. They need to train, encourage, support, and assist the end users in obtaining the applications they need. Box 14.1 lists functions that should be carried out by the information center, divided into two groups: those performed by the analysts or consultants who work with the end users, and those performed by a technical support group or person.

The size of the information center staff varies greatly depending on the number of users supported and whether the consultants *develop* the applications together with the users or insist that users do their own development.

BOX 14.1   Functions that should be carried out by an information center

By the Consultants:

- Training the users to employ the tools and create applications.
- User encouragement, education, and selling.
- Continual assistance in improving the effectiveness of end-user computing.
- Generation of applications (without programmers) in conjunction with users.
- Generation and modification of prototypes.
- Specification of changes to prototypes that may be needed to make them into working systems.
- Cognizance of future maintenance problems and selection of techniques and controls that will avoid them.
- Consulting on user problems.
- Debug support when something goes wrong.
- Determining whether a proposed application is suitable for information center development, and selecting the software and methods.
- Demonstrations of information center capabilities to users, including senior management.
- General communication with senior management.
- Communication with traditional DP development.
- Ensuring that the data used conform to the corporate data models.
- Close links to the data administrator(s) in defining and representing data, and evolution, if necessary, of the data models.
- Providing input to the various stages of information engineering.
- Maintaining a catalog of available applications and data bases.
- Coordination to prevent duplicate or redundant application development.
- Creating Class IV data bases, and initiating *the extraction* of data into information retrieval facilities.
- Assisting the user in locating the data he needs. Arranging to have data converted where this is necessary.
- Assisting the user in obtaining authorization to access the required data.
- Conducting user-group meetings for users to interchange experience, and workshops to develop proficiency in better techniques and user self-sufficiency.

Box 14.1 *(Continued)*

- Administrative assistance to help users obtain a terminal, ID, password, workspace, and so on.
- Operation of schemes for motivating users.
- Tracking the benefits to the organization.
- Promoting the information center facilities and benefits at all levels in the organization.

By the Technical Specialists:

- System setup and support.
- Dealing with technical and software problems.
- Selection of languages and software and the versions of those which are used.
- Ongoing evaluation of software products that might be used and their possible applications.
- Assistance in choosing techniques or software for a given application (the job of the techniques analyst).
- Selection of hardware where departmental minicomputers or microcomputers are used.
- Communication with vendors.
- Monitoring system usage, and planning future resources.
- Charge-back to users.
- Tuning or reorganizing an application for better machine performance.
- Auditing system usage and application quality.
- Ensuring that the users have the terminal they want and appropriate network access.
- Providing backup, recovery, and archiving. End-user data on peripheral systems can be included in the overall backup and recovery plan.
- Advising when traditional systems needing maintenance should be redeveloped with information center techniques.

Some corporations have started an information center with a low-level commitment and allowed it to grow. In some small operations the staff members carry out all the support functions in Box 14.1; there is no division into technical and consultant staff. The staff play a role which is similar to that of an IBM systems engineer.

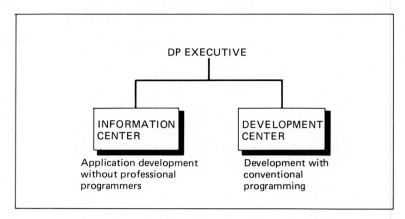

Figure 14.10   Two-part DP development organization.

One large bank started this operation with a manager, assistant manager, two professional staff, and a clerical coordinator. The manager was an enthusiast of the software used, had a technical background, and was chosen because he wanted to do the job. The assistant manager was an ex-operations shift supervisor with no programming or systems background. It was argued that he was going to guide users who also had no technical background, so it would be an advantage for him to have gone through the learning process relatively recently.

This information center (which is called by a different name) is a low-key operation with a low budget compared to the bank's overall DP budget. In other cases a much more aggressive move has been made into this form of operation with a tough executive heading it who believes that a high proportion of new application development can be done with techniques that bypass conventional DP programming and analysis.

DP ORGANIZATION   Information centers have assumed different roles and been managed differently in different organizations [5]. The author discusses them more fully elsewhere [6].

Some corporations have divided DP development into two parts, an *information center* and a *development center* (Fig. 14.10). Both use on-line tools for developing applications. The *development center* uses tools for on-line programming and debugging, on-line data dictionaries, on-line specification and documentation, and on-line productivity aids. The programmer may be able to insert nonprocedural code into sections of otherwise conventional programs.

Extending this organization, there may be two other parts to DP, also on-line (Fig. 14.11). Figure 14.11 shows some of the tools required by these groups. Chapter 19 discusses the tools desirable for maintenance.

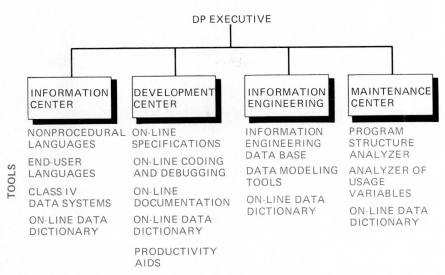

Figure 14.11 Extension of Fig. 14.10. Some of the desirable tools are shown.

REFERENCES

1. M. V. Zelkowitz, A. C. Shaw, and J. D. Gannon, *Principles of Software Engineering and Design* (Englewood Cliffs, NJ: Prentice-Hall, Inc., 1979).

2. J. Martin, *Fourth-Generation Languages,* Savant Technical Report 25, Savant Institute, Carnforth, Lancashire, UK, 1982.

3. J. Martin and C. Finkelstein, *Information Engineering,* Savant Technical Report 22, Savant Institute, Carnforth, Lancashire, UK, 1981.

4. J. F. Rockart, "A New Approach to Defining the Chief Executive's Information Needs," Center for Information Systems Research, M.I.T., Alfred P. Sloan School of Management Report CISR 37, WP 1008–78, Cambridge, MA, 1971.

5. R. B. Rosenberger, "The Information Center," SHARE Proceedings No. 56, Session M372, March 1981.

6. J. Martin, *Application Development Without Programmers* (Englewood Cliffs, NJ: Prentice-Hall, Inc., 1982).

15 PREPROGRAMMED APPLICATION PACKAGES

INTRODUCTION   It is often better to buy rather than build an application, especially if a well-designed, well-documented package is available that is not too expensive because it has substantial sales. More and more of these are becoming available. They represent one of the largest revenue sources of the software industry.

During the 1970s the total independent software industry revenue for application packages grew from almost 0% to 4% of the total of computer users' expenditures on programs. The percentage will rise during the 1980s to perhaps 10% or higher.

Perhaps the biggest unforeseen danger with application packages is the difficulty of maintenance. Most business applications change substantially with time and the package has to be modified. Often the customer has to make the modifications.

If the modifications have to be made in a language such as COBOL, PL/1, or FORTRAN, this requires much work. To facilitate maintenance, excellent documentation and clean design of the package are needed. These characteristics need to be examined when the package is bought.

In some cases the maintenance programming that is necessary is more expensive and takes more time than creating and maintaining the entire application would have taken with an application generator or a fourth-generation language. Potential users should compare the cost of application generation with the cost of purchasing and maintaining packages.

One large corporation used a payroll package for paying all employees. A complicated union negotiation changed the methods of calculating pay and benefits. The corporation reacted to this by making other changes of its own in the pay structure. The result was that suddenly the package could not handle the payroll. It proved to be so difficult to modify as required that a new payroll program had to be written, with considerable delays. There are many other such cases. Some giant insurance companies can be found processing many claims by hand because the applications cannot adapt to a sudden change in government regulation.

In these cases the applications could have been created fairly quickly with fourth-generation languages. In the long run this would have been cheaper than a difficult-to-maintain package.

Often users change their requirements for types of reports. In this case a preprogrammed package with a highly flexible generator may be the answer.

NIH SYNDROME

In many large corporations the percentage use of preprogrammed application packages is low. The percentage is larger in small corporations. Corporations with fewer than 100 employees are often entirely dependent on application packages and have greater flexibility than large organizations in adapting to the packages. One giant multinational corporation which we studied used no application packages until 1979 and then used them only in a few isolated areas. It spent hundreds of millions of dollars per year on application development, but only a few thousand on packages.

The reasons usually given for not using packages include "our organization is unique," "the packages do not fit our requirements," and "we do it differently." In some cases the differences are genuine. In some there is the NIH syndrome—an opposition, not overtly stated, to using anything Not Invented Here. In other cases, particularly in small corporations, it pays to change the administrative methods and paperwork to fit the packages.

Substantial problems have been experienced with application packages, and it is necessary to watch out for the pitfalls. Nevertheless, we feel that most corporations are not making as much use of packages as they should.

PACKAGES ARE IMPROVING

As the market for packages increases, software houses can afford to spend more money on them and make them better. They design them with more parameters which can be selected and varied. Good parameterization is the key to making packages fit into organizations with as little change in procedures as possible, and to avoiding subsequent maintenance expenses.

In the early 1970s the largest use of application packages was probably that for airline reservations. The predominant package was IBM's PARS (Program for Airline Reservation Systems) and IPARS (International PARS). Various additions to these were created and marketed by certain airlines. PARS and IPARS had a major effect on IBM's sale of hardware to the airlines. This degree of application packaging success was not repeated at the time with any other industry. The reasons it worked with airlines were that the reservation application was very precisely defined and essentially the same for all international airlines; there was already substantial cooperation between airlines because this was necessary for booking multiairline journeys; the application was very complex and expensive to develop; and IBM made the package the basis of its worldwide marketing and teleprocessing design for airlines.

Whereas airline reservations may look the same around the world, production control, budgeting, planning, and so on, differ from one corporation to another. On the other hand, inventory control, invoices, purchase orders, and such are sufficiently similar from one organization to another that packages with a good choice of parameters for varying their actions could satisfy these applications in a vast number of corporations.

Nevertheless, such packages had remarkably little success until the late 1970s, when concern about DP costs swung increasingly from hardware to application development. It was easy to underestimate the differences and complexities in these and other applications.

Now there are many thousands of software packages available. Their variety is tremendous. The total revenues from standard packages are increasing at about 30% per year, and the prices of packages are dropping as competition and market size grow. That growth rate may increase as the quality, diversity, and general acceptance of packages increases.

Box 15.1 gives examples of some of the types of packages that are available.

TRAINING AND ADAPTABILITY

The installation of an application package often needs adjustments by the purchaser and sometimes by the vendor. Teamwork between the purchaser and the vendor is sometimes essential for success. This teamwork requires the following essentials:

1. Willingness of the purchaser to make adjustments in his methods so that the package is fully usable

2. Willingness of the vendor to make adjustments to the package, for a fee, when needed

3. Willingness of both to work together as a team, with appropriate personal resources, to make needed adjustments

4. The vendor's commitment to training

Sometimes the sum paid to the vendor for training and adaptation of the package is greater than the cost of the package itself.

Perhaps the biggest problem with purchased packages is underestimating the adjustments that are needed. The user sometimes assumes that the software will run itself.

The input and output of a package are often unfamiliar to the users.

BOX 15.1   Typical examples of available application packages

Accounting
  Banking
  General
  Tax
  Trust
Accounts payable
Accounts receivable
Airline reservation
Application development aids
Architecture

Banking systems
Bill-of-material processing
Bond and stock management

CAD/CAM
Check processing
Commercial loans
Computer-aided design
Computer-aided instruction
Computer management aids
Construction
  Accounting
  Job costing
Conversion aids
Correspondence control
    systems
Customer information file
    (CIF)

Data-base management
    systems
Data management systems
Demand deposits
Distribution systems
Document/text processing

Education
Engineering
  Electrical
  Mechanical
  Space

Financial
  Control/planning
  General
  Management
  Forecasting and modeling

General ledger
Government
  Federal
  Local
  State
Graphics

Health care
Health insurance
Hospital management
  Accounting
  Administration
Hotel management
  Accounting
  Reservations

Information storage and
    retrieval
Installment loans
Insurance
  Accounting and billing
  General
  Life and health
  Property and liability
Inventory control
  Management
  Manufacturing

Job accounting
Job costing
Job performance measure-
    ment systems

Letter writing/mailing systems
Liability insurance
Library systems

BOX 15.1 *(Continued)*

Life and health insurance
Loans
   Commercial
   Installment
   International
   Mortgage

Mailing/correspondence lists
Management sciences
Manufacturing
Mathematical/statistical
Medical and health care
Modeling
Mortgage and loans

Order entry

Payroll, general
Performance measurement
Personnel systems
Petroleum industry
Preprocessors, computer
   language
Production control
Project control and planning
Property and liability
   insurance

Process control

Query languages

Real estate management
Remote job entry
Report generators
Resource management
Route scheduling

Sales and distribution
Savings systems
Scientific
Securities management
Statistical and modeling
Stock portfolio management

Tax accounting
Teleprocessing systems
Text/document editors
Time-deposit accounting
Trust accounting

Utilities accounting

Word-processing systems
Work in progress

Substantial training and familiarization are needed in its use. The user department may have considerable adjustments to make. The vendor, who has much experience with the package, should give advice on how to make the installation as successful as possible.

It is often desirable to operate an earlier system (often manual) in parallel with the package until the package has settled into full operation and all the necessary adjustments have been made.

The vendor sometimes forgets or underestimates the uneasiness of a new user or difficulty in learning and adjusting to the package. Considerable patience and handholding is needed as the package is being phased into use.

SOURCES OF SOFTWARE

There are five types of sources of software:

- Computer manufacturers
- Software houses
- Software brokers
- Time-sharing companies
- User groups and individual users

● Computer Manufacturers

Until the 1970s IBM and other manufacturers provided software free in order to sell machines. When IBM "unbundled" and began to charge for its software, this gave the whole software industry a boost. Now it is clear that a substantial part of computer manufacturers' revenue will be from application software.

The manufacturers offer a bewildering array of application products. Prospective users should apply the same rigorous evaluation procedure to them as to software from other sources.

Some application packages from manufacturers are "silent salesmen" which will force the user to add more memory, more terminals, or use a particular data-base management system such as IMS. Nevertheless, it can be much more economical to use such packages than to write your own.

Packages are *essential* for many small customers. The accounting package on the IBM System/34, for example, contains about 80 programs for statements, trial balances, and so on. It costs $30 to $40 per month. To write what a typical customer needs in this area would be likely to cost about $50,000 to $100,000.

Like other manufacturers IBM passes on to customers the benefits of packages developed within IBM internally, by IBM field employees, and by customers. IBM has two categories for the latter type of software products:

1. Field-developed programs (FDPs)
2. Installed user products (IUPs)

An FDP is a product that has been developed by IBM in the field, but not as part of a planned software product. It is available through IBM to its customers.

An IUP is similar, but is written by IBM customers. IBM agrees to maintain it *with limited support*. Naturally, the type of product is carefully analyzed by IBM before it appears on the market.

● Software Houses

Software houses are tending to move away from contract programming, which was once their lifeblood, to the development and mass distribution of packages. The highest-selling packages have been *extremely* profitable.

Some best-selling packages have been created by small companies formed by one or a group of individuals who know a particular application area extremely well. A substantial number of individuals have become millionaires through doing this. The software industry therefore has many small firms as well as large ones. Some of the very small firms have excellent products but shaky management. Some of them may not be in business five years from now.

Programmers are noted for being colorful and unpredictable and they sometimes form companies in their own image. A programming manager recently described a career programmer as one who returns after lunch. Sometimes they form companies designed to make a quick killing and quick retirement.

Their customers should protect themselves by *insisting that source code and good documentation of the product is held in escrow* so that it becomes available to customers if the firm ceases to function. The law and contracts for software are discussed in the following chapter.

● Software Brokers

Because excellent products are being created by cottage corporations, there is a need for software brokers. Most new, small software corporations cannot handle worldwide marketing. Often they do not want to be bothered with the administration necessitated by success. A software broker, like a publisher, handles sales, service, and administration and pays royalties to the software creators. It may help the creator in legal matters and protect him from taxes on worldwide sales. Like a rock star, the software creator can burst into fashion, have sales that rocket for two years, then fade and lose a potential fortune in taxes unless a corporate structure protects this fortune.

The software broker can also protect the users of software by helping to ensure quality, good documentation, and no loss of source code. Brokers may convert good packages so that they run with multiple machines, operating systems, terminals, and data-base management systems. Some software brokers provide installation of the packages. However, in some cases they provide little or no maintenance.

● Time-Sharing Companies

Time-sharing organizations make software available via teleprocessing. Accessing software in this way is dropping in cost and becoming easier because public data networks are spreading. Many countries around the world now have easy access to time-sharing computers in North America and to a lesser extent in Europe.

For some applications time sharing is a way to try out a package before committing to purchase. Sometimes the use is perceived as being temporary or intermittent, so time sharing may always be cheaper than purchase. Some corporations end up spending much more money for time-sharing a package than they would have spent on its purchase.

For packages used infrequently or intermittently, the cost of time sharing should be compared in detail with that of leasing or buying the package.

A rapidly growing area of time sharing is the use of public data banks. Use of this information may be combined with the use of software which manipulates it, searches it, or generates reports.

• User Groups and Individual Users

User groups are playing an increasingly important part in information exchange and making programs available to members. They also play a role in liaising with manufacturers not only on software but on hardware as well.

Some individual users who have developed an excellent application keep it proprietary; others make money by selling it. In the 1970s one nationalized airline sold the software it developed and made more profit doing so than it did from flying airplanes. (If only it could have given up its addiction to flying airplanes, it would have been highly profitable!)

When obtaining a package or program from a user group or individual user, be sure to ascertain all details relating to support, documentation, quality of the product, and characteristics which affect its maintainability. User groups vary considerably and care should be exercised when purchasing application development products.

An important role of user groups and industry associations ought to be to develop standards. Standards are needed so that data can be exchanged between corporations without conversion and so that packages can be used throughout an industry. An insurance broker ought to be able to access many insurance companies through its terminal rather than having a different terminal for each insurance company, for example. Purchase orders, invoices, and other documents ought to be standardized and exchanged directly between application software products in different firms.

INFORMATION ABOUT APPLICATION PACKAGES

Information about packages can be obtained from computer vendors, software houses, industry groups, and periodicals. Organizations such as Datapro and Auerbach provide listings and surveys of packages. They often include detailed surveys from users, and their findings are valuable. A good indication as to the use and acceptance of a particular product is the number of users and the date of first installation. For example, a product introduced five years ago with 1000 users could be considered very successful, whereas a similar product with five users should cause further research to be made.

Two major international directories of software are now published [1,2]. These provide detailed 1000-page summaries of a great many packages.

DEVELOP OR BUY?   A careful analysis is required by the application under consideration before a decision is made as to whether to develop the application programs or to buy a package.

There are several considerations other than cost:

- Consider the functional characteristics of the application itself. How complex is it? What is the priority of implementation? What is the time scale for development?

- A long development backlog may be a good enough reason to consider a package. In-house projects may take several years to develop and may go seriously over budget at the end of it. An application software package should be implemented in a month or two at a fixed price.

- Often some aspects of the in-house development never reach a programmer's coding pad for a variety of reasons, whereas the content of software packages is well known and defined.

- Do the application data have close links to other applications, for example, in a data-base environment? Can the data-base administrator accommodate the package with some form of bridge between it and the data-base systems?

- Sometimes senior management resists the whole idea of purchasing applications from outside sources. One way around this problem is to present the clear economic advantages and point out that programming staff will be free to concentrate on more important areas of application development.

- Documentation, which is so often neglected with in-house development, can be a necessary prerequisite for the purchase of a software package. It is also a good indication of the quality of the product itself.

PITFALLS   Box 15.2 lists the main pitfalls of packages. One pitfall results from insufficient care in fitting the package to the user needs. There may be subtleties that were not perceived in the rush to purchase the package, and a bad fit causes severe maintenance problems later.

Sometimes the package does a good job when first installed but the user needs changes, or the system changes, and substantial maintenance is required. Some packages are designed for maintenance and some are a nightmare to maintain.

BOX 15.2   Pitfalls of application packages

- The package is insufficiently parameterized and does not fully adapt to changes in requirements.
- DP modifies the package when it is installed and subsequent maintenance becomes almost as expensive as with in-house application programs.
- Expensive maintenance becomes necessary later when the hardware, operating system, terminals, or network are changed, or when the user requirements change.
- The package is difficult to maintain due to poor documentation, lack of hooks for user-created code, ill-structured design, absence of source code, excessive complexity, low-level languages, or poor-quality coding.
- The package has been made difficult to maintain because it has been tinkered with and modifications made which are ill documented and difficult to understand.
- The package does not fit in with the corporate data-base implementation and strategy.
- The software house that owns the package ceases operations.

Some package users have modified the package when it was first installed and later have found it expensive to maintain the combination of the package and in-house changes. The vendor often develops the package in ways that invalidate home-made modifications. Because of such troubles some DP organizations have decreed that packages *cannot* be tinkered with by in-house programmers; if changes are needed, they must come from the package vendor.

Possibly in the future, packages will be written with application generators so that they are easy to modify by users. This would be very valuable for certain applications. Even packages written in conventional code can benefit from using report generators.

Many corporations have a corporate-wide data-base plan with which the proposed package is incompatible. Many packages use their own files, not data bases. Increasingly, package vendors are adapting them to use data-base management systems, but even then their fields and records do not conform to those of the data administrator. Some corporations have solved this by modifying the data their packages use so that the data conform to the corporate data structures.

In some cases a package can exist in isolation, but often it must pass data to other information systems. Sometimes it must link into a data-base environment. Some package users have modified their packages so that the field structures are the same as those in their corporate or data-base data dictionaries. It is often preferable to avoid modifying the package and use external conversion routines which convert the data to data-base form. This type of link between packages and a data base is shown in Fig. 15.1.

Some manufacturers' application packages are written for that manufacturer's DBMS alone. IBM's impressive set of applications for production

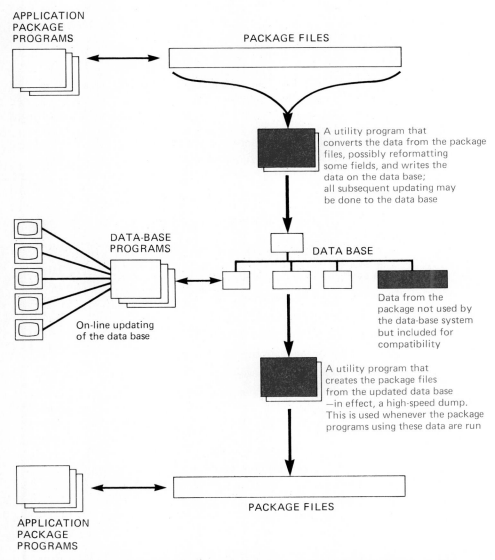

Figure 15.1   Utility programs may be written to link purchased application packages to a data-base environment.

control, COPICS, is written for IMS only, as are many other IBM packages. Cullinane Inc. has created a conversion tool, called ESCAPE, so that these and other programs can be converted automatically to run with an IDMS data base.

Only in few cases have package creators tried to fully accommodate the needs of a data administrator.

A particular danger is that of the software house ceasing to exist and the source code disappearing with it. As commented, users should insist that the source code be well documented and held in escrow in case the software house fails.

**ACQUIRING
A PACKAGE**

Selecting an application package should be approached systematically using a formal, logical procedure. Box 15.3 lists suggested steps in acquiring a package.

If a very detailed list of requirements is drawn up, it may be difficult to obtain a package which fits them. Some compromise is often needed in fitting the application to the package. It is desirable to minimize future

BOX 15.3   Steps in the acquisition of an application package

- List the present and future requirements of the application in detail.
- Survey *all* available packages for that application.
- Examine their documentation.
- Check whether they are sufficiently parameterized.
- Check whether they have adequate aids to maintenance.
- Draw up a short list of suitable packages.
- Examine the vendor. Will it provide adequate service?
- Talk to users of these packages.
- Can the package link into the corporate data-base plans?
- Conduct benchmarks if performance is critical.
- Allow end users to use them on a temporary basis if the end-user interface is critical.
- Write an appropriate contract (see the next chapter).
- Monitor use of the package.

maintenance problems, so a thorough listing should be made of how the application needs may change in the future.

Information on related packages should be gathered from all available sources: Datapro reports, Auerbach reports, software directories (e.g., Refs. 1 and 2), consultants, user groups, salesmen, trade journals, and so on.

The documentation of the package should be examined thoroughly. Is it well documented? Is it sufficiently parameterized? Will it need modification, now or in the future? Is it easy to modify? Is it designed for maintenance? What may be the future cost of maintaining the package?

A short list of possible packages may be drawn up based on the answers to these questions. A number of packages will not reach the short list for reasons such as price, availability, disk space, machine configuration, and not fitting the users' needs.

The vendor of the package may be examined to see whether it is likely to give suitable service. Will the vendor be prepared to make modifications? Will the vendor help install the package? What future development of the package is planned? Could the vendor go out of business or cease to support the package? Would this matter? In some cases the purchaser is prepared to take over support and maintenance of the package.

It is particularly valuable to talk to users of the package before acquiring it. The vendor should be asked for a list of users. Users should be asked about any delays, numbers of bugs encountered, response times, vendor service, and so on. They should be asked how they would like to see the package improved.

Can the package fit into the corporate data-base plans? Does it use a DBMS? Does it have a data dictionary? Is it designed to be adapted into data-base environments? If not, does that matter?

Where performance is critical, as with high-volume runs, different packages may be benchmarked employing the user's data. Where the end-user interface is critical, selected end users may be allowed to use the package, or different packages, for a period, to see whether they find them user friendly and effective. There is often a great difference between the user reactions to packages for the same application.

Corporate lawyers may become involved in negotiating the contract. They should ensure protection in the event of the vendor ceasing to operate. Sometimes it is desirable to drive a hard bargain to ensure adequate support. The legal process is necessary, and we discuss it fully in the following chapter, but it should not be taken to extremes. One software house selling a package for $12,000 estimated that the firm it was selling to had spent more than that on legal fees in acquiring the package and the lawyers had caused a harmful delay of many months.

The vendor's help may be needed in installing complex packages. A plan should be drawn up for this. A considerable period of vendor advice and handholding may be needed when the package is first in operation.

After a period, the operation of the package should be reviewed. Statistics may be collected on performance, or errors. Any operational inefficiencies should be identified and corrected with the help of the vendor. In some cases an agreement with the vendor, and possibly a contract, may be made for improvement of the package. The performance of the vendor may be analyzed and recorded if additional packages might be purchased from him in the future.

REFERENCES

1. The *International Directory of Software 1982* is available from CUYB Publications Ltd., 430–432 Holdenhurst Road, Bournemouth BH8 9AA, England; or 633 Third Avenue, New York, NY 10017.

2. The *ICP Software Directory* is available from International Computer Programs, Inc., 9000 Keystone Crossing, Indianapolis, IND 46240; or Deanery Street, Park Lane, London W1Y 5LH, England.

16 CONTRACTING FOR MAINTAINABLE SOFTWARE

SOFTWARE CONTRACTS   A powerful approach for building maintainability into software supplied by an outside organization is to build it into the contract. This approach applies to both custom-developed software and to standardized software packages. A contract is a written, binding agreement between the software vendor (supplier) and the software user (customer) that can be used to define explicitly the terms of software function, quality, and support. The more explicit, the better.

The purpose of a contract is to explain the relationship between the parties and to prevent problems (which may lead to costly and lengthy litigation) by formally defining the vendor and user responsibilities. A common rationalization against the need for such formality is that it is unnecessary since most of us most of the time tend to honor our commitments and to act in good faith. Therefore, a verbal "handshake" agreement ought to be sufficient. Although the first statement is usually true, the conclusion does not necessarily follow. Most disputes do not arise because a party has failed to do as he promised, but rather because of matters never discussed or included in a written contract. A common example is user reliance on statements made in vendor-published material but not included in the contract. The user assumes that the vendor is bound to perform according to these statements, but the vendor claims they are merely "puffing" or advertising [1]. To settle this dispute, the parties probably end up in court, where neither side really wins because of lost time, money, and opportunities.

A fundamental rule for acquiring externally supplied software is that *a written contract is essential*. In any good contract, all important promises and commitments are carefully considered, mutually agreed upon, and explicitly stipulated in writing. In a good software contract, the support functions and responsibilities and all deliverables that are needed to use and to maintain the software are defined in the greatest possible detail. Besides being detailed, the contract should be understandable and avoid the use of generalized or subjective standards and requirements.

Software is available in several forms. It may be bundled or unbundled, vendor-supplied or distributed by an independent software house, proprietary or public, purchased or leased. Custom-built software is usually sold, whereas packaged software is usually licensed. The license is probably nonexclusive and nontransferable, and may be perpetual with a one-time charge or may be offered for a term with or without the opportunity to renew. Whether the software is sold or licensed, the customer should be confident that the software will be usable and maintainable over its expected lifetime. This is a major objective of the contract.

Although the software may be standardized, the contract need not be. On the contrary, it should be customized to meet the requirements of a particular organization. The contract should describe the software in detail, such as its capabilities, its form, its components, and its requirements; should specify the requirements needed to maintain the software, such as test facilities, computer configuration, personnel requirements, and revalidation tools; and should define measurable quality requirements, such as source code and documentation standards and performance capabilities.

MAINTAINABILITY OF PURCHASED SOFTWARE AND LEASED SOFTWARE

For software that is purchased, maintainability is assured by requiring an acceptance test at installation time. Final payment for the software is not made until the acceptance test is passed and approved by the customer. If the software is unacceptable, the contract should allow its return to the supplier within a prespecified period of time after installation at no charge to the customer. One possible acceptance clause is the following:

> The Customer shall have a reasonable time not to exceed thirty (30) days to accept the software and its associated deliverables after installation. If the software or any of its deliverables are deemed unacceptable by the Customer, Customer shall within such thirty-day acceptance period return the unacceptable software and its associated documentation in the same form and quantity as originally received with a description of why it is unacceptable. Supplier shall refund any amounts paid for such software, or Supplier will replace unacceptable software within a mutually agreed-upon time period with no charge to the Customer.

A description of the acceptance test should be clearly defined in the contract. For example, a software benchmark test should be executed on the customer's computer system as part of the acceptance test. Also, a checklist of deliveries should be included as part of the acceptance test. The checklist should include not only what is to be delivered, but also the form, the quantity, and the quality (e.g., source code for all programs plus relevant documentation, user training, all agreed-upon modifications to a package, together with the responsibility and deadlines for making them).

Quality source code, user training, and documentation are extremely important to ease of use and maintenance of the software. Without them, it will be impossible for the user to use or maintain the software effectively over a period of time. If the user assumes that there will be no need to change the software once it is installed, his expectations are probably unrealistic and he will most certainly be disappointed. If he wishes to protect his investment, the user must prepare for maintenance support by stipulating what is required.

Maintainability is further assured by requiring a warranty period and remedies for breach. For most purchased software, the period ranges from 30 days to one year effective after installation *and* acceptance test approval [2]. Terms of the warranty should be precisely defined, as in the following example:

> Programs are warrantied by the Supplier from the date of acceptance by the Customer against all latent defects for the period of one year. During this period, any error discovered by the Customer will be repaired by the Supplier or a temporary bypass around the problem will be provided by the Supplier within three days after receipt of notification of the error(s) with no charge to the Customer.

To clarify implied contract warranties (such as claims made in vendor materials), it is important to attach to the contract all vendor letters, proposals, and published specifications or to at least make reference to them in the contract. In this way many misunderstandings between the user and the vendor concerning vendor promises may be avoided.

To improve the protection afforded by warranties, remedies for breach should be clearly defined. This will increase the user's leverage in convincing the vendor to provide the services that have been promised. This is particularly important for the small customer who must compete with larger customers for the supplier's attention. Due to rapid growth rates, many software suppliers have difficulty acquiring additional personnel and other resources quickly enough to meet their expanding needs. This may lead to customer support problems. Usually, it is the small customers that will suffer first because they represent less revenue to the supplier. However, a strong contract specifying remedies for breach by the supplier will help even the smallest customer keep the supplier's attention.

The normal remedy is that the supplier must repair or replace deficient software within a specific time period at the supplier's expense [3]. When repair or replacement is not too costly and is feasible, this is precisely what should be done. Unfortunately, this is not always the case. It simply may not be feasible for the supplier to repair or replace the software within the agreed time period (e.g., the supplier is itself a licensee of the software and the master licensee is no longer in business). In this case, the supplier should be required to otherwise compensate the customer for the breach. For example:

> Each time the Supplier fails to meet warranty obligations as described in this contract, the Customer shall be entitled to one additional month of support under the terms of this contract at the expiration of this agreement or a credit issued in subsequent billings.

Another possible remedy for breach is the right to terminate the contract. Usually termination is not a viable remedy because, at the very least, it will probably cause interrupted use of the software, which in turn may impair the user's ability to continue operating his business.

SOFTWARE MAINTENANCE SUPPORT

For software that is leased, software maintenance is normally included within the lease agreement. For software that is purchased, an optional maintenance service agreement is usually available. As with the purchase contract, it is extremely important to define explicitly the terms and conditions of acceptable maintenance service within the contract. Nebulous terms such as "Supplier will provide its best effort to maintain software in good operating condition" should be avoided because they cannot guarantee even a minimal level of acceptable support.

The customer is dependent on the software to perform certain functions for his organization and, furthermore, he is dependent on the supplier to maintain that software in good working order—especially in the case where the customer does not have access to the source code and/or is not allowed to modify the software. This dependence makes it extremely difficult for the customer to terminate a relationship with a supplier even when the supplier's service is unsatisfactory. Defining in detail in the contract the supplier's maintenance support responsibilities will help the customer control this dependency and gain some leverage in dealing with the supplier. A great deal of emphasis should be placed on providing very detailed contract provisions describing the expectations of the parties, the required standards of performance, and the remedies available to the parties. Four provisions are suggested:

1. Reliability guarantee
2. New release clause

3. Renewal option

4. Termination clause

RELIABILITY GUARANTEE

Below is a typical example of a reliability guarantee defined by a software supplier:

> Noting that Supplier is not responsible for failure to render maintenance service, Supplier agrees to keep the software in working order, to make necessary adjustments and repairs, and to provide standard software upgrades. Furthermore, Supplier agrees to perform maintenance services to correct errors within a reasonable time after the request for service is received.

This clause is too vague to guarantee adequate maintenance support and is therefore unacceptable to the customer. A more acceptable reliability guarantee specifies how quickly the supplier can be expected to respond to a request for service, how quickly a software error will be repaired after it is reported, the methods for correcting software errors, and the penalties incurred by the supplier if the reliability guarantee is not met. In the example below, the reliability guarantee is clearly defined in terms of mean time to repair (MTTR):

> Supplier will maintain a four-hour response time (over any thirty-day period during the term of this contract) to Customer requests for remedial (error correction) maintenance service. The basic maintenance fee entitles the Customer to maintenance service between the hours of 8 a.m. and 5 p.m., Monday through Friday, excluding stated holidays.
>
> If a Customer shall discover an error in the licensed software programs as delivered to Customer that prevents the licensed programs from performing substantially in accordance with the User Manual, Customer shall notify Supplier of the error and upon request by Supplier will deliver to Supplier its analysis and sample runs exhibiting the error. Upon receipt of such notification, Supplier shall within three business days respond at its option in one of the following ways and deliver to Customer:
>
> 1. An updated version of the program which corrects the error. The program will be delivered in the same form and quantity as the original versions and shall be accompanied by the appropriate updated documentation.
>
> 2. Procedures for avoiding the apparent error until such error is corrected in a subsequent release of the program.
>
> If Supplier fails to correct properly reported errors as described in the above paragraphs of this contract and Customer informs the Supplier of this breach in writing accompanied by supporting documentation within 60 days of the

breach, Customer is entitled to one month additional support under the terms of this contract at the expiration of this agreement or a credit issued in subsequent billings.

Other important reliability considerations are the availability of error status in information and maintenance support personnel. Knowing the status of all outstanding system errors will help the user utilize the software more effectively. A clause such as the following should be included in the contract:

> Supplier shall provide to Customer routine bug status reports on a quarterly basis to specify all known outstanding bugs in the current version of the software.

In the case of software systems whose correct and continual performance is critical to the customer, the availability of qualified maintenance support personnel should be discussed in the contract. For example, the contract should require minimal qualifications for maintenance support personnel (e.g., knows the programming language in which the software is written) and a limitation on personnel changes (e.g., someone who has previous experience developing or maintaining the system is always available).

NEW RELEASE CLAUSE

Since software packages are periodically updated by the supplier to correct deficiencies and to incorporate new features, the software lease agreement should assure the customer knowledge of and access to new releases of the software. For example:

> The Supplier shall notify the Customer of the availability of newer versions of the software and within 60 days of receipt of written request from the Customer supply Customer with this newer version. The new version will be provided to the Customer without charge except for the cost of duplication, delivery, and installation in the same form and quantity as originally delivered. The supplier shall provide free updated documentation in the form of new revision manuals or changed pages in current manuals consistent with the original documentation supplied and reflecting the changes included in the new version of the software.

Portability can be threatened if the operating requirements change with the new release. For example, a larger computer configuration may be required to support this new version or a different programming language may be used. Also, usability can be affected. If the command structure is changed in the new version, some commands may no longer be valid, forcing users to learn a new set of commands. If documentation is not updated to reflect the changes in the new version, user confusion and frustration can result. In addition, reliability can be impaired if new releases are not thoroughly tested before they are made available to users. Finally, if new releases are offered too frequently, the user may have difficulty keeping up with the changes. Too many releases are often a warning signal of an unstable product whose evaluation is not being adequately planned or controlled. On the other hand, if new releases are offered too infrequently, the user may have difficulty waiting for needed error repairs and enhancements. Too few releases are often a signal that the vendor has turned his primary attention to other, newer products and that the future support of this product is limited.

To avoid these problems, the customer should have the option of upgrading to a new release or continuing to use the current release:

> If the Supplier has notified the Customer of the availability of a newer version of the software which is compatible with the version of the software that the Customer is currently using, the Customer will have six (6) months to update to this newer version. If the Customer fails to upgrade by the end of this period, the Customer will be billed for maintenance service on a time and material basis according to the Supplier's current fee structure. If the newer version is not compatible, the Supplier will continue to maintain the Customer's current version with no additional charge to the Customer during the term of the contract. The Customer should recognize that a refusal to accept any new version may prevent the Customer from conveniently using subsequent releases.

In addition, the contract may stipulate that new releases are offered at regular as well as announced intervals. Most vendors offer one or two new releases per year.

Finally, many vendors establish Beta test sites to reduce reliability problems. A Beta test site is a customer who has volunteered to use a new version of the software before it is officially released to all customers. The function of the Beta test site is to help the vendor discover errors in the new release. For his help the customer is usually offered additional vendor support or a reduced maintenance fee.

RENEWAL OPTION   To ensure maintainability the user should be given a guarantee that the supplier will maintain the software throughout its useful lifetime. The longer the term of the contract, the more assurance the user will have. However, because of inflation and the desire to continue to make a profit, suppliers tend to restrict fixed-price maintenance support commitments to shorter terms. The term of a lease agreement typically ranges from one to five years. In the case of a longer term, the contract is usually renewable each year during the term. In the case of a shorter term, an option to renew the contract at the end of the term should be given to the user. Often, suppliers are willing to commit to providing maintenance support for an extended period at the "going rate," perhaps with a cap on year-to-year increases. For example:

> This agreement shall be for a term of five years following the Commencement Date. Effective each anniversary date, the charges set forth herein shall be adjusted to reflect the then current Supplier's rate for maintenance service.

TERMINATION CLAUSE

In the case of leased software, the customer is totally dependent on the supplier to provide maintenance support. Without access to the source code, the customer cannot correct errors or make modifications. As long as the supplier provides adequate maintenance support, there is no problem. But what happens if the supplier fails to perform according to the terms of the contract or decides to discontinue maintenance service? Exercising a penalty is certainly possible, but may not help the user to continue to utilize the software effectively. Instead, it may be more useful for the customer to obtain the source code and program documentation and to maintain the software himself or choose another software vendor to do so. There should be a clause in the contract allowing the customer to terminate the contract without a penalty if a breach of contract is caused by the supplier. Also, there should be a clause to allow the customer to obtain the source code in the event that the supplier ceases to do business (e.g., bankruptcy):

> In the event that the Supplier decides to terminate this agreement for reasons other than the Customer's failure to perform or observe any of its obligations under the terms of this agreement, the Supplier agrees to make available to the Customer without charge the source code and its accompanying documentation for all licensed programs. Further, in the event that neither the Supplier nor any successor to the business of the Supplier is ready, willing, and able to fulfill the obligations of the Supplier under the terms of this agreement, the Supplier agrees to make available to the Customer without charge the source code and its accompanying documentation for all licensed programs.

USER PERSPECTIVE

The software contract discussion thus far has been from the user's perspective. In addition to the contract provisions described in previous sections of this chapter, a software contract should provide the following user protections [3]:

1. *Quiet enjoyment.* The uninterruptable right to use a correctly functioning system.

2. *Unrestrained use.* The right to transfer the system or to use it to the benefit of subsidiaries, affiliates, or successors.

3. *Integration with other systems.* The right to interconnect this system and/or its associated data with other systems not necessarily supplied by the vendor.

4. *Backup.* The right to copy the system and its associated documentation for backup purposes.

5. *Need-to-know access.* The right to disclose the system and its documentation to personnel, software support vendors or consultants, and equipment maintenance vendors.

VENDOR PERSPECTIVE

A good contract fairly represents all parties involved. Protecting each party's interests establishes a mutually beneficial relationship in which promises and commitments are more likely to be honored. It is to the user's advantage to negotiate a contract that protects the rights of his supplier since his ability to use the software is dependent on the continued well-being of his supplier. The supplier is as eager as the user to use the contract to build a solid foundation for a long-term relationship. From the supplier's perspective, the contract should contain the following provisions [3]:

1. *Timely payment.* right to timely payment of fees owed to the supplier by the customer

2. *Proprietary rights protection.* assurance of owner's proprietary rights to system

3. *System transfer restrictions.* right to restrict system transfer within or outside the customer organization to maximize return on investment

4. *Limitation of liability.* right to restrict remedies for damages (including consequential and direct) that can be claimed by the customer

5. *Termination.* right to early termination for business convenience with notice and with some cancellation charge paid to the customer

Box 16.1 contains an example of an actual software license agreement. The agreement was written by the software vendor and of course favors the vendor's viewpoint. Although the agreement is complete in that it covers all the basic software issues, a prospective user probably would not find it acceptable in its present form. For example, from the user's perspective, the warranties and remedies offered are inadequate. Expecting the vendor to supply the user with a completely acceptable software contract simply is not realistic. The user should consider a vendor-supplied contract as a starting point for obtaining a usable and maintainable externally supplied software system. Through negotiation and compromise, a serious user and a reputable vendor should be able to arrive at a mutually acceptable agreement.

BOX 16.1   ABC software system license agreement

1. Agreement

The Supplier indicated on the signature page hereof "Supplier" agrees to provide Subscriber/Licensee "Customer" with services and systems, all of which are hereinafter referred to as the "ABC System" provided for herein in accordance with the provisions hereof. It is understood that the Customer includes its subsidiaries and affiliates.

2. License

Supplier hereby grants Customer a nontransferable, nonexclusive license to Company's ABC System on a Customer owned-or-operated computer system for the sole and exclusive benefit of Customer and located as described in Paragraph 23, and Customer agrees to pay the sums set forth in Paragraph 22.1 on account of such license.

3. Magnetic Tape

Supplier will supply to Customer one (1) magnetic tape containing the object code of the ABC System and three (3) copies of Installation and Application Manuals covering the installation, application, and use of the System. The version of the ABC System and the format of the magnetic tape is specified in Paragraph 26. By agreement between Supplier and Customer, other media may be substituted for magnetic tapes. Customer agrees to pay Supplier for its direct cost necessarily associated therewith at Supplier's prevailing prices.

4. Computer System

Customer agrees to install the ABC System and a computer system which is operated for the exclusive use of Customer, which computer system will meet or exceed the specifications set forth in Exhibit CS attached hereto and incorporated by reference herein.

5. System Installation

If a price appears in Paragraph 22.2, Supplier agrees to supply, and Customer agrees to pay such amounts as therein provided, con-

BOX 16.1 *(Continued)*

sulting services to assist Customer in the installation of the ABC System and Customer's computer system and to train Customer's personnel in the use of the ABC System. Consulting services in addition to the number of man-days shown in Paragraph 22.2 shall be provided to and paid for by Customer in accordance with Paragraph 20 hereof.

6. Program Maintenance

This paragraph shall apply only if payments in Paragraph 22 are not delinquent.

6.1. If Customer shall discover an error in the coding or logic of the ABC System as delivered to Customer which prevents the ABC System from performing substantially in accordance with the Application Manual pertaining thereto, Customer shall notify Supplier of error and upon request by Supplier will deliver to Supplier its analysis thereof accompanied by complete program, model, and data listings and sample runs exhibiting the error. Upon receipt of such notice, Supplier shall, within 10 days, respond at its option in one of the following ways and deliver to Customer:

6.1.1. An updated version of the ABC System which corrects the error. The ABC System shall be in the same form and quantity as originally supplied to Customer in exchange for the tapes, documentation, and data originally delivered, or

6.1.2. Procedures for avoiding the apparent error until such error is corrected in a subsequent release of the ABC System.

6.2. Company shall periodically notify Customer of the availability of newer versions of the ABC System which Supplier has released for use by its Customers generally and shall, within 60 days of receipt of written request by Customer, supply Customer with such newer version. The materials shall be provided to Customer, without additional charges to Customer, except for cost of duplication, delivery, and installation, in the same form and quantity as originally delivered.

6.3. If, pursuant to Paragraph 6.2, Supplier has notified Customer that a version of the ABC System which is compatible with the computer system described in Exhibit CS hereto but more

(Continued)

BOX 16.1 *(Continued)*

recent than the version then installed at Customer's location is available without further charge except for duplication, delivery, and installation, then within six months of such notice, Customer shall pay Supplier the charges specified in Paragraph 20 hereof for any program maintenance services performed by Supplier with respect to such older version of the ABC System.

6.4. The Customer shall assist Supplier in its performance under this paragraph by allowing Supplier to use Customer's computer system, models, data listings, and sample runs to reproduce and/or correct the reported error and to install and check updated versions of the ABC System.

6.5. Paragraph 6 shall not apply to program maintenance services rendered by Supplier if the rendering of such services is required due to Customer changes to models, data, procedures, or computer environment, and any such services will be provided by the Supplier at the charges specified in Paragraph 20 hereof.

6.6. In the event neither the Supplier nor any successor (by operation of law or otherwise) to the business of Supplier is ready, willing, and able to fulfill the obligations of Supplier under the terms of this System License, Supplier agrees to make available to the Customer without charge the source code of the ABC System, provided, however, that as long as the Supplier or any such successor shall be proceeding with due diligence and in good faith to fulfill such obligations, it shall be deemed to be ready, willing, and able to fulfill the Supplier's obligations hereunder. In the event such source code is made available pursuant to the terms of this Paragraph 6.6, the provisions of Paragraph 16 relating to confidential information shall apply to the Customer's use of such source code, except that the provisions of Paragraph 16.6 shall not prohibit Customer's modification of such source code for its own use.

7. Purposely Omitted

8. Testing

The installation Manual supplied Customer includes test procedures and programs designed to verify proper ABC System performance. Successful operation of the specified test programs and procedures shall be deemed conclusive evidence of successful installation and operation of the ABC System.

BOX 16.1 *(Continued)*

9. Invoicing

Supplier shall periodically render invoices to Customer which shall be due and payable upon presentation, and Subscriber agrees to make payment to Supplier as provided herein in lawful money of the United States. All amounts unpaid after 30 days shall bear interest at the maximum rate allowed by law. In the event that any invoice is not paid by Customer within 30 days after its date, Supplier may, at its sole option and discretion (reserving cumulatively all other remedies and rights under this Agreement and law), terminate this Agreement.

10. Reimbursement

In addition to the prices set forth elsewhere herein, Customer shall, upon receipt of invoice, reimburse Supplier for travel, living, and out-of-pocket expenses reasonably incurred in conjunction with the rendering of services hereunder. It is understood that such reimbursement shall include the actual charges incurred by Supplier plus 15 percent of such actual charges in partial reimbursement for indirect costs associated therewith.

11. Taxes

The charges listed in the Agreement do not include sales, use, personal property, excise, or similar taxes. Consequently, in addition to the charges specified herein, the amount of any present or future sales, use, personal property, or similar tax applicable to such charges shall be paid directly by Customer or shall be paid to Supplier upon receipt of Supplier's invoice therefore.

12. Communications and Terminals

Customer shall be responsible for providing data terminals, communications facilities, telephone charges, and other supporting services, except as otherwise specified herein.

13. Attorney's Fees

In the event suit is brought under this Agreement to enforce any provision hereof, the party in default shall pay reasonable attorney's fees to the prevailing party.

(Continued)

BOX 16.1 *(Continued)*

14. Assignment—Other Use

This agreement is for the sole use and benefit of Customer, as set forth in Paragraph 23 of this Agreement, and for no other person or location. No assignment, delegation, or other use of any right or duty under the Agreement may be made by Customer without the written consent of Supplier. Any assignment, delegation, or other use attempted to be made without such written consent shall be void for all purposes, and any such purported assignment by Customer shall entitle Supplier to terminate the Agreement and/or to assess such additional fees as may be applicable.

15. Warranty—Limitations of Liability

15.1. Supplier represents and warrants that it is the owner of the ABC System and has the right to permit Customer to use the same. THERE IS NO OTHER WARRANTY HEREUNDER, EXPRESSED OR IMPLIED, OF ANY KIND OR NATURE WHATSOEVER REGARDING THE SYSTEM OR ITS USE. Supplier shall not be liable for any incidental or consequential damages, whether foreseeable or not, even if Supplier has been advised of the possibility of such damages, resulting from or in any way connected with the use of the ABC System, including, but not limited to, delays or failures in computer operation.

15.2. The Supplier shall defend any suit or proceeding brought against the Customer and shall pay any adverse judgment entered therein as far as such suit or proceeding is based upon a claim that the use of the ABC System furnished by the Supplier under this Contract constitutes infringement of any copyright or patent, provided that the Supplier is promptly notified in writing and given authority, information, and assistance (at the Supplier's expense) for the defense of same; and the Supplier shall, at its own expense and at its option, procure for the Customer the right to continue to use said ABC System, or to modify it so that it becomes noninfringing, or to replace the same with a nonfringing installation. The foregoing shall not be construed to include any agreement by the Supplier to accept any liability whatsoever in respect to copyrights or patents for inventions including more than the ABC System furnished hereunder, or in respect of copyrights or patents for methods and processes to be carried out with

BOX 16.1 *(Continued)*

the aid of said ABC System, except those which are inherent in said system as furnished. The foregoing states the entire liability of the Supplier with regard to copyright and patent infringement.

16. Confidential Information

16.1. Customer acknowledges the proprietary rights of Supplier in and to the ABC System, including, but not limited to, computer programs, user manuals, other supporting material and data, identifying symbols, passwords, user numbers, and security symbols, and further acknowledges that such are properly considered to be trade secrets in that they involve processes and compilation of information which are secret, confidential, and not generally known to the public, and which are the product of Supplier's own expenditure of time, effort, money, and creative skills. Customer also acknowledges and agrees that use of the ABC System of Supplier is furnished during the term of the Agreement to Customer on a confidential and secret basis for the sole and exclusive use of Customer and not for resale, and agrees that it will not use, publish, disclose, or otherwise divulge to any person, except necessary officers and employees of Customer, at any time, either during or after the termination of the Agreement, or permit its officers or employees to so divulge any such information regarding the ABC System, without the prior written consent of an officer of the Supplier, except that Customer is authorized hereby to reproduce information derived from the ABC System for its own internal use by authorized officers and employees. Notwithstanding the foregoing, the proprietary and secret information covered hereby may be disclosed by Customer to a third party, person, firm, or corporation if such disclosure is unavoidable because of its or their access to or control of Customer's computer, provided that this sentence shall not be deemed to permit any use of the ABC System which would otherwise be prohibited by Paragraph 16.5 hereof. In the event any such information is so disclosed, Customer agrees that any unauthorized use or disclosure of such information by such third party, person, firm, or corporation may be treated by Supplier as an unauthorized use of disclosure by Customer, and Customer shall remain liable therefore. Nothing herein shall be deemed to limit any rights of Supplier under copyright, patent, or other law.

(Continued)

BOX 16.1 *(Continued)*

16.2. Supplier agrees that, without the prior written consent of an officer of Customer, it will not disclose to others nor will it permit its officers or employees to so disclose any technical or accounting data or proprietary information or confidential business information of Customer.

16.3. The preceding provisions of this Paragraph 16 shall not apply to any data, information, item, or other matter which is in the public domain at the time of disclosure to Supplier or Customer, or which is thereafter disclosed to either, as a matter of right by a third person or persons, or which thereafter passes into public doman by acts other than the unauthorized acts of Supplier or Customer, or which is in the possession of either party at the time of its disclosure by the other.

16.4. Customer agrees that all tangible objects containing or relating to the trade secrets described in this Paragraph 16 are the sole and exclusive property of Supplier, and upon termination of the Agreement for any reason, Customer will forthwith return to Supplier the user manuals, instructions, and related material which were furnished to Customer hereunder, and shall not retain any copies for its use or for any purposes.

16.5. Customer shall use the ABC System solely and exclusively for its own purposes and shall not, without the prior written approval of Supplier, either allow any third party, person, firm, or corporation to use the ABC System or itself use the ABC System for purposes of any such third party whether or not Customer is compensated therefor.

16.6. Without limiting anything contained in this Paragraph 16, Customer agrees that it will not modify or permit anyone to modify any part of the ABC System. This Paragraph 16 shall survive termination of this Agreement.

17. Force Majeure

Should any circumstances beyond the control of Supplier or Customer ("Event of Force Majeure") occur which delays or renders impossible the performance of its obligation hereunder, such obligation shall be postponed for such time as such performance necessarily has had to be suspended or delayed on account thereof or canceled, if such performance necessarily has been rendered impossible thereby. Events of Force Majeure shall include, without

BOX 16.1 *(Continued)*

limitation, accidents, acts of God, strikes or other labor disputes, acts, laws, regulations, or rules of any government or governmental agency, and any other similar circumstances beyond the control of the Supplier or Customer.

18. Notices

Any notice or communication required or permitted to be given hereunder shall be sufficiently given when received by the other party and must be delivered or mailed by registered mail, postage prepaid, or sent by cable, charges prepaid, in each case properly addressed to the addresses of the parties indicated on the signature page of this Agreement, or at such other address as may hereafter be furnished in writing by either party hereto to the other party, and such notice shall be deemed to have been given as of the date so delivered, mailed, or sent.

19. Governing Law

This Agreement shall be subject to acceptance by the Supplier and shall be governed by and construed in accordance with the laws of State, U.S.A. In case any one or more of the provisions contained in this Agreement shall be invalid, illegal, or unenforceable in any respect under any applicable statute or rule of law, such provisions shall be deemed inoperative to the extent that they are invalid, illegal, or unenforceable, and the remainder of this Agreement shall continue in full force and effect. The parties hereto agree to replace any invalid, illegal, or unenforceable provision with a new provision which has the most nearly similar permittable economic effect of the invalid, illegal, or unenforceable provision.

20. Consulting, On-Call

In addition to services provided for elsewhere herein, Supplier will perform on-call consulting and programming services for Customer, and Customer shall pay the Supplier its normal daily rates then existing for such services. In addition to such daily charges, Customer shall reimburse Supplier in accordance with Paragraphs 9 and 10 hereof for reasonable travel, living, and out-of-pocket expenses calculated in accordance with Supplier's normal practice as set forth in such paragraphs.

(Continued)

BOX 16.1 *(Continued)*

21. Base Agreement

If Customer and Supplier have previously entered into an ABC System Agreement providing for Customer's use of the ABC System over a commercial time-sharing service network ("Base Agreement"), Program Use charges under such Base Agreement shall be terminated upon receipt of the initial License Fee specified in Paragraph 22.1 hereof. Customer shall continue to pay all other charges specified in the Base Agreement.

22. Prices

Description	Price	Payment Due
22.1 License Fee	$_____ per month	Upon execution of this License and monthly in advance thereafter.
22.2 System Installation A maximum of _____ man-days.	$_____ total	Monthly as expended. Invoices due upon receipt.
22.3 Other Charges	As provided	Upon receipt of invoice.

23. Location of Use

This License is for installation and use of a single computer system of Customer located in _____ .

24. Effective Date

The effective date of this License is _____ .

25. Terms

Unless sooner terminated by Supplier in accordance with the provisions hereof, the minimum term of this License is 5 years. Upon expiration of such minimum term, the License shall automatically renew for successive annual terms unless terminated by Customer's written notice to Supplier at least 60 days prior to the expiration of such minimum term or renewal period.

26. System Version and Tape Format

The ABC System, Version _____ , will be supplied for installation under this License. Magnetic tapes will be in the following

BOX 16.1 *(Continued)*

format:

9 Track
1600 BPI

27. Entire Agreement

This Agreement states the entire agreement of the parties. Except as herein expressly provided to the contrary, the provisions of the Agreement are for the benefit of the parties hereto solely, and not for the benefit of any other person, persons, or legal entities. No waiver, alteration, or modification of any of the Provisions of this Agreement shall be binding unless in writing and signed by a duly authorized representative of Supplier and of Customer and expressly referring to this Agreement.

ACCEPTED FOR SUPPLIER
ABC SOFTWARE, INC.
U.S.A.   ACCEPTED FOR CUSTOMER

_____   _____
Name   Name

_____   _____
Title   Title

_____   _____
Date   Date

EXHIBIT CS
TO LICENSE AGREEMENT

The computer system configuration referred to in Paragraph 4 is set forth herein.

Hardware:

Machine
Model
Real memory
Storage devices
Paging devices
Tape devices
Card reader
Printer

(Continued)

BOX 16.1 *(Continued)*

Software:

Operating system
Version
Release
Compiler(s)
Minimum real or virtual
Memory available to user

Initialed for Identification:

| _____ | _____ | _____ |
| Supplier | By | Date |

| _____ | _____ | _____ |
| Customer | By | Date |

**SUMMARY
OF SOFTWARE
CONTRACT
CLAUSES**

Box 16.2 summarizes the contract clauses normally included in a software agreement [4–6]. Although the list is general and is not intended to be all-inclusive, it is helpful in pinpointing the critical issues that should be addressed in a software contract. Careful consideration of each of these issues will help avoid ambiguities that might result in contract disputes and surprising judicial interpretations.

To date, only a limited number of software cases have been tried in court. Thus far, the usual outcome is that if the contract is ambiguous, the court tends to favor the user but limits the vendor's liability to that which is specified in the contract [5].

REFERENCES

1. S. Segelstein, "Use of Project Management Techniques in Data Processing Contracts—An Aid in Project Control and Dispute Resolution," in *Computer Law 1981,* Commercial Law and Practice Course Handbook Series No. 267 (New York: Practicing Law Institute, 1981), pp. 109–124.

2. "How to Buy Software Packages" (Delran, NJ: DATAPRO Research Corp., 1978), Report 70E–010–20g.

BOX 16.2   Software contract clauses

General Clauses

- Name and Addresses of Parties
- Effective Date of Contract
- Term of Contract
- Governing State Clause
- Arbitration Clause for Resolution of Disputes
- Survival Clause
- General Notice Clause
- Force Majeure
- Warranties
- Breach of Agreement and Remedies
- Limitation of Liabilities
- Rights upon Termination

Software Specific Clauses

- Payment
- Expenses
- Taxes
- Total Price
- Options to Buy
- Options to Renew
- Delivery and Installation
      Penalties for Delivery Failure
      Time for Installation
      Availability of Installation Assistance
- Acceptance of Software
      Description of Acceptance Tests
      Failure to Accept
- Performance Specifications
- Computer System Requirements
- Documentation
      Operations Manuals
      User Manuals
      Systems Documentation
      Availability of Future Documentation

(Continued)

BOX 16.2 *(Continued)*

- User Training
- Warranties and Remedies for Breach
    Performance
    Quality
    Revision Rights
    Copyright, Patent, or Proprietary Right Infringement
    Guarantee of Ownership
- Software Ownership Rights/Usage Rights
- Protection of Confidential Information
- Maintenance of Software
    Reliability Guarantees
    Remedial Maintenance Support
    New Releases and Provisions for Updates
    Right to Modify Software
- Source Code Availability and Access
- Assignment

3. D. Brooks, "System Contracts," in *Computer Law 1981,* Commercial Law and Practice Course Handbook Series No. 267 (New York: Practicing Law Institute, 1981), pp. 161–219.

4. R. Raysman, "How to Negotiate Contracts with Software and Data Service Vendors," in *IPC Directory—Business Management: Industry Specific* (Indianapolis, IND: International Computer Programs, Inc., 1980), pp. IX–X.

5. C. H. Reddien, "Legal Aspects of Software Development," in *Software Engineering* (Englewood Cliffs, NJ: Prentice-Hall, Inc., 1979), pp. 485–552.

6. D. H. Brandon and S. Segelstein, *Data Processing Contracts* (New York: Van Nostrand Reinhold Company, 1976), pp. 109–123.

17 PERFORMING PROGRAM MAINTENANCE

IMPROVING THE MAINTENANCE PROCESS

Many of our maintenance problems have grown out of a mistaken belief that program maintenance is substantially different and generally easier than program development, and therefore requires less planning, less experienced personnel, less sophisticated tools, and less management control. On the contrary, program maintenance work is often more challenging than new development projects.

The maintainer is expected to comprehend programs that were probably written by someone else and make program modifications without jeopardizing program correctness or integrity. Often this must be accomplished in a very short time without the aid of proper documentation and modern programming tools. Also, program maintenance typically involves a variety of analysis and programming tasks such as [1]:

- Reviewing program requirements and specifications
- Interviewing end users and developers
- Examining programs and documentation
- Determining the cause of program errors and where program changes should be made
- Evaluating the possible side effects resulting from a program change
- Coding program changes
- Revalidating programs
- Updating program documentation and libraries

The difficulty of the maintenance function arises from problems such as:

- Poor quality of the original program
- Inadequate documentation
- Limited tools
- High learning curve due to the increasing size and complexity of new software systems

It also arises from the characteristic of most programs to require change continually and the difficulty of controlling negative side effects arising from change. A series of haphazardly made program patches and changes can quickly lead to a maintenance mess and program obsolescence.

Making programs more easily maintainable is one method of minimizing the maintenance burden. An equally important method is to improve the maintenance process.

Regardless of improvements in program quality and program development technologies, much maintenance still has to be done and is a major burden for DP installations and software houses. Certain types of main-

BOX 17.1 Ways to improve the maintenance process

- Provide a program modification procedure that uses structured techniques.
- Encourage flow of communication among the end users, maintainers, and developers.
- Establish and enforce programming and documentation standards.
- Improve documentation for existing programs.
- Perform maintenance audits to check the correctness and quality of maintenance work.
- Increase end user involvement and responsibility in the maintenance process.
- Batch maintenance requests rather than make program modifications in a piecemeal fashion.
- Emphasize careful and thorough retesting and revalidation when a program is modified.
- Provide continuous training for maintainers in new software technologies and knowledge of the application area.

tenance (error corrections and adapting to new computing environments) can and should be controlled by improving program quality. But other kinds of maintenance (changes and enhancements requested by users) must and should be done. Since it is not possible to eliminate all maintenance work, a more reasonable objective is to minimize the effort by improving the maintenance process. Box 17.1 summarizes the approach suggested.

BASIC MAINTENANCE FUNCTIONS

Three functions are involved in performing program maintenance (see Fig. 17.1):

1. Understand an existing program
2. Modify an existing program
3. Revalidate a modified program

Performing maintenance first and foremost requires an understanding of the program—its functional objective, its internal structure, and its operational requirements. If the maintainer does not thoroughly understand the program to be maintained, he runs a great risk of jeopardizing program quality by unknowingly introducing new program errors each time he attempts a program fix or change.

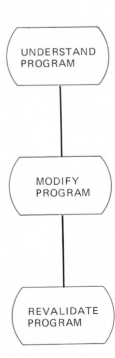

Figure 17.1 Three basic functions are involved in performing program maintenance. Performing program maintenance requires, first and foremost, an understanding of the program. Modifying a program involves creating new logic to correct an error or to implement a change. Revalidating a program checks the correctness of the new logic and that the program as a whole still functions correctly.

Modifying a program involves creating new program logic to correct an error or to implement a change and incorporating that logic into the existing program. The maintainer must make certain that the new logic does not destroy program integrity or increase program complexity.

Whenever software is modified, its correctness should be revalidated. The maintainer should perform selective retesting to demonstrate that not only is the new logic correct but also the unmodified portions of the program remain intact and the program as a whole still functions correctly. Assuming that even a small change will work as intended and therefore does not require testing is almost certainly a mistake that will lead to program deterioration.

A TOP-DOWN APPROACH TO UNDERSTANDING EXISTING PROGRAMS

The maintainer should be given an opportunity to become familiar with a program before he is given an assignment to modify it or make an emergency repair. Familiarity with a program implies an understanding of the overall program function, its basic components, its stability, and its ability to be easily and correctly modified. A top-down approach is recommended (see Fig. 17.2):

1. First become familiar with the overall program purpose and the overall flow or control from component to component. Identify the basic data structures as well as the processing components of the program. If this program is part of a system of programs, understand its function within this system.

2. Then become immersed in the details of how the program works by identifying what each component does and how it is implemented in the code. A component may be a data file, a program subroutine, a program module, or simply a piece of program code that can be logically grouped together.

3. As you learn about the program, document what you learn.

The two traditional sources of information about existing programs are the program source listing and the program documentation. There have been problems with the quality of both. In the case of source listings accessibility and readability are commonly experienced problems. In the case of documentation, availability, accuracy, and completeness are major problems.

Particularly valuable for understanding programs are interactive maintenance tools that allow the maintainer to explore the control structure and use of variables. One such tool is Amdahl's MAP, described in Chapter 19.

PROGRAM SOURCE LISTING

The current source listings should be readily accessible to the program maintainer, but in practice this is often not the case. All too frequently

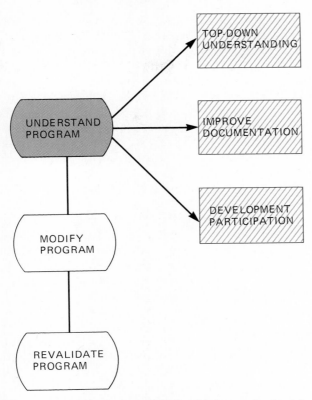

Figure 17.2 A top-down approach should be used when becoming familiar with an existing program. First become familiar with the program at a general level of understanding; then try to understand the details. When becoming familiar with an existing program, document what is learned, concentrating on improving high-level program documentation. When possible, participate in the program development process to learn about the program.

the complete source listing or the current version of the program cannot be located. This situation not only complicates the maintainer's job but also reduces the maintainer's chance of successfully modifying the program. Better management control procedures (e.g., applying IBM's Development Library Concept to the maintenance environment) and automated source management libraries (e.g., NIC's SLICK or Pansophic's PANVALET) can be used to solve this problem.

Readability is another common problem. Many existing program listings are simply impossible to read. When they were originally written, the programs were not written with readability in mind. Furthermore, when they were changed, the programs were not changed with any regard to preserving the original program style or design concept. Hence, the listings became a conglomeration of discordant pieces requiring an incredible and tedious effort to decipher. For this reason many software professionals believe that any program has a finite life [2]. Also for this reason, the program maintainer often prefers to rewrite the entire program rather than attempt to understand someone else's code. The latter is a reasonable solution in some cases, but more often it is not. The new replacement program may not be any easier to read than the original program. When the next maintainer is assigned to the program, he too may feel the need to rewrite it using his own programming style or favorite language. Repeatedly rewriting the program is usually not cost-effective. Instead, it may be more useful to rewrite only those portions of the program that are particularly abstruse and troublesome.

Automated tools can help improve program readability. Cross-reference listings, symbol tables, and other aids provided by the compiler (assembler) can assist the program reader. Automatic flowcharters, reformatters, documentors, and structuring engines can be used to transform the source code into a more readable format (e.g., General Research Corp.'s RXVP; Catalyst Corp.'s COBOL Engine; Caine, Faber & Gordon's FORTRAN Engine).

PROGRAM DOCUMENTATION

Good documentation is a powerful tool for the maintainer who must understand programs written and modified by many different programmers over the years: not only documentation explaining *what* the program does but also *why* it is essential to gaining this understanding. High-level program documentation (such as overview documentation and module comment blocks, described in Chapter 9) is probably the most helpful in familiarizing the maintainer with the current status of the program and its internal workings. Historic documentation is equally important in explaining how and why this program has evolved to its present state. Emphasis should be placed on gaining an overall picture of the program and the whys behind it. Understanding the broader background issues can help the maintainer resolve the confusion that occurs when the original design concept and documentation no longer reflect the present program status.

The program development journal, program error history, and the program maintenance journal are all extremely helpful in reconstructing program evolution, in pinpointing chronic problems, and in suggesting future evolution directions (see Chapter 8).

In reality, however, it is unlikely that complete, up-to-date documentation will be available. For many existing programs, no documentation exists or the documentation that does exist is so out of date that it is of no use and may even be misleading. As part of studying the program, the maintainer should create or update the documentation, concentrating on high-level documentation rather than instruction-level comments.

Freedman and Weinberg refer to this as the *fix and improve* approach. The objective is not just to change a program to fix an error or implement a modification, but also to improve its future maintainability [3]. Automated tools such as flowcharters, module invocation analyzers, data flow analyzers, and cross-reference reports speed up the redocumentation process.

THE MAINTAINER'S PARTICIPATION IN PROGRAM DEVELOPMENT

In addition to studying the source listing and program documentation, participation in the development process is another very valuable way for the maintainer to become familiar with a program.

The maintainer should participate actively in the program development process by offering maintainability guidelines to the developers, by gathering testing and error information, and by conducting maintainability acceptance audits. Waiting until the operation and maintenance phase to learn about a program, to make support preparations, or to ensure maintainability greatly increases the risk of not being able to effectively and efficiently perform program maintenance.

Besides the maintenance acceptance review (see Chapter 4), the software maintainer should be encouraged to participate at three other points during program development (see Fig. 17.3).

1. Design checkpoint review

2. Coding checkpoint review

3. Testing phase

DESIGN PHASE PARTICIPATION

The design review offers the maintainer the first opportunity to evaluate the program quality and to determine maintenance support requirements. The capability of being easily modified is a critical aspect of program quality that must be designed into the program. Based on previous experiences in making program modifications, an experienced program maintainer can suggest typical ways in which the program can be expected to change. Being aware of changes that have occurred in similar applications may help developers design a more easily modifiable program. Also, considering future change possibilities may help developers determine the degree of generality versus flexibility to be designed into the program. *Generality* allows the program to provide a diversity of functions which may be changed without modifying the program, while *flexibility* allows a program to be modified

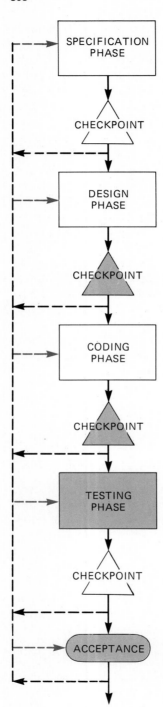

Figure 17.3 The program maintainer should participate actively at strategic development process points—design checkpoint review, coding checkpoint review, testing phase, and program acceptance review—to ensure future program maintainability.

easily [4]. An optimum program design balances the appropriate degree of each to meet present and future needs most effectively.

To ensure the quality of maintainability, the following design guidelines are suggested [5, pp. 29–69]:

1. Introduce generality by designing the program to:
   (a) Execute on different hardware configurations and under different operating systems
   (b) Operate on different input/output formats
   (c) Function in a subset mode performing a selected set of features
   (d) Operate with different data structures or algorithms

2. Introduce flexibility by designing the program to:
   (a) Allow a module to perform only *one* unique function
   (b) Isolate specialized functions into separate modules
   (c) Provide module interfaces that are insensitive to changes

To test the quality of maintainability quality, checklists and measures (see Chapter 3) can be applied to the design. For example, the complexity of the design can be evaluated by measuring the complexity of several randomly chosen program modules. If the complexity of these modules exceeds the recommended limit, the maintainability of the design should be examined before development is allowed to continue. Also, change exercises can be performed. Using some examples from the program future features list, the design should be modified to incorporate these changes. If a major redesign of the program is required, other possible design approaches should be considered before development is allowed to continue.

CODING PHASE PARTICIPATION

The coding phase review offers the maintainer another opportunity to ensure program maintainability. The objective of the coding phase is to produce program code that is reliable, readable, and maintainable. If the code is not understandable, it cannot be maintained effectively.

The source code should be audited for compliance to the organization's coding and documentation standards. If it does not meet these standards, the developers should be required to rewrite the code. For example, automated structure checkers can be used to evaluate the structuredness of the code. In addition, the complexity of each module can be calculated to assure that complexity limits are not exceeded.

TESTING PHASE PARTICIPATION

The program maintainer should actively participate in the creation of the program test plan. When the test plan is developed, the maintainer should be given an opportunity to review it and make suggestions as to how the testing process might be improved. A comprehensive test plan should be created during the design phase and should contain [5, pp. 29–69]:

1. Testing objectives
2. Testing approaches and strategies (e.g., top-down testing)
3. Test tools
4. Testing, problem reporting, error correction, and retesting procedures
5. Testing acceptance criteria

Furthermore, the maintainer should actually participate in the testing phase by executing some of the tests to give him firsthand experience with the program. Since the program will be retested each time it is changed during the maintenance phase, the maintainer should have copies of the test plan, the test data, and the test results produced during development testing. Then, when the program is modified during the maintenance phase, it can be retested with these test cases, and the results can be compared.

Besides conducting tests, the maintainer should gather information on the number and types of errors found during development testing. A program that is difficult to test is often difficult to maintain. Error information can help pinpoint portions of the program that are error-prone and difficult to modify. A test history should be compiled for each program tested (see Chapter 8).

MODIFYING EXISTING PROGRAMS

Modifying existing programs is the most basic maintenance function and perhaps the most challenging of all programming activities. It involves three steps (see Fig. 17.4):

1. Devise a plan for changing the program (i.e., design the program change/debug the program).
2. Alter the program code to incorporate the change.
3. Evaluate the impact of the change.

Not only must the programmer make certain that the new logic is correct but also that the unmodified portions of the program remain intact and that program as a whole still functions correctly. It is this second aspect of modifying a program that often proves to be the more difficult. The new logic needed to make the change may involve adding, deleting, or rewriting only a few lines of code, but determining the impact of this change on the other portions of the program may involve a detailed study of the entire program.

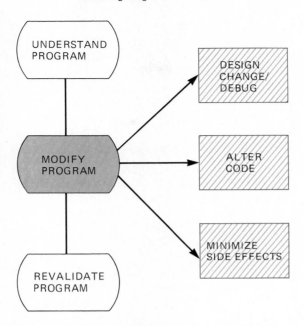

Figure 17.4 Modifying existing programs is perhaps the most challenging of all programming activities. It involves three steps: (1) design the program change, (2) alter the program code to incorporate the change, and (3) evaluate the impact of the change and minimize unwanted side effects.

Unanticipated and undesired "side effects" have resulted from even apparently simple program changes [6]. An active label, subroutine, or macro may be accidentally deleted. A data value may be inadvertently changed. Memory usage may be unknowingly increased. In many cases the side effect may be so subtle that it remains undetected long after the change has been made. When it is finally noticed (perhaps because the program produces incorrect output), the change that causes the problem may be extremely difficult to pinpoint.

Side effects are a primary cause of program deterioration during the maintenance phase. For this reason the objective of modifying software cannot be simply to make a change correctly, but must include modifying the program in such a way that:

- Program quality is not harmed.
- Program style and integrity are preserved.
- Future program changes can be easily made.
- Program users are not adversely affected.

DESIGNING A PROGRAM CHANGE   If the task is to correct an error, the maintenance programmer must first locate the cause(s) of the error (see Chapter 18) and then determine how to rectify the program by changing the appropriate logic. If the task is to change or enhance the program, the maintenance programmer must develop the new logic needed and then determine how to alter the program appropriately.

A top-down approach is recommended for designing a program change:

1. First, the entire program is reviewed at a general level by studying each module, the module interfaces, and the data base.

2. Next, in steps, the modules and data structures to be changed (and those modules and data structures affected by the change) are isolated.

3. Finally, the internals of each module and data structure to be changed (or affected by the change) are studied in detail. The change is then designed specifying the new logic and any existing logic that must be altered.

Some guidelines for designing a program change are listed in Box 17.2.

CHANGING PROGRAM CODE   The objective when changing program code is twofold:

1. Correctly and efficiently code the change.

2. Eliminate any unwanted side effects from the change.

The first part of this objective can be achieved by following the guidelines listed in Box 17.3. However, achieving the second part may be more difficult. Side effects are a serious problem because they are often very difficult to recognize and may have widespread and costly ramifications.

Freedman and Weinberg divide side effects into four categories [6]:

1. Code (e.g., active label changed or deleted, active subroutine changed or deleted, timing relationships altered, memory usage increased, efficiency decreased)

2. Data (e.g., flag or condition changed, overlay altered, field or record size modified)

3. Documentation (e.g., new error message incorrect, documentation does not match program function, default condition changed)

4. Miscellaneous (e.g., clerical procedures modified, job control changed, rerun procedure changed, system usage cost increased)

The first two types of side effects affect mainly the program itself and are commonly referred to as the *ripple effect*. The last two types have a broader impact since they may adversely affect other programs, the operations staff, and the end users. Freedman and Weinberg suggest making a

BOX 17.2   Guidelines for designing a program change*

- Examine alternative designs seeking a design for the change that is compatible with the original design philosophy of the program.
- Strive for design simplicity, choosing the design alternative that modifies the fewest modules, the least complex modules, and the fewest global variables.
- Choose a design that meets generality requirements in terms of its ability to be used in various versions of the program, with different operating systems and on different hardware configurations.
- Choose a design that meets flexibility requirements in terms of its ability to isolate specialized functions into separate modules and to provide module interfaces that are insensitive to further changes.
- Choose a design that will not degrade program quality, in particular future maintainability. Determine the compatibility of the change with other changes that are likely to be requested in the future.
- Describe the design in terms that are testable and include test methods.
- Consider changes in processing time, storage requirements, and operating procedures.
- Consider the effect of the change on human engineering and interruption to user service, as well as cost and time to implement.
- Document the what's and why's behind the design chosen.

*These guidelines are based on Ref. 5, pp. 150–153.

checklist of possible side effects and then using this list to review a program change for each type of side effect.

CONTROLLING THE RIPPLE EFFECT FROM A CHANGE

The ripple effect occurs when changes to one part of a program affect other parts of a program [5, pp. 154–157]. This happens because of the interdependence that can exist between program modules. Modules that share common functions or data are interdependent. For example, several modules may call a common subroutine or may reference a global variable. Any change made to a common subroutine or global variable may alter the internal processing of any module that accesses it. The more interdependent the program modules are, the more complicated it becomes to determine the ripple effect from even a seemingly simple pro-

BOX 17.3   Guidelines for changing program code

- Become familiar with the overall flow of control in the program before attempting to make even a one-line change. (Yourdon)
- Make changes with the greatest caution. (Yourdon)
- Do not change more than necessary just for the sake of changing. (Yourdon)
- Introduce structured code if it is possible to do so without destroying original program style and consistency. (Van Tassel)
- Do not attempt to share program variables that already exist. Instead, create new local variables. (Yourdon)
- Create multiple routines rather than common routines for "almost duplicate" functions. (Mc Clure)
- Use automated tools such as on-line programming aids, code auditors, automatic flowcharters, and so on. (Mc Clure)
- Keep records of what changes were made, why the changes were made, warning of potential troublespots, suggestions for future changes, and any other appropriate comments. (Yourdon)
- Employ defensive programming (i.e., program can self-detect errors) by inserting error checking around the new code. (Glass and Noiseux)
- Consider the effect of the change on human engineering and interruption in user service. (Mc Clure)
- Have a code inspection performed to audit software quality and compliance to standards by someone other than the maintenance programmer who coded the change. (Mc Clure)
- Update the program documentation to reflect the changes and keep the premodified version of the program code. (Mc Clure)

gram change. Not being able to determine completely the ripple effect arising from program changes is a major cause of software quality deterioration during the maintenance phase.

Since any program change has the potential to ripple through the module in which the change is made and across module boundaries into many other modules, the possible ripple effect arising from a program change must be carefully examined. Usually, this involves a manual search through the code beginning with the module(s) in which the change is made and continuing on to all modules sharing global variables or common routines with this module(s). Depending on how many modules and variables must be examined, the search can become very tedious and time consuming.

BOX 17.4 Guidelines for controlling ripple effect*

- Change as little as possible.
- Change as few variables as possible and, in particular, as few global variables as possible.
- Consider changes in processing time, storage requirements, error probability, complexity, and impact on other versions of the program.
- Determine compatibility with original design concept and future software changes.
- When a common module is changed, examine all modules that invoke this common module to determine if they are affected by the change. Also, examine all modules that are invoked by the common module to determine if they are affected by the change.
- When a local variable is changed, examine the code in the module referencing that variable to determine if the function performed by this module or if any other variables referenced in this module are affected by the change. Remember that a change to one variable may indirectly affect other variables if their value is determined in part by the changed variable.
- When a global variable is changed or affected by a change, examine all modules referencing this global variable to determine if they have been affected by the change.
- When multiple changes must be performed to a program, order the changes in the following manner.

  1. Group the changes by module.
  2. Plan the sequence of modules to be changed by following a top-down approach, that is, change the main-line module first, then its descendants, and so on.
  3. Change one module at a time.
  4. For each module changed, determine the ripple effect of the change before changing the next module in the sequence.

---

*These guidelines are based on Ref. 5, pp. 133–162.

Module coupling is one measure of module interdependence [7]. When modules are very interdependent (e.g., one module makes an unconditional transfer of control to a label within the boundaries of another module), they are called *tightly coupled*. Great care should be taken when changing the code in such a module since the change is likely to affect the internal processing of any other modules that are tightly coupled with the changed module. Box 17.4 lists some guidelines for determining and controlling the ripple effect from a program change.

Cross-reference maps, storage maps, and traces provided by many compilers, automatic flowcharters, and execution flow tracers can help identify the ripple effect from a change.

REVALIDATING EXISTING SOFTWARE

Whenever a program change is made, the program should be revalidated to demonstrate that the change has been made correctly and that the program as a whole still functions correctly (see Fig. 17.5). Often there is a tendency to skip or minimize this step, especially when the change consists of only a few lines of code. However, this tendency must be avoided because it can quickly lead to the deterioration of even a very reliable high-quality program. Studies by Boehm show that a programmer has only a small chance of correctly changing a program on the first attempt. For example, if the change involves fewer than 10 source statements, the probability of correctly changing the program on the first attempt is 50%, but if the change involves as many as 50 statements, the probability drops to only 20% [8]. If the programmer does not even bother to test the change, the chance of introducing a program error is almost certain.

A revalidation procedure should be designed for each program or system of programs. Program error properties and complexity measures should be used to identify the most error-prone and most complex program modules so that the revalidation effort can concentrate on these modules as well as the ones in which the changes were made.

The procedure should be kept simple and aided by automated tools such as cross-reference listers, test data generators, and file compare utilities. Automated tools can provide improved organization of the revalidation process, can measure the thoroughness of testing, and can relieve the programmer of many routine, tedious chores.

Most important, the revalidation procedure must be used. Each time a program is changed, the procedure should be followed. Weinberg warns that a programmer who finds no or a few errors in early tests may stop testing prematurely [9]. To guard against this tendency he suggests that a plan specifying test cases and test results be prepared in advance, preferably by someone other than the program tester. Box 17.5 suggests some additional revalidating guidelines.

Revalidation should closely resemble the original program validation process, using the same (or similar) test cases and test data as those used when the program was originally developed. Then results from the original

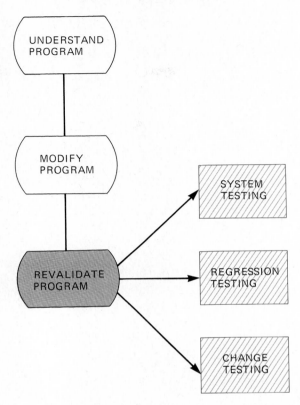

Figure 17.5 To revalidate a changed program, test both the modified
and the unmodified portions of the program following these steps: (1)
test for program failure first by performing system tests, (2) test the
unmodified portions of the program by performing regression tests,
and (3) directly test the modified portions of the program.

testing effort and the retesting efforts can be compared to reveal any unexpected discrepancies.

   Increases in the number of errors detected and in the effort needed to
detect and correct errors is often the first sign that program quality is
deteriorating and that future maintenance of the program will require more
effort and more resources. Error increases may indicate that the changes
were made too hastily, or that program documentation, technical tools,
or programmer experience were inadequate. Furthermore, they may indicate
that the side effects from the change were not recognized, that retesting was
inadequate, or that the quality of the original program was poor.

   Comparing errors discovered during revalidation with previously dis-

BOX 17.5   Guidelines for revalidating a program

- Since maintenance programmers tend to concentrate their testing effort on the changes they made and tend to ignore the unmodified portions of the system, use the following testing approach to avoid this problem:

  1. Do not allow the maintenance programmer who made the change to be the only person who revalidates the program.

  2. Test for program failure first. Then test the unmodified portions of the program. Finally, test the modified portions of the program.

- Prepare a standard set of test cases and expected test results in advance and use this test set as part of the program revalidation process. When possible, use the same test cases and data as were used when the program was originally developed, in addition to some new revalidation tests.

- Use automated tools to aid the revalidation process.

- Involve the end users in the revalidation process by encouraging them to perform revalidation tests independently.

- Record the number and types of errors discovered during the revalidation process and compare the results with previous testing efforts to evaluate possible program deterioration.

covered errors can help identify maintenance problems. This information can be used to suggest improvements in both the program development process and the program maintenance process as well as the need for more advanced software tools. In addition, it can help extend the program life. Once identified, the modules that are the most error-prone can be rewritten to improve the future maintainability of the program.

REFERENCES

1. G. Parikh, "Some Tips, Techniques, and Guidelines for Program and System Maintenance," in *Techniques of Program and System Maintenance* (Lincoln, NE: Ethnotech, 1980), pp. 69–74.

2. C. Liu, "A Look at Software Maintenance," *Datamation,* Vol. 22, No. 11 (November 1976): 51–55.

3. D. Freedman and G. Weinberg, "Maintenance Reviews," in *Techniques*

of Program and System Maintenance (Lincoln, NE: Ethnotech, 1980), pp. 57–59.

4. D. Parnas, "Designing for Ease of Extension and Contraction," *IEEE Trans. on Software Engineering,* Vol. SE-5, No. 2 (March 1979): 128–137.

5. C. McClure, *Managing Software Development and Maintenance* (New York: Van Nostrand Reinhold Company, 1978).

6. D. Freedman and G. Weinberg, "A Checklist for Potential Side Effects of a Maintenance Change," in *Techniques of Program and System Maintenance* (Lincoln, NE: Ethnotech, 1980), pp. 61–68.

7. G. Myers, "Selections from Composite/Structured Design," in *Techniques of Program and System Maintenance* (Lincoln, NE: Ethnotech, 1980), pp. 205–206.

8. B. Boehm, "Software and Its Impact: A Quantitative Assessment," *Datamation,* Vol. 19, No. 5 (May 1973): 48–59.

9. G. Weinberg, *Psychology of Computer Programming* (New York: Van Nostrand Reinhold Company, 1971), pp. 247–251.

18 DEBUGGING

THE CASE OF THE MISSING PERIOD

Gloria was one of the best programmers at the British American Insurance Company. But as sometimes happens to even the best programmer, Gloria was having a bad week. She had almost completed her part of the new on-line Claims System when an elusive bug brought her progress to a halt. Gloria was determined that no bug would get the best of her, so she searched through listings, test runs, and dumps to find the problem. Although her coworkers offered help, she refused, claiming that it would take too long to explain the program and the problem to someone else. By the time another programmer became familiar enough with her problem to be of any real help, she would certainly have it solved.

Then finally after a week of searching, Gloria asked Ted, another programmer at BAI, to look at her program. After a few minutes explanation of the program logic from Gloria and several more minutes to review the code, Ted pointed out the bug. There was a missing period at the end of an IF statement. The compiler had not detected the mistake and the indentation had camouflaged it.

Gloria was both relieved and humiliated. How could she have studied her own program for a whole week without seeing such an obvious mistake!

Gloria's experience is a common one among programmers. Although the error was very minor, it had cost BAI a week of valuable programmer time.

THE CASE OF THE $18.5 MILLION HYPHEN

On July 22, 1962, the U.S. Mariner I Space Rocket was launched on mankind's first effort to explore the planets, a mission to Venus. The rocket deviated from its course and ground control gave the order to blow it to pieces. Later, an investigation revealed that the software was at fault. Although the programs had been thoroughly tested, not all errors were discovered. The omission of a single hyphen from one computer program had gone unnoticed and had caused the whole mission to be scrapped. The cost to the American taxpayer was $18.5 million [1].

Some revealing experiments have been performed on the debugging process. Researchers have used both professional programmers and programming students to gain a better understanding of which debugging methods are most useful. The results are both disappointing and surprising. First, the inability of experienced programmers to detect even obvious errors is alarming [2]. Second, computer-based debugging by the original programmer appears to be one of the least efficient debugging methods [3]. Third, no single method used alone is very good [2].

In general, programmers are not very successful in finding errors. They do not know where to look and often waste a great deal of effort looking in the wrong place. They do not know what errors are most likely to occur. They do not know when they have isolated all aspects of an error and how to track its total effect throughout the program. When they are looking in the wrong place, they find it difficult to look elsewhere because their thinking becomes fixed on one possible cause.

Even in situations where experienced programmers have been given information about the number and the location of program errors, the programmers have been unable to find all the errors. Debugging seems to be very dependent on the individual programmer. In some instances, inexperienced programmers are more successful than experienced programmers at finding errors. Also, when different programmers independently debug the same program, they are likely to find different errors.

DEBUGGING METHODS   There are two basic debugging methods:

1. Individual debugging
2. Group debugging

In individual debugging, one programmer works alone to find the error(s); in group debugging, two or more programmers work together to find the error(s). For each method, there are many variations. For example, an individual may use a computer-based debugging approach which relies mainly on studying the results from program execution tests. Or, an individual may use a non-computer-based method in which the program listing is studied (desk debugging). On the other hand, a group of programmers may choose to walk through the program listing together in an attempt to discover the error.

In his experiments, Myers found that the most cost-effective method for finding errors was to employ two programmers who work independently of one another and later pool their results. This method proved equally cost effective (in terms of cost per error found) to a single-person method because of little overlap in the errors found by both programmers [4, pp. 129–130]. Fagan performed experiments with group inspection techniques at IBM. He found that group walk-throughs/inspections were a more effective debugging method (in terms of programmer time and computer time) than when the original programmers each debugged their own code individually [4, pp. 28–29].

Since the ability to detect different types of errors varies depending on the method used and the individuals involved, a combination approach is probably best. Based on the results of debugging experiments and studies, the following debugging method is suggested:

1. Two individuals work independently to locate the error using a computer-based testing approach interspersed with individual desk debugging. (These individuals are not the same persons who wrote or changed the code.)

2. Then, the two individuals pool their findings by performing a walk-through review of the program and the error evidence each has gathered.

3. Automatic debugging tools are used to aid the process.

Using more than one debugging method and more than one debugger may seem too extravagant a suggestion when many systems and programming departments are suffering from personnel shortages. But it is a very practical suggestion because this approach will not only enable programmers to find more errors sooner but will also provide an environment in which supportive feedback from peers, programming education, and programmer communication can be enhanced. A better program and better programmers will result.

PROGRAM DEBUGGING TOOLS

Which debugging tools are the most useful? Is the source listing the only essential debugging aid? Are dumps of any use? Does an on-line debugging environment improve programmer effectiveness?

Shneiderman suggests the following list of debugging aids [4, pp. 112–113].

- Source code listing
- Detailed program specification
- Program flowchart
- Output listing
- Trace of statements executed and variable values
- Access to terminal for program execution
- Clues to type or location of error

He places the source listing at the top of the list, claiming that it is the most important debugging aid. Experiments by Gilb support Schneiderman's claim by showing that simple source code reading is more effective than use of test data in finding errors [5]. Also, Van Tassel believes that desk checking a source listing can be as effective as studying program dumps [6]. Weinberg suggests that automatically generated flow diagrams can be used to supplement code reading [7].

Box 18.1 lists a set of tools that aid the debugging process. Selection of appropriate debugging tools depends on the problem to be solved and the debugger's personal preference. However, the important point here is that the availability of a powerful set of debugging tools can greatly affect the amount of debugging effort expended. For example, Van Tassel claims that the use of good debugging compilers (e.g., University of Waterloo's COBOL WATBOL and FORTRAN WATFIV, Cornell University's PL/1 and PL/C, and IBM's PL/1 Checkout Compiler) can reduce the debugging effort by half [6]. A debugging compiler more thoroughly checks for syntax errors by examining the interaction of instructions as well as the correctness of each single instruction. Also, it performs checks such as out-of-range subscripts and uninitialized variables during program execution.

LOCATING PROGRAM ERRORS

The last item on Shneiderman's list of debugging aids lists clues to the type or location of the error.

Traditionally, programmers have spent too much time looking for errors in the wrong places. Myers found that programmers focused their attention on normal processing at the expense of considering special processing situations and invalid input. Weinberg found that programmers have difficulty finding errors because their conjectures become prematurely fixed, blinding them to other possibilities.

Knowing what types of errors are likely to occur and where they are likely to occur in the program can avoid these problems and greatly simplify the debugging process. Two techniques are suggested:

1. Studying the program error properties
2. Measuring program complexity

PROGRAM ERROR PROPERTIES

Each program has an error property identifying which parts (modules) of a program are most error-prone and what types of program errors are most likely to occur. These properties are established during program development because most developers have a favorite subset of programming constructs they use repeatedly and also have certain programming errors that they make

BOX 18.1   Debugging tools and aids

- Debugging compilers (e.g., University of Waterloo's COBOL WATBOL and FORTRAN WATFIV, Cornell University's PL/1 and PL/C, IBM's PL/1 Checkout Compiler, Stanford University's ALGOL W).

- Cross-reference listers (e.g., TRW's DEPCHT, DPNDCY, FREF for FORTRAN programs).

- Storage map (i.e., a common compiler option).

- Source code reformatters (e.g., ADR's MetaCOBOL).

- Automatic flowcharters (e.g., TRW's FLOWGEN for FORTRAN programs).

- Automatic documentors (e.g., General Research Corp's RXVP, Amdahl's MAP).

- Structuring engines (e.g., Catalyst Corp.'s COBOL Engine; Caines, Farber & Gordon's FORTRAN Engine).

- Executive monitors and performance monitors (e.g., TRW's PPE).

- Code optimizers (e.g., IBM's PL/1 Optimizing Compiler).

- Structure checkers (e.g., TRW's CODE AUDITOR for FORTRAN programs).

- Decision table processors.

- Data dictionaries.

- Automated librarians (e.g., NIC's SLICK).

- Data management systems.

- Test data generators (e.g., TRW's ATDG).

- Test case generators (e.g., General Research Corp.'s RXVP for FORTRAN programs).

- Compiler error checking features (e.g., IBM COBOL USE command, IBM PL/1 ON SIZE ERROR command, DEC BASIC-PLUS).

- File compare utilities.

- Language debug packages for dumps, flow trace, variable trace, subroutine trace, subscript checks, and display (e.g., Stanford's ALGOL W, IBM's COBOL and PL/1).

- On-line debuggers providing on-line breakpoints, restarts, and modifications (e.g., DEC BASIC-PLUS).

- Language conversion packages.

- Programmer's workbench (e.g., UNIX).

repeatedly. Unless a major program rewrite is performed, these properties remain generally unchanged throughout the life of the program.

Error properties can be determined by studying the program errors found during development testing and the maintenance phase. Boxes 18.2, 18.3, and 18.4 list the error information that should be recorded and studied.

Herndon and Keenan studied the program errors that were discovered during the testing of a real-time communications system [8]. In total, 200 errors were found. The errors were categorized according to the cause of the error:

- *Specification error:* incomplete or incorrect design specification
- *Programming error:* faulty design, logic, and code
- *Testing error:* invalid test procedures

BOX 18.2

ERROR REPORT

ER NO _____

Reported by: _____

Date reported: _____

System name: _____

Severity of error:

_____ High: system does not function

_____ Medium: system functions, but not satisfactorily

_____ Low: system functions, but with minor irregularities

Symptomatic description of error:

_____

_____

_____

_____

BOX 18.3

ERROR CORRECTION DATA

System names(s)   _____

Program names(s)   _____

Type of error:

_____   Specification error   _____   Debugging error

_____   Design error   _____   Testing error

_____   Coding error   _____   External error

_____   Clerical error   _____   Other _____

Explanation of cause of error

_____

_____

_____

_____

_____

Life-cycle phase during which error corrected:

Development	Maintenance
_____ Specification	_____ Change/enhancement
_____ Design	_____ Rewrite
_____ Coding	_____ Error correction
_____ Testing	(of another error)

Number of modules changed: _____

Number of lines of code added and/or changed: _____

Number of compiles: _____

Number of tests for revalidation: _____

Total number of test runs: _____

Test data available: _____   _____

                        yes   no

(Continued)

BOX 18.3 *(Continued)*

Modules Changed   Number of Times Previously Changed

_____   _____

_____   _____

_____   _____

_____   _____

Times to detect and correct errors: _____ worker-hours

Difficulty of detecting and correcting error:

_____ Low: less than 4 worker-hours

_____ Medium: 4 worker-hours to 16 worker-hours

_____ High: greater than 16 worker-hours

Code style:

_____ Structured

_____ Unstructured

- *External error:* hardware failures or problems in other systems that interface with the system

The majority (58%) of the errors found in the communications system were programming errors. Specification errors accounted for 19% of the errors found, external errors for 13%, and testing errors for the remaining 10%. Using this historical error information, we can predict that future problems with this communications system will probably be caused by programming errors.

Schneidewind and Hoffman also performed programming experiments to study program errors [9]. They categorize errors according to the following error types:

- *Design error:* communication error, data design error, etc.
- *Coding error:* syntax error, design misunderstanding, etc.
- *Clerical error:* manual input error, mental error, etc.
- *Debugging error:* inappropriate use of debugging tools, etc.
- *Testing error:* inadequate tests, misinterpretation of results, etc.

BOX 18.4 Error categories

I. Design Error

1. Missing cases or steps
2. Inadequate checking/editing
3. Initialization error
4. Loop control error
5. Misunderstanding of specifications
6. Incorrect algorithm (e.g., math error)
7. Timing problems
8. Failure to consider all data types

II. Coding Error

1. Misunderstanding of design
2. I/0 format error
3. Control structure error (If, Perform)
4. Syntax error
5. Incorrect subroutine usage
6. Initialization/reinitialization error (e.g., flag)
7. Indexing/subscripting error
8. Naming inconsistency
9. Inadequate checking/editing
10. Error in parameter passing
11. Using wrong arithmetic mode
12. Overflow, underflow, truncation

III. Clerical Error

1. "Slip" of the pencil (misspelling)
2. Keypunch/data entry

IV. Debugging Error

1. Insufficient or incorrect use of test cases/data
2. Negligence
3. Misinterpretation of error source/debugging results

V. Testing Error

1. Inadequate test cases/data
2. Misinterpretation of test results
3. Misinterpretation of program specifications
4. Negligence

VI. External

1. Hardware failure
2. Software reaction to hardware failure
3. Problems in other systems that interfaced with this one

VII. Specification Error

1. Incomplete or ambiguous specification
2. Incorrect problem definition

The error type that occurred most frequently was clerical, followed by coding, design, and, finally, testing errors. It is interesting to note that the design errors were caused by the neglect of extreme conditions (i.e., extreme numeric values which cause underflow or overflow or exceed any limits). This agrees with Myers' findings that programmers tend to concentrate on normal processing situations at the expense of off-normal situations. As a general debugging guideline, the programmer should focus the debugging search on examining extreme conditions rather than normal processing. Box 18.5 lists some additional debugging guidelines.

In error discussions, the emphasis is often placed on specification/design errors rather than clerical/coding errors because these errors are more difficult to detect and correct, and because many clerical/coding errors are detectable during compilation. However, clerical/coding errors cannot be entirely ignored by the debugger, for two reasons. First, although they are easier to detect and correct, often more coding errors are made than design errors. This was the case in both the Herndon and the Schneidewind studies. The result is that the total amount of effort expended detecting and correcting clerical/coding errors may equal or even be greater than the effort expended detecting and correcting specification/design errors. Second, many clerical/coding errors (e.g., uninitialized variable, out-of-range subscript, nontermination of loops) are not detectable by the ordinary compiler.

When searching for a program error, the programmer should not dismiss the possibility that its cause may be a syntax error or a misunderstanding of how the language works. A debugging compiler can greatly aid the programmer in locating these types of errors.

PREDICTING ERROR-PRONENESS

Program complexity can be used to measure error-proneness by predicting where errors are most likely to occur (in which modules) and the types of errors that are most likely to occur. Knowing the types of errors and where they are likely to occur can be used to select an optimum debugging strategy and tools, leading to the detection and correction of more errors sooner and at lower cost.

McCabe's cyclomatic number has been found to have a significant relationship with program error occurrence. As defined in Chapter 3, the cyclomatic number is calculated by counting the number of program compares:

$$\text{cyclomatic number} = \text{number of compares} + 1$$

Program errors are more likely to occur in program modules having a high cyclomatic number (> 10) than in modules having a low cyclomatic number. In addition, a high cyclomatic number is associated with design errors,

BOX 18.5　Debugging guidelines

- Do not use a random approach to debugging. Begin by excluding the unlikely sources of the error. First eliminate the simple cases, and then move on to the more difficult cases [6].

- Insolate one error at a time [6].

- Employ defensive programming by making program errors easy to locate with the use of debugging code embedded in the program (e.g., printout of selective variable values, logic traces, "end-of-program logic" message). After debugging is completed, leave the debugging code in the program by changing each debugging statement into a nonexecutable comment so they are available for future use but do not interfere with normal processing [6].

- Carefully study actual program output, comparing it to samples of expected output. Many errors are observable in the output listings [2].

- Focus attention on data handled by the program rather than solely on program processing logic. Focus on boundary and invalid-input conditions when checking for data-related errors [2]. Check data type, data value ranges, data field sizes, and data value.

- Use the most powerful debugging tools available and a variety of debugging methods (e.g., computer-based and non-computer-based) to avoid becoming locked into considering only one possibility too prematurely.

- Keep a record of errors detected and corrected, noting where the errors occurred in the program and the types of errors that were found, since this information can be used to predict where future errors will occur [10].

- Measure program complexity. Programs (modules) with high complexity have greater propensity for error and will probably require more time to detect and correct errors. Programs (modules) with high complexity are more likely to contain specification/design type errors, whereas programs (modules) with low complexity are more likely to contain clerical/coding-type errors.

- Use programs of artificially seeded errors to train programmers in debugging techniques and then give them immediate feedback on all seeded errors, showing them what they missed [2].

whereas a low cyclomatic number is associated with coding errors. The desk checking debugging method and nonexecution debugging tools such as a debugging compiler are very helpful in finding coding errors. A group walkthrough and execution debugging tools such as tracers and on-line debuggers are recommended for finding design errors.

REFERENCES

1. G. Wallace, D. Wallechinsky, A. Wallace, and S. Wallace, *The Book of Lists #2,* (New York: William Morrow & Co., Inc., 1980), p. 486.

2. G. Myers, "A Controlled Experiment in Program Testing and Code Walkthrough/Inspections," *Communications of the ACM,* Vol. 21, No. 9 (September 1978): 760–768.

3. B. Knight, "On Software Quality and Productivity," in *Technical Directions,* IBM FSC, (July 1978), pp. 21–27.

4. B. Schneiderman, *Software Psychology* (Cambridge, MA: Winthrop Publishers, Inc., 1980).

5. Gilb,

6. D. Van Tassel, *Program Style, Design, Efficiency, Debugging, and Testing* (Englewood Cliffs, NJ: Prentice-Hall, Inc., 1978), pp. 176–237.

7. G. Weinberg, *Psychology of Computer Programming* (New York: Van Nostrand Reinhold Company, 1971), pp. 247–251.

8. M. Herndon and A. Keenan, "Analysis of Error Remediation Expenditures During Validation," 3rd International Conference on Software Engineering, May 1978, pp. 202–206.

9. N. Schneidewind and H. Hoffman, "An Experiment in Software Error Data Collection and Analysis," *IEEE Trans. on Software Engineering,* Vol. SE-5, No. 3 (May 1979): 276–286.

10. H. Mills, "Software Development," *IEEE Trans. on Software Engineering,* Vol. SE-2, No. 4, (December 1976): 265–273.

19 TOOLS FOR MAINTENANCE

THE NEED FOR MAINTENANCE TOOLS If all programs to be maintained were well documented and cleanly structured, and used third-normal-form data models and data dictionaries for generating the programmers' data, the task of the maintainer would be much easier. If most commercial applications used fourth-generation languages and were structured and documented with action diagrams, much of today's maintenance burden would not exist. The problem for most maintainers is that they have to maintain ill-documented code that is covered with patches with no comprehensible structure and that has data representations buried in the program code. It is a major detective operation to find out how the program works, and each attempt to change it sets off mysterious bugs from the tangled undergrowth of unstructured code.

The tool the maintainer needs most is an interactive code analyzer that will help him to understand how the code works and to predict the side effects of modifications.

The maintainer spends much time in the following tasks:

1. Looking for a Structure

There may be several different types of structure that need to be understood:

- Procedural structure
- Control structure
- Data structure
- Input/output structure

These structures may be difficult to perceive and follow in the existing code.

2. Understanding Data Aliases

A single data area may be referred to by multiple names. Data areas may overlap.

3. Following Data Flow

Where do data values originate? Where are they used after they have been set?

4. Following Control Flow

All the control flows have to be understood, and the consequences of executing each path. The path may use GOTOs, hidden switches, and be extensively patched.

5. Looking for Patterns

The maintainer needs to discover patterns and ask questions such as: "Where is this message produced?"

6. Understanding Differences Between Versions of a Program

Why is one version correct and another not? How does a change effect different versions? In what ways do they differ?

AMDAHL'S MAP   A tool called MAP from the Amdahl Corporation is designed to support the six maintenance tasks listed above [1]. The manual does not say what "MAP" stands for, but we are sure the reader can easily fit words to the acronym. MAP enables the maintainer to examine COBOL programs interactively at a terminal screen.

The tool operates in two phases: the LOAD phase and VIEW phase. The LOAD phase processes the program, conducts research into how it works, and stores information about it which can be interrogated during the VIEW phase. The user can examine the program interactively during the VIEW phase and can produce a variety of views and charts on the screen, showing how the program works.

Among these charts are the following:

- ## Structure Chart View

This view gives an overall picture of the program. PERFORMed procedures and CALLed programs are displayed as boxes in a hierarchy chart. The user can traverse the chart, examine data interactions between the boxes, and mark the boxes on the screen for future reference.

- ## Source Code Views

The source code can be viewed in various ways. The user can scroll through the source code, exclude lines, and mark lines. He can ask questions about where variables are used, control flow, and so on, and see the answers displayed by the appropriate code being highlighted.

- ## Control Trace

The control trace displays the procedural structure of a program. The user can follow the branches, loops, and paths which the program follows, and find how switches are used, and can ask questions such as: "How can I get there from here?"

- ## Data Trace

The data trace can answer questions such as: "Where is this variable modified?" "Where is this variable used next?" "Where did the value in this variable come from?" It tells where any variable is used, modified, or referenced. It thus helps the user to determine which control paths are relevant, what data aliases must be examined, and what statements might modify a variable.

- ## Version Comparison

MAP can display the differences in source code between two versions of a program. This information can be manipulated on the Difference Display so that interesting differences are more evident.

- ## Subset Facility

Subsets of a program can be displayed, for example:

- Input/output
- Data definitions
- Data manipulation (assignment of values to data items)
- Control

- Procedure calls
- Labels
- Comments

- **Search Facility**

MAP can search through the program to find variables or answer other questions about the program.

STRUCTURE CHART

Figure 19.1 shows a program structure chart created by MAP's analysis of the program. It shows the *call* relationships among the subprogram units within the program. Here "call" refers to any method of invoking a unit, including PERFORM and CALL statements, and the INPUT and OUTPUT clauses of SORT and MERGE statements.

MAP draws hierarchical pictures of these relationships. The *called* unit is drawn underneath the *calling* unit. The left-to-right ordering of subordinate boxes is based on the ordering of calling statements in the program. If a unit is called by more than one other unit, it will appear more than once on the chart. In this case it is marked with an asterisk. Unit 14, for example, appears twice in Fig. 19.1.

The structure chart, like other MAP charts, is usually too big for one terminal screen. MAP creates a virtual screen that may be longer and wider than the terminal screen. To view the larger virtual screen, the terminal screen is scrolled over it like a viewing window. The virtual screen is of such a size that it can be printed. It is also called a page.

The user is given a variety of commands with which he can move around the structure chart and learn various facts from it. There are both graphical commands and a LIST command for displaying tabular information about the units. The user can print either individual screens or the whole chart.

Like moving a cursor, MAP's attention can be on one box on the chart at a time. Map writes "* current" at the bottom of this box. Unit 1 is the *current* box in Fig. 19.1. Various commands for examining or manipulating the chart change the *current* box. MAP scrolls the chart so that the current box is within the viewing window. The user can scroll away from this to examine other parts of the chart. Sometimes the subordinates of a box are on a different virtual screen. In this case MAP writes *"see page x"* below the box.

The word *entry* is written above a box which is an entry point to the chart, as with unit 1 in Fig. 19.1. The word *exit* is written below a box that exits the program. The word *recursive* is written below a box that calls itself (directly or indirectly).

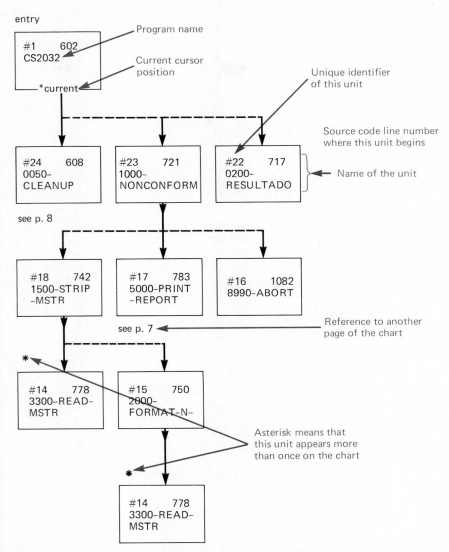

Figure 19.1 Structure chart displayed by Amdahl's MAP tool. The chart may occupy many virtual screens (pages).

The commands for manipulating the structure chart enable the user to traverse it along its arrows, to scroll around it, to set up marks on it, to adjust the drawing of the chart, and to carry out various types of searches. The search commands employ the *source* code. The user can tell MAP to search for source statements of a particular type, for variables, or for patterns of characters.

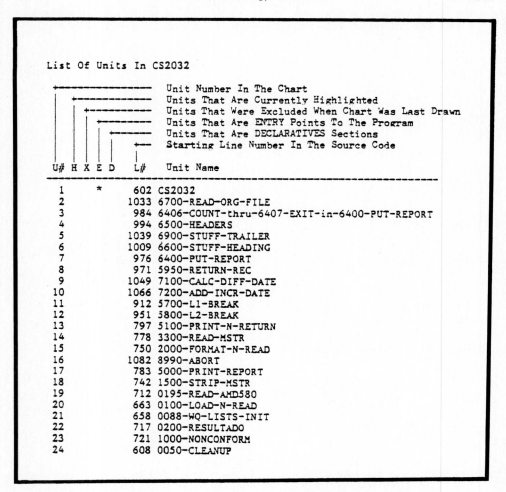

Figure 19.2 LIST display showing the program's unit. Part of this program is shown in the structure chart of Fig. 19.1.

Figure 19.2 shows the output of the LIST command, which lists all units in a program. Part of the program in Fig. 19.2 is in the structure chart of Fig. 19.1.

VIEWING THE SOURCE CODE

MAP's *source code view* allows the user to explore the data flow, control flow, procedure interfaces, and generally how the program functions. The user can browse, search, compare versions, trace calling sequences, find out where variables are modified, and so on.

The user may examine the whole program, or one of the units in Fig. 19.1. He may ZOOM IN to a PERFORMed paragraph in the code. The screen display then excludes all other source code. The user may ZOOM OUT to a high-level view from which the current view was derived.

Whereas in the *structure chart view* the object of *current* examination is a box (program unit), in the *source code view* it is a line of source code. Many *source code view* commands operate with the current line of code to produce effects. Many commands move to a different *current* line.

Particularly useful among the commands that search the source code are the *trace* commands. There are two types of trace: a *data trace* and a *control trace.*

DATA TRACING

Data traces enable the users to find out what happens to variables. The variables traced can be simple variables, and also files, groups, tables, table elements, or any legal COBOL reference.

A data trace does not display the sequence of the source code but rather the sequence in which lines of code employ the data item that is being traced. The *current* line of code may be 350 and the next line 157 because that is where the data item is *next* used in the program control sequence. There may be more than one "next" use of the data item.

If the program uses a REDEFINE, giving the data item a different name, this will be traced. Also, if a subroutine returns a different data item derived from the original, this will be indicated.

The user may start the trace at any point by moving the cursor to that position in the source code.

There are three types of data trace:

- *Use:* where the value of a variable is read
- *Modification:* where the value of a variable is set or modified
- *Reference:* both of the above

The trace may procede in a forward or backward direction.
Combined, these give six data trace commands:

	Forward	Backward
Use	NEXTUSE	PREVUSE
Modification	NEXTMOD	PREVMOD
Reference	NEXTREF	PREVREF

The NEXTUSE command, for example, shows all statements reachable from the current statement which could *use* the variable in question. The

PREVUSE command shows all statements that could reach the current statement and *use* the variable in question. Similarly, the NEXTMOD and PREVMOD relate to statements that could *modify* the variable; and NEXTREF and PREVREF relate to statements that could *reference* the variable.

The result might be too wide-ranging. The user can limit any MAP search with various types of "filters." For example, the command

    ! 312 - 375   I FIND MOVE ALL

would look at source code lines 312 to 375 for all occurrences of the pattern "MOVE." If this statement is combined with a trace, it limits the result to statements 312 to 375, which contain the pattern "MOVE."

CONTROL TRACE

Whereas a *data trace* shows statements that use or modify variables, a *control trace* shows the control flow statements such as GOTO, PERFORM, IF, ELSE, CALL, RETURN, and so on. It provides a mechanism for simulating conditions and branches, and therefore for following a control path.

A FORWARD CONTROL TRACE lists all possible paths forward from the current statement. A BACKWARD CONTROL TRACE lists all possible paths that could have reached the current statement. DESTINATION commands show possible paths from the current statement which could reach a given destination—how can you get *there* from *here*?

The range of such traces can be limited with a variety of filters. The user may pick one of the many paths to or from the current statement and display the source code statements on that path. MAP will show which program units contain statements in any given control path.

FIND

A group of FIND commands will search backward or forward through the text of the source code, looking for given character strings or patterns.

DEAD CODE

The data trace can be employed to look for unused variables. The control trace can be employed to look for unused program statements.

VERSION COMPARISONS

Two versions of source code can be compared by MAP. A variety of commands can be used for this comparison. Figures 19.3 and 19.4 are comparison displays, one the old version and one the new version of the source code. The two columns of statement numbers on the left show which statements

```
 <unit name>                              <short message>
 ==> _<primary command input>
 OLD     NEW        <long message>-------------------------------
 *********************** TOP OF UNIT ***********************
 000001 000001 0050-CLEANUP                        SECTION
 000002 000002    MOVE SPACES TO WQ-AMD580-LISTS-GRP.
 000003 000003    PERFORM 0088-WQ-LISTS-INIT VARYING WQ-NDX1
 000004 000004       FROM +1 BY +1
 000005 000005       UNTIL WQ-NDX1 > WQ-MAX-NUM-OF-JOB-CODES
 000006 000006    AFTER
 000007 000007    WQ-NDX2 FROM +1 BY +1
 000008 000008       UNTIL WQ-NDX2 > WQ-MAX-NUM-OF-GRADES.
        DELETE       ...          1 line excluded
 000010 000009    OPEN INPUT JOB-AMD580-NULLS-FILE.
        DELETE       ...          1 line excluded
 000012 000010    IF W2-EOF-JOB-AMD580-NULLS-FILE = '1'
 000013 000011       MOVE 'DDNAME CS2032C, FILE EMPTY'
 000014 000012                        TO WX-ABORT-TEXT
 000015 000013    PERFORM 8990-ABORT.
        FROM         ...          2 lines excluded
 TO     000014    PERFORM 0195-READ-AMD580.
 TO     000015    PERFORM 0196-COMPUTE-AMD580.
 TO     000016    PERFORM 0197-CHECK-AMD580.
 TO     000017    IF IJ-NUMBERS IS ALPHANUMERIC
 ADD    000018       EXHIBIT NAMED IJ-NUMBERS 'DATA NOT NUMERIC'
        DELETE       ...          5 lines excluded
 000023 000019    PERFORM 0195-READ-AMD580 UNTIL IJ-NUMBERS
```

Figure 19.3   This figure and Fig. 19.4 show comparison displays of two versions of a program. The code of the old version is shown in this figure.

are changed. The programs may be large, so MAP can display a comparison in which all lines that are the same in the two versions are excluded. Figure 19.5 shows this.

Tools for program creation and testing have been in use for many years. Tools such as MAP for helping maintain programs have been surprisingly neglected. Today, MAP works with source code. In a surprising number of cases the source code has been lost. It is desirable to have a tool like MAP which also works from object code.

GENERAL RESEARCH CORP.'S RXVP

The Karlsruhe Nuclear Research Center had many FORTRAN systems, some as large as 75,000 lines of code. These needed extensive modification and maintenance. Karlsruhe used an automated test and documentation tool, RXVP, developed by the General Research Cor-

```
<unit name>                                        <short message>
==> _<primary command input>
OLD     NEW      <long message>--------------------------------
************************* TOP OF UNIT ***********************
000001 000001 0050-CLEANUP                              SECTION
000002 000002    MOVE SPACES TO WQ-AMD580-LISTS-GRP.
000003 000003    PERFORM 0088-WQ-LISTS-INIT VARYING WQ-NDX1
000004 000004       FROM +1 BY +1
000005 000005       UNTIL WQ-NDX1 > WQ-MAX-NUM-OF-JOB-CODES
000006 000006     AFTER
000007 000007       WQ-NDX2 FROM +1 BY +1
000008 000008          UNTIL WQ-NDX2 > WQ-MAX-NUM-OF-GRADES.
000009 DELETE SET WQ-NDX1 WQ-NDX2          TO +1.
000010 000009 OPEN INPUT JOB-AMD580-NULLS-FILE.
000011 DELETE PERFORM 0195-READ-AMD580.
000012 000010 IF W2-EOF-JOB-AMD580-NULLS-FILE = '1'
000013 000011    MOVE 'DDNAME CS2032C, FILE EMPTY'
000014 000012                          TO WX-ABORT-TEXT
000015 000013    PERFORM 8990-ABORT.
000016 FROM   PERFORM 0195-PROCESS-AMD580.
000017 FROM   IF IJ-NUMBERS IS ALPHANUMERIC OR SPACES
 TO              ...                 4 lines excluded
 ADD             ...                 1 line excluded
000018 DELETE    DISPLAY 'THIS IS FOR DEBUG PURPOSES'
000019 DELETE    DISPLAY 'UP TO THE TEST FOR IJ-NUMBERS'
```

Figure 19.4 Code of the new version of the program shown in Fig. 19.3.

poration. This proved an immense aid in making program modifications that would otherwise have been impractical. The tool also generated a substantial portion of the program documentation.

RXVP provided information on the data flow and module invocation structure in the complex programs. This made it possible to investigate thoroughly the impact of modifications on the entire program, and to trace possible side effects. In addition, it was helpful in static error detection. It enabled them to find uninitialized variables quickly, or variables whose values were set but never referenced.

RXVP analyzes FORTRAN code and produces a data base containing information about the program. Using this data base, the following documentation reports can be generated:

1. Source code listing

2. Module invocation structure

3. Cross-reference report

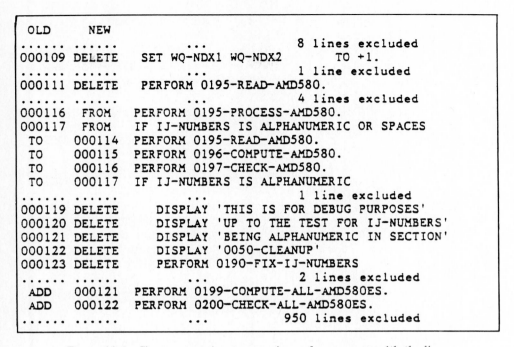

```
OLD       NEW
......  ......           ...              8 lines excluded
000109 DELETE     SET WQ-NDX1 WQ-NDX2       TO +1.
......  ......           ...              1 line excluded
000111 DELETE     PERFORM 0195-READ-AMD580.
......  ......           ...              4 lines excluded
000116  FROM      PERFORM 0195-PROCESS-AMD580.
000117  FROM      IF IJ-NUMBERS IS ALPHANUMERIC OR SPACES
  TO    000114    PERFORM 0195-READ-AMD580.
  TO    000115    PERFORM 0196-COMPUTE-AMD580.
  TO    000116    PERFORM 0197-CHECK-AMD580.
  TO    000117    IF IJ-NUMBERS IS ALPHANUMERIC
......  ......           ...              1 line excluded
000119 DELETE     DISPLAY 'THIS IS FOR DEBUG PURPOSES'
000120 DELETE     DISPLAY 'UP TO THE TEST FOR IJ-NUMBERS'
000121 DELETE     DISPLAY 'BEING ALPHANUMERIC IN SECTION'
000122 DELETE     DISPLAY '0050-CLEANUP'
000123 DELETE     PERFORM 0190-FIX-IJ-NUMBERS
......  ......           ...              2 lines excluded
  ADD   000121    PERFORM 0199-COMPUTE-ALL-AMD580ES.
  ADD   000122    PERFORM 0200-CHECK-ALL-AMD580ES.
......  ......           ...              950 lines excluded
```

Figure 19.5 Chart comparing two versions of a program, with the lines that are common to both versions excluded.

4. Common block matrix

5. Test coverage analysis reports

The basic program documentation is a source listing. For all program modules, a source code listing is generated in a standardized and easy-to-read format.

In the module invocation structure report, all invocations to each module from other modules and all invocations from this module to other modules are listed. The statement number of the invocation is also listed.

A global cross-reference report is also provided. For each variable the modules in which the variable appears, the statement number, and the type of reference are listed.

In addition, the data flow between modules via the COMMON blocks is described in the common block matrix. It identifies in which modules the individual common blocks occur and whether or not at least one variable of the COMMON block is referenced in that module.

When the program is executed, a graphic report displays the branches executed in each specified module. Also, a summary report in which the number of calls, the number of branches executed, and the percentage of test coverage by the test cases is given for all modules and for the complete system. Unexecuted branches are listed separately.

Amdahl's MAP and General Research's RXVP are two examples of newer, more powerful software tools. There are many other tools that are less sophisticated but widely used, such as structure checkers, source code reformatters, and test data generators.

An amazing number of maintenance programmers work without good tools, presumably being unaware of their existence.

SOFTWARE TOOLS   Throughout this book many different software tools—from programming languages and data-base languages to automatic documentors—have been suggested to aid the program maintenance process. Good tools are important because their use can greatly improve both program quality and programmer productivity. For example, the choice of a compiler can greatly affect productivity. According to Van Tassel, a good debugging compiler can cut debugging time in half [3]. In terms of software tools, reliability is equated with goodness. Although program developers and maintainers should be provided with the most powerful tools available, Mills stresses that reliability is even more crucial than pure power [4]. Reliable tools promote good work habits and reduce stress.

Categories of software tools include the following:

- System design tools
- Data-base design tools
- Analysis tools
- Programming tools
- Testing and debugging tools
- Maintenance tools
- Measurement and monitoring tools
- Documentation tools
- Data dictionaries
- Librarians
- Data-base managers
- Report and chart generators
- Screen design aids
- Dialogue generators
- Application generators
- Auditing tools

Most tools currently in use are related to design and program development. Tools for maintenance are very important but have often been neglected.

The design and development tools do help with subsequent maintenance because in making programs easier to create they also make them easier to change. They often result in fewer hidden bugs. Nevertheless, most maintenance teams badly need tools like Amdahl's MAP.

An essential characteristic of good tools is user friendliness. Tools should accommodate the user by providing clear diagnostics, error recovery, HELP subsystems, easy access, and portability.

Boxes 19.1 to 19.4 list some examples of good software tools currently available.

THE PROBLEMS WITH TOOLS

Although a great variety of tools are widely used, there are some problems. They lack uniformity, completeness, and compatibility. No system has a complete set of tools available. Many tools that are available are system dependent and language dependent. Moreover, tools available on the same system for the same language may be incompatible. For example, one tool may require an input format that is different from the output format produced by a related tool.

It is sometimes said that to employ one tool is great; to employ two tools is terrible. This comment is made because many tools are incompatible and bridging their incompatibilities is more work than it is worth. What is needed is a set of compatible tools forming a software environment.

SOFTWARE ENVIRONMENTS

Software environment is the term used for an integrated set of tools supporting each phase of software development, maintenance, and migration to new technologies. Its primary objective is to raise the quality of software while lowering the price. Its secondary objective is to improve the software work environment by automatically handling much of the drudgery work of programming and freeing programmers for more creative activities.

Because there are many different types of software work, what is needed is not just one software environment but many different environments designed to meet the particular needs of each software activity—production, maintenance, management, verification and validation, documentation, and so forth.

One type of software environment is a *programming environment.* It aids programmers in the development, integration, and execution of program modules. The tools provided by a programming environment typically include an operating system, utility programs, programming language compilers/interpreters, editors, debugging aids, documentators, a file management system, and project management tools.

BOX 19.1 Examples of programming tools

Product	Query Language	Report Generator	Graphics Generator	Application Generator	High-Level Programming	Vendor	Machine Type	On-Line?	Suitable for End Users?	Data Base?
ACE	√	√				Relational Inc. San Francisco	DEC/PDP	√		Relational DB
ADAM				√		Intelligent Machine Corp.	Own machine			
ADF		√		√		IBM	370/0S	√		For IMS applications
ADMINS/11			√	√		Admins Corp.	PDP/11	√	√	Its own files
ADPAC						ADPAC Computer Languages Corp.	IBM	√		
ADRS (APL-based)	√	√			√	IBM	370	√	√	DL/1
ADS-ONLINE	√	√		√	√	Cullinane	Various	√		IDMS DB
APG	√	√				I.O.S.B. Inc.	DEC	√		Its own files
APL					√	Various	Various	√	√	
APL-DI					√	IBM	370	√	√	DL/1: IMS
APL-PLUS	√	√			√	STSC	Various	√	√	
ASI INQUIRY	√	√				App Software Applications Software Inc.	370	√		Queries IMS
ASI-ST							IBM			
ASRES	√	√				University of Georgia	360	√		Its own files
BASIS	√	√				Batelle Inc.	Various	√	√	Conventional files
BLOOM	√	√				I.D.B.S. Inc.	IBM	√	√	IDBS DB
CAFS	√	√		√	√	ICL SERIES	2900	√	√	Its own associative information retrieval system
COBOL Program Generator						Black/Prime	PRIME			
COMPOSE-II						Compusource	Data Gen.			
CONTEXT C-705	√	√				Context Systems	370	√		Its own files
CS4	√			√		Databaskonsult, Sweden	DEC/IBM			Associative records

Product	Vendor	Machine	Data files
DATA ANALYZER	Prog. Products	370	Its own files
DATATRIEVE-11	DEC	PDP/11	Its own files
DIRECT	BANCOHIO	Honeywell	Its own files
DISPLAY INF. FAC.	IBM	S/38	For S/38 DB
D.L.A.	E.M.I. Ltd.	Various	Its own files
DMS	IBM	370/8100	DL/1 and its own files
DRS-11	Synoco Ltd.	DEC	Its own files
EASYTRIEVE	Pansophic	Various	IMS, TOTAL, ADABAS
ELIAS	IBM	IBM	DL/1
EQUS	IBM	S/3, S/32	Its own files
EXTRACTO	OPTIPRO Ltd.	370	Its own files
FILETAB	N.C.C. Ltd.	Various	Conventional files
FLEXTRACT	Faulkner	Various	Its own files
FOCUS	Information Builders	370	Its own files
FORTH	Forth Inc.	Various	Conventional files
GENASYS	Generation Sciences	IBM	
General Information Systems	IBM	370	Its own DB
GIS	IBM	Various	DL/1; IMS
GRS	Enterprise Corp.	PDP	Conventional files
HARVEST	I.D.S.B.	DEC/IBM	Its own files
IBM BRADS	IBM	5110/20	Its own files
IBM 3790 QUERY	IBM	370	Its own files
ICES	UNIVAC	UNIVAC	Its own files
IDEA	Data General	Data Gen.	Its own files
IDEAL	A.D.R.	IBM	DATACOM/DB
IDL	Britton-Lee	Various	Relational DB
IIS Data Logger	Int. Inf. Sys.	DEC	Its own files
IMDOC	M.A.G.	370	Its own files
IMS FASTON	IBM	370	IMS
INFORMAT	M.R.P.	NOVA	Its own files
INGRES	Relational Tech.	PDP/IBM	Relational DB
INNOPAK	Innovators Inc.	Datapoint	Conventional files

(Continued)

BOX 19.1 (Continued)

Product	Query Language	Report Generator	Graphics Generator	Application Generator	High-Level Programming	Vendor	Machine Type	On-Line?	Suitable for End Users?	Data Base?
IN? QUIRY	✓	✓				Informatics	370	✓		IMS and its own files
INSCI	✓	✓				Information Science	Various		✓	Its own files
INSYTE	✓	✓				Remote Comp.	Burroughs	✓		Its own files
INTELLECT	✓	✓				Artificial Intelligence	IBM	✓	✓	ADABAS, others
IQ	✓	✓				Management Group	Various	✓	✓	IDS, IMS, total
IRS	✓	✓				Sigma Data	370	✓		Its own files
ISA/OAS	✓	✓				ISA Corp.	370	✓		Its own files
JPI DIS	✓	✓				University of Georgia	UNIVAC	✓		Its own files
LINC		✓	✓	✓		Future Systems	Burroughs	✓	✓	Its own DB
LIRS	✓	✓				University of Georgia	370	✓	✓	Its own files
MAESTRO	✓	✓			✓	SOFTLAB	Various	✓		Conventional files
MANTIS				✓	✓	CINCOM	IBM	✓		Total, IMS, others
MAPPER	✓	✓		✓		UNIVAC	1100	✓	✓	Its own files
MARK V	✓	✓		✓		Informatics	IBM	✓	✓	IMS
MAXIMUS						Maximus	Data Gen. and Eclipse			
MDBS III	✓	✓			✓	MDBS INC.	Various	✓	✓	Its own DB
MDQS II	✓	✓				Honeywell	60/66	✓	✓	Its own files
MICRODATA REALITY	✓				✓	Microdata	Reality	✓	✓	Its own files
MRS	✓	✓		✓		INFOPAC	370	✓	✓	Its own files
MUMPS					✓	Mass. Gen. Hospital	Various	✓		Its own DB
NATURAL	✓	✓		✓	✓	Software AG	IBM	✓	✓	ADABAS
NCR TOTAL IQ	✓	✓				NCR	NCR	✓	✓	Total
NOMAD	✓	✓	✓			Nat. C.S.S.	IBM	✓	✓	Its own relational DB
ON-LINE ENGLISH	✓				✓	Cullinane	370	✓	✓	IDMS and its own files

Product				Vendor		Hardware			Files / DB
ORACLE	√	√						√	Its own relational DB
PRO	√			Business EDP Services		Burroughs	√		Its own files
QL SEARCH	√			QL Systems		370	√	√	Its own files
QUEO IV	√	√		Computer Tech.	√	Prime	√	√	Its own DB
QUERY-BY-EXAMPLE	√	√		IBM		370/4300	√	√	Its own relational DB
QUERY S/3	√	√		IBM		S/3	√		S/3 files
QWICK QUERY	√	√		C.A.C.I.		Various	√	√	Its own files
RAMIS II	√	√	√	Mathematica	√	370	√		Its own DB
RAPID/3000	√	√	√	Hewlett-Packard	√	H.P.	√		Relational DB
RAPPORT	√	√		Logica		Various	√		Its own relational DB
RDM	√	√		I.T. Inc.	√	PDP	√		Conventional files
RECALL	√	√	√	Data Man SY.		370	√		Its own files
REQUEST	√	√		Automation Artificial Intelligence		Various / IBM, Honeywell	√		Its own files
ROBOT	√				√	Various	√		
RPG II	√	√		IBM		Various	√		Conventional files
RPG III	√	√		IBM		S/38	√		For S/38 files and DS
S/34 UTILITIES	√			IBM		S/34	√		Uses S/34 files
S/38 DBMS	√	√		IBM		S/38	√		For S/38 DB
SAS, GRAPH	√	√	√	SAS		IBM	√	√	Its own files
SEED	√	√		I.D.B.S. Inc.		IBM	√		IDBS DB
SL/1	√	√	√	THORNE		370	√		Defines its own files
SQL/DS	√	√		IBM		IBM	√	√	Its own relational DB
STAIRS	√			IBM		Various	√	√	Its own information retrieval system
STRADIS	√	√		McDonnell Douglas		Various	√		Conventional DB
SYS/38 QUERY	√	√		IBM		S/38	√	√	Its own DB
T-ASK	√	√		CINCOM		370	√	√	Total
TCS/1700	√			Dedicated Systems		Burroughs	√	√	Its own files
TELL-A-GRAF	√	√	√	ISSCO Inc.		Various	√	√	Its own files
TIS	√	√		CINCOM		Various	√	√	Conventional DB
UCC/FCS	√	√		U.C.C. Corp.	√	Various	√		Its own files
UFO	√	√		Oxford Software	√	IBM	√		Conventional files
USER/11	√			N. County National Computing Industries		PDP/11	√	√	Uses its own DB
WORK TEN	√	√				IBM	√		

BOX 19.2 Testing and debugging tools

- Debugging compilers (e.g., University of Waterloo's COBOL WATBOL and FORTRAN WATFIV, Cornell University's PL/1 and PL/C, IBM's PL/1 Checkout Compiler, Stanford University's ALGOL W).
- Cross-reference listers (e.g., TRW's DEPCHT, DPNDCY, and FREF for FORTRAN programs).
- Storage map (i.e., a common compiler option).
- Source code reformatters (e.g., ADR's MetaCOBOL).
- Automatic flowcharters (e.g., TRW's FLOWGEN for FORTRAN programs).
- Automatic documentors (e.g., General Research Corp.'s RXVP, Amdahl's MAP).
- Structuring engines (e.g., Catalyst Corp.'s COBOL Engine; Caines, Farber & Gordon's FORTRAN Engine).
- Executive monitors and performance monitors (e.g., TRW's PPE).
- Code optimizers (e.g., IBM's PL/1 Optimizing Compiler).
- Structure checkers (e.g., TRW's CODE AUDITOR for FORTRAN programs).
- Decision table processors.
- Data dictionaries.
- Automated librarians (e.g., NIC's SLICK).
- Data management systems.
- Test data generators (e.g., TRW's ATDG).
- Test case generators (e.g., General Research Corp.'s RXVP for FORTRAN programs).
- Compiler error checking features (e.g., IBM COBOL USE command, IBM PL/1 ON SIZE ERROR command, DEC BASIC-PLUS).
- File compare utilities.
- Language debug packages for dumps, flow trace, variable trace, subroutine trace, subscript checks, and display (e.g., Stanford's ALGOL W, IBM's COBOL and PL/1).
- On-line debuggers providing on-line breakpoints, restarts, and modifications (DEC BASIC-PLUS).
- Language conversion packages.
- Programmer's workbench (e.g., UNIX).
- Static analyzer (e.g., Amdahl's MAP, General Research Corp.'s RXVP).
- Dynamic assertion processor.
- Test execution verifier.
- Test-harness generator.

BOX 19.3 Program documentation tools

- Cross-reference listers, symbol tables (compiler generated).
- Automatic flowcharters and structure charters (RXVP, MAP, FLOWGEN).
- Reformatters/indenters (ADR's MetaCOBOL).
- Automatic documentors (RXVP, MAP).
- Structuring engines (Catalyst's COBOL Engine; Caine, Farber & Gordon's FORTRAN Engine).
- Module invocation analyzers (RXVP, MAP).
- Data flow analyzers (RXVP, MAP).
- On-line editors.
- Source management libraries (NIC's SLICK, Pansophic's PANVALET).

BOX 19.4 Software quality measurement tools

Quality Characteristic	Measurement Tools
1. Understandability	Structure checkers
	Automatic flowcharters
	Execution path tracers
	Automatic complexity analyzers
2. Reliability	Execution path tracers
	Automatic complexity analyzers
3. Testability	Automatic flowcharters
	Execution path tracers
	Automatic complexity analyzers
4. Modifiability	Automatic complexity analyzers
5. Portability	Standard-language-version compiler
	Structure checkers
6. Efficiency	Structure checkers
	Performance monitors

BELL LAB'S UNIX   Bell Lab's UNIX is the most widely available programming environment [5]. UNIX is basically a time-sharing operating system supported by an extensive set of tools. UNIX provides a general environment since it can support different programming languages and different programming methodologies. One particularly powerful feature of UNIX is that it allows the programmer to move easily from one system to another. For example, while editing a program, the programmer can suspend editing to invoke the mail program. When he has finished answering his mail, he can return to editing his program. Because UNIX is easy to use, it encourages the user to pick and choose from a powerful tool kit as well as to share user-developed procedures and data bases with other users. Underlying the power of UNIX is a consistent design philosophy employing a single uniform file system.

Programming environments such as UNIX have been designed primarily to support program development efforts. In some cases they provide such a powerful tool kit that it is often possible to avoid programming completely. Since they concentrate on coding and testing aids, they are also very useful in the program maintenance environment.

WORKBENCH   Eventually, as software continues to improve, we will probably see a wide diversity of tools designed to work together on line, aiding both the developer and maintainer. The tools will constitute a development and maintenance workbench. The software effort needed to create this is massive.

Meanwhile all maintenance programmers should know that maintenance tools exist today and their usage is a fraction of what it should be.

REFERENCES

1. Amdahl Corp., *Amdahl MAP Version 1.0 User's Guide.*

2. W. Geiger, "Test and Documentation System for FORTRAN Programs," in *Practice in Software Adoption and Maintenance* (Amsterdam: North-Holland Publishing Company, 1980), pp. 143–156.

3. D. Van Tassel, *Program Style, Design, Efficiency, Debugging, and Testing* (Englewood Cliffs, NJ: Prentice-Hall, Inc., 1978), pp. 183–187.

4. H. Mills, "Software Development," *IEEE Trans. on Software Engineering,* Vol. SE-2, No. 4 (December 1976): 265–273.

5. B. Kernigham and J. Mashly, "The UNIX Programming Environment," *Computer,* April 1981, pp. 12–24.

20 MANAGING THE MAINTENANCE FUNCTION

MANAGEMENT METHODS FOR MAINTENANCE
For many organizations, the program maintenance function is out of control. Reutter comments that "maintenance often has the outward appearance of being a helter-skelter, uncoordinated activity rather than a planned, methodical, controlled, necessary business function of any organization committed to computerized data processing" [1].

While program development has received a great deal of attention from management, maintenance has been almost totally ignored in the hope that it would disappear as a result of new, improved software technologies. Although the majority of the systems and programming effort is spent on maintenance, management has little knowledge of what activities comprise the maintenance function, what is the source of most maintenance work, and what is the most effective staff organization structure for performing maintenance.

Project management disciplines such as the chief programmer team and checkpoint reviews have been used with great success to improve the program development process. Experience has shown that good management can make the difference between project success and failure. In project after project, following sound management practices has helped keep development projects on schedule, has improved the quality of the programs produced, and has increased job satisfaction.

However, these same practices have not been applied to managing the program maintenance function. Traditionally, program maintenance has been treated differently from new development. Because it has been viewed as less difficult and less important, maintenance has been performed by less experienced DP personnel with less management supervision. The result is that management problems often outweigh the technical problems of performing program maintenance.

BOX 20.1 Management methods for maintenance

- A change control procedure, including a change review board, a user charge-back system, and a program quality control audit step, can be used to control the costs and risks associated with changing programs.

- A separate maintenance staff can be formed as a method for increasing programmer productivity and controlling the effort and costs associated with performing program maintenance.

- A scheduled maintenance approach, in which the new release concept used for systems software is also applied to application programs, enables better planning and management of maintenance work.

- Programming teams can provide the same benefits to maintenance as they provide to new development—improved program quality, increased programmer productivity, and job enrichment.

Solving the technical problems may provide temporary relief to the maintenance burden, but in the long term does not control rising maintenance costs. To control costs the program maintenance function must be properly managed. The project management disciplines used to control program development can and must be used to control program maintenance. Box 20.1 suggests some management methods for maintenance.

CONTROLLING
PROGRAM
CHANGES

The outstanding management problem for the maintenance organization is controlling program changes. The management of changes in an effective and economical manner requires an understanding of why a change is needed, of the effort required to make the change, and of the impact of the change on program quality and user satisfaction. A first step in managing change is to record change information. This information is useful in deciding to approve or reject a change request, in planning for the long-term maintenance effort required for program support, and in studying the capability of a program design to accommodate changes.

A second step is to institute a change control procedure to monitor changes. This ensures that change requests will be handled in a professional manner. Each individual requesting a change should be notified of the status of the request in a timely fashion regardless of whether the change request is accepted, rejected, or temporarily tabled.

JUSTIFYING A PROGRAM CHANGE

Program change requests come from the user community, from the program development group, from the maintenance group, from the operations group, and from management. These requests, depending on the reason given for the change, can be classified into Swanson's three maintenance categories [2]:

1. *Corrective changes:* changes to correct program failures, performance failures, and implementation failures
2. *Adaptive changes:* changes to adapt a program to changes in the data requirements or the processing environments
3. *Perfective changes:* changes to enhance performance, improve cost effectiveness, efficiency, or maintainability

Regardless of the requester or the change category, no request should result in a program modification without careful consideration. Even a simple change can have subtle yet very serious ramifications on program quality and user satisfaction. Also, many changes cannot be justified in terms of increased usability or performance improvements. For example, users often tend to exaggerate their needs for a particular enhancement, and then after the enhancement is implemented, it is seldom used [3]. Finally, change requests should be considered in the context of other change requests and how they relate to the program life-cycle plan. For example, a similar request may have been submitted by several different requesters. On the other hand, different requesters may suggest changes that are incompatible with each other or incompatible with life-cycle goals.

When considering a change, questions such as the following should be addressed [4]:

1. Is the maintenance objective to preserve a single version of the program for all user groups or to allow different versions to support different user groups?
2. Is there a plan to replace this program in the near future?
3. Will this change alter the original scope and purpose of the program?

Each time a program is changed, there is a risk of introducing additional errors into the program and of jeopardizing program quality. Although this risk can be reduced by building a well-structured, easy-to-change program, it is always present to some degree because of the complex nature of programming. Therefore, a basic guideline for managing program change is that a program should *not* be changed unless the change can be justified in terms of a set of meaningful, explicit criteria.

The justification for corrective changes is straightforward. Usually, the change will be made on the justification that the program must function correctly. In some cases, however, the cost or the effect on the rest of the program may be so great compared to the minor inconvenience resulting from the failure that the user may choose to tolerate the failure rather than risk introducing new problems or modifying present operating procedures.

The justification for adaptive changes and perfective changes may be more complicated since the benefits compared to the cost of implementing and the risk of degrading quality may be difficult to evaluate. The specific justification criteria depend on the needs and priorities of a particular organization, but generally should include:

- Total cost of the change
- Staff requirements to implement the change
- Elapsed time needed to implement the change
- Disruption to current service and operating procedures
- Retraining needed for operation personnel and user groups
- Impact on program integrity
- Compatibility with program life-cycle plan
- Ramifications on future changes to the program

Emphasis should be placed on those criteria that measure the long-term effect on operations and maintenance costs rather than on satisfying the user or improving performance for the short term with an apparently low-cost modification. Decisions to change programs that are based on a response to user pressure or that rely on the maintenance programmer's personal scheme for performance tuning have helped turn even high-quality programs into a maintenance nightmare.

CHANGE CONTROL PROCEDURE

The excuse that maintenance tasks cannot be planned, since it is impossible to predict when a critical failure requiring immediate attention may occur, applies only to a small percentage of all maintenance work. The majority of maintenance work is done in response to change requests that can be controlled and planned.

An essential management tool for controlling program change is a formal change control procedure whose purposes are:

- To study how the program changes, and to plan for support needs.
- To provide a follow-up procedure for every request with a report to the requester of the planned change or the reason for rejecting the request.
- To ensure that changes are planned and scheduled to allow maintenance tasks to be planned and scheduled.

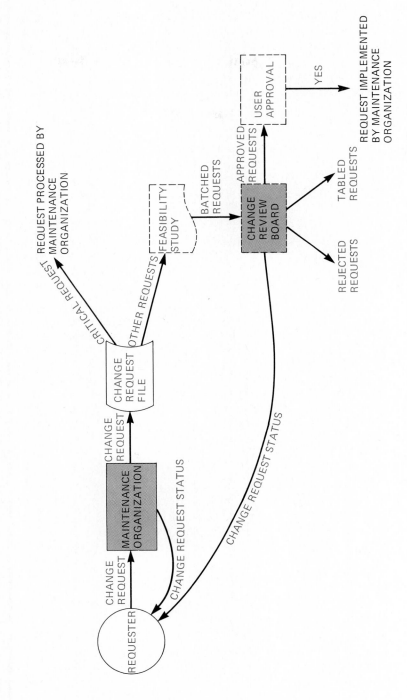

Figure 20.1 A change control procedure is a management method to control the risks and costs associated with changing programs.

A change control procedure is shown in Fig. 20.1, and a sample change request form is shown in Fig. 20.2. This is an outline of a general procedure to serve as a guide in developing a change control procedure for a particular maintenance organization. For some organizations, it may be too detailed, for others not detailed enough. The key point is that every maintenance organization requires some type of formal change procedure to control the change requests and to serve the requester in an expedient manner.

CHANGE REVIEW BOARD

A formal change control procedure allows for increased user control over program changes. As part of the change procedure, each change request is assigned a priority code, such as the following:

0	Tabled	Should be reconsidered for a later release
1	Critical	Should receive immediate attention ahead of currently scheduled maintenance tasks
2	Important	Should be placed at the end of the list of tasks to be performed for this program
3	Optional	Should be placed at the end of the list of tasks that, time and resources permitting, should be performed for this release

Critical requests are attended to immediately by the maintenance staff. Other requests are collected for periodic review by a change review board. The change review board includes user representatives as well as DP members. The board is responsible for deciding the fate of change requests based on long-term DP goals, user needs, and cost considerations. Before being reviewed by the board, change requests are studied by the maintenance staff to determine the effort and time needed to make each change, the impact of the change on other programs, the cost of the change, and so forth.

Many organizations have found that creating a change review board whose members represent different functional areas within the organization can eliminate possible bias toward some applications and can help resolve conflicting change requests. For example, one user group may request a program enhancement that will make the program too expensive for other groups to use.

CHARGE-BACK SYSTEM

Related to the concept of a change review board is the concept of a charge-back system. Users are not only given the opportunity to choose the changes they most need, but they also pay for these changes.

The goals of a charge-back system are cost recovery for the DP orga-

CHANGE REQUEST

Requester: _____ Date: _____

Application: _____ Program: _____

Type of Change

_____ Corrective

_____ Adaptive

_____ Perfective

Reason for Requesting Change

_____

_____

_____

Date Change Needed: _____

Priority Number

_____ 0 Tabled
_____ 1 Critical
_____ 2 Important
_____ 3 Optional

Approvals

User _____ Date: _____

Recommendation _____

_____

Maintenance Leader _____ Date: _____

Recommendation _____

_____

Change Review Board _____ Date: _____

Figure 20.2 An example of a Change Request form.

nization and more effective allocation and regulation of computer resources and DP personnel [5]. There are many different types of charge-back schemes. The most common is a system in which costs are allocated back to users/departments based on utilization. Use formulas identifying resource and personnel units and a series of unit rates are developed to calculate usage costs.

The institution of a charge-back system for production program changes is a method for controlling maintenance costs. The charge-back system gives the users an economic incentive to be more selective with their change requests.

A charge-back system tends to introduce more formality into the change control process since the DP organization usually produces an estimate of what a requested change will cost and then the requester must approve the change before it is actually implemented. A major benefit of this added formality is better information to plan maintenance work and manage maintenance resources.

Also, a charge-back system can favorably affect user attitudes. Users tend to become more knowledgeable about how to use their programs and take more interest in planning for future computing needs and changes. As a consequence of having more control over their applications, users seem to be more satisfied.

On the other hand, a charge-back system can discourage user innovation in computer usage and force users to do without program changes that could greatly improve their productivity [6]. More affluent departments may be able to afford program changes, whereas less affluent areas may find even a small program change an unaffordable luxury.

For many organizations a charge-back system is too expensive to implement and operate. In their DP surveys, Lientz and Swanson found that charge-back systems are most commonly used in larger DP organizations handling many change requests [7, pp. 33–66].

PROGRAM QUALITY CHECK

A formal change control procedure can be used to protect program quality. Even the most diligent maintenance programmer is often tempted to bypass programming standards in the interest of saving time. This practice can have a disastrous effect on program integrity and future maintainability. Including an audit step in the change procedure can ensure that programming standards have not been violated and that program documentation has been properly updated. Before a program change is implemented on the production version of the program, the maintenance manager or maintenance audit group should check it and approve it. This practice should apply without exception every time a program is changed.

SCHEDULED MAINTENANCE

Scheduled maintenance is a method of managing the maintenance function in which the new-release concept used for systems software and software packages is also applied to typical DP application programs. Instead of changing a program as each request is received, the program is changed only according to a predetermined maintenance schedule. For example, maintenance work for the inventory control programs may be scheduled during the spring quarter of each year. Users and maintainers are aware of this schedule. Although change requests for these programs are collected all year, they are held for consideration just before the spring quarter begins. Then a study is done by the maintenance staff to determine the feasibility and costs of implementing the requested changes. Based on a recommendation from the maintenance staff and the approval of the users and the change review board, the changes are implemented during the spring.

The determination of an appropriate new-release schedule for each application should be based on considerations such as program stability, program error-proneness, and the number of program change requests. This information is available from the program change history generated by the change control procedure.

Lindhorst cites several benefits of using scheduled maintenance [8]:

1. By consolidating the changes to be made, program modification can be performed more efficiently (e.g., documentation is updated only once).

2. Since the users know their requests will not be acted on immediately, they may give more careful consideration to which changes they really need.

3. By batching together all the change requests for one program, the impact of the changes can be more thoroughly evaluated.

4. Knowing which applications will be maintained during which months of the year enables management to plan more effectively and to prioritize maintenance projects.

Emergency program repairs and changes will still be performed on an as-needed basis. Since these tasks account for only a small portion of all maintenance work, the scheduled maintenance approach allows the maintenance function to be managed much in the same way as new development projects. Maintenance requests involving the same application can be grouped together to form a programming project. In this environment, project management concepts, such as team programming, can be applied.

A SEPARATE MAINTENANCE ORGANIZATION?

Is it better to have a separate staff for carrying out maintenance, or to integrate maintenance into the work of the development staff?

Although most DP organizations do not segregate maintenance from new development into a separate organization, those organizations that do claim that programmer productivity and morale as well as management control are increased. In their DP surveys, Lientz and Swanson found that less than 20% of the DP organizations studied had created a separate maintenance organization and those that did were usually the larger DP departments [7, pp. 15–32].

There are good arguments for and against segregating the maintenance function [9]. The opposition fears that establishing a separate maintenance staff may cause morale problems since no one wants to work on maintenance. Also, for most organizations, there are too few experienced personnel for it to be practical to consider dividing them into two separate organizations.

On the other side, supporters argue that a separate maintenance staff can resolve the conflict that programmers face when they must split their time between new development assignments and maintenance requests. Further, a separate maintenance organization allows management to institute more formal controls to track change requests, quality problems, and maintenance costs.

Some organizations have solved the morale problem of a separate maintenance organization by offering special incentives to maintainers, such as higher salaries, more training programs, or opportunities to specialize in a particular maintenance function or application area.

Other organizations have instituted a personnel rotation plan in which every two years programmers and analysts are given a six-month assignment in the "other" organization. This enables maintainers to get firsthand development experience and developers to get maintenance experience. Since everyone works on maintenance, the maintenance stigma disappears.

Another variation is that when a new system is released, some developers "escort" it into the maintenance organization. The converse is that during system development, some maintainers are assigned to the development team.

Different approaches are suitable for different DP organizations. The key is to choose an approach that allows personnel responsibilities and assignments to be clearly defined and individual achievements to be clearly recognized and rewarded.

THE PERSONALITY OF MAINTAINERS

A strong argument for having a separate maintenance team is that the personality of the good maintainer tends to be different from that of the good designer.

The good maintainer likes to investigate problems and does so with meticulous care and skill. Like a detective he tracks down the control structures of programs and finds out why patches and switches have been inserted and what can change variables. He is a tinkerer, a skilled mechanic, but may have little originality.

The good designer is a creative person, looking for new or better procedures. He should be able to communicate well, understand the users problems, and think up solutions. He may be bored by maintenance work with its meticulous tracking through detail. He enjoys the structures he creates but does not enjoy investigating the minute detail of other people's structures.

A good writer is often a lousy editor, and a skilled editor is often a poor writer. The same is true with system creators and maintainers.

The good maintainer has special talents which are badly needed and he should be paid well for putting them to use. He enjoys his work, whereas the creative programmer is frustrated by maintenance. The creative programmer is proud to say: "I did it my way." Toward the end of a project he yearns to create something new. The good maintainer adapts to other people's methods, finds out how they work, and adjusts them.

The good maintenance manager builds up a team of people with appropriate personalities for maintenance. He has them trained to investigate programs, provides them with good tools, draws out their talents, and makes them feel special.

REFERENCES

1. J. Reutter, "Maintenance is a Management Problem and a Programmer's Opportunity," AFIPS Conference Proceedings on 1981 National Computer Conference (Chicago), Vol. 50, May 4–7, 1981, pp. 343–347.

2. E. Swanson, "The Dimensions of Maintenance," IEEE 2nd International Conference on Software Engineering, Proceedings (San Francisco), October 13–15, 1976, pp. 492–497.

3. D. Parmas, "Designing for Ease of Extension and Contraction," *IEEE Trans. on Software Engineering,* Vol. SE-5, No. 2 (March 1979): 129–137.

4. W. Cave and A. Salisbury, "Controlling the Software Life Cycle—The Project Management Task," *IEEE Trans. on Software Engineering,* Vol. SE-4, No. 4 (July 1978): 326–334.

5. J. Follman, "An Explanation of Computer Changeout Mechanisms and Their Effect on How People Behave," Management Information Systems Working Paper 6-80, Graduate School of Management, Northwestern University, June 1980.

6. T. Ravese, "Change-back in the Distribution Network," Computer Science Working Paper, Computer Science Department, Massachusetts Institute of Technology, Cambridge, Mass., January 1980.

7. B. Lientz and B. Swanson, *Software Maintenance Management* (Reading, MA: Addison-Wesley Publishing Co., Inc., 1980).

8. W. Lindhorst, "Scheduled Program Maintenance," in *Techniques of Program and System Maintenance* (Lincoln, NE: Ethnotech, 1980), pp. 133–136.

9. "Easing the Maintenance Burden," *EDP Analyzer,* Vol. 19, No. 8 (August 1981), pp. 1–6.

21 MAINTENANCE TEAMS

PROGRAMMING TEAMS

Team programming structures have been used with great success to develop high-quality programs in a reasonable amount of time. They provide the organizational structure and project controls needed to manage analysts and programmers who must work together to build a program or system of programs.

Egoless programming, the chief programmer team, and the structured walk-through are among the most popular team programming concepts. They are people-organization tools whose purpose is to improve programming by enhancing communication and program visibility and by increasing programmer productivity and job satisfaction.

EGOLESS PROGRAMMING

Egoless programming is the oldest and the simplest team organization structure. Its basic operating premise is that everyone connected with a program development effort must work together to build the best possible program [1]. It stresses an open, democratic environment where personal worth is separate from errors in one's work.

Egoless programming removes the program from the analyst's and the programmer's private domain by encouraging exchange and review as a normal part of the development process. For example, before compilation, a programmer asks at least one other programmer to read his code and check it for errors. Also, each programmer consults with other team members to exchange programming style ideas and to learn how to use new programming tools.

The philosophy of egoless programming is that allowing programmers to view their programs as an extension of their ego is dangerous and nonproductive. Because programmers internalize the code they write, their errors are less obvious to them than to others. Encouraging a sharing of the programming process helps programmers find more errors sooner and results in programs that are not only more likely to be error-free, but also more likely to be readable.

This type of environment tends to reinforce the team spirit. By reading one another's code, the total program becomes more familiar to the entire team and becomes team property, instead of one individual's private possession. The result is a better integrated program that is less dependent on a single individual. Further, egoless programming provides an excellent learning environment. All team members, from the most experienced to the least experienced, exchange code. By sharing code, the programmers can learn new programming techniques and algorithms and discuss style and efficiency questions in a nonhostile atmosphere.

Egoless programming does not suggest specific functional responsibilities for the various team members; instead, the responsibilities assigned to individual members are determined by the capabilities of each member and the tasks at hand. In this type of democratic organization, team leadership may rotate among the team members depending on the particular skills most needed at various points in the project.

CHIEF PROGRAMMER TEAM

In contrast to the democratic structure of egoless programming, the chief programmer team (CPT) employs a strict organizational structure in which discipline, clear leadership, and functional separation are stressed [2]. The goals of the chief programmer team are to structure program development work into well-defined tasks, to provide an environment in which state-of-the-art tools can be used, and to ensure that at least two people understand every line of code in the program.

In the CPT, the function of each member and the relationship between members is explicitly defined. As shown in Fig. 21.1, the nucleus of the team consists of two experienced programmers, called the chief programmer and the backup programmer, and a clerical assistant, called the programming secretary. Additional programmers are added to the team at the discretion of the chief programmer. In some forms of the CPT, a project administrator is also included in the nucleus group. The size of a CPT ranges from 7 to 10 members.

The *chief programmer* is the undisputed technical leader of the team. In the eyes of management, he is directly responsible for the technical success of the project. His tasks include the development of the program specification and design documents, the coding and testing of the critical portions of the program, and the guidance of the other team members in the coding and testing of the remaining portions of the program. In the strictest form of the CPT, the chief programmer designs, codes, and tests every line of code in the

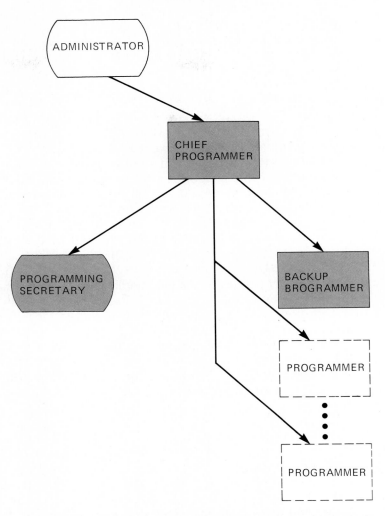

Figure 21.1　The chief programmer team is a formal team organization structure that stresses discipline, clear leadership, and functional operations of tasks. The nucleus of the team consists of two experienced program developers, called the chief programmer and the backup programmer, and a clerical assistant, called the programming secretary.

program. In modified forms of the CPT, the chief programmer directly codes and tests only the critical portions of the program himself and supervises the coding and testing of the remaining portions of the program.

The *backup programmer* is the backup leader of the team. Because he is totally familiar with all aspects of the project, he is prepared at any time to take over project leadership in the event that the chief programmer cannot continue. He participates in all important technical decisions, although the chief programmer has the last word in all decision making. The tasks of the backup programmer include the development of the test plan and research activities for the chief programmer.

The *programming secretary* is the clerical member of the team whose principal responsibility is to keep all project documentation current and visible throughout the project. His tasks include the maintenance of all program libraries, test data, test results, and project documents.

The use of standards, a development support library, and state-of-the-art software engineering tools is considered an essential component of the CPT concept. The CPT concept formalizes the egoless programming concept in several ways. First, instead of rotating team leadership, the chief programmer assumes permanent technical leadership. With a visible leader, management controls can be more easily implemented, communication with outside groups can be simplified, and deadlock situations in decision making can be avoided. Second, instead of informally assigning tasks, functional responsibilities are clearly delineated by the specific function each member is assigned in the CPT organizational chart. With individual responsibilities defined, the contribution of each individual's efforts can be more fairly evaluated. Finally, instead of relying on code exchange to improve program visibility, a programming secretary and a library management system are used to make the most current version of the program visible to the team, to management, and to the user throughout the project. With current information readily available, a more accurate picture of project status can be reported to management and to the user.

STRUCTURED WALK-THROUGH

The *structured walk-through* is a set of formal rules for reviewing program development progress. It can be used during any phase of the program life cycle to determine schedule breakdowns, to identify development problems and system errors, and to provide a constructive learning environment. Many different types of materials, such as functional specifications, system and program designs, code, or program test plans and results, can be reviewed during a walk-through.

There are strict rules for a structured walk-through defining who should participate, the roles and responsibilities of the participants, and the format to be used. The basic rules for a structured walk-through are [3] :

1. A walk-through is *not* used to review an individual's work performance; it *is* used to review program quality and project progress.

2. Each person attending a walk-through must function in the reviewee, reviewer, or recording secretary role.

3. The reviewee conducts the meeting, since it is his work that will be reviewed.

4. The reviewee is responsible for distributing the material to be reviewed to all the reviewers prior to the meeting.

5. The walk-through should not exceed two hours.

6. During the walk-through, problems may be identified, but *not* corrected.

There are four sequential steps followed when conducting a structured walk-through. First, each reviewer is asked to point out any problems discovered when initially reviewing the material. Second, the reviewee gives an overview description of the material. Next, the reviewee walks through the material in a step-by-step fashion noting the problems mentioned by the reviewers. Finally, assignments are made to investigate and correct problems discovered during the walk-through.

Structured walk-throughs are a good, safe way for developers to seek out assistance from their peers in critiquing their work. The structured walk-through philosophy is that everyone's work should be reviewed in the interest of building the best possible program, and that everyone's ego should be protected by directing criticisms at the work, not the individual.

MAINTENANCE TEAMS

Programming teams have been used primarily in the development of new programs rather than for the maintenance of existing systems. Are teams also useful in the maintenance environment?

Since many maintenance tasks involve changing only a small portion of a program, they require less time and less personnel. Perhaps, then, a team approach is not appropriate for program maintenance. If one individual can do the job, how can a team be justified? The answer is simply that programmers work more effectively when they check one another's work and when they can learn from one another.

Although programmers as a group have the reputation of being loners—individuals who prefer to work alone undisturbed by others—they do *not* perform as effectively when they work alone. For example, when changing even a few lines of code, a programmer working alone has only a small chance of correctly making the change on the first attempt [4]. Programming experiments have shown that the programmer working alone to debug his own program code is the least effective debugging method [5]. Just as everyone else, programmers have great difficulty seeing their own mistakes. By working with others, they are likely to find more errors sooner and to do the job at less cost.

A team approach is not only appropriate but strongly recommended for the maintenance environment. It is especially appropriate when used in conjunction with the scheduled maintenance approach (see Chapter 20).

Programming teams can provide the same benefits to maintenance as they provide to new development efforts—improved program quality, increased programmer productivity, and increased job satisfaction. For example, egoless programming encourages doing the best possible work to gain peer approval. The chief programmer team allows for specialization (e.g., debugging expert), which is especially useful in the maintenance environment, where the variety of tasks can be even greater than in a development environment. Also, the chief programmer team offers a promotion path to motivate team members.

However, this does not mean that programmers should never be allowed to work alone. Certainly, there are many tasks, such as designing a program change or rewriting a program module, where it is most efficient to assign one individual. What it does mean is that programmers should have all their work reviewed by someone else to ensure its correctness, quality, and completeness.

Two types of maintenance teams are suggested:

1. Short-term (temporary) teams
2. Long-term (permanent) teams

TEMPORARY MAINTENANCE TEAMS

The temporary maintenance team is an informal structure created to perform a specific task such as debugging a program, reviewing an enhancement design, or conducting a quality control audit. It is patterned after the egoless programming concept where programmers work together to solve problems and where leadership rotates depending on the task assigned. A structured walk-through format is used to minimize the time required by each participant and to ensure that efforts are focused on solving the problem rather than on criticizing individuals.

PERMANENT MAINTENANCE TEAMS

The lack of a formal organization structure for performing maintenance has greatly contributed to problems with program quality, programmer morale, and user satisfaction. An organizational structure that can provide the following is needed:

- Allow for technical specialization among program maintainers
- Establish communication channels between the program maintainers and the outside organization, including management, user groups, and program developers
- Encourage an open, egoless atmosphere in which new software technologies and tools can be mastered and applied
- Avoid dependency on one individual to maintain a program
- Perform periodic audit checks to preserve program quality

A more formal, more permanent maintenance team can help meet these needs. Like the program development team, the program maintenance team requires the leadership, the specialization, and the open, egoless atmosphere that is offered by the chief programmer team.

A maintenance team is assembled for the duration of the production life of the programs it supports. Although individual membership in the team changes, the team itself continues to exist as long as its programs. This provides continuity of support throughout the production life of the program.

As shown in Fig. 21.2, the maintenance adaptation of the chief programmer team consists of a maintenance leader, a co-leader, a user liaison, a maintenance administrator, and, optionally, a group of maintenance programmers [6].

The *maintenance leader* is directly responsible for technical program support. He reports to the maintenance administrator, and the rest of the maintenance team reports to him. The maintenance leader is an experienced systems analyst, is trained in project management, and is knowledgeable in the program application areas.

The *co-leader* of the maintenance team is the assistant to the maintenance leader. He can assume team leadership in the event that the maintenance leader leaves the team. Like the maintenance leader, he is an experienced systems analyst, a trained project leader and is knowledgeable in the program application areas. He performs the liaison function with the development staff of the systems and programming department and with other teams. He is responsible for tracking the development of new programs slated to be supported by his team. During the development phases, he attends each checkpoint review, defines program maintainability acceptance criteria, audits the program for compliance to these criteria, and gathers information needed for maintenance support preparations.

During the maintenance phase, the co-leader continues to interact with the program developers. He reports feedback on the program's behavior as a production program. For example, he reports error frequency rates, problems with program quality, actual changes compared to changes predicted by the developers, and so forth. This type of feedback is critical for program developers since it can confirm or raise serious doubts about the value of various software engineering tools and techniques employed and the resulting program quality.

Since a large portion of maintenance work is generated by user requests, the *user liaison* function is extremely important during the maintenance phase. The user liaison is a specialist in the application area and is responsible for communications between the user groups and the maintenance team. The user liaison serves as a buffer protecting the maintenance team from direct and continual user interruptions. Funneling user requests through the user liaison provides a mechanism for controlling change requests as well as identifying long-term user needs.

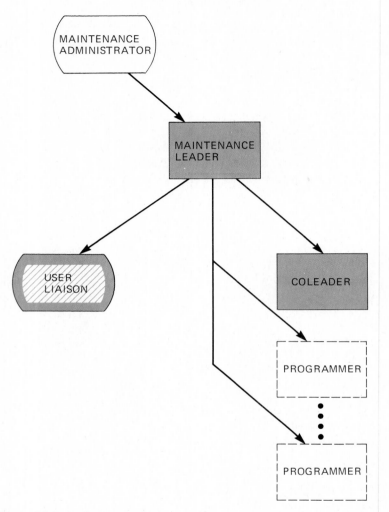

Figure 21.2 The maintenance team is a group of programmers and analysts assembled to perform maintenance support for a program during its production life. The structure of the team is patterned after the chief programmer team concept. Its nucleus consists of a maintenance leader and a co-leader.

The *maintenance administrator* function is performed by the supervisor of the maintenance staff. He is the administrative head of the maintenance team with hiring/firing/promotion responsibility for all members of the team. He provides the communication link with management. Usually, one maintenance administrator has charge of several maintenance (and perhaps, development) teams.

The *maintenance programmers* are responsible for diagnosing program problems and modifying programs under the direction of the maintenance leader. Technical training for maintenance programmers should be similar to that provided for development programmers. Also, specialization should be encouraged. Besides developing coding, debugging, and testing skills, the maintenance programmer should be encouraged to develop skills in the areas of performance tuning and error analysis and an in-depth knowledge of the application areas.

MAINTENANCE ASSIGNMENTS

Not all maintenance programmers should be programmer trainees since many maintenance assignments involve difficult and critical programming tasks. Allowing inexperienced programmers to modify complex programs without experienced supervision has caused program quality degradation and has hastened the obsolescence of many programs.

Assigning very difficult tasks to inexperienced personnel or assigning very straightforward tasks to experienced personnel may result in increasing program complexity. In the case of an inexperienced programmer, additional complexity may be introduced because the ripple effect of the modification is not properly evaluated. In the case of an experienced programmer, additional complexity may be introduced as a consequence of attempting to make the program, and also the assignment, more interesting.

Not only program complexity but also programmer productivity is affected by the choice of personnel assigned to a particular task. Normally, the more experienced the programmer, the more quickly the task can be accomplished. In some cases, if the task is beyond the experienced level of the programmer, it will never be completed. However, the assignment of very simple tasks to experienced personnel also runs the risk of the task never being completed. In this case, the experienced programmer may indefinitely set aside simpler tasks in favor of working on more challenging problems.

MAINTENANCE TEAM STAFFING

Using a similar team structure in both the development area and the maintenance area allows easier exchange of personnel in both directions. Assigning development personnel to the maintenance area can reduce the learning curve for large systems/programs and improve the quality of maintenance personnel. Also, forcing software developers to maintain the programs they build reinforces the necessity of developing high-quality, maintainable programs.

Not only should development personnel be assigned to the maintenance area, but also maintenance personnel should be assigned to the development area. Rotating software personnel between the two groups will create greater flexibility in staffing, improve overall personnel experience levels, create a sense of appreciation for the technical expertise required in both areas, and lessen the stigma attached to performing maintenance tasks.

The effort required to maintain a program varies over time and with changes to the program [7]. Because of scheduling constraints and unforeseen development problems, software programs are seldom really completed during the development portion of the life cycle. The implementation of less critical system functions, final documentation, and performance tuning are often postponed until the maintenance phase. A more modest version of the program is temporarily released to the user, while enhancements are performed to upgrade the program to its intended capabilities level. This, together with correcting errors not discovered during development, causes the maintenance effort for a newly released program to be initially high and then decrease until the next major release of the software occurs, and then this cycle is repeated (see Fig. 21.3).

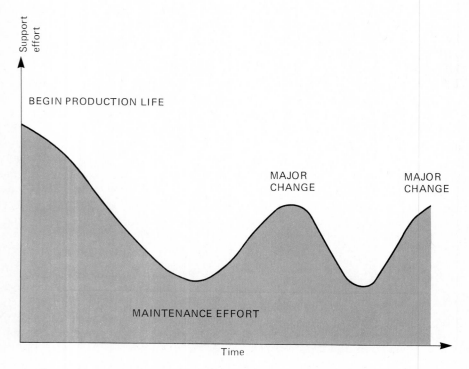

Figure 21.3 The effort needed to support a production program varies over time and with changes in the program. Usually, a program requires more support after its initial release to the operations and maintainance phase and after each major update during its production life.

To provide for the greater maintenance support needs of a newly released program, some members of the original software development team can accompany the program into the maintenance phase. Lientz and Swanson refer to these individuals as *maintenance escorts* [8]. This is usually a temporary assignment ending when all program development work has been completed in terms of reliability, efficiency, and maintainability requirements. The escorts then return to the development staff.

In some cases, however, the maintenance escort may become a permanent member of the maintenance team. For example, the backup programmer from the development team may be promoted to the leadership position of the maintenance team. Since he is intimately familiar with the program, he is an ideal candidate to direct maintenance activities, especially when the program is first released for use as a production system. In some companies, development programmers are assigned to the maintenance teams for a six-month period after a program is released to the operations and maintenance phase.

CONTRACTING AND EXPANDING THE MAINTENANCE TEAM

The maintenance team can be contracted to accommodate small maintenance efforts or expanded to accommodate large efforts. For small programs/ systems, the maintenance leader and co-leader can work jointly, checking one another's work and debugging the program. Probably, they would be responsible for supporting several programs. For large programs and systems, a hierarchy of maintenance teams can be formed, where each team specializes in a particular portion of the system or a particular set of maintenance functions (e.g., design or revalidation). The co-leader from each team can act as the communication link between the teams and one overall maintenance administration can direct and coordinate all maintenance efforts.

REFERENCES

1. G. Weinberg, *The Psychology of Computer Programming* (New York: Van Nostrand Reinhold Company, 1971), pp. 67–94.

2. F. T. Baker and H. Mills, "Chief Programmer Teams," *IBM Systems Journal,* Vol. 11, No. 1 (1972): 56–73.

3. "Structured Walk-Throughs," in *Improved Programming Technologies Management Overview,* IBM Data Processing Division Systems Marketing Installation Productivity Dept., August 1973.

4. E. Yourdon, "Managing Structured Techniques," in *Techniques of Pro-*

gram and System Maintenance (Lincoln, NE: Ethnotech, 1980), pp. 125–128.

5. B. Shneiderman, *Software Psychology* (Cambridge, MA: Winthrop Publishers, Inc., 1980), pp. 86–90.

6. C. McClure, *Managing Software Development and Maintenance* (New York: Van Nostrand Reinhold Company, 1981), pp. 164–174.

7. B. Lientz, E. Swanson, and G. Tompkins, "Characteristics of Application Software Maintenance," *Communications of the ACM,* Vol. 21, No. 6 (June 1978): 466–471.

8. B. Lientz and E. Swanson, *Software Maintenance Management* (Reading, MA: Addison-Wesley Publishing Co., Inc., 1980), pp. 173–174.

22 PLANNING FOR FUTURE MAINTENANCE

INTRODUCTION Once a system is debugged, most of its future maintenance will be caused by changes of various types. The more these changes can be planned for and understood, the more their impact can be minimized.

Management at all levels needs to recognize the cost and permanence of the maintenance function and to plan for it. The plan needs to consider both the maintenance of existing systems and new systems with new technology. A proper balance between maintenance and new development can be planned by understanding the patterns of DP growth. These in turn should follow the pattern of corporate change and growth.

As the number of programs and files grows, so too will the maintenance burden unless active measures are taken to plan for it and migrate to systems designed to minimize maintenance. To forge ahead without considering maintenance implications is a very expensive mistake.

A NEW SOFTWARE What is required is a new, broader perspective of
LIFE CYCLE the software life cycle emphasizing change, maintenance, and migration to new technologies. The current view of the life cycle divides software work into two discrete phases wherein software is first developed and then used and maintained. In reality, however, the software life cycle is one of *continuing development* that extends throughout the entire cycle. Most applications programs used by industry continually evolve to meet new corporate needs and to take advantage of new technologies.

Furthermore, as shown in Fig. 22.1, the life cycle must be expanded to include a termination/replacement phase. For the great majority of applications, a point of diminishing returns will be reached. Usually, this will happen

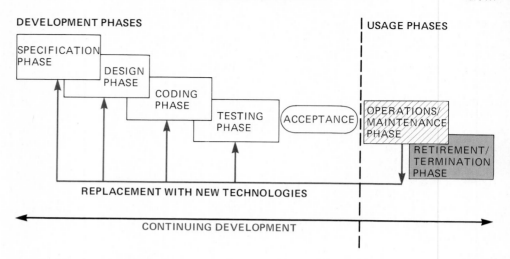

DEVELOPMENT PHASES   USAGE PHASES

Figure 22.1 The current view of the software life cycle divides software work into two discrete phases wherein software is first developed and then used and maintained. In reality, however, the software life cycle is one of continuing development. What is needed is a broader view of the life cycle, emphasizing change, maintenance, and the need to eventually replace or terminate programs.

within 10 years. User demands for more application flexibility at a lower operational cost will eventually dictate that the software be replaced.

The need for replacement will be signaled by a growing user dissatisfaction and an increasing maintenance effort. The enhancement request list will grow at a faster rate than new changes can be incorporated into the existing programs. Changes will require more effort and take more time than previously, even though the program documentation is fairly good and the maintenance programmers are knowledgeable.

PROGRAM REPLACEMENT

Program replacement or termination is a normal and necessary part of program maintenance and the software life cycle, but the inclination has been to resist replacing existing application programs. The past investment is so great that it is difficult to cost-justify a replacement plan. Furthermore, the current view of software suggests that if a program is designed right, is implemented correctly and efficiently, and is taken care of properly, it can have a perpetual life. Although software does not wear out in the same way as hardware, program designs in a sense do wear out. They are outgrown by the organizations they serve when, over the years, these organizations change and grow.

Ignoring the need to replace software compounds the maintenance

burden. It is a shortsighted, penny-wise mistake that in the long term will cause enormous problems and expenditures. Running an organization with outmoded, expensive-to-operate programs is like using an antique car to drive to work every day. It can be done, but you sure have problems.

Besides being expensive in terms of user costs, programming costs, and hardware costs, avoiding software replacement can cause serious opportunity losses. One large insurance company lost countless potential new clients because it took weeks to respond to simple requests for policy information [1].

If a company is forced to replace its antiquated programs in a very short time, rather than gradually over the years, the costs may be overwhelming. One life insurance company had to spend $25 million for new hardware and software in 2½ years [1].

Stuck with outmoded programs, such companies tend to resist changing them, knowing how expensive the cure will be. But eventually the day of reckoning arrives.

PLANNING FOR MAINTENANCE

The first step in avoiding such an expensive cure is to recognize that almost all application programs eventually must be replaced. The second step is to plan for it as part of planning for maintenance. In commercial data processing, the plan should include the migration to modern technologies with data models and fourth-generation languages.

DP organizations that feel there is no way out of a growing maintenance burden have not explored all the alternatives available. Since most maintenance work is discretionary, it does not necessarily have to be done. Furthermore, it does not have to be done by patching and changing old programs.

What are some of the choices?

1. Do not accommodate all maintenance requests.

2. Accommodate a maintenance request by changing an existing program. As a byproduct of making the change, improve the future maintainability of the program.

3. Do not change the existing program. Instead, develop another program to accommodate the maintenance request.

4. Replace the existing program with a new program that takes advantage of new technologies, particularly data-base systems.

5. Redevelop with new technology using corporate-wide information engineering—strategic data planning, data modeling, action diagrams, fourth-generation languages, data management systems, and information center development where practical.

Which choice is best depends on many factors. If the decision is based *only* on maintenance considerations, it probably will not be the best one. It may satisfy the requester in the short term, but in the long term it will not minimize future efforts and costs.

Maintenance decisions ought to be made based on a well-thought-out comprehensive strategy that considers the goals of the entire DP function and the overall business plan. To devise this strategy the following steps should be taken:

1. Study the overall business plan.
2. Evaluate the status of current key application systems.
3. Understand the stages of DP growth.
4. Migrate to information engineering methodologies.

THE BUSINESS PLAN

The business plan for a company always has implications for the DP organization and for maintenance. Without understanding where the company as a whole is going, DP management cannot develop a workable plan for controlling future maintenance costs.

If a manufacturing company plans to introduce a new product line over the next three years, this will most certainly lead to many changes in many applications. Inventory control, manufacturing control, order processing, and payroll systems, just to mention a few, may require changes to handle the new product line. Knowing, for example, that the MRP (Materials Requirements Planning) programs must be changed to accommodate the new product line may indicate a good time to replace the batch MRP system with a new on-line system that can provide more timely and complete information at less cost.

Or, if a company plans to acquire several new subsidiaries over the next five years, the existing application systems will probably be affected. Any plans to perform major enhancements to these systems should take into account the impact from a new subsidiary. It may even be advisable to delay major enhancements until the computing requirements of the new subsidiaries are better understood.

THE NEED FOR LONGER-RANGE VISION

Failure to take into consideration the overall directions of an organization causes systems to be created which are doomed to expensive maintenance. Consider a long, cumbersome, wagon train trekking across America in the 1870s. It is venturing into unknown territory through mountainous country. Its leader sends a scout ahead to view the terrain. From the hilltops he can see a river ahead, and a dangerous chasm. The present course of the wagon train will lead it into trouble. The scout finds a better course, but it is expensive to change; many wagons will have to be backtracked a long way.

The present course of the wagon train seemed appropriate when it was originally established. It was based on the best knowledge available. The sooner the scout finds out about the future terrain, the lower the cost of change will be.

Most application development is done without sending out a scout. The need for change often comes as a surprise. The change has to be made in a hurry and is then expensive. One large brokerage house had a budget of $30 million for new application programs over a three-year period to catch up with competition [1]. DP management had become aware much too late of what competition was doing.

Often when we automate, the systems analysis technique draws diagrams of the *current* data flows and procedures. The same procedures are automated with only minor changes—changes visible to the wagon train driver without sending out a scout. Often the analyst looks at only one department or functional area without learning how the data employed affects other areas. Often there is no real thought about how network and database operation should change the procedures.

To have the vision of the wagon train scout, we need to take into account the strategic directions and objectives established by senior management. Senior management often have not communicated these to DP, being unaware of the problems of DP maintenance. DP, on the other hand, often have not asked, because of a parochial viewpoint. DP and senior management often proceed in ignorance of the effect their decisions have on one another.

To automate existing systems without awareness of how the organization may change is to condemn it to the procedures of the past. Often such automation is less capable of change than the manual procedures it replaces. The computer rigidifies the obsolete procedures so that the organization is unable to respond in a timely fashion. The computerized system, designed to be the servant of the organization, has become the master.

THE APPLICATIONS PORTFOLIO Not all programs contribute equally to the maintenance burden. Weinberg claims that for most DP organizations an 80/20 rule is operating [2]. In general, 80% of the effort is spent maintaining less than 20% of the program code. Rewriting or replacing this 20% can substantially reduce future maintenance costs. Weinberg refers to this as the *worst-first maintenance approach*.

To apply the worst-first approach, DP management must take inventory of all its existing application systems. A list of all programs in each system should be made and the following information compiled for each program:

1. Effort spent maintaining the program during each year of its production life
2. Program age (based on when the program was originally developed)
3. Programming languages in which the program is written
4. Program error information, indicating any increases in the number of errors occurring and the difficulty of correcting errors
5. Program change information, indicating any increases in the number of changes requested and the difficulty of making changes
6. User satisfaction survey, indicating whether the users feel the program is generally useful or used at all
7. Maintenance programmers' opinion about the difficulty of maintaining the program and its overall quality
8. Conformance of the program to corporate data models
9. Difficulties in interfacing the program with other systems because of lack of conformance to corporate data models

This information can be used to suggest candidate programs for replacement. Programs which are written in a language that is no longer used or known by the programming staff should be put on the replacement list. Programs which are experiencing many errors or causing much user dissatisfaction should also be listed. Programs which were originally developed over eight years ago should be listed since technology will have advanced so greatly over the years that these programs are probably inefficient and generally outmoded.

Certainly, these are not strict rules but only guidelines for identifying possible programs to be partially rewritten, completely replaced, or terminated. No action should be taken unless it makes sense as part of the long-term DP plan and it can be cost-justified.

Lientz and Swanson refer to this information as the applications portfolio [3]. DP management and the company computer steering committee should monitor the applications portfolio in the same way they monitor other capital expenditures. When setting priorities, approving DP budgets, and reviewing new development proposals, the portfolio should be consulted. Decision models should be used to evaluate the current and future benefits and costs together with the risks of rewriting or replacing existing application programs. With a better understanding of the trade-offs and options, management can more effectively allocate resources between new development and maintenance activities.

MIGRATION TO INFORMATION ENGINEERING

Many DP organizations have adapted a data-base planning philosophy. They have set out to replace the chaotic data which exist in their own systems with data which are in third-normal-form and to use corporate-wide entity analysis [4]. They have a data administrator who employs a data dictionary and data modeling tool.

The problem with strategic planning of data is that the old applications use data which are differently represented and structured. The old applications coexist with the new environment of systems that employ the data models.

It is fortunate that most of the old applications do *not* have an indefinite lifetime. A time arrives when they will be redeveloped using the data models. The corporate systems steadily evolve encompassing more and more of the old applications into a framework of common data representation.

As this migration occurs, newer technologies are used, selected for their ability to speed up application development, lower the costs of maintenance, and enable end users to generate their own reports, information, and procedures. The new methodologies discussed in Part III of this book are used wherever practical.

Figure 22.2 extends Fig. 22.1 to illustrate the migration to information engineering methodologies.

JUSTIFYING PROGRAM REPLACEMENT

Cost justification of a program rewrite or replacement may not be as difficult to show as expected. When operating costs, maintenance costs, and user costs are considered, a new program may prove much less expensive than the old version.

Yourdon claims that in most cases the maintainability of the new program will be improved by at least a factor of 2 and possibly by as much as a factor of 10 over the old program [5].

Further, the replacement program can be developed at a much faster rate. The original program can serve as a sort of *prototype* defining many of the program requirements. This prototype, together with the experience of using and maintaining the program, eliminates the need for lengthy requirements and specification documents, so the requirements analysis and specification phases can be performed more quickly. Subsequent development phases can also be performed more quickly. As Yourdon explains:"The new designers are, in a sense, able to stand on the shoulders of the original designers and see a better way of approaching the problem" [5].

Replacement efforts can be performed at a rate of 20 to 25 debugged statements per day instead of the usual 10 to 15 statements [5].

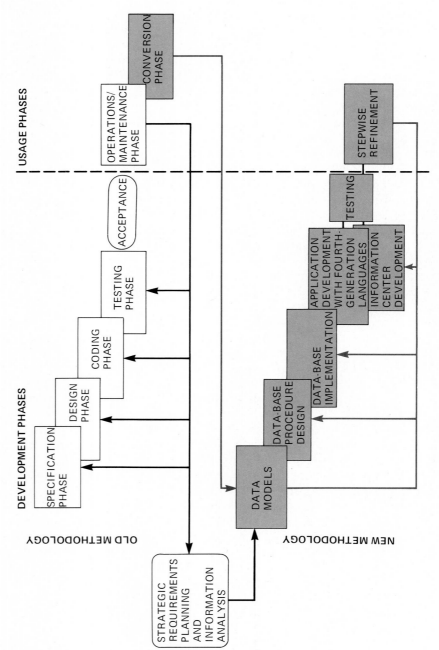

Figure 22.2 It is necessary to plan for the conversion of data-processing systems built with old methodologies to the new methodologies of information analysis, data modeling, application generators, fourth-generation languages, data management systems, and information centers.

Much higher productivity rates can be achieved with fourth-generation languages, especially nonprocedural languages. Also, the users can do much of the work. Most enhancement maintenance relates to output reports and correlations of data. The users can be trained to employ query languages, report generators, graphics packages, and languages for manipulating data. They can do their own calculations on the data and build tables and charts showing "what if?" situations[6].

The use of fourth-generation languages should be encouraged not only because they offer such huge productivity gains and allow much of the enhancement work to be transferred to users, but also because they greatly improve maintainability. If replacement programs are coded in third-generation languages, such as COBOL or PL/1, they will soon present the same maintenance problems as their predecessors. Even if the programs are initially very reliable and well structured, they will be difficult to maintain since they are written in hard-to-maintain languages. Programming professionals will be needed to provide maintenance support.

With nonprocedural languages, enhancements can be made simply, a step at a time. Interactive stepwise refinement becomes a way of life, often accomplished by end users or analysts working with them and not involving lengthy programming investigations and changes.

Another feasible option is to replace programs with vendor-supplied software packages.

THE SIX STAGES OF DP GROWTH

Nolan has observed that many DP organizations exhibit a similar pattern of growth passing through six stages to reach ultimate maturity [7]. Figure 22.3 shows the six stages of growth.

Different organizations are currently at different stages of growth. As yet, most organizations have not entered the last stage. Most organizations are probably somewhere in the middle stages. Looking ahead, this means that DP is headed for rapid growth as more organizations enter stage 4.

Nolan claims that understanding the DP growth pattern can help management more effectively plan for and control the DP function. First, management must determine in which stage its DP organization currently stands. Then, it can determine an effective plan for moving on to more advanced stages. This plan must be compatible with the overall business plan in terms of realistic expenditures, and concentrate on the application areas that are most critical is achieving corporate goals.

Stage 1, initiation, is the introduction of DP activities, often tentative and naive in the beginning.

Stage 2, contagion, is characterized by growing awareness and excitement about the potentials of DP. In an atmosphere of little management awareness and control, many new applications are created.

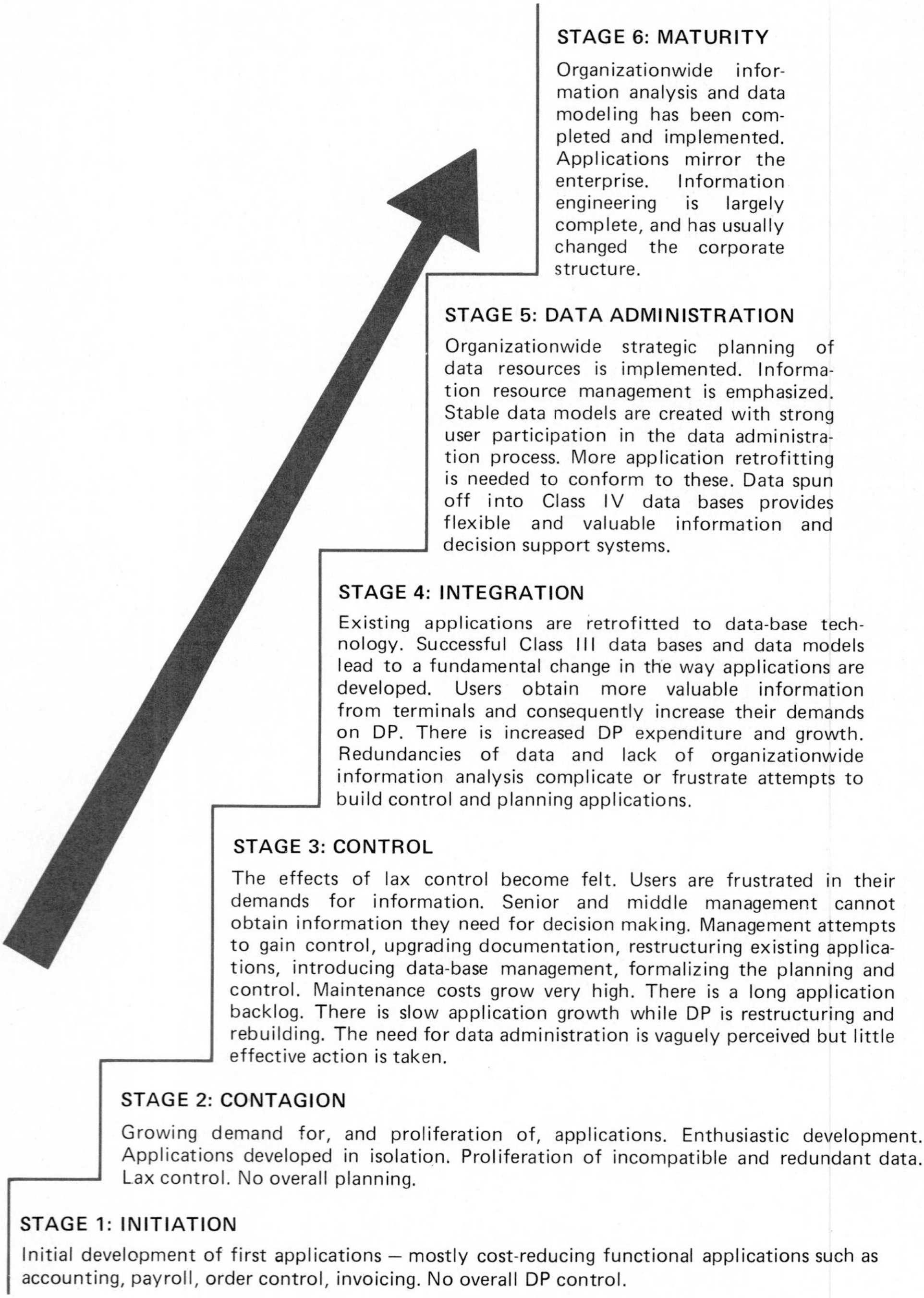

STAGE 6: MATURITY

Organizationwide information analysis and data modeling has been completed and implemented. Applications mirror the enterprise. Information engineering is largely complete, and has usually changed the corporate structure.

STAGE 5: DATA ADMINISTRATION

Organizationwide strategic planning of data resources is implemented. Information resource management is emphasized. Stable data models are created with strong user participation in the data administration process. More application retrofitting is needed to conform to these. Data spun off into Class IV data bases provides flexible and valuable information and decision support systems.

STAGE 4: INTEGRATION

Existing applications are retrofitted to data-base technology. Successful Class III data bases and data models lead to a fundamental change in the way applications are developed. Users obtain more valuable information from terminals and consequently increase their demands on DP. There is increased DP expenditure and growth. Redundancies of data and lack of organizationwide information analysis complicate or frustrate attempts to build control and planning applications.

STAGE 3: CONTROL

The effects of lax control become felt. Users are frustrated in their demands for information. Senior and middle management cannot obtain information they need for decision making. Management attempts to gain control, upgrading documentation, restructuring existing applications, introducing data-base management, formalizing the planning and control. Maintenance costs grow very high. There is a long application backlog. There is slow application growth while DP is restructuring and rebuilding. The need for data administration is vaguely perceived but little effective action is taken.

STAGE 2: CONTAGION

Growing demand for, and proliferation of, applications. Enthusiastic development. Applications developed in isolation. Proliferation of incompatible and redundant data. Lax control. No overall planning.

STAGE 1: INITIATION

Initial development of first applications — mostly cost-reducing functional applications such as accounting, payroll, order control, invoicing. No overall DP control.

Figure 22.3 Six stages of growth in data processing as identified by Nolan [7]. When information engineering is applied early enough it can circumvent some of the problems in this growth and lessen maintenance costs.

446

Toward the end of stage 2, the enthusiasm tends to turn to frustration as the effects of lax control become felt. Applications do not work as anticipated. They do not link together, so overall control data cannot be derived.

Stage 3, control, attempts to put controls into place. Management becomes cost conscious of the DP function. Planning, controlling, and organizing for future growth are emphasized. Controls such as programming and documentation standards are introduced. Computer steering committees and user charge-back systems are instituted.

Maintenance costs usually grow high in stage 3. Old applications and data are restructured. The application backlog grows long. The rate of development slows down and user frustration spreads seriously.

Stage 4, integration, sees the growth of data-base and data communications usage bring more terminals and more services to the users. As users perceive what is possible from terminals, their demands for information and new applications grow. The terminal access brings new needs to change procedures and integrate systems. Class III data bases lead to fundamental changes in the way applications are developed—a swing from procedure-centered development to data-centered development.

Stage 5, data administration, emphasizes the overall planning of data resources. Stable data models are created with much participation by end users. Data throughout the corporation become planned and represented in data dictionaries and data models.

Stage 6, maturity, is a goal rather than a reality yet for most organizations. It refers to a situation where functional systems are automated and employ common data models. The information needed by all managers is made available. The organization thus operates with all elements informed and integrated.

PROGRESS
THROUGH
THE STAGES

The six stages of growth provide important insights on what opportunities and pitfalls may lie ahead. Organizations may use the stages to measure their progress and to benefit from the experience of other more advanced organizations.

A growing maintenance burden can change and stifle the pattern of DP growth. Because of maintenance, some companies find that their DP growth has stopped. They are stuck in stage 2 or 3. There seems to be no way out. With DP resources almost totally directed toward keeping current production programs running, they cannot look toward the future.

Unless radical management action is taken, such companies will remain stuck indefinitely, and the business ramifications may be disastrous. The only way out is migration to new technologies. Management must be resigned to cut its losses and to make a commitment to move on. A careful plan must be devised to determine which new technologies will be most useful, to train

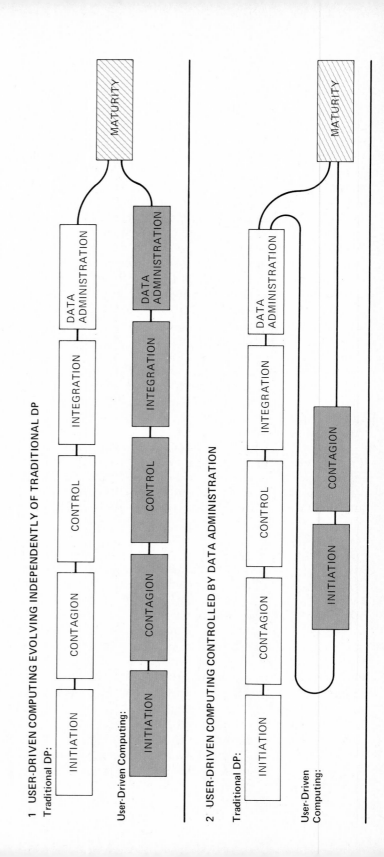

1 USER-DRIVEN COMPUTING EVOLVING INDEPENDENTLY OF TRADITIONAL DP

Traditional DP:

| INITIATION | CONTAGION | CONTROL | INTEGRATION | DATA ADMINISTRATION |

User-Driven Computing:

| INITIATION | CONTAGION | CONTROL | INTEGRATION | DATA ADMINISTRATION |

MATURITY

2 USER-DRIVEN COMPUTING CONTROLLED BY DATA ADMINISTRATION

Traditional DP:

| INITIATION | CONTAGION | CONTROL | INTEGRATION | DATA ADMINISTRATION |

User-Driven Computing:

| INITIATION | CONTAGION |

MATURITY

3 A NEW ORGANIZATION DEVELOPING INFORMATION SYSTEMS WITH DATA ADMINISTRATION AND STRATEGIC PLANNING FROM THE START

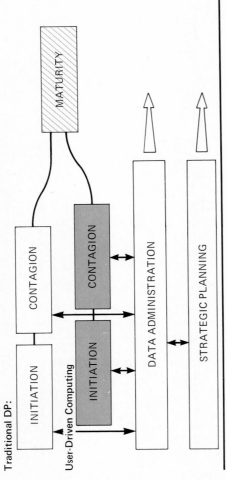

Figure 22.4 Patterns of growth with user-driven computing. The third is the most desirable but needs top management understanding from the start.

DP personnel and end users in the new technologies chosen, to reorganize DP, and to control future growth. The plan should provide long-term goals against which DP progress can be measured. It should also specify the immediate actions necessary to get things moving. Finally, management must implement the plan and remain committed to it.

INTRODUCTION OF FOURTH-GENERATION LANGUAGES   Nolan's classic article on the six stages of growth was written before the widespread use of fourth-generation languages. These languages tend to bring the spread of user-driven computing. Information centers may grow up to support user-driven computing.

Often user-driven computing does not learn from the history of conventional computing. It passes through the same stages of growth. Initial experimentation with fourth-generation languages and data systems succeeds and leads to contagious growth *without* controls or data administration. This causes future maintenance work and redevelopment of the user-driven systems.

It is better if user-driven computing becomes widespread after data administration has formalized the data definitions, representations, and normalized records. This is shown in the center of Fig. 22.4. When that pattern exists many systems that were developed with older methods can be migrated across to the fourth-generation languages and data management systems.

If an organization were setting out to develop its data processing from scratch today, it would be well advised to establish a data administration function from the beginning. It should follow the steps of information engineering shown in Fig. 14.3. Controls would be put into place before the contagion stage had gone too far, as shown in Fig. 22.4. Prespecified computing and user-driven computing should proceed simultaneously, both using fourth-generation languages where possible and both taking steps to minimize future maintenance problems.

REFERENCES

1. M. Buss, "Penny-Wise Approach to Data Processing," *Harvard Business Review,* July–August 1981, pp. 111–117.

2. G. Weinberg, "Worst-First Maintenance," in *Techniques of Program and System Maintenance* (Lincoln, NE: Ethnotech, 1980), pp. 119–121.

3. B. Lientz and E. Swanson, *Software Maintenance Management* (Addison-Wesley Publishing Co., Inc., 1980), pp 149–174.

4. J. Martin, *Strategic Data Planning Methodologies,* Savant Technical Report 12, Savant Institute, Carnforth, Lancashire, UK, 1980.

5. E. Yourdon, "Structured Maintenance," in *Techniques of Program and System Maintenance* (Lincoln, NE: Ethnotech, 1980), pp. 211–213.

6. J. Martin, *Application Development Without Programmers* (Englewood Cliffs, NJ: Prentice-Hall, Inc., 1981), pp. 33–58.

7. R. Nolan, "Managing the Crisis in Data Processing," *Harvard Business Review,* March–April, 1979, pp. 115–126.

23 STRATEGIC PLANNING AND MIGRATION

INTRODUCTION We have stressed that the factors which most affect maintenance costs lie in the *design* phase of systems.

Seen from the programmer's viewpoint, he should write code designed for maintenance. Seen from the analyst's viewpoint, he should use structured techniques, diagrams, and documentation, which help the maintainer. Seen from the data-base designer's point of view, he should create stable data structures and use software which facilitates change.

There is a much higher viewpoint—the overall strategic planning of how DP should evolve in an organization. Many of the most expensive aspects of maintenance have arisen because strategic planning has been neglected.

An objective of strategic planning is to make the pieces of information systems fit together where they need to. Most systems will evolve, and as they evolve they still must be able to interchange data. This requires both logical and physical compatibility. The need for interfaces and interchange among separate systems has often been grossly underestimated. Because of incompatibility, changes have to be made, and these changes can be very expensive.

THE NEED FOR
TOP-LEVEL
PLANNING
It would be unthinkable to build a battleship without an overall plan for the entire ship. Once the overall plan exists, separate teams can go to work on the components. Corporate information engineering is not much less complex than building a battleship, yet in most corporations it is done without an overall plan of sufficient detail to make the components fit together.

The overall architect of the battleship cannot conceivably specify the detailed design of the guns, electronics, or other subsystems. These have to be developed by different teams working autonomously. But imagine what would happen if these teams enthusiastically created their own subsystems without any coordination from the top.

The DP world is full of inspired subsystem designers who want to be left alone. Their numbers are rapidly increasing as minicomputers proliferate and end users learn to acquire their own facilities. In many cases they are doing an excellent job. However, the types of data they use overlap substantially and this is often not recognized. The subsystems need to be connected together, but often this cannot be done without conversion. Conversion, when the need for it becomes apparent, is often too expensive to accomplish, so incompatible systems live on, making it difficult or impossible to integrate the data that management need.

Good system design avoids excessive complexity. Corporate information systems ought to be composed of discrete modules, each of which is simple enough to be efficiently designed, completely understood by its design team, low in maintenance costs, and susceptible to high-productivity development methods (such as the use of high-level data-base languages). But the modules must fit together and they will not do so unless designed with planning from the top, with appropriate design tools.

THE DEPARTMENT OF DEFENSE ABIC CONCEPT

Sometimes the experience with complex systems in the military is years ahead of corporate computer application, and lessons learned with military systems filter down to civilian practice. SAGE and AUTOVON, for example, taught the world much about real-time and transmission systems. More recently, enormous expenses have been incurred because of the incompatibility of multiple systems. The systems have to be retrofitted or redesigned so that they can interface with one another—a maintenance activity on a grand scale.

In the 1970s, for example, the U.S. Department of the Army developed many separate systems which are referred to as Battlefield Automated Systems (BAS). In a war these systems need to work together, interchanging certain information. Information needs to be extracted from multiple systems for higher-level command and control functions.

The systems were independently developed, as indeed they must be, and the problems of information exchange requirements were addressed in various studies and directives under the general guidance of the Army Tactical Command and Control Master Plan (ATACCOMAP) and the ARTADS Interface Management Plan (AIMP). However, after separate systems had been implemented, it became clear that these studies were not detailed enough. The separately developed systems did not work together as they should. Major changes were needed to improve their interoperability and enhance their value to the commanders. These changes, however, were exceedingly expensive and difficult to make.

There had been a large-scale proliferation of independent systems, but insufficient detail in planning how the systems would work together. This situation is now becoming common in industry and government, especially with the spread of minicomputers and separate network systems. The Department of the Army described the result as "an inefficient and uneconomical situation" in which necessary information exchange between automated systems is often not possible [1].

A solution was devised: the Army Battlefield Interface Concept (ABIC) [2]. The ABIC was devised to identify interface and interoperability requirements among U.S. Army battlefield systems. It provided architectural guidance for system developers. It addressed the retrofitting of existing systems so that they could cooperate. It organized the funds needed to develop software *and hardware* facilities that would enable separate systems to interface and work together. The 1978 ABIC addressed 48 battlefield automation systems. The 1979 ABIC addressed 100.

FUTURE PLANNING   The expense of retrofitting was great, and the danger of having systems that would not work together was alarming. To prevent this situation from recurring in the future, the ABIC plans in detail the interfaces and interoperation of systems for seven years in the future. Each year the top-down plan is rolled forward. The 1980 ABIC addressed all systems required to interwork in 1987; the 1981 ABIC addressed 1988; and so on.

With ABIC, the U.S. Army moved from individual systems development to a functionally integrated approach to development. Integrated network planning and management is done, standards are developed and enforced, and data formats, definitions, and exchange requirements are planned. Common software and commonality of systems configurations are used where necessary to aid the horizontal and vertical interoperability of systems. A philosophy of optimization of the whole is advocated even where it may be at the expense of one or more individual systems.

THE DANGER OF   The danger with highly integrated systems plan-
INTEGRATED   ning lies in our inability to understand in detail the
SYSTEMS   future system requirements. Although it is de-
PLANNING   sirable to design systems so that they can work
together, it is *entirely impractical* to plan or understand all the systems that an enterprise will need. Totally integrated systems are far beyond our capability, and almost all attempts to build them have failed catastrophically.

What is needed instead is freedom for user areas to employ their own initiative in creating the systems they need, but they still must obey certain laws. They make *their systems conform to a set of rules which permit them to interchange data, now and in the future.*

To permit interoperability, two design characteristics are needed. First, the separate systems should have an interface with a common network so that they can interchange data. Second, they should employ compatible data in their files or data bases, structured according to a common data model.

If appropriate standards for networking and data can be created so that they are reasonably stable, individual systems can be created by relatively small teams covering areas of operation each narrow enough to be well understood and sharply focused.

The object of future planning, then, should not be a grand all-embracing design, but rather a stable infrastructure into which small modular designs can be connected. The grand all-embracing design is too complex, with vast numbers of interactions doomed to vast numbers of changes all entangled and expensive. The infrastructure should be the *minimum* set of standards needed to enable the separate modular systems to interoperate.

FOGHORNS

The smaller and more independent the subsystems are, the better. This can be illustrated with an analogy.

Imagine a large and very noisy foghorn. If the foghorn is blowing during any given millisecond there is a 50% chance that it will be silent in the next millisecond.

Imagine that a place has many such foghorns. Any foghorn may or may not be connected to any other foghorn. If a foghorn is silent, it remains silent unless one of the foghorns to which it is connected is blowing. If one or more foghorns to which it is connected are blowing, there is a 50% chance that it will blow in the next millisecond (with a small allowance for transmission delay).

The stable state of this system is when all foghorns are silent. The world is at peace. However, if someone should start one foghorn, that may set off other foghorns to which it is connected.

Someone sounding a foghorn represents a demand for maintenance. How much noise ensues depends on the patterns of interconnections.

If the foghorn is connected to only *one* other foghorn, the pair of them will fall silent on average in 2^2 milliseconds (i.e., 4 milliseconds).

If the foghorn is connected to *ten* other foghorns, they will all tend to rouse each other. The system will become silent only when all of them by chance happen to be silent at the same millisecond. This will take about 2^{10} milliseconds on average (i.e., about 1 second).

If the foghorn that is blown is connected to a *hundred* other foghorns, the system will again reach equilibrium only when all 100 are by chance silent. This will take of the order of 2^{100} milliseconds, or 10^{19} years. The age of the universe itself is only about 10^{10} years. 2^{100} milliseconds is a billion times the age of the universe.

If we want to build a system with many foghorns we had better be sure that the patterns of interconnections are severely limited. The difference between 10 and 100 foghorns is startling!

Suppose that there are 10 foghorns, *all* interconnected to each other, and *all* blowing at once. They will become silent in just over a second, on average. We can live with groups of 10.

However, imagine that we are instructed to build a worldwide system with many thousands of foghorns. The only reasonable way to do it is to cluster the foghorns into subsystems each small enough to stabilize quickly. One cluster may be connected to many other clusters, but each cluster must solve its own maintenance problems without interfering much with the other clusters.

Maintenance in one cluster may turn on *all* the foghorns in another cluster, but provided that this is only one event, the other cluster will recover in about 1 second. It may turn on all the foghorns in 10 clusters, but provided *each* cluster is self-contained, *each* will recover in 1 second or so.

This property of being self-contained and independent is very important. We sometimes describe the separate subsystems as loosely coupled (meaning largely independent) or tightly coupled. In a tightly coupled system any of the 10 foghorns blowing in one cluster might affect all the foghorns in the other clusters. Then we would be back to a recovery time of 2^{100} milliseconds or so. A stable system must be able to adapt subsystem by subsystem.

Structured programming seeks to reduce complexity, and hence maintenance, by a principle of *divide and conquer.* Divide a program into functionally coherent modules, each of which can be maintained largely independently of the others. Complex system design should similarly divide and conquer.

**DESIGN OF
DISTRIBUTED
SYSTEMS**

The designers responsible for distributed systems in an enterprise should have two contrasting images in their minds. One is of a plate of spaghetti on which if you pull one piece of spaghetti every piece on the plate is moved. The other is an image of separate, autonomous nodes, each appearing to be simple to its users—the complexities being hidden under the covers. The network interconnecting them is standard, flexible, and also appears to be simple, and like the telephone network, its complexities are hidden under the covers. The complexities under the covers are much greater than most systems analysts imagine, so they should not be modified or tampered with in any way.

Box 23.1 lists factors in the overall design of distributed systems that affect maintenance.

BOX 23.1   Factors in distributed system design which affect maintenance

Good Design of Distributed Systems	Bad Design of Distributed Systems
• Overall system complexity is decreased by distribution.	• Overall system complexity is increased by distribution.
• Interfaces between subsystems are simple and small in number.	• Complex, convoluted patterns of interaction exist between subsystems.
• The functions of the subsystems are largely self-contained.	• Many functions cross subsystem boundaries.
• End-user processors are autonomous to a substantial degree.	• End-user processors have complex relationships with distant processors.
• The distributed processors all conform to common system interfaces and standards.	• The distributed processors are selected by different groups without central coordination.
• Off-the-shelf fully supported system software is used without modification.	• Software is created or modified to permit interlinking of otherwise incompatible systems.
• The distributed processors give the end users powerful facilities for access to data, report generation, and application development.	• The distributed processors have to be programmed in low-level languages.
• End users have autonomy in application development where this is useful.	• Only centralized application development is permitted.
• A common high-level network architecture is used which is reliable and flexible. [3].	• Random low-level teleprocessing links are used; or a rigid clumsy network architecture.
• One network is used throughout.	• Separate incompatible network architectures are interlinked.
• Application development and maintenance is a dominant design concern.	• Only conventional programming is used for application development.
• The peripheral processors need no elaborate system skills, and changes can be easily affected.	• The peripheral processors need systems programmers and system changes are complex to make.
• The design of data is centrally coordinated, except where those data are usable by only one location.	• Incompatible versions of the same data are used at different locations.

BOX 23.1 *(Continued)*

Good Design of Distributed Systems	Bad Design of Distributed Systems
● Careful attention is paid to data-base design, location, and use.	● Data-base management systems are not used.
● Stable logical data-base design is used employing third-normal-form and canonical structures (Chapters 6 and 7).	● Casual, logical record design is used without canonical synthesis.
● Data dictionary control is used for data in all locations.	● No data dictionary is used, or it applies only to a centralized location.
● An effective balance is designed between what ought to be centralized and what ought to be decentralized.	● Restrictive centralization; or uncoordinated implementation by user departments.

NETWORKS   Desirable properties of a computer network are that it should be autonomous, trouble-free, and easy to use, like the telephone network. Machines should be able to plug into it simply at any location and transmit to any other location it serves. Unfortunately, much software for networking does not have these properties. Some software is complex, needs careful network planning, and is rapidly evolving. Many machines cannot connect to it. Worse, it is incompatible with network software from other vendors. Because of this, careful planning is needed to avoid maintenance problems [4].

It is often tempting to solve the problems of incompatibility by writing teleprocessing monitors, modifying the network software, or writing software to interlink machines. This activity is almost always doomed to expensive maintenance later because the vendors' software is rapidly evolving. From all the experience we can observe, we believe that customers should never modify vendors' networking software or write their own if they can possibly avoid it. Find off-the-shelf software solutions even if they restrict, for the time being, the configurations that can be used. The attempt to create unique network solutions has almost always turned out to be far more expensive than expected, and often in the long run does more to restrict the configurations that can be used than following the vendors' evolution.

How, then, can two vendors with incompatible network software be employed? Their networks should be kept separate, and where records must be passed between them this should occur in a simple, loosely coupled fashion. There are various ways in which networks can be loosely coupled. Tapes or disks may be passed off-line between the machines. A machine of one network may emulate a standard input/output peripheral of a computer on another network. Simple start-stop or binary synchronous links may connect the different machines (with software support). Both types of machines may connect to a local-area network or computerized branch exchange, which does protocol conversion.

MIGRATION PATH   Both software and hardware are likely to continue to evolve rapidly. While improving what is possible with computers, this evolution can worsen maintenance problems if not handled appropriately. To lessen the problems, most manufacturers have a migration path planned for their customers' systems evolution. The total elapsed time to create a new-architecture computer is typically about six years, so manufacturers have their product lines planned some years ahead without necessarily revealing them.

If a customer follows the migration path of a major vendor, this will usually lessen the system maintenance costs. It pays a customer to try to understand the migration paths of his vendors. The more he understands the future evolution, the more he can design to minimize maintenance.

Some vendors, including IBM, do not reveal their future product plans except in generalizations. The customer then needs to decide whether a partially blind commitment to the vendor's migration path is worthwhile. With IBM it often *is* in reducing system maintenance but has other effects on application creation which need to be evaluated.

Often a customer locks himself out of his vendor's migration path without understanding the maintenance implications. A vendor may be designing complex software to link distributed systems, for example, and the customer installs foreign front-end processors which will not operate with the new software when it arrives. The vendor may be planning an active data dictionary designed to drive a future data-base management system, teleprocessing facilities, and very high level languages, but the customer installs a foreign data dictionary which cannot be used in this way. Migration-path planning should be discussed with the vendors with the objective of avoiding expensive maintenance later.

SYSTEM KLUGES   It is desirable to avoid lashing together hardware and software combinations that are each evolving separately. One bank installation, for example, has a mainframe without its own data-base management system. A DBMS from a software house is used with no data dictionary. A different teleprocessing monitor is used with

BOX 23.2　Examples of system problems that lead to expensive maintenance and can be avoided with top-down planning

- Machines are difficult to interconnect by telecommunications because they use different line-control procedures.

- Computer network architectures of different manufacturers are fundamentally incompatible.

- Even if compatibility can be achieved in the transport network, fundamental incompatibility exists between manufacturers' software external to the transport network.

- Different types of data-base software are incompatible (even without considering distributed data bases).

- File structures are expensive (sometimes prohibitively so) to *convert* to other file structures, or to data-base structures.

- Technology is evolving rapidly, and migration to better technology may be difficult in a distributed environment unless planned for.

- Even if all the software is compatible, severe problems may arise from incompatible data fields and data structures due to inadequate data administration in an organization.

- Office automation terminals cannot be connected to data-processing facilities.

terminals from still other vendors. This combination is clumsy and fraught with software problems. It is a nightmare to make any changes. The middle management of the bank became very dissatisfied at not obtaining the applications they needed, and adopted a policy of implementing microcomputers. These, however, needed to extract data from and pass data to the mainframe, so further linking of systems became needed.

System kluges—hardware/software combinations that incur high future maintenance costs—tend to arise because of absence of strategic planning. Box 23.2 lists examples of system problems that lead to expensive maintenance but which can be avoided with top-level planning.

STRATEGIC PLANNING

Strategic planning for computer systems ought to look some years into the future, create a view of what facilities will be needed at that time, and then ask the question: "How do we get from here to there?"

Getting from here to there needs to be done in a succession of projects each of which has a high chance of success. The facilities created by each project should link together where necessary, but the interactions between the projects should be minimal, as described above. Each project should be as small and modular as possible, able to be completed by a small team in a reasonably short time. Strategic planning should seek to subdivide the enterprise requirements into small projects, each autonomous except for the conformity to the overall plan.

The view of the future cannot identify all user needs with clairvoyance. What we need instead is to design an infrastructure which permits the autonomous growth of independent projects. If we were designing a new form of city for the future we could not possibly know how people would live or what type of houses they would want. We *could* design the street layout, the transportation system, the public utilities, the library facilities, the shopping areas, the theaters and services. People and entrepreneurs would be free to build their own houses and design their own life-styles within this planned infrastructure.

FOUR ASPECTS OF THE INFRASTRUCTURE

There are four major aspects to the infrastructure for corporate electronic systems:

1. Corporate network planning
2. Architecture for distributed processing
3. Information engineering
4. Office automation planning

For each of these areas the planning needs to be done in sufficient detail that it gives implementable standards for the individual project developers. The knowledge required is different in these four areas and so a different person may be responsible for each. The skills required for the information engineering planning described in Chapter 14 are, for example, quite different from the skills required for network planning or office automation planning. In some large corporations four separate efforts have been conducted relating to these four planning areas.

Network planning should be concerned with all telecommunications—voice, data, electronic mail, teleconferencing, wide-area networks, and local-area networks. It needs to plan the protocol conversion mechanisms which permit devices with different link-control procedures to intercommunicate [4]. Eventually a ubiquitous, highly flexible, data networking facility needs to be built in an enterprise. There are multiple options for how this might be done and they need long-term planning. In the past, many enterprises have planned their networks inadequately. This has resulted in multiple incompatible teleprocessing systems and the need for later conversion, which is sometimes extremely expensive.

The conversion (maintenance) due to absence of planning is often much more than mere access method conversion. The terminals have to be changed to achieve common networking protocols and this causes the terminal dialogue to have to be changed in application programs. Changing the terminal dialogue often results in changes to record structures. These records are used by multiple applications.

Distributed processing standards [3] are broader in scope than network standards. The architectures for distributed processing encompass complex functions over and above the transmission subsystem. The planning for distributed processing includes selection of the software architectures to be used. Proliferation of software needs to be avoided because different architectures tend to be incompatible at the higher levels and are often evolving in different ways. If more than one type of architecture is used, the planning needs to design which zones of the enterprise use which architecture and how they interlink.

Information engineering [5] plans the data used in an enterprise and creates data models, as described in Chapters 6, 7, and 14. This usually has more effect on future maintenance costs than the other areas of strategic planning.

Office automation planning attempts to determine what office-of-the-future facilities will be required. Word processors, electronic mail systems, electronic filing and archiving systems, intelligent copying machines, terminals for document display, and so on, need to interconnect and hence need top-down planning. Random uncoordinated purchase of office systems leads to high future expenses for conversion or replacement. The office terminal of the future needs to access data processing facilities as well as office automation facilities. Combined software is often needed for office automation and DP. Both classes of facilities need to share local area networks, exchanges, and often wide-area networks. Failure in top-down planning of office automation has resulted in DP facilities having to be changed as well as office automation facilities, with consequent costs in program maintenance.

TOP MANAGEMENT INVOLVEMENT   Strategic planning needs top management involvement for two principal types of reasons.

First, the plans which are put together are often counterpolitical—they cut across separately managed areas, and middle managers are often jealous of their empires. Without top management directives, all manner of arguments will be devised for deviating from the plans.

Second, the enterprise, its information needs, strategic direction, and geographic locations are likely to change. Top-level managers know best what changes are likely or desirable. They know what new business areas are possible. They understand the factors critical for success of the enterprise, which relate to the planning of information resources.

Just as in the Department of Defense ABIC approach, the top-down plans need to be reviewed every year and rolled forward. ABIC looks forward seven years. This may be too long a planning horizon for some corporations, especially as the rapid rate of technology evolution makes the future more blurred. Five years seems an appropriate horizon for most corporations. The strategic infrastructure takes a long time to build, so a horizon shorter than five years may be insufficient for network and distributed system planning.

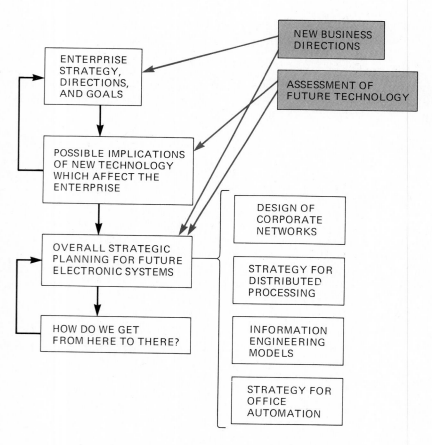

Figure 23.1 Strategic planning for corporate electronic systems.

SUMMARY   In general, the better the view of the future when systems are built, the lower future maintenance costs will be. End users, especially with fourth-generation languages, need a high level of spontaneity in creating new procedures and generating information. This can happen much better when network, terminal, and data system planning has been thorough and well implemented. Figure 23.1 illustrates the breakdown of strategic planning that is generally necessary.

Strategic planning for DP is an activity that involves the highest levels of management. All levels, from programmer to president, should be made aware of the costs, inflexibility, and lost opportunities associated with program maintenance, and be made aware of the role each can play in the solutions to the problem.

REFERENCES

1. Headquarters, U.S. Department of the Army, letter DAMO-RQ, November 3, 1977; subject: "Interface Requirements."

2. Headquarters, U.S. Department of the Army, requirements definition for an "Army Battlefield Interface Concept" (ABIC), November 1977.

3. J. Martin, *Computer Networks and Distributed Processing* (Englewood Cliffs, NJ: Prentice-Hall, Inc., 1981).

4. J. Martin, *Design and Strategy for Distributed Processing* (Englewood Cliffs, NJ: Prentice-Hall, Inc., 1981).

5. J. Martin and C. Finkelstein, *Information Engineering,* Savant Technical Report 22, Savant Institute, Carnforth, Lancashire, UK, 1981.

INDEX

DP'S CONCEPTUAL PRISM
THE JAMES MARTIN BOOK

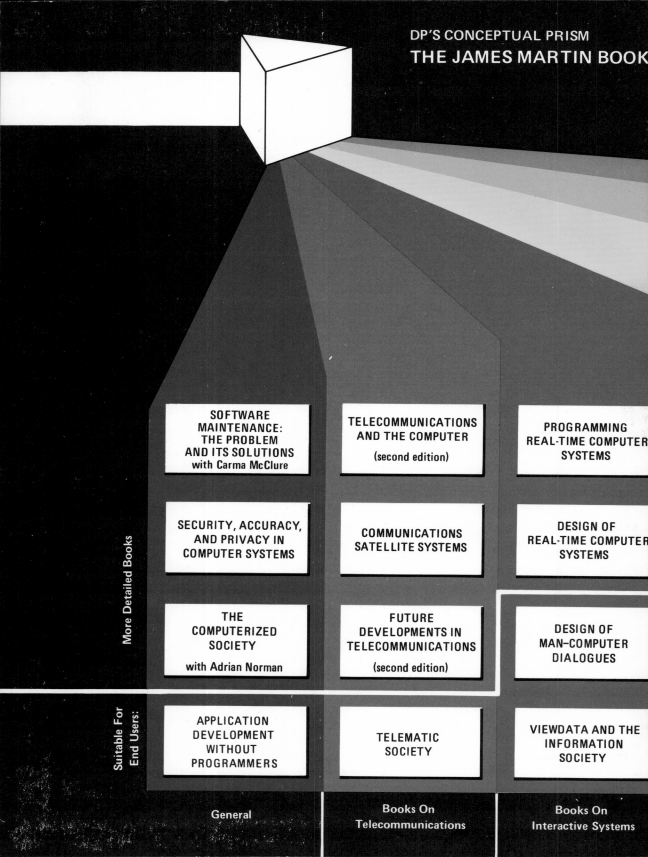

More Detailed Books

SOFTWARE MAINTENANCE: THE PROBLEM AND ITS SOLUTIONS with Carma McClure	TELECOMMUNICATIONS AND THE COMPUTER (second edition)	PROGRAMMING REAL-TIME COMPUTER SYSTEMS
SECURITY, ACCURACY, AND PRIVACY IN COMPUTER SYSTEMS	COMMUNICATIONS SATELLITE SYSTEMS	DESIGN OF REAL-TIME COMPUTER SYSTEMS
THE COMPUTERIZED SOCIETY with Adrian Norman	FUTURE DEVELOPMENTS IN TELECOMMUNICATIONS (second edition)	DESIGN OF MAN–COMPUTER DIALOGUES

Suitable For End Users:

| APPLICATION DEVELOPMENT WITHOUT PROGRAMMERS | TELEMATIC SOCIETY | VIEWDATA AND THE INFORMATION SOCIETY |

| General | Books On Telecommunications | Books On Interactive Systems |